LIFE IN TRANSIT

JEWS IN POSTWAR LODZ, 1945-1950

Studies in Russian and Slavic
Literatures, Cultures and History

Series Editor: Lazar Fleishman

LIFE IN TRANSIT

JEWS IN
POSTWAR LODZ,
1945-1950

SHIMON REDLICH

BOSTON 2010

Library of Congress DATA

Redlich, Shimon.
  Life in transit : Jews in postwar Lsdz, 1945-1950 / Shimon Redlich.
    p. cm. -- (Studies in Russian and Slavic literatures, cultures and history)
  Includes bibliographical references and index.
  ISBN 978-1-936235-21-6 (hardback)
  1. Jews--Poland--Lsdz--History--20th century. 2. Holocaust survivors--Poland--Lsdz--
    History--20th century. 3. Redlich, Shimon. 4. Holocaust survivors--Israel--Travel--
    Poland--Personal narratives. 5. Holocaust, Jewish (1939-1945)--Personal narratives.
    6. Lsdz (Poland)--Biography. 7. Lsdz (Poland)--Ethnic relations. I. Title.
  DS134.62.R43 2010
  940.53'18092--dc22
  [B]
                            2010043240

Copyright © 2010 Academic Studies Press
All rights reserved

ISBN 978-1-61811-818-9

Book design by Adell Medovoy

Published by Academic Studies Press in 2010
28 Montfern Avenue
Brighton, MA 02135, USA
press@academicstudiespress.com
www.academicstudiespress.com

For my teachers and friends from the Hebrew Ghetto Fighters' School in Lodz

TABLE OF CONTENTS

PREFACE AND ACKNOWLEDGEMENTS	ix
A NOTE ON TRANSLITERATION	xii
MAPS	xiv
1. MY LODZ MEMORIES	1
2. POSTWAR LODZ	29
3. JEWS IN POSTWAR LODZ	53
4. FRIENDS, ACQUAINTANCES, STRANGERS	87
5. SURVIVING	109
War: The First Days	120
The Eastward Trek	123
Inside Russia	125
In the Soviet South	133
Returning to Poland	138
In the Ghettos	140
In the Camps	143
On the Aryan Side	146
6. THE ZIONISTS	151
7. THE OTHERS	181
EPILOGUE	203
CONCLUDING REMARKS	211

BIOGRAPHICAL NOTES	215
NOTES	223
1. My Lodz Memories	223
2. Postwar Lodz	223
3. Jews in Postwar Lodz	226
4. Friends, Acquaintances, Strangers	231
5. Surviving	233
6. The Zionists	236
7. The Others	239
ARCHIVES LIST	242
BIBLIOGRAPHY	243
INDEX	253

PREFACE *and*

ACKNOWLEDGEMENTS

THE IDEA OF WRITING ABOUT POSTWAR LODZ HAD ALREADY GERMINATED while I was working on my Brzezany book.[1] The basic premise of both projects was to place my personal memories within a wider historical context. I lived in Brzezany as a child for the few prewar years and then during the war. We moved to Lodz in the summer of 1945, and left for Israel in early 1950. Thus my adolescence, in a large industrial city in central Poland, was completely unlike my childhood years in a picturesque and pastoral small town in the eastern Polish borderlands. Whereas as a child in Brzezany I had to face the tragedies of the War and the Holocaust, my Lodz years coincided with a significant and meaningful period in the history of the Jews in Poland immediately after the war.

For decades, the lives and fates of the survivors in the immediate postwar years were insufficiently researched and discussed. They were overshadowed by the tremendous events of the War and the Holocaust on the one hand and by the emergence of Israel on the other. Zionist-oriented historiography has tended to accept a rather simplified, almost predestined, formula of "Holocaust and Redemption." The few in-between years got lost somehow. The prevailing and stereotyped image of Holocaust survivors was primarily one of passive and helpless remnants of vibrant Jewish communities. It is only since the 1990s that this perception has begun to be challenged. My study of Jews and Jewish life in postwar Lodz is, in a way, part of this novel approach.

Lodz, in the years 1945-1950, was the major urban center of Jewish population in Poland. A basic feature of Jewish life in postwar Lodz, as it was throughout postwar Poland, was its fluid and transitory nature. Yet, despite the ever-shifting scene, there was a strong sense of vitality and purpose. Although some research on postwar Jewish life in Poland has been emerging recently, studies of specific locations are rather scarce. As for research of the history of Jews in Lodz, the few studies that have been published focus on prewar Lodz and on the Lodz Ghetto. Very little has been written on Jews and Jewish life in postwar Lodz.

---

[1] *Together and Apart in Brzezany: Poles, Jews, and Ukrainians, 1919-1945* (Bloomington and Indianapolis: Indiana University Press, 2002).

In some ways, my mental and emotional journey to postwar Lodz has been similar to my return to prewar Brzezany. Both were happy periods in my life. Unlike those who view the early postwar years as a rather sad postscript to the war's tragedy and trauma, I've always recalled my postwar Lodz years fondly. One reason for this, perhaps, is the fact that my Lodz years were preceded by the Holocaust and followed by emigration and adjustment to a new life in Israel.

My physical return to Eastern Europe has been facilitated by the fall of Communism. I've made repeated trips to Warsaw and Lodz. While the memories of Jewish Warsaw were unearthed and discussed there increasingly in the course of the 1990s, a similar process has begun in Lodz only in the last few years.

As I did in *Together and Apart,* I decided to base my Lodz book both on conventional sources and on interviews with people who lived in the city in the postwar years. I sought to check, verify and confront my adolescent postwar Lodz memories with the memories of others who lived there at the same time. I was curious to find out whether my Lodz impressions, mostly positive and pleasant, were correct. The very act of meeting with and listening to people who shared my Lodz experience was moving and gratifying. Historians are reluctant to make use of life stories, because it often brings up the familiar charge of lack of objectivity. Having gone through enough formal documents, I've become increasingly convinced that they too do not always tell us the objective "truth." I am convinced now even more than in the past that individual voices are highly significant in the writing of history, no less than the more conventional and traditional sources.

Since most of my adolescent life in postwar Lodz took place in a Jewish-Zionist milieu and since most of the Jewish writings deal with that milieu, I was determined to include others in my study too: the Communists and the assimilationists. Unlike the Brzezany book, which discusses the Polish-Jewish-Ukrainian triangle, the Lodz book centers primarily on Jews. I also faced a structural dilemma. Whereas the Brzezany book covers a quarter of a century, the Lodz book deals with less than five years. It made sense to present my Brzezany story chronologically. The Lodz story centers mostly upon the major aspects of Jewish life during the postwar years. Initially, I intended to write only about the early postwar years in Lodz, but as my research and interviews progressed, I came to realize that Jewish life in postwar Lodz could not be comprehended unless the wartime background of those who survived the war and the Holocaust, was also presented.

Preface

* * *

IN RESEARCHING AND WRITING THIS BOOK I'VE BEEN ENCOURAGED AND assisted by friends and colleagues. When *Together and Apart* — a blend of historical and personal narratives — was first published, I was quite apprehensive. The positive reception of that book by both professional historians and ordinary readers vastly surpassed my expectations. It has encouraged me to continue along similar lines.

I am deeply indebted to my colleague, friend and neighbor, Professor Yuval Lurie, with whom I discussed my Lodz project during our numerous "walking seminars." I appreciate his critical approach and his insightful suggestions. Professor Gaby Schreiber encouraged me to persist. Professor Jerzy Tomaszewski sent me a document concerning my Hebrew school in postwar Lodz, and helped me in the early stages of the Lodz project. Professor Matityahu Mintz, who was an emissary of Hashomer Hatzair in postwar Poland, suggested some interesting interviewees and was kind enough to share his personal memories with me. Professor Joanna Michlic shared her research on Lodz in the post-Communist era with me. Henryk Grynberg, a friend and a contemporary of my Lodz years, gave me much of his time and attention. Dr. Maurice Preter shared with me his interest in and enthusiasm for *Undzere Kinder*, a Yiddish film produced in postwar Lodz, which his father and I had participated in as child actors. Professor Gaby Finder, who researched the history of that film, has become a close friend.

I shared the idea of the Lodz project with Prof. Antony Polonsky and Prof. Padraic Kenney. Both made helpful comments. I also discussed the Lodz project with Prof. Mordechai Altshuler and Prof. Omer Bartov. Prof. Janusz Wrobel and Prof. Leszek Olejnik assisted my research in Lodz. Mr. Ryszard Bonislawski walked the streets of contemporary Lodz with me, pointing out the geography of postwar Jewish Lodz. Prof. Halina Goldberg introduced me to her parents, who had remained in Lodz through all those years. While in Warsaw I was frequently hosted by my longtime friends Professor Ludwik Czaja and Professor Jolanta Brach-Czaina. I spent some very pleasant times in Lodz with my friend Dr. Kaja Kazmierska and her family.

I deeply appreciate Sir Martin Gilbert's enthusiastic response to my Lodz book and his preparation of the maps. Ms. Roni Bluestein-Livnon of Ben-Gurion University's Geography Department assisted me in preparing the map of postwar Lodz. I would also like to thank Mr. Zeev Baran,

Honorary Consul of Poland in Jerusalem, for letting me examine his collection of *Mosty*.

Invaluable help has been extended to me by those who searched for relevant materials in Polish libraries and archives. My special thanks go to Ms. Ewa Kozminska-Frejlak in Warsaw and to Ms. Katarzyna Szafranska in Lodz. Mr. Wojciech Lasota, Dr. Joanna Nalewajko-Kulikov and Mr. Radoslaw Peterman were also of great help. Mr. Roman Zakharii conducted several interviews for my Lodz project, for which I am thankful. My former student at Ben-Gurion University, Mr. Boaz Vanetik, conducted a search at the Yad Yaari Archive in Israel. I would also like to thank the staffs of the Library and Archives at Yad Vashem, Jerusalem, of ZIH, the Jewish Historical Institute in Warsaw and of the IPN Archive in Lodz. The meetings and interviews with my Lodz classmates were moving and educating. I also learned a lot from other people who lived in postwar Lodz and were willing to share their wartime and postwar memories with me. I thank them all.

Assistance for my Lodz project was graciously extended by the Israel Science Foundation and by the Rabb Center for Holocaust Studies at Ben-Gurion University and by Professor Jimmy Weinblatt, Rector of Ben-Gurion University.

I appreciate very much Dr. Saadya Sternberg's editorial assistance. I am grateful to Margo Schotz for preparing the manuscript for publication and to Yossi Regev for his help with computer-related problems.

Professor Lazar Fleishman of Stanford read the manuscript and recommended its publication. The staff of Academic Studies Press was most helpful and cooperative.

I profoundly thank my wife Judith who for years has shared my passion for and obsession with Brzezany and Lodz. I also appreciate the interest in my research and travels of my daughters, Shlomit and Efrat. Hopefully, I will some day be able to take my lovely grandchildren, Oria, Shay and Alon to Brzezany and Lodz.

Modi'in, June 2010

A Note on Transliteration

Transliteration has been simplified for the convenience of the reader. Hebrew, Russian and Yiddish titles were translated into English. Polish diacritical marks have been omitted.

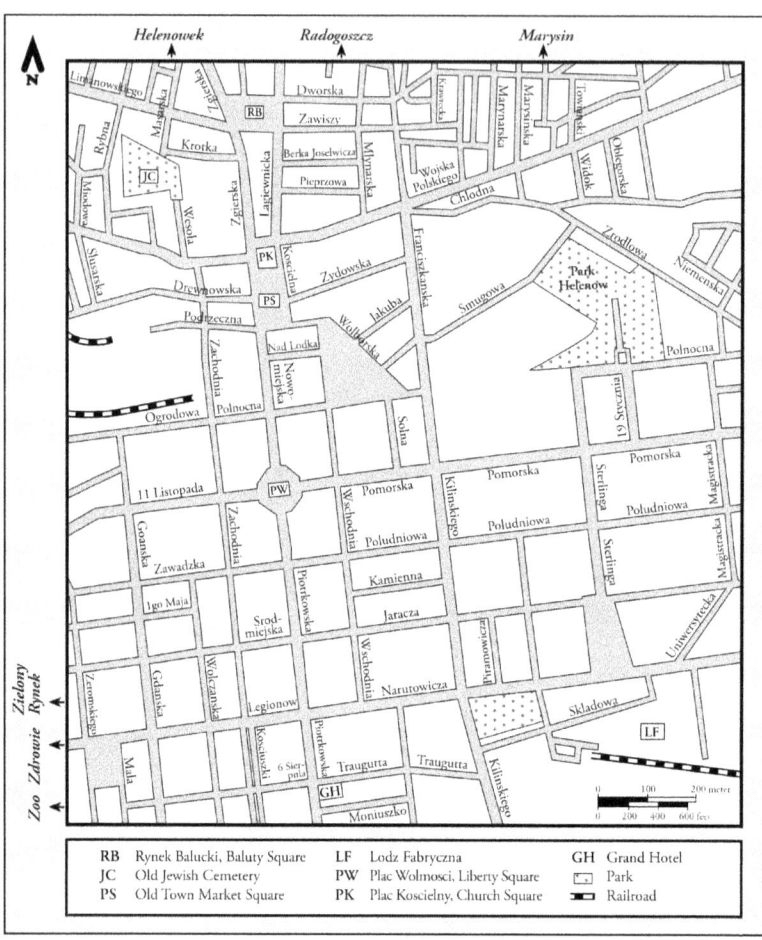

Postwar Lodz.

Wartime and postwar Poland, showing the locations mentioned in this book.

The Soviet Union, showing the locations mentioned in this book.

1

MY LODZ MEMORIES

I RETURNED TO LODZ, AFTER 37 YEARS, IN APRIL 1987. My host in Warsaw at the time was Karol, who with his father Stanislaw were friends of my Grandpa Fishl before the war. Indeed, they were so faithful to him, and so courageous, that they helped us with food during the war itself, when we were hiding in the empty, half-ruined Brzezany ghetto. I lived in Brzezany, in eastern Galicia, up to age ten, and have always cherished the memory of the first six, "normal," years of my life there, before the arrival of the Germans. I was a happy, secure and loved child when the Germans occupied Brzezany in the summer of 1941, and it is to those few normal prewar years that I always return for solace and hope. At the same time, however, Brzezany is for me a site of loss and trauma. My father, along with Grandpa Fishl and numerous members of our family, were either deported from there to the Belzec death camp or shot and buried in the local Jewish cemetery.

In German-occupied Brzezany we first lived in the ghetto, and then, following its liquidation, hid in the nearby village of Raj until the summer of 1944 when the Red Army arrived. We left Soviet-Ukrainian Brzezany, as it was now referred to, a year later and settled in Lodz, where we stayed for nearly five years before departing for Israel. Karol and his family moved to Poland as well, but for many years there was no contact between us. My first contact with him was made only in the early eighties, and he arrived in Israel in May 1986 to be awarded, together with his late father, the title of Righteous Gentile. Karol planted a tree at Yad Vashem. A year later, on Easter Monday, I traveled with him from Warsaw to Lodz.

It was a gray, cold and drizzly morning. The trip took less than two hours. I had been thinking about, imagining and dreaming of Lodz for some time, sensing that a return might become real. And here was the mid-city train terminal, Lodz Fabryczna, much smaller than in my memory. After a five-minute taxi ride we were on the corner of Gdanska Street and 1go Maja, May First Street. I had often thought about this corner house, and now here I was, facing the Gdanska Street entrance. The street was completely deserted, nothing but dilapidated buildings. The small palace opposite "my" house — the "palacyk" which I knew served as a music conservatory — was all black and gray. The sight was depressing. As I approached "my" house, I felt dizzy, experiencing an eerie sense of being catapulted back in time. I started checking the list of the tenants' names at the entrance as if expecting to find somebody I had known there years earlier. Then I walked to a neighboring house, on the other side of the street where some of our acquaintances used to live, and looked for their names. I hardly noticed the group of teenagers standing farther back in the courtyard. Suddenly I was all wet. The remains of a bucketfull of ice-cold water was running down my neck. I was instantly hurled back into postwar Lodz. I was being chased by Polish teenagers. Now and then: in the very same streets. Breaking into my immediate reaction of anger and fear, Karol apologized and reminded me of the ancient Polish custom of Lany Poniedzialek — Wet Easter Monday.

I do not recall a prevailing atmosphere of anti-Semitism in postwar Lodz, as some of my Lodz friends and schoolmates do. Some incidents, though, have remained in my memory. I'm walking home in the late afternoon, along Narutowicza Street. It's almost dark. Suddenly two Polish boys, older and bigger than me, appear out of nowhere and push me into a building entrance. They slap me and disappear. I do not recall any words being spoken or shouted, though I'm sure that they must have called me names. Another memory: It's a bright summer afternoon, on the left side of 1go Maja. I'm walking toward Wolczanska Street. Two or three boys surround me and start calling me names. This time, for some reason, I'm not scared. Feelings of anger and rage overcome me instantly. I reach into my pocket, pull out a penknife and draw the blade. They run away and I chase them.

I never thought I would return to Poland. The first time I became aware of a real prospect of doing so was in the mid-1980s. In an Israeli newspaper I had read a short, emotional poem by a very unlikely author, Professor Shlomo Avineri, a political scientist from the Hebrew University. He had just returned from his first postwar visit to his hometown in Poland. Avineri wrote: "To return to the town of your birth and feel like landing on Mars." [1] Yehudit Hendel, an Israeli writer whose parents left Warsaw for Palestine before the Second World War, traveled to Poland in the fall of 1986 and told the story of her visit in a series of radio talks in early 1987. I was fascinated by her torn emotions and her strong urge to travel to Poland, which ultimately prevailed. "I was scared and my first impulse was to refuse. But suddenly it all began to move, and soon I couldn't think about anything except going to Poland. Suddenly I felt I had to go to Poland, and yet, at the same time, I felt a tremendous hesitation. All that baggage we drag around with us from Poland. Suddenly I was plunged into a vortex of dread and regret, and memory, and longing to forget, and hatred."² Eva Hoffman's return to Poland was of a completely different kind. In her *Exit Into History* she wrote: "I was born in Poland and got my primary schooling there. I emigrated in early adolescence, but for a long time afterward, Poland remained for me an idealized landscape of the mind. It stayed arrested in my imagination as a land of childhood sensuality, lyricism, vividness, and human warmth."³

My own first return to Poland, as well as subsequent visits, differed from that of most Jewish and Israeli travelers to that country. Jews and Israelis looked, almost exclusively, for camps and cemeteries. For me Poland was not only a place of murder, death and mourning. It was landscapes, language and culture as well. I did go to Auschwitz, Treblinka and Majdanek, but I also spent time with my Polish friends, Karol and the Czajas. Ludwik Czaja, a professor of informatics, and his wife Jola, a professor of philosophy, both of whom I had met while on a sabbatical in the US, were mountain climbers on a nearly professional level. I went with them year after year to Zakopane, and we climbed the Tatras. Unlike most Jews traveling to Poland, I experienced it as a place where one could meet friends and go on a holiday.

Another kind of "return" to postwar Lodz was the reunion of former students of the Lodz Hebrew School in Tel-Aviv, in the early fall of 1997. The idea was mine, and a few of my Lodz friends were ready to implement it. We succeeded in getting together some 80 people, almost all residing in Israel. Two arrived for the occasion from abroad: Hanka Rydel from Montreal and Dr. Yossi Shalev-Spokojny from Las Vegas. I recalled Hanka as one of the prettiest girls in our school. Now she was a quite well-to-do, chain smoking Canadian whose former beauty still showed. Spokojny used to be a rather shy and withdrawn kid, pampered by his parents. He became a successful eye doctor in the gambling capital of America. A few of our former teachers, now in their mid- and upper-eighties, showed up as well. Among them were Baruch Kaplinski, our first principal, and our gym instructor, Captain Binyamin Majerczak.

Kaplinski, a retired lawyer and a Biblical scholar, started by quoting from the *Book of Psalms*: "I was young and now I'm old." Then he told us how our school had started. He had arrived in Lodz from a Nazi labor camp in the spring of 1945. Fortunately for all of us, he soon thereafter met Antek Zuckerman and Zivia Lubetkin, both ardent Zionists and participants in the Warsaw Ghetto uprising. "Towards the end of our chat Antek asked me whether I would do something for the Zionist Labor movement. He suggested that I set up a Hebrew school in Lodz, modeled on the prewar Tarbut Hebrew schools. Although I was doubtful about the whole thing, I agreed. Antek asked me to name the school after the Ghetto Fighters. "Bravo!, I responded, there couldn't be a better idea."[4]

Natan Gross was there too. In postwar Lodz he was a young, freshly-minted film director. He filmed *Undzere Kinder (Our Children)*, the only Jewish feature film to be made in postwar Poland. Since his Lodz years, Natan has directed numerous films, mostly documentaries, has written books and contributed regularly to the only Israeli Polish newspaper, the Nowiny-Kurier. At our gathering, in the Diaspora Museum, Natan pulled out a piece of paper and read a poem about orphaned Jewish children which he had written back in 1946. Excerpts from *Undzere Kinder*, in which some members of the audience had participated, were screened. The reunion ended with the singing of Hebrew songs, accompanied by an accordion. Some of them were the first Hebrew songs we had learned in our school on Poludniowa Street.[5]

My return to Lodz was in some ways different from my return to Brzezany, where I'd had a happy childhood before the war, and then gone through loss and trauma during the Holocaust, but in other ways resembled it. I had a strong urge to "return" to both. I always recalled my time in Lodz as a rather happy period in my life and kept, on the whole, good memories of those five years. I longed to return to my childhood town of Brzezany, but I was also drawn to Lodz, the city of my adolescence.

Four of us had survived our experiences in Brzezany: my mother, her younger sister Malcia, Malcia's husband Vovo and me. My extended family, more than a hundred people, were either deported to the Belzec death camp or shot and buried in mass graves at the old Jewish Okopisko cemetery overlooking Brzezany. We departed from Brzezany on a hot and humid midsummer day, in 1945. We were part of the mass exodus of prewar Polish citizens who were allowed and urged to leave Soviet Ukraine and to resettle in the so-called Ziemie Odzyskane, The Recovered Lands, in western Poland. We rode in a roofless freight train with a few passenger cars in the front, surrounded by our few meager possessions and bundles of dry straw. For me, a boy of ten, it felt like a summer vacation and smelled of adventure. The train rolled slowly through picturesque countryside landscapes. From time to time big, heavy raindrops preceded an occasional violent midsummer storm. For me it was fun; for the grownups, not so much. On top of the usual difficulties of relocation, Malcia was in the last weeks of her pregnancy. Vovo secured a seat for her in one of the passenger cars. The first sizeable towns on the Polish side of the new postwar border were Krosno and Jaslo. It was in one of them that Malcia and Vovo got off the train. My aunt expected to give birth very soon, and they didn't want it happening on the train.

I have no recollections of the remaining part of that voyage, but it must have taken a week for the train to reach Lodz, on its way to western Poland. I do not recall my arrival in Lodz, but I do know from family stories that while my mother continued the long journey to The Recovered Lands, I was left in Lodz. It must have been early autumn. I stayed with distant relatives from Brzezany, the Wagszals. My immediate surroundings had changed drastically: from a small-town neighborhood in eastern Galicia with a green countryside nearby I had come to a gray Polish metropolis. Lodz was known for years as the "Polish Manchester." Already in the 19th century, it was one of the biggest centers for the cotton industry in Europe. I do not recall its smoking red-brick chimneys, but I do remember that a white shirt would turn gray in a matter of hours out in the streets. To me this did not make the damnest difference.

I must have been separated from my closest family for some time. My mother was in Chojnow, not far from the new Polish-German border, where numerous Brzezanyites were resettled in previously German households. Vovo went back to the town in southeast Poland, where Malcia gave birth. I was alone with my relatives, Dr. Wagszal's family. Decades later, sipping coffee at the Ben-Gurion University Faculty Club, I heard from Nurit, Dr. Wagszal's daughter-in-law, about how the Wagszals used to act as benefactors and sponsors for their "poorer relatives." This was an eye-opener for me. Lipa and Pepka Wagszal willingly extended help and guidance, but at the same time made it quite clear that "they knew best." Dr. Wagszal enrolled me in the newly founded Hebrew school. Lodz at the time had a Yiddish school as well, but the doctor, who was an ardent Zionist, decided that I should receive a Hebrew and Zionist education. He even decided that I should change my last name, from a German-sounding one into Hebrew. Thus, instead of Redlich — "honest" in German — it became Tsadik, "righteous" in Hebrew. I still cherish an old, brownish, handwritten, report card from the Lodz Ghetto Fighters' Hebrew School, stating "Shimon Tsadik, born in 1935, attended the second grade in the school year of 1945/46." I studied Hebrew, the Pentateuch, Math, Polish and Music. My grades were "very good." The report card was signed B. Kaplinski, Principal. In subsequent report cards my name reverted to its original form. Apparently my mother didn't approve of Dr. Wagszal's decision.

It was already getting cold outside when Malcia and Vovo arrived one day at the Wagszals. Nobody spoke to me explicitly about it, but somehow I grasped from hushed conversations that the newborn baby girl had caught a severe cold on the train to Lodz and died of pneumonia. It is quite possible that Vovo brought the tiny body to the Wagszals, wrapped in white cloth. I don't know to this day whether some sort of a funeral was held, and where this baby was buried. I never asked and nobody offered any information on this sad subject. Only now, more than sixty years later, am I aware what a tragedy it must have been, particularly for my aunt Malcia. She had lost a baby two years earlier, when she and Vovo were hiding at Tanka's. Tanka, a Ukrainian peasant woman in her late twenties at the time, whose husband was sent for forced labor in Germany, fell in love with my uncle Vovo, a very attractive man. The relationship between Vovo and the two women was extremely complex. Tanka agreed to hide them, and later to hide myself and my mother as well, on the condition that Vovo would divorce Malcia after the War. When Vovo and Malcia sought refuge in Raj after the liquidation of the Brzezany ghetto, Malcia was already pregnant. When she went into labor Tanka left the house and stayed away for hours. When she returned, the newborn infant was dead.

Vovo departed soon for Chojnow, to make arrangements with my mother to settle in Lodz. The two of us — Malcia, a thirty-year-old woman, and a boy of ten — were thrown together, once again at the mercy of "others." In this quite uncomfortable situation, we presumably drew solace from each other. I became a "substitute" for my aunt's lost child, and she a temporary, "surrogate" mother to me. This closeness between the young aunt and her nephew wasn't entirely new. Already in prewar Brzezany, Malcia who was significantly younger than my mother, had spent many hours with me while my mother was busy in the family store. Now, at the Wagszals, we were drawn to each other once more, forming a sort of "conspiracy" in the relatively affluent household of our relatives. One of my most pleasant memories of those gray and dark early evening hours in Lodz is of sharing cookies and cake with Malcia on the dark staircase leading to the Wagszals' apartment.

Vovo and my mother arrived in Lodz a couple of weeks later, and we settled into what would be my home for the next four years: 33 Gdanska Street at the corner of 1go Maja. It was a grayish, rectangular, four-storey building with two entrances, one on Gdanska and another on 1go Maja. The cobblestoned court, closed in on all sides, formed a small open inner space where people met and children played. Our closest neighbors were the Polish concierge next door and his son. I don't recall the son's name, but I do recall quite distinctly how he tried to educate me. He drew a profile contour of the lower parts of two human bodies, male and female, in a classical "spoon" position. This was quite exciting for a boy of ten or eleven; otherwise I would have forgotten it long since. A family living on the opposite side of the courtyard invited me once for kutia, a traditional dish served at Christmas. I can still taste those sweet poppy seeds.

Ours was a ground floor apartment, with windows facing 1go Maja Street. One of my close friends, the short, stocky, muscular, and mischievous Heniek Napadow, used to climb into the apartment through one of those windows. To the right of the apartment entrance was a permanently dark kitchen, where for some time we kept our young German shepherd, Diana. I recall her leaps and bounds each time I returned from school. A long, dark corridor led to two rooms, separated by a door. Initially all of us stayed in the first room. The other was occupied by two strangers, a father and a son. Their last name was Burzynski, and the son's name was Natek. I soon learned that both were survivors of the Lodz ghetto. They showed me stamps and coins from the ghetto, and used to hum a popular ghetto song in Yiddish about Rumkowski, the King of the Jews: "Rumkowski, Chaim, er git uns klain — Haim Rumkowski feeds us straw." I can barely recall the father, seeing in my mind's eye just his balding, gray head. Natek was a tallish, unattractive, pockmarked, lean young man who wore polished black boots. He became my mentor in the art of step dancing, and also took me once or twice to a Zionist youth organization. I distinctly recall sitting with Natek high up on the balcony of the Wlokniarz cinema hall on a Saturday or Sunday morning. The speaker at the podium was the renowned Soviet-Jewish writer and journalist Ilya Ehrenburg, then on a tour of Poland. Natek told me to stand up and yell something about Jews desiring to go to Palestine. Decades later, I researched Ehrenburg's activities and writings concerning the War and the Holocaust in the newly accessible Soviet archives. I read dozens of letters written to Ehrenburg from all over Russia, and from the front lines as well, in which ordinary people, mainly Jews, wrote him of their despair and hope.

My life in Lodz in those few postwar years centered on three locations: the apartment on 33 Gdanska Street, the Hebrew school on 18 Poludniowa Street, and the Hashomer Hatzair youth movement building on 49 Kilinskiego Street. These were my most intimate spaces in that big city, whose outer reaches I scarcely knew. This was my personal Lodz geography. The numbers 33 and 49 remained engraved in my memory for decades; the school address was blurred, until other, older people, along with archival documents, reestablished it. Part of the problem was that the names of some of the streets in Lodz had changed. Poludniowa became in time Rewolucji 1905 r., the 1905 Revolution Street. A few years ago a small plaque was placed on the corner of Piotrkowska and Rewolucji 1905 r., mentioning the original name. When I first saw it during one of my Lodz visits, it made me feel good, as if an authentic piece of my past had been restored.

Another site I kept recalling was Piotrkowska Street, the main thoroughfare of prewar and postwar Lodz. I remembered it as bustling and crowded, lined with stores on both sides. One particular memory fragment: it's a bright, sunny day on Piotrkowska. I'm walking with Heniek, the "expert" on girls. We are giving "grades" to passing females, and Heniek comments on our decisions. Two locations on the corner of Piotrkowska and Poludniowa streets were significant for me: my uncle's taxi stand, and a coffee shop U Turka — At the Turk's.

It was quite unusual for a Jewish boy to have an uncle who was a taxi driver. Vovo owned a second-hand Citroen with the taxi number 23, one of those Lodz numbers which I had retained. Years later I gained visual proof of this memory when an old-time friend presented me with a photo I'd given him a long time ago. I'm standing at the fender of that old, gray Citroen, the number 23 within a circle painted on its door. I'm holding the leash to my beloved dog, Diana, and look very happy.

U Turka, At the Turk's, held another pleasant, sensual memory. It was based on looks, smells and tastes. They baked the best cakes in town, and I was an enthusiastic connoisseur. Sometimes Malcia and I would stop in and buy two pieces of their exquisite chocolate tart, which we devoured immediately, but more often, Vovo would show up at home at the end of his workday, when we were already in bed, and deposit on the table a rectangular gray box with that same delicious treat inside. Decades later, when I walked the streets of Lodz, I tried to verify these memories as well. I set out from the Grand Hotel with Pan Ryszard, the top tourist guide on "Jewish geography" in Lodz, early on a sunny Sunday morning. One of the central points of interest for me was, of course, U Turka. Ryszard told me that the Turk's last name was Erol and that he had three sons who still lived in Poland. The origin of the family had actually been in the Crimea, and "the Turk," Mr. Erol, was Catholic. He came to Lodz to do business, at which he succeeded quite well. He died sometime in the 1980s. If I had visited Lodz two or three years earlier, I could have met him.

My memories of the Gdanska Street apartment are split and sporadic. At one point we acquired a huge printing machine, which was deposited in the cellar. It printed kerchiefs in very bright colors and in various patterns. It would roll from side to side, and those kerchiefs would emerge. At other times big packs of cloth would be brought into the apartment. Then the cloth was delivered to tailors who turned it into suits and trousers. The reigning color, as far as I recall, was gray. Mother and Aunt Malcia would stand for hours on Zielony Rynek, the Green Market, and sell those suits and pants. This must have been before Vovo became a taxi driver.

Another memory from Gdanska: Since early childhood I had suffered from headaches, a trait I must have inherited from my father. I'm lying on a sofa or a bed, my temples throbbing with pain. There were no painkilling pills yet, so instead I'd fasten a tight wet cloth around my head. At times thin cool slices of a raw potato were inserted between the cloth and my burning forehead. My pain would then be somewhat eased. At other times, particularly in the evenings, I would stare at the lit windows of a building across the street, and this would gradually lull me to sleep.

When I got really sick my mother would ask Dr. Redlich to come and see me. I recall him, somewhat vaguely, as a balding, black-haired, thick-browed, middle-aged man. He lived at that time nearby on 1go Maja. Doctor and later Professor Franciszek Redlich was a distant relative. Although I was never a "roots seeker" and genealogy did not interest me in particular, I did try to establish some biographical facts concerning my namesake. Fredzio, as they used to call him when he was young, was born in Brzezany in 1896. His family was one of the very few assimilated Jewish families in town. He graduated from the local high school, the Gimnazjum, before the First World War, and started studying medicine. During the war he served as a medical assistant in the Austrian army, and after receiving his MD in Vienna, he specialized in pediatrics in Lwow, becoming one of the town's leading pediatricians. Years later I met people my age, both in Israel and abroad, who as children had been patients of my relative. One of the most unexpected and astounding stories about Dr. Redlich came from Joanna Szczesna, an ex-Solidarity activist and a leading journalist at Gazeta Wyborcza, in Warsaw, who told me that Dr. Redlich had saved her life in postwar Lodz.

In Lwow, Dr. Redlich married the divorced wife of a Polish army officer who hid him during the German occupation. After the war they, like us, settled in Lodz. From his official biography I learned that Dr. Redlich headed the Department of Pediatrics in the Lwow Ghetto hospital, and later was a prisoner at the Janowska labor camp, from which he eventually managed to escape.[6] After the war he served on the faculty of the newly-founded Lodz University. He obtained his professorship there in the early 1950s, and became, as he had been in prewar Lwow, one of the town's leading pediatricians. He held many additional posts and was awarded numerous distinctions for his service to the community. He was sixty-eight when he died. When I interviewed Marek Edelman, one of the legendary leaders of the Warsaw Ghetto Uprising and a cardiologist by profession, I was surprised to hear that one of his mentors at the Lodz University School of Medicine had been my relative. When Professor Redlich became ill with heart disease, Edelman treated him. I was also intrigued by the fate of Dr. Redlich's only son. I knew from my days in Lodz that the doctor had a son my age, but while talking to Edelman and inquiring, as I often did when speaking to people who knew my relative, he couldn't tell me much, only that Dr. Redlich's son had left Poland. The stories seemed to have a tragic ending, but I have never found any specific details.

Some of my most pleasant Lodz memories are of the outings to the Zdrowie Recreation Park and to the City Zoo. These took place, usually, on weekends with nice, sunny weather. We would walk around the place or row a boat. One of my Lodz photos shows me standing on the pier, with Salek and Moniek Pomerantz on either side of me, and the water shimmering in the background. The three of us are bare-chested. The Pomerantz brothers, and other boys I knew, enjoyed swimming. I didn't. Our gym instructor at the Hebrew School, Captain Majerczak, taught us "dry swimming." Essentially, we lay belly-down on chairs and moved our hands and legs to his instructions. I never dared try this in real water. I have remained a lousy, water-fearing swimmer, limited to the breaststroke, and even that mainly in water I can stand in, should I become too scared. I do not recall the Lodz Zoo in detail, but I still cherish a photo showing a real elephant with us, four smiling Jewish youngsters, "riding" on its back. I'm the first one, holding on to the elephant's neck. Heniek Napadow sits behind me, his hands on my shoulders.

When some years ago an American-Jewish guest scholar at Ben-Gurion University discussed the fate of Jewish children during and after the Holocaust, and painted a starkly dark and depressing picture, I dared to challenge her, and argued that in spite of everything, there were also some bright and happy moments — at least in my postwar years in Lodz. The photo with the elephant was clear-cut proof of that. There were also outings to nearby forests, either with our teachers or with Hashomer Hatzair counselors. Most of my friends used to go to Hashomer Hatzair summer camps. I was never allowed to join them. My mother and the others in our small family must have been protective and afraid to let me out of their reach.

The most popular entertainment in postwar Lodz was the cinema. I was pleasantly surprised when in the Lodz Municipal Archive I discovered documentation confirming the impressions and memories of my adolescent self.[7] For decades I remembered the names of Lodz cinemas. The most popular films were postwar Polish productions, such as *Ulica Graniczna* (*Border Street*), or *Zakazane Piosenki* (*Forbidden Songs*). There were, of course, many Soviet films too. Of the American ones I vividly recall *Gunga Din*. I also went at least once to a performance of the Yiddish Theatre headed by Ida Kaminska. It was "Mirale Efros," with Kaminska in the leading role.

Some of my most exciting and happiest memories were from Hashomer Hatzair, the Zionist youth movement, at 49 Kilinskiego Street. When I returned to Lodz in April 1987 and went to see the building again, I was immediately shocked and depressed. The entrance gate was gray and black, with large patches of soot. The courtyard looked even worse, with the rusting corpse of a car, all four wheels missing, in its center. An elderly Polish couple came down the stairs, and we exchanged a few words. The man, on that early Easter Monday morning, was quite tipsy. I could smell the alcohol on his breath. When I asked whether they recalled any Jews living there, they said yes, there was a family, and they left for Palestine. I was astounded. Was this really the place that was once so full of life and vigor? I recalled many joyous moments on Kilinskiego Street, and when I met decades later with Fayvl Podeh, the first postwar leader of the Hashomer Hatzair in Lodz, he confirmed my memories. "Yes, the youngsters would march around the room with a white and blue flag and sing Hebrew songs. It was not only Zionism. We had to warm up in the unheated quarters at Kilinskiego. Then, there were discussions, recitations, book readings." [8]

I must have joined Hashomer Hatzair either in the fall of 1945 or in early 1946. An old, blurred picture shows five boys facing what must have been a boxlike street camera, on the cobble-stoned corner of Kilinskiego and Narutowicza. All are wearing heavy second-hand winter coats made of rough cloth. Behind them, resting his hand on my shoulder, is Moshe the madrich, our counselor. Even in this small, creased picture, one can detect his nicely carved, gentle face. He wears some sort of a battle-dress, fashionable in the first postwar years. We adored him. Although I do not recall our meetings, talks and outings in detail, his image remains imprinted in my memory.

WE MET AGAIN IN JERUSALEM, ACCIDENTALLY, IN THE EARLY 1960S. I WAS about to leave for the US, for graduate studies at Harvard. Moshe told me that he was studying at the Hebrew University. He must have been around forty at that time. When I returned to Israel a few years later, I was told that Moshe had committed suicide. After that point I thought about him intermittently. His life and death fascinated me. I'm not sure why. He reminded me of my pleasant Lodz years, of the youth movement on Kilinskiego. But his was also a story of high drama and tragedy, or at least, that's the way I perceived it. Finally, I decided to reconstruct Moshe's relatively short life and its tragic end by talking to people who knew him.

I called Moshe Lewin, an eminent retired professor of history in Philadelphia, and we had a long talk. It turned out that he knew Moshe Shmutter as a young boy, and had kept in touch with him for many years. The Lewins and the Shmutters were friends in prewar Vilna. Mishka Lewin was four years older than Moshe. He reminisced: "We used to walk together in a nearby forest, and young Poles attacked us there quite often. I had to defend him, since he was small. I would engage them with my stick while Moshe was running away. He couldn't protect himself then. Later he ended up even taller than me. He was a good-looking youngster. He was a student at the Vilna Tarbut Hebrew high school."[9]

Beniek Miznmacher met Moshe in Lodz, sometime in 1946. They lived in the same "shituf," a collective apartment, at 72 Wschodnia Street, and even shared the same room. "We weren't fully aware of it, but Moshe wasn't 'all there' already during the Lodz times. One day he was given money to buy food for all of us. Instead, he brought a couple of exorbitantly expensive oranges. "They have all the necessary vitamins," he argued, "and this is more important than food." Both Mishka Lewin and Beniek Miznmacher recalled that Moshe was very talented, and was known for writing poems and short stories. [10]

Pinhas Zayonts was fifteen when he arrived in Lodz with a group of youngsters at the Hashomer Hatzair kibbutz, on Kilinskiego 49. He recalled Moshe very vividly. "He was a lively young man. He entertained us, and tried very hard to make us feel happy. I recall a winter outing near Helenowek — a bonfire, Hebrew songs, dancing the hora. Moshe was dancing with the kids. He was excellent in communicating. Perhaps the rather insignificant difference in age, made him acceptable. He seemed to be one of us. We trusted him and confided in him. Moshe had that special quality of empathy, and made us open up. When I told him shortly and haltingly what happened to my parents during the war, he embraced me." [11] Those teenage boys and girls, who survived the war either in Nazi-occupied Poland or in faraway places in Soviet Russia, longed for somebody to trust, for adult models in their shattered lives. There was also a vague erotic element in the relations between the young counselors, male and female, and the youngsters who adored them. The fact that many of these boys and girls had lost one or both parents, and had no family, made such emotional and romantic tendencies even more pressing and urgent.

Zipora Horowitz, then Fela Rozenstein, a survivor of Majdanek, told me that she was one of those teenage girls at Hashomer Hatzair who had a crush on the handsome madrich. "There were rumors that Moshe was in love with the beautiful and talented Dziunia, one of the female counselors, who used to recite Pushkin." Moshe recognized Zipora on a Jerusalem street a few years later, in the early fifties. He was glad to meet her. Since she herself was already at that time a madricha in the Hashomer Hatzair movement in Israel, Moshe offered his experience and advice. "He did not look well, and lived in a rundown place in a Jerusalem convent. I wasn't too eager to meet with him again." [12]

And then there was, of course, the sad and tragic story of Moshe's end in Israel. Mishka Lewin told me that he was constantly worried about Moshe. "He could never focus on one particular matter. He would start something, leave it and start something else. His mental and emotional problems erupted a few years after he came to Israel. He lived in various places, but he always came for visits. It was increasingly obvious that he suffered from some sort of paranoia. He used to tell me that he was constantly surrounded by 'agents,' and talked about it for hours." Mishka Lewin was told, apparently by Moshe's younger brother, that while traveling one day in a public taxi, a sherut, Moshe decided that the people sitting nearby must be "agents," whom he dreaded. He forced the door and jumped. During our long-distance overseas conversation, Lewin kept repeating, "We lost him, it was our loss."[13]

I became obsessed with the need to establish how Moshe actually died. His death somehow fascinated me. It was like solving a sad, but still interesting and meaningful, puzzle. The most exhaustive and reliable source of information was Moshe's brother-in-law Zeev, or "Vovke" as his Vilna friends used to call him. I met with him in a senior citizens' home on the outskirts of Tel-Aviv. Vovke, in spite of his age, was vigorous and highly excitable. His memory wasn't bad at all. "I recall Moshe as a boy of 12 or 13, in prewar Vilna. The Shmutter siblings, Rachel, Moshe, and their younger brother Binyamin, were excellent athletes. They were always referred to as 'the Shmutters.'" Vovke met them again in wartime Russia, in Tashkent. He had just completed his service in the Red Army, and fell in love with Rachel, Moshe's beautiful older sister. She spotted him at a victory ball, on May 9, 1945. She was then 21 and he was 23. "Moshe was 18 or 19 at the time, somewhat naive in his enthusiastic, vociferous support for Zionism. I advised him to shut up and to leave Russia as soon as possible."[14]

Moshe arrived in Lodz in early 1946, and immediately became active in the local branch of Hashomer Hatzair. Vovke and Rachel arrived in Lodz in May, and Moshe arranged for them to stay at a Hashomer Hatzair collective on Poludniowa. Then they left for Germany, where

Vovke worked for the UNRRA. Within two or three years they arrived in Israel. Vovke recalled that he was very eager at the time to leave Poland. As early as his trip from Russia to Lodz he had overheard a Polish woman at the Krakow rail station complain "Stalin takes our coal and sends us Jews."

When I asked Vovke whether Moshe ever told him about his experience as a youth counselor, he recalled some of Moshe's impressions. "He told me of children shattered by the war, and of one girl in particular who refused to join their outings to a nearby forest. 'I am scared of forests,' she kept repeating. It turned out that her family had been murdered in a forest. Moshe tried to restore a somewhat normal way of life to those youngsters. He was an excellent educator and was very successful in his work. He had a good sense of humor, with children as well as with adults."

According to Vovke, Moshe arrived in Israel sometime in 1949, and served for nearly two years in the Israeli army. Then he started studying Law at the Hebrew University, in Jerusalem. It must have been 1951 or 1952. At the same time he worked in a court, as translator: his knowledge of Yiddish, Russian and Polish seems to have come in handy. However, as in other endeavors, he did not persist in his studies for long. For some time he was involved in archeological digs at Massada and became increasingly involved in leftist politics. His Zionist-Marxist ideology was supplanted by Communism. It is not clear whether he became a card-carrying member of the Israeli Communist Party, but, according to Vovke, he was constantly participating in Communist meetings and demonstrations. He also wrote for the Israeli Communist daily *Kol Haam*, under the pen name "Moshe Oshres." It was during that time that Moshe began to associate with the Russian-born, pro-Communist Israeli poet Alexander Pen. According to Vovke "they used to drink together and discuss politics and literature. Although Moshe knew rather well the realities of life in Soviet Russia, he was ready to overlook everything, while becoming increasingly critical of Israel." It is quite possible that Moshe had an idealized image of the new Zionist state and society.

While living in a student dormitory Moshe began to realize that his room was being searched when he was out. At one point, a young woman he had come to know confessed that she was sent to follow him and inform on him. Moshe was, apparently, hemmed-in by his own radical ideology and politics, by an oversuspicious and anti-Communist Israeli security establishment that possibly monitored him, and by his growing mental and emotional idiosyncrasies. "I sensed already then, that Moshe was ill. I didn't know whether this was schizophrenia," Vovke confided. "It was impossible to convince him to seek professional help. He was once hospitalized in a psychiatric hospital. Then, he was granted a leave for a few days, and never returned."

The last episode in Moshe's life, as related by Vovke, was a truck accident. It was sometime in 1964. "Moshe was missing for a week and nobody knew where he was. I suspected that something bad had happened. And then I got a call from Abu Kabir, the Pathology Institute, to come and identify his body. We were devastated. Later they showed me the police report. Moshe had been waiting at a bus stop. A huge semitrailer passed by and Moshe was actually 'erased' under its wheels. I was quite convinced that this was no accident. I suspected that this was suicide. During the trial that followed, the driver's lawyer presented a number of previous 'near accidents,' in which Moshe had been involved. The charges against the driver were dropped. His insurance company covered the funeral expenses. Only the immediate family participated in that funeral. Moshe's mother, Zipora, was never told about his tragic death, and was fed all kinds of stories. When she died she was buried next to him, in the old Segula cemetery in Petach-Tikva."

When I asked Vovke about Moshe's relations with women, he told me that his brother-in-law was incapable of ever maintaining a steady, normal relationship. "At one time he was involved with an attractive young woman. She came to Israel from Iraq in the early 1950s. She was educated, and a Communist. But it didn't last. Moshe was a very handsome man, but he deteriorated. During his last few years he abstained from women altogether." For me, Moshe will always remain the young, sensitive, good-natured and good-looking, ultimate youth counselor, the "madrich."

A MOST MEMORABLE RECOLLECTION I HAVE IN CONNECTION WITH Hashomer Hatzair was a trip to Warsaw, for the unveiling of the Ghetto Fighters Monument, in April of 1948. We traveled by night train, fully dressed in Hashomer Hatzair garb, blue shirts with white laces. Next morning we marched in the streets of the ruined Polish capital. I recall flags and speeches, and, of course, the impressive granite monument in the grandiose style of wartime Soviet Social Realism. The sculptor, Natan Rapoport, had lived in Russia during the war and was influenced by contemporary Soviet art. Almost forty years later, in April 1987, on my second day in Warsaw, our tourist group was driven to the same site, and by chance there was another ceremony in the front of the monument, with hundreds of young Israelis holding blue-and-white flags. Many wore blue shirts with white laces. What a coincidence!

My uncle Vovo told me that he got his first job in Lodz with Michal Mirski, chief editor of the postwar Yiddish newspaper *Dos Naje Lebn*. Vovo seems to have worked for a while as Mirski's personal chauffeur, driving him around town and probably on occasional trips to Warsaw. I recall one such trip, when Vovo took me along. Then one day he was fired. That's when he became a taxi driver. Vovo was in a way a surrogate father and male role model for me, though he was probably quite different from my actual father. He cared a lot about his appearance, combing and brushing his curly blond hair for hours. He would whistle popular tunes and knew how to dance. He must have been quite illiterate — I never saw him reading a newspaper or a book. He used to drink on occasions and almost always became sick as a result. He was a physical man who believed in spanking, and acted on his beliefs more than once. His palm would leave burning red marks on my skin. At the same time, he was a good and caring person. Women liked him, and he didn't shy away from an affair or two. I still recall a saying he used to repeat: "I'm not a professional porter, but I do pick up a valise from time to time." Malcia must have suffered. I faintly recall her shouting at Vovo and crying when she was in a bad mood. I did not pay much attention to this.

And then there was the Solarz incident. I must have been playing with some friends in and out of the Gdanska Street apartment. It was a pleasant summer afternoon. Vovo was hosting an acquaintance, a driver. When he was about to leave, the man noticed that his briefcase was missing. I do not recall the details, or the exact sequence of events, but I do recall that we went to the house of one of the boys who'd been playing with us. I remembered his last name for decades: Solarz. It must have been the end of the day and the room was quite dark. My uncle asked some questions and the missing briefcase materialized. Then, right there, in front of Solarz and his family, Vovo gave me the worst beating of my life, or at least that is what I remember. Was he right? Why did he do it? What did it signify for me? It is quite clear that he held me responsible for what happened, since it was one of my playmates who'd swiped the briefcase. It is possible that I would have forgotten the beating if it had happened, as other spankings did, inside the four walls of our apartment. What insulted and enraged me was the humiliation in front of others, some of them people whom I'd only just become acquainted with.

The only time I can recall trips away from the Gdanska Street apartment was during the summers. My mother and relatives did not let me go to summer camps, like some of my closest friends did, but I did have trips to Kolumna or Helenowek. To Kolumna we would go together, the whole family. To Helenowek I would be sent alone. The Jewish-Polish writer Henryk Grynberg succinctly describes postwar Kolumna in his autobiographical novel: "green and yellow wooden villas with glass-covered porches, surrounded by pine forests." Most of these houses were built by Lodz Jews before the war. Now they served as a modest summer resort of sorts for the few local survivors and other Jews who settled in postwar Lodz. [15]

Although Henryk's description of Kolumna is from the early fifties, it looked, smelled and sounded quite familiar to me too. I clearly recall the local river with young Jewish men and women splashing each other and having a good time. A slim, dark and particularly good-looking woman, one of Vovo's acquaintances, was wearing hot pants. Summer, vacation and a certain frivolity were in the air. All of this was very unlike gray, urban Lodz. Henryk goes on to describe his adventures in Kolumna in the summer of 1952, when he was sixteen, noting that it was right then and there that he lost his virginity, to a Gypsy woman twice his age. A few years earlier, my photograph was taken in Kolumna. I cherish that image to this day: I must have been twelve or thirteen, and looked like a child.

I stayed for one summer in Helenowek. This was a Jewish children's home in a wooded area, on the outskirts of town. My memories are fragmented, sometimes showing a pleasant place surrounded by trees, and at other times appearing as a quite new, strange and sometimes scary experience. I'd rarely been on my own before, separated from my mother, from Malcia and Vovo. It was a boys' place: boys of different ages slept in one room, took showers together. It was the first time that I saw male bodies in the nude. Some older boys I recall finding quite attractive. I was rather small for my age, longed for my mother and eagerly awaited her Sunday visits. A memory: a group of boys, including myself, is standing at the entrance to the main building, gazing out to the long shaded alley where our Sunday guests are supposed to appear. When I detect my short, limping mother among them, one of the boys, Chaim, remarks viciously: "Here comes a wobbling duck." I was angry enough to kill him for his nasty remark, but I don't recall saying anything or hitting him. The offence and rage of that moment remained buried inside me for years. Chaim, incidentally, like me, was one of the child-actors in *Undzere Kinder*, which was filmed in Lodz after the war. Whenever I watched that film it reminded me of my irritating memory of him.

Close to sixty years after the Helenowek incident I received an unexpected e-mail message from Dr. Maurice Preter, Chaim's son. I had just published an article in which I mentioned my experience as a child actor in *Undzere Kinder*, and he'd happened to read it. Preter is a young psychiatrist practicing in New York, with a deep interest in the Holocaust. He wrote to me that he used *Undzere Kinder* "to teach professional audiences about childhood trauma, the transmission of traumatic experiences and the Shoah." A day later he phoned me, and since I was about to travel to Boston, we arranged to meet there. I was quite uneasy before we met. I wasn't sure whether I should tell him about the Helenowek incident. We had lunch in a noisy fish restaurant in Cambridge, Massachusetts, and immediately seemed to hit it off. We shared an interest in the past, especially in postwar Lodz. I told Maurice about some of my Lodz memories, including the one involving his father, and learned a thing or two about his father's family. It turned out that Chaim Preter had lived in the Soviet Union during the war. His father, Moshe, whom Maurice was named after, was drafted by the Red Army and was killed in the Battle of Smolensk in the summer of 1942. Chaim also had an infant brother who perished, apparently of hunger. Then, a lonely man from their Polish hometown joined Chaim's mother, and after the war the family settled in Lodz. Shortly thereafter, young Chaim, who was apparently a difficult boy, was sent to the Helenowek Children's Home. So, according to Maurice, there must have been strong feelings of loss and abandonment. Finally I was able not only to recall but also to understand Chaim's behavior in those days. My age-old rage suddenly subsided, melted away. I no longer hated, but rather pitied this handsome, bitter young boy. Chaim's story also helped me understand how lucky I was. In spite of my personal loss and trauma, I've never been abandoned. And though I lost my father, I was always with my mother, who never remarried after the war.

I WAS AN AVID READER AND DEVOURED BOOKS. MEMORY FRAGMENTS: I'm standing on a ladder in a lending library, apparently the one on the right side of Narutowicza Street, toward Kilinskiego; I'm asking the librarian to recommend some powiesci zyciowe — life stories. Biographies still interest me. I also used to read popular Polish historical novels by Sienkiewicz, such as *Potop* (*The Deluge*) and *Ogniem i Mieczem* (*By Fire and Sword*), as well as *The Three Musketeers* by Dumas. It seems that my extensive readings in Polish during my adolescence in Lodz gained me a solid, if mostly passive, fluency in that language. This would come in handy in the late 1980s, when I began visiting Poland.

THE HEBREW GHETTO FIGHTERS' SCHOOL WAS A LOCATION OF MUCH significance in my adolescence. Years later, whenever I visited Lodz I was drawn as though by a magnet to the entrance of 18 Poludniowa Street. The place was now shabby and repulsive. When I returned there for the first time, in 1987, two old Polish women showed up, and I engaged them in reminiscences about the postwar years. They told me that the place had become a low-rent apartment building. During another visit, when I approached it from the corner of Piotrkowska Street, I noticed two unshaven men with an old bicycle standing and talking in front of the gate. A large grafitti scrawl of a Star of David adorned the entrance. I took a picture from a "safe" distance and walked away. It is amazing how in contemporary Lodz one block makes such a difference. Renovated Piotrkowska Street is now a modern pedestrian mall, with stores, cafes and restaurants. Rewolucji 1905 r. Street, formerly Poludniowa Street — one block down — is almost a slum.

In the mornings I would leave via the Gdanska Street gate, turn right, walk a block or two, turn left, walk for another 2-3 blocks, cross Piotrkowska and finally get to Poludniowa Street. The school was on the second floor of what before the war seems to have been an ordinary apartment building. I recall a few teachers: Liberman, Rashal, Melamed. Some were respected, others we had epithets for. Melamed, short and bespectacled, was dubbed "Krupka" after a funny character from a cartoon series in the local evening newspaper. Another was nicknamed "Alojzy brodawka," because of a wart — brodawka in Polish — on his chin or forehead. I've kept, through all these years, a formal class photo taken in December of 1948, on the eve of his departure for Israel. An engraved dedication on the photo's bottom says: "For eternal memory, to our teacher I. Geverts, on his aliya to Israel, 6th grade." The six of us are seated and standing around him. Perhaps one or two are missing. Another teacher was our gym instructor, Majerczak, who would at times appear in his Captain's uniform. At the time he was still serving in the Polish Army. I would meet him next only in the late 1990s, at the school reunion in Tel-Aviv. He was quite excited and happy to be surrounded again by his "pupils." My Polish teacher, Karola, remains distinct in my memory. Short, dark and strict, she would demand that we recite perfectly the various noun declensions in Polish. As I walked back home from school I would go over the various declensions time after time. If I make only a few grammatical errors when speaking Polish today, it is Karola's achievement.

My favorite teacher was Israel Glantz. He taught us music, painting and crafts. To whatever extent I can draw for my grandchildren anything resembling a house, or print reasonable Hebrew letters, it is Glantz's legacy.

A most exciting and uplifting experience was the school choir which Glantz headed. Most of the songs were in Hebrew, but here and there a Yiddish song might slip into our repertoire. Our choir must have been quite good, as we were asked to provide the musical accompaniment to *Undzere Kinder*, the only Jewish feature film produced in postwar Poland. At one time the school was putting on a production of Shulamis, a Yiddish play by Goldfaden. I recall playing a black boy, wearing blackface. There were also all kinds of celebrations, usually accompanied by recitals. I must have been good at that, since on each occasion I was asked to memorize and perform a poem or two.

A most vivid and exciting memory from my "acting career" in Lodz was the filming of *Undzere Kinder*. It starred the two popular Yiddish comedians Dzigan and Schumacher. The director was Natan Gross. The most touching and emotional parts of the film were the survival stories re-enacted by three children living in a Jewish children's home. I was one of them. It must have been Glantz who recommended me to Gross. I was thirteen at the time, and the filmmaking was a unique experience and an adventure. Although there were long hours and repeated takes, I enjoyed it immensely. My text was in Yiddish, but since I wasn't fluent in that language they wrote it all up in Polish letters for me to memorize.

A considerable part of *Undzere Kinder* was filmed in Helenowek. I particularly recall the joyous ending, when the two actors leave the children's home, surrounded by happy faces. The film tells the story of Dzigan and Schumacher as they arrive at the Home, and, at night, peek through keyholes and listen to the children telling each other what had happened to them during the war. I am one of those children. I am dressed in striped pajamas and speak Yiddish as if it were my mother tongue. A flashback shows me hiding behind a closet, in a Polish doctor's apartment. And then, when German boots are banging on the steps, I decide to look for a better solution. I dramatically throw myself on a carpet, wrap it around myself and roll away. This wasn't, of course, the real story of my survival. The amazing thing was that at the time of the filming I did not for a moment even consider that the two stories were related to each other within the wider context of the Holocaust. For me it was pure fun. *Undzere Kinder* was never screened in Poland. It was first shown in Israel in the old Eden cinema in Tel-Aviv, apparently in 1951. By that time I was already in Israel, and proudly went to see it with my aunt Rachel. The next showing was in the Tel Aviv Cinemateque, in 1981. One day, unexpectedly, I got a call from Gross, who invited me for a special showing of the film. The event was sponsored by the Tel-Aviv Municipality. The most popular Israeli daily reported that "yesterday the heroes of the film watched themselves as they were 32 years earlier."[16]

A lasting memory from my school years in Lodz has been A.G. We used to share a first-row bench at the school on Poludniowa Street. I would often walk her home, and we must have gone to the movies a couple of times. Her proximity in the classroom excited me day by day. Our knees touched from time to time, and this was bliss. She used to wear a shiny dark blue school outfit and a striped beet-colored T-shirt. She must have been twelve or thirteen at the time. I could still sense her budding young breasts. Once, during a gym session she missed a jump over a wooden "donkey" and was hit between the legs. I became extremely worried that something dangerous could have happened to her. When I interviewed A.G. almost sixty years later, she did not recall any of those things.

Unlike some of my more outgoing and audacious friends, I never experienced an actual, close relationship with a girl. There was perhaps one fleeting exception: a rather heavy teenage girl with a sweet face. She must have been either a neighbor or a visitor. A split-second memory: we sit close to each other on a couch or bed in our Gdanska Street apartment. I lean over her and touch her, and it's pleasant. Nothing more. When I spoke recently with Heniek he told me how he and others would go "hunting" for girls. I didn't even know about it at that time.

IN THE FALL OF 1949, WE BEGAN MAKING ARRANGEMENTS TO LEAVE LODZ for Israel. The Hebrew school, Hashomer Hatzair, and our correspondence with close relatives in Israel, had made this a wholly natural and expected step. In addition to the Zionist and Palestine-oriented instruction at school and the activities at Hashomer Hatzair, I would listen from time to time to Israeli radio. As the reception was very poor, I used to cover my head and the radio with a blanket to block out noises. Through the hums and cracks, it felt as if the Hebrew words and songs were coming from another planet. It was exciting. I would later hear some of these songs issuing from the loudspeakers of "Galila," the ship that brought us to Israel.

Benny Wittlin, a cousin of ours from Toronto, arrived for a short visit sometime in 1946 or 1947, and there was some talk of our going to Canada. And even before that we'd almost set out illegally for Germany: Ben-Zion, a close friend of Vovo's who had arrived from Russia, recommended that we leave with him. Just then I got sick with the mumps, and Vovo refused to go. Ben-Zion left for Germany, lived there for some time in DP camps, and then emigrated to Canada. We stayed on in Lodz for another three years. All this can demonstrate how certain crucial decisions were made on an instantaneous basis in those years.

In late 1949, I went on a trip from Lodz to Wroclaw with a group from Hashomer Hatzair. Expectations were high among us that we would be soon leaving Poland for Israel. Hashomer Hatzair, like other Zionist organizations, was winding down its activities. What lingered in my memory for years was that get-together of Hashomer Hatzair in Wroclaw, formerly German Breslau. We walked through streets that were almost entirely devastated. I was exhausted from the long train journey from Lodz. My only memory of that meeting was a crowded room, with people talking about Eretz Israel. We were apparently sitting on the floor, leaning on each other. I felt a female hand touch and caress my face. It was to remain for many years a most cherished erotic, sensual memory.

I recall a train trip to the Israeli Legation in Warsaw. I went there with my mother to arrange our exit papers. We sat in a darkly furnished waiting room and I leafed through some Hebrew journals. I distinctly recall one of them, Dvar Hashavua. It was richly illustrated, and I was quite impressed. Then came the packing and other preparations for the long journey. We made our final departure, from the Lodz Fabryczna midtown train station, in January of 1950.

1. Author at the entrance to 49 Kilinskiego Street, Lodz, April, 1987.

2. The Lodz Hebrew school reunion, Tel-Aviv, 1997. From left to right: author, Natan Gross, Baruch Kaplinski.

3. A group of Hashomer Hatzair youngsters with their counselor Moshe Shmutter, Lodz, 1946. First on the right: author.

4. Moshe Shmutter (on the right) with his younger brother Binyamin. Lodz, 1946. Courtesy of the Mitznmacher family.

5. Author at 33 Gdanska Street. Lodz, winter 1948.
6. Author with his dog Diana at the taxi of his uncle Vovo.

7. In the Lodz zoo. First from the left: author. Second from the left: Heniek Napadow.

8. In the Zdrowie recreation park in Lodz. From left to right: Shlomo (Salek) Pomerantz, author, Moshe (Moniek) Pomerantz.

9. An outing of Hashomer Hatzair near Lodz. First row, lying down: two unidentified boys. Second row, sitting, from left to right, second: author, third: Moshe (Moniek) Pomerantz. Third row, first right: Eliezer Zalkind. Fourth row, standing, from left to right, third: Shlomo (Salek) Pomerantz, fourth: Aharon Zalkind, sixth: Heniek Napadow.

10. Playing volleyball in Helenowek. First left: Chaim Preter. Center, staring down: author. Second right: Rysiek Lubelski. Courtesy of Chaim Preter.

11. Sixth grade of the Lodz Hebrew school with their teacher I. Geverts, on the eve of his emigration to Israel, December 1948. First row, sitting, from left to right: Rachel Kuperhand, I. Geverts, Karola Proport, author. Second row, standing, from left to right: Ada Gibraltar, Moshe (Moniek) Pomerantz, Shlomo (Salek) Pomerantz, Josef Spokojny, Tsila Wierzba.

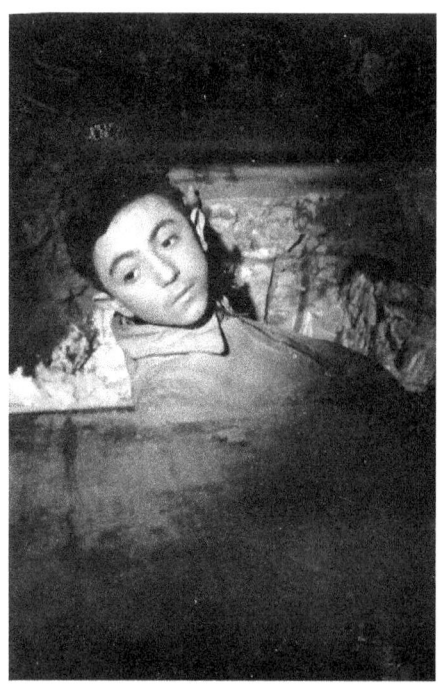

12. Author as child actor in the Yiddish film *Undzere Kinder* (*Our Children*) — Lodz, 1948. Courtesy of Natan Gross.

13. A sequence to *Undzere Kinder* shot in Tel-Aviv in the early 1950s. From left to right, first: Shoshanka, sixth: Moshe (Moniek Pomerantz), seventh: Shimon Dzhigan, eigth: Lidia Schumacher, ninth: Israel Schumacher, tenth: author.

2

POSTWAR LODZ

POLAND SUFFERED TREMENDOUS LOSSES DURING THE SECOND WORLD War. The material devastation was immense, and the country's demography, geography and politics went through extreme upheavals and shifts. Soviet and Nazi occupations caused a catastrophe and wiped out a considerable portion of the Polish elite. With significant changes to its borders, the effects of the Holocaust, and the massive, mostly forced, population movements, Poland lost its two largest minorities: the Ukrainians and the Jews. Millions of Germans were forced to leave the newly-incorporated, formerly German western territories. Poland was turned into an almost mono-ethnic society. It became, in a sense, a different country.

Approximately two million Poles and three million Polish Jews lost their lives as a result of the War. Out of the 24 million Poles who survived the War, 5 million were left outside its borders. Half of them were scattered throughout the world, and the other half lived in eastern Poland, annexed by the Soviet Union and prewar Russia. Most of the prewar Polish citizens living under Soviet rule at the end of the war were repatriated, primarily to the ex-German Recovered Territories, in the immediate postwar years.

People were returning to Poland from forced-labor and concentration camps in Germany, from their wartime relocation to the Soviet Union, and from the West. Others, in much smaller numbers, were leaving Poland, mainly for political reasons. There was also a considerable internal migration, mostly from the countryside to cities: a full quarter of the inhabitants of Poland changed their places of residence during the 1940s. Poland of the immediate postwar years was clearly a country in flux.

Additionally, living conditions in the entire country had changed significantly. The urban population was affected more by the war than the people of the countryside. Such major centers as Warsaw, Lwow, Vilna, and Poznan had either been devastated or fallen to the Soviet Union. Malnutrition and stress affected large parts of the population. The death rate was higher than before the war, and disease and alcoholism were widespread.

The war, as well as the postwar demographic, economic and political upheavals, had far-reaching results. Traditional structures and patterns of life were eroded and social ties within families and among neighbors were weakened. However, at the same time, new opportunities were created, especially for the young and those of proletarian and peasant origin. Prewar professionals and officers, who initially did not support the new regime, started adjusting to the new circumstances and filling various state, local and army positions.

The political transformation of postwar Poland into a Communist-Stalinist state was gradual. The Communist takeover aimed to crush any legal opposition and to destroy the illegal Home Army network. By the end of 1945, close to six thousand terrorist events took place, killing more than 7,000 persons. Alongside the anti-Communist political-military opposition, there was also the common banditry that had typified wartime Poland. Repressions, conducted by the Communist security apparatus, were harsh, with thousands imprisoned and executed. The internal security establishment, guided and supervised by Soviet personnel, swelled substantially within a relatively short period of time.

One of the first steps toward Communist control was the so-called "Referendum," conducted in June 1946. The Communist-dominated National Council, the KRN, sought to demonstrate that Poles basically approved of the postwar geographical and political changes. The Three Times Yes Referendum campaign was bolstered by both mass propaganda and intimidation. The January 1947 elections, in which the Communists used United Front tactics, resulted in a victory of the Communist-dominated Democratic Bloc. The new Government formed in February was clearly under the influence of the PPR, the Polish Communist Party, and within the PPR, the Moscow-oriented section gained the upper hand. From that point, the Communist Party continued to consolidate its control of state and society. In December of 1948 the PPR merged with the PPS, the Polish Socialist Party, to form a single political entity, the PZPR, the Polish United Workers Party, which would dominate the Polish political scene for years to come. Its membership grew steadily. The Party was particularly interested in mobilizing the support of the young, and several youth organizations were amalgamated into one massive, Communist-oriented youth movement, the ZMP — Zwiazek Mlodziezy Polskiej — the Union of Polish Youth. In the years 1949-1950 Poland underwent further Sovietization and Stalinization. The profound changes within the country were also marked by a growing isolation from the West.[1]

Postwar Poland's economy and society were in the process of reconstruction. Criticism of and disappointment with the "new Poland," which was increasingly under the sway of Communist Russia, were balanced by enthusiasm and support for an optimistic and future-oriented vision of the country. Increasing that enthusiasm was the fact that the new political and administrative establishment employed an impressive number of people. At the same time, economic problems and difficulties, including poverty and in particular a lack of food, resulted in widespread dissatisfaction. A wave of strikes erupted in a number of industrial centers, the largest of them taking place in Lodz in August-September 1945. More than a hundred strikes broke out over the course of 1946. An improvement in the standard of living in 1947, and the tightening of state control, brought these workers' strikes to an end.

As we have seen, the country's mood in the immediate postwar years was mixed. The war had ended with a victory over Hitler's Germany and the country was being rebuilt: in some places, such as devastated Warsaw, rebuilt literally from scratch. However, victory and reconstruction were also followed by the growing domination of Stalin's Russia. For many Poles this was "defeat in victory."

A basic concept in the political discourse of Poland in the early postwar years was that of a mono-ethnic state. Despite the ideological and political conflicts within postwar Polish society, and the criticism of the increasingly Communist and Soviet-oriented regime, the idea of a mono-ethnic Poland served as a unifying factor. The principle of mono-ethnicity and the undisputed Polishness of the newly established state, as well as the impressive gains along its western borders, eased the acceptance of the territorial losses in the east. The fact that prewar Poland had contained sizeable ethnic minorities was now considered a source of instability and a major element in the disintegration of the Second Polish Republic. The atrocities of the Second World War, the impact of Nazi ethnic policies, Nazi attitudes and Nazi policies toward Jews in particular, as well as Polish images of and prejudices against Jews connected with the Soviet occupation of the eastern borderlands, accentuated Polish preferences for an "utterly Polish" Poland.

The War resulted in mistrust and hostility of Poles towards the "other," be that "other" German, Ukrainian or Jew. Prevailing anti-German attitudes were used by the Communist leadership to integrate Polish society and gain popular support. Anti-German sentiment served the legitimization of the new order quite well. Official patriotic slogans accompanying the ethnic cleansing of the previously German lands were now attractive even to prewar Polish nationalists. Recent memories of the bloody Polish-Ukrainian conflict along the eastern borderlands under the German and Soviet occupations created attitudes of hostility towards the Ukrainians. In spite of the almost total annihilation of Polish Jewry, anti-Semitism became a prevalent feature of postwar Polish society. Although anti-German, anti-Ukrainian and anti-Jewish attitudes had their roots in pre-war Poland, they were considerably aggravated by the war. The regime's attitudes and policies in respect to non-

Poles differed, at least to some extent, from those of Polish society at large. Whereas Germans and Ukrainians were suspected, hated and mistreated by both state and society, the Jews, although disliked by many Poles, were relatively favored by the regime.[2]

Lodz, known for its textile industry, was one of the few large Polish cities not affected by the wartime bombardments and devastation. Still a village in the early 19th century, Lodz became the second largest city of interwar Poland. During the second half of the 19th century it rapidly modernized. Its population grew from a few thousands in the 1830s to 672,000 in the late 1930s. There was a steady and massive influx of newcomers. Throughout the 19th century and the first decades of the 20th century it was populated mainly by Poles, Jews and Germans, and it acquired a multi-ethnic and multi-cultural flavor. Its population on the eve of the Second World War was 57% Polish, 34% Jewish and 9% German. The Jewish population of Lodz increased from a few thousands in the 1830s to 233,000 in 1939.[3]

The essence of this fast-growing urban conglomerate has been succinctly described in both Polish and Jewish literature of the late 19th and early 20th century. The Polish Nobel Laureate Wladyslaw Reymont spoke in his *Ziemia obiecana* (*Promised Land*) of the dynamic and socially cruel realities of Lodz. The constantly inflowing settlers held high hopes for their future and were usually confronted with inhuman capitalism and personal alienation. Israel Joshua Singer, the older brother of Isaac Bashevis Singer, depicted Lodz in his Yiddish novel *The Brothers Ashkenazi* in a similar manner. The city bred conflicts of all sorts: between brother and brother, between owner and worker, between Gentile and Jew. Joseph Roth, in a short novel set in Hotel Savoy in Lodz in the immediate post-World War I years, presented the dramatic fates of the hotel's guests within the wider context of war and revolution.

There was a continuity over time in the pattern of urban settlement of the town's three main ethnic groups. Poles tended to inhabit the outlying neighborhoods, while Germans and Jews lived mostly in the town center. The second half of the 1930s witnessed growing tensions among Poles, Jews and Germans.[4]

Lodz has always been a place of great contrasts. Textile factories, workers' housing and industrialists' mansions marked its landscape. Industrial areas of the city, such as the huge Poznanski factory complex, were located right in the midtown area. Not far from the impressive and elegant mansions of its affluent industrialists spread cobbled alleys and courtyards crowded by workers' tenements. The dominant colors were dark gray and brick red. Lodz was often referred to as "the evil city" by critics of its fast industrialization and urbanization, ruthless capitalism and lack of historical and esthetic values. Nevertheless, it was always a dynamic industrial and urban center, marked by an intense vitality: Arthur Rubinstein, the renowned pianist, and Julian Tuwim, an outstanding modern Polish poet, have both held and expressed strong sentiments towards Lodz, the city of their childhood.

The hub of downtown Lodz has always been Piotrkowska Street, stretching south of Plac Wolnosci, Liberty Square. It was lined by stores, restaurants and coffee houses. Most of the theaters and numerous cinemas were located on or around Piotrkowska. The oldest hotel in Lodz, the Hotel Polski, or Polish Hotel, was located on Piotrkowska, around the corner of Plac Wolnosci. In 1945 it served as the headquarters of the Soviet Army that was stationed in the city. The most elegant and prestigious hotel has always been The Grand, on Piotrkowska, a few minutes walk from Plac Wolnosci. Another impressive hotel was The Savoy, on a narrow side street, just around the corner from The Grand. In the early postwar years The Savoy hosted the "Pickwick" literary club bar, which was highly popular with literati and artists of all sorts. An American-Jewish journalist who visited Lodz in the summer of 1946 found Piotrkowska bustling and noisy. "The stores were open, the cafes lively, the streetcars crowded."[5]

North of Plac Wolnosci, beyond Plac Koscielny, Church Square, the four-kilometer-long Piotrkowska turned into Zgierska Street. East of Zgierska sprawled the Baluty neighborhood, inhabited mostly by poor Jews. This is where the Lodz Ghetto was located. It was the second largest ghetto in Poland. After the deportations and deaths, there were still close to 70,000 Jews living in the ghetto in mid-1944. Most of them were deported to Auschwitz in August. Less than a thousand Jews survived, hiding in the desolate ghetto area. It is estimated that 7000-10,000 Jews from Lodz survived in the camps in Germany. Some of them returned to Lodz, while others stayed on in Germany, mostly in DP camps, and eventually left for Palestine/Israel or North America.[6]

Lodz retained its character as an industrial and proletarian city in the postwar years, but lost its multiethnic and multicultural flavor. Most of its prewar Germans disappeared. Its Jewish population was drastically diminished, and most of those Jews who settled in Lodz in the postwar years were not original *Lodzer Yidn* — Lodz Jews. The official postwar Communist image of the city cultivated its "proletarianism" and its "Polishness." Former industrialists' mansions and villas now housed various institutions of the Communist state. Still, at least in the bleak early postwar years, Lodz was a bustling urban centre, attractive to shoppers from all over Poland. For a while it also served as an unofficial "interim capital," while Warsaw was being rebuilt.[7]

As might be expected, the demographic profile of Lodz changed dramatically during the war and in the early postwar years. The total population of Lodz was 680,000 on the eve of the German invasion. A majority, close to 390,000, were Poles. The 233,000 Lodz Jews constituted a third of the city's population. Its 60,000 Germans constituted less than 9%. The total population of Lodz shrank considerably during the German occupation. Its Jewish population, including Jews deported to the Lodz Ghetto from various locations in Germany and other German occupied cities, was almost totally annihilated. The Polish population declined as some Poles were sent to forced labor and concentration camps. At the same time, the German population of Lodz — which became part of the German Reich and was renamed Litzmanstadt, to commemorate the World War I German General Karl Litzmann — rose to about 100,000. These were local prewar Germans as well as Germans from the Reich and *Volksdeutsche*. Many Lodz Germans escaped westward in the weeks preceding the arrival of the Red Army. In May 1945, three months after liberation, the population of Lodz reached only 422,000, slightly over 60% of its prewar population. Now, however, an overwhelming majority — 380,000 — were Poles. Germans were still the next nationality group, around 33,000. As a result of the influx of Jewish survivors and Jewish returnees from the Soviet Union, the number of Jews in Lodz in the summer of 1945 reached 20,000. The overall Lodz population was increasing rapidly. Over half a million people lived in Lodz in early 1947, out of which 25,000 were Germans. Whereas the German population was steadily decreasing, the number of Jews — despite the fact that many of the newly-arriving left after a relatively short stay — increased to about 30,000 during the summer of 1946. Although Lodz had lost its prewar multiethnic character, every tenth inhabitant was non-Polish during the immediate postwar years. As it was before the war, Lodz after the war was predominantly proletarian. Out of nearly 224,000 employed inhabitants in early 1948, close to 180,000 were laborers.[8]

Lodz was liberated on Friday, January 19th, 1945, by the First Belorussian Front Group, headed by Marshal Zhukov and the First Ukrainian Front Group, headed by General Lelushenko. The city was encircled by the Russians from the north and the south. The westward direction was left open, to ease the German retreat and avoid prolonged street battles. In the vicinity of Lodz the Soviet Air Force bombed mainly road and railroad junctions. Soviet tanks reached the northwest outskirts of town during the night between the 17th and the 18th. Some small-scale street fighting, including skirmishes in midtown around the Lodz Fabryczna railroad station, continued throughout the 19th, the official liberation date. The liberation of Lodz, during which there were hardly any civilian casualties, was marred by the murder by the retreating Germans of hundreds of Polish prisoners in the Radogoszcz labor camp. The Red Army Military Command in Lodz was established on Sunday, January 20th, and an "operational group" representing the Polish Temporary Government, headed by Colonel Ignacy Loga-Sowinski, arrived in Lodz on the same day. A joint meeting of Government and Communist Party representatives was held at the Grand Hotel on Monday. As a result, Loga-Sowinski assumed the leading position in the local Party apparatus, whereas Kazimierz Mijal became the head of the civilian administration. He was elected as Mayor of Lodz in early March, 1945.[9]

Red Army soldiers and officers were mostly welcomed by the local Polish population, at least during the first few days. Red and white-red flags were displayed at entrances to buildings. Piotrkowska, renamed Hitlerstrasse during the German occupation, was filled now to the brim. "It was 10 a.m. Gigantic tanks were parked on Plac Wolnosci and one could see Soviet and Polish soldiers. The crowd went wild with joy. People danced and cried."[10] The welcome and enthusiasm of the crowds was directed primarily towards Polish soldiers and officers and Polish military symbols. Close to 30,000 people massed for a rally in the Poniatowski Park on January 23. The main speaker was Loga-Sowinski, dressed in a Polish Army uniform. In his speech he emphasized the town's "proletarian" pedigree: "Only Lodz, the capital of the Polish proletariat, could burst forth with such universal, spontaneous enthusiasm."[11]

Vasily Grossman, the renowned wartime Soviet journalist and writer, who arrived in Lodz a short while after its liberation, wrote: "Lodz. Five hundred factories and plants. Directors and owners have fled. At the moment they are managed by workers. The electric power station, trams, railway are working at full power."[12] The textile industry was nationalized soon after liberation. A considerable portion of the factories resumed production in the month of February. Some workers spontaneously formed temporary management committees to prevent looting. In numerous factories, workers initially received their wages not in money but in products, such as food, clothes and coal. The municipal Committee of the PPR, the Communist Party, assumed a central role in factory management. Mijal, the Mayor, and heads of the security establishment in town were frequent visitors at the Lodz PPR Committee headed by Loga-Sowinski. At the same time, retail commerce stayed in private hands. Numerous small foodstores, bakeries, restaurants and coffee shops opened in the center of town.[13]

In spite of the increasing normalization of everyday life, armed opposition by the political underground as well as plain banditry still prevailed for some time around Lodz, mainly in the outlying districts. MO

(Citizens Militia) locations were attacked and militiamen were killed. Empty, formerly German apartments and houses were looted.[14] An operational security group was dispatched to Lodz as early as January 20, 1945, and the appointed head of the Public Security Office in Lodz and Lodz Province, Mieczyslaw Moczar, arrived a few days later. Moczar, then in his early thirties, was born in Lodz in 1913, joined the Communist Party there and was imprisoned just before the War. He was released a short time after the War began and lived in Soviet-occupied Bialystok, where he was apparently recruited by the NKVD. During the German occupation Moczar was active in a number of Communist partisan units in central Poland. He returned to his native Lodz with the rank of Colonel. Starting in December 1945, Moczar was also a member of the PPR Central Committee. As chief security boss in Lodz during the next three years, Moczar became infamous for his ruthlessness toward political opponents and striking workers.[15]

The major tasks of the Lodz security establishment under Moczar were to eradicate any political opposition to the new regime and to control industry. During the summer and early fall of 1945, dozens of anti-Communist underground units were liquidated in the Lodz Province. A special security operational group of 1000 men consisting of Internal Security personnel, Polish Army soldiers, Soviet soldiers, and Polish militiamen was established in April 1946. Its activities, including numerous arrests, seriously damaged the still-existing underground. More than a hundred people were executed. Moczar personally participated in the apprehension and investigation of those arrested and earned his reputation as a cruel opponent of the underground. One of the underground organizations issued a death verdict against him. Moczar's achievements won him a promotion to the rank of Brigadier General in the summer of 1947. The nearly total liquidation of armed resistance in the Lodz Province coincided with Moczar's transfer to a position in the Security Ministry, in Warsaw, in the summer of 1948.

Moczar and his security apparatus were very active in the June 1946 Referendum and in the January 1947 elections. A list of 8,000 trusted persons to oversee the Referendum had been prepared by the Lodz Province Security Office. Moczar's people applied pressure, including threats of arrest; even some PPS activists were arrested. People were summoned to Security offices and terrorized to vote the "right" way. The Lodz PPR leadership praised local Security activists for their "militant" stance.[16]

Lodz Security was also involved in the suppression of student protests. A most dramatic event in postwar Lodz was the murder of Maria Tyrankiewicz, a second year student in the Dentistry Department of Lodz University. Her body was found in one of the city parks, on the evening of December 14, 1945. Rumors quickly spread accusing Red Army soldiers stationed nearby of rape and murder. These rumors fed on the fact that the murderer was not apprehended. Anti-Soviet moods intensified among local students. Lodz Security authorities pressured for an immediate and "quiet" funeral. However, a crowd of close to 2,000 students maintained a vigil around the casket, and eventually, a funeral procession of about 6,000 students from various academic institutions marched through the city's main thoroughfares, including Piotrkowska, in the morning hours of December 19. Leading the funeral procession were the University Rector, Professor Tadeusz Kotarbinski, and the Academic Priest, Father Rostworowski. Student delegations from other cities attended as well. Some of the marchers clashed with Security personnel and with the militia. On the way back from the cemetery a group of students gathered in front of *Glos Robotniczy* — The Workers' Voice — the PPR newspaper building. Windows were smashed and the police started shooting in the air. Dozens of students were arrested that evening in the University dormitories. During the next few days Lodz newspapers ran a campaign aimed at "brawlers" and "neofascist" students. Workers' meetings in various textile plants condemned "reactionary elements among the academic youth." In spite of the official criticism against students, at least some public support for them was apparent. Thus, tram drivers all over the city refused to charge students for some time. Another clash between students and the militia occurred in May of 1946, in connection with the 3rd of May, Constitution Day. Following a church ceremony, a group of students marched along Piotrkowska Street shouting "Long live Mikolajczyk" and "Down with the PPR." Militiamen shot at the marchers. One student was killed and a few were wounded. Workers were utilized once more to condemn the protesters.[17]

A major source of unrest in Lodz in the early postwar years was the tendency for massive workers' strikes, mainly in the textile industry. Lodz had its working-class traditions based on syndicalism, skill, nationalism and gender. The war had introduced women into the workforce to a considerable extent. The first postwar strikes erupted as early as May of 1945. In July there were twenty-three strikes. The main issues had to do with food supply, high prices and low wages. The private market that still existed in food and clothing gave rise to widespread notions of injustice among workers. A Ministry of Information and Propaganda report stated that "The Lodz worker cannot accept the fact that his children can only gaze at cake from afar, and he is not satisfied that one like himself who works hard earns so little, while some parasite makes big money."[18] August and September of 1945 witnessed a wave of strikes in Lodz and vicinity. As part of a near-general strike between the 7th and 25th of May, 1946, some 25,000 workers stopped production in thirty factories. Tram workers struck several times throughout 1946. The most massive and final wave of strikes began at the Poznanski Plant, in September 1947, and soon spread to other factories. Within days 26,000 workers were on strike. The winter of 1947/48 marked the final repression of large-scale labor unrest.[19]

Although the Red Army was initially greeted as a liberator from Nazi occupation, attitudes toward the Soviet Union and the Soviet-supported PPR were quite negative. One of the most popular political parties in postwar Lodz was the PSL — the Polish Peasant Party, headed by Mikolajczyk. There were 50,000 PSL members in the Lodz district in late 1945. Rumors played a significant role in the shaping and spreading of anti-Soviet attitudes. One of the most repeated rumors, especially on the eve of the January 1947 elections, was that additional Red Army units were about to be stationed in Poland. Grafitti stating "Stalinie, tys maczal rece w Katynie" (Stalin, you bloodied your hands in Katyn) appeared in Lodz in May 1948.

The public mood of postwar Lodz was affected by the massive influx of people from all over Poland. Lodz, a city hardly touched by the wartime devastation, but which had lost most of its German and Jewish population, became a desirable site for resettlement. Communist Party functionaries, writers, artists, students and academics now preferred Lodz to other cities. This, in turn, affected the locals and the returning prewar inhabitants. National and ethnic hostility was directed mainly towards Germans and Jews. Public trials of former Nazi bureaucrats stirred strong anti-German emotions. The influx of Holocaust survivors and Polish Jews returning from the Soviet Union, as well as widespread beliefs that the new Communist structures were permeated with Jews, resulted in an increase of anti-Semitism. One report cited a rumor that "50,000 Jews have been brought to Lodz and they are favored in the *aprowizacja* (food supply)." In Radomsko, a city south of Lodz, a rumor spread in the summer of 1946 that 10,000 Jews would be settled there, and local inhabitants would be banished from their apartments.

Jews became the scapegoat of Polish economic and political grievances. They were accused of shirking factory work and preferring white-collar jobs. One official report stated: "The worker wants to see the Jew around him, but as a worker, not as a director... The worker is outraged that all higher positions are taken by Jews who steal and then escape with the money abroad." Three thousand workers were on strike for two days in mid-1945 in the Biederman textile plant against the appointment of a Jewish director. Women workers were among the most outspoken critics at workers' meetings. They complained that since Jews had special privileges in the supply and distribution of food, Polish children had to go without milk. Anti-Jewish accusations claimed that a high percentage of the top ranks of the UB, the Security apparatus, had been occupied by Jews.

Anti-Semitic moods intensified in Lodz in the wake of the Kielce pogrom and the subsequent trial of its perpetrators, in July 1946. Official meetings in Lodz factories were convened to condemn the pogrom. However, most workers were rather apathetic and only a small number were ready to sign resolutions. When the press, nevertheless, reported that there was "massive" workers' support for the proposed resolutions, anti-Jewish and anti-regime sentiments increased. Strikes broke out in some factories. Some Lodz Jews sensed a pre-pogrom atmosphere. Official reports in late July 1946 spoke of a tense situation.[20] However, despite several anti-Semitic incidents, there was no pogrom in postwar Lodz.

Lodz was the most significant cultural center in Poland in the immediate postwar years. Its proximity to Warsaw, which was in the process of reconstruction, and the availability of apartments and office spaces, attracted writers, artists and academics. Adolf Rudnicki, the Polish-Jewish writer and essayist, recalled that "Lodz, with its thousand chimneys, smoky, narrow, wooden and ugly, offered empty apartments left by Germans and a desk to work at." The new regime also favored Lodz, a "proletarian" and "red" city. Former residents of devastated Warsaw, people repatriated from the eastern borderlands, former inmates of concentration camps and a few Poles returning from the West swarmed to the "substitute capital." Despite the war and its national and personal tragedies, there was energy and vitality in the air. According to Rudnicki, "It hasn't been easy to forget the spring and summer of 1945. After the lifeless [war] years, the gates to life reopened. People met and embraced in the middle of the street at any time of the day. In this ugliest of Polish cities, which history turned for a while into a second capital, we worked as never before."[21]

Lodz became a media and publishing center. The first post-occupation newspaper printed in Lodz was *Wolna Lodz*: it appeared less than a week after liberation, but it didn't last long. The following weeks and months witnessed a steady increase in the number of dailies and periodicals of various kinds. Eight newspapers, fifteen weeklies and 27 monthlies were being published in Lodz in 1946.[22] The most political and most regime-oriented were the dailies *Robotnik, Glos Robotniczy, Glos Ludu* and *Polska Zbrojna*. A popular weekly paper was the satirical *Szpilki*. The most popular daily newspaper was the *Express Ilustrowany*. A leading journal on theater arts was *Lodz Teatralna*. The most outstanding ideologically Marxist journal was the *Kuznica*. Its editorial group included Jan Kott, Mieczyslaw Jastrun, Adam Wazyk, Adolf Rudnicki and Kazimierz Brandys. Another cultural and academic publication was *Mysl Wspolczesna*, initiated by a group of Lodz University professors. Its Chief Editor was the leading young Marxist philosopher Adam Schaff. The most significant Polish postwar publishing house, actually a publishing empire, *Czytelnik*, arrived in Lodz from Lublin on January 30, 1945 and was installed on Piotrkowska. Its boss was the indefatigable Jerzy Borejsza, a leading figure in postwar Polish Communist culture.[23]

Lodz also became a significant academic center. Unlike Krakow and Warsaw, Lodz lacked a university tradition. The only institution of higher learning in prewar Lodz was the socialist-oriented Wolna Wszechnica Polska. It resumed its activity in March 1945. A Government decision to found both a university and a polytechnic in Lodz was signed in May of that year. During its first academic year, that of 1945/46, Lodz University had an attendance of more than seven thousand students. University Rector was the renowned Polish philosopher Tadeusz Kotarbinski and among its philosophy students was the future philosopher, Leszek Kolakowski. Another student who would later achieve nationwide fame was Maria Janion. Students arrived from all over Poland. Many were demobilized soldiers, former partisans and former camp inmates. Still others were former inhabitants of the eastern borderlands and returnees from the Soviet Union. The average age was higher than before the war. Special preparatory programs were opened for those lacking the Matura — the high school matriculation certificate.[24]

Postwar Lodz had a lively literary scene. Public meetings with writers in Sienkiewicza Park became quite popular. The literati would meet in the various coffee houses. Close to two hundred writers settled in Lodz with the assistance of the government and the local authorities. Among them was Wladyslaw Broniewski, who left the Soviet Union with General Anders' Army, lived for the latter part of the war in Jerusalem and arrived in Lodz in early 1946. Julian Tuwim, a native son of Lodz who spent the war years in the Americas, moved to Warsaw after it was over but continued to nourish a strong personal and sentimental attachment to the city of his childhood. Tuwim's mother, who had stayed in Lodz during the German occupation, was thrown from the window of her apartment on Kosciuszko Avenue and was buried in the Lodz cemetery. In a poem published in 1949, Tuwim mourned his mother and spoke of his and his mother's Polish-Jewish identity:

> There is in the Lodz cemetery
> In the Jewish cemetery
> The Polish grave of my mother
> My Jewish mother
> The grave of my mother the Pole
> My mother — the Jewess...[25]

Postwar Lodz became a leading center for the theater. First rehearsals for a review performance began just days after liberation, and "This is Our Lodz" was warmly accepted by the public in early February 1945. Seats were sold out in Lutnia Hall; people stood in the aisles. When the actors appeared on the stage dressed in their shabby clothes, suitcases in their hands, the audience started crying. The first professional theater to settle in a prewar theater building on Cegielniana Street was the Polish Army Theater. It premiered with Wyspianski's "Wedding" in late March. Soon the Lodz City Theater staged performances. It also opened a drama studio in the Poznanski Palace on Gdanska Street, which it shared with the Lodz Conservatory. The satirical Syrena Theater on Traugutta Street opened its doors in December. Thirteen theaters performed in Lodz in 1946. Its four drama theaters had thirty premier performances in the course of 1948. Close to 800,000 theater tickets were sold in 1946. Only slightly more than half of that number had been sold by Lodz theaters in 1938, when its population was considerably larger. This difference could be attributed to the postwar "hunger" for art and entertainment, as well as to the state-subsidized ticket prices and new social strata of theater-goers.[26]

THE RENOWNED POLISH THEATER DIRECTOR LEON SCHILLER, WHO HAD been imprisoned during the war in German concentration camps, arrived in Lodz in late 1945 and joined the Polish Army Theater. "When Leon Schiller appeared in the overcrowded rehearsal hall on the theater's ground floor wearing a battledress stretched tightly over his already prominent round belly, his familiar bald head shining, my heart lept into my throat," recalled Erwin Axer. Schiller's work in postwar Lodz began with "Easter," a brand new play focusing on prewar Polish-Jewish relations and on the Holocaust. The most acclaimed play Schiller directed in Lodz at the Army Theater was the comic opera *Krakowiacy i Gorale*, Cracovians and Highlanders. Schiller left Lodz in 1949, following his appointment as director of the Teatr Polski in Warsaw. He confided in Adolf Rudnicki a few years later: "In Lodz I spent a few beautiful, unforgettable years. I had my second youth there. I was utterly happy."[27]

Despite, and perhaps because of, the difficulties of everyday life, the few modest restaurants and coffee houses located along and near Piotrkowska Street became an integral part of the postwar intellectual and artistic milieu. A most popular meeting place for actors, mainly those from the Polish Army Theater, was Mocca, on 31 Piotrkowska Street. Some considered it to be a replacement for the famous prewar Warsaw literati coffee house

Ziemianska. Writers and editors mostly frequented Fraszka. Others met at the Pickwick Club on Traugutta Street, on the first floor of the Savoy. Among the writers who frequented the Pickwick were Brandys, Kott, Dygat, and Rudnicki. The youngest went to Albatros, where they could dance the boogie-woogie. Still another place to have a bite and a chat was Kasyno. Lodz had its social track: dinner in Kasyno, a short stopover in Albatros and an end to the evening at the Pickwick Club, all, of course on Piotrkowska.[28]

The most popular form of mass entertainment in postwar Lodz was film. Sixteen cinemas were already functioning there in 1945. Close to 4.7 million tickets were sold between March and December of that year. Twenty cinemas were active in 1946 and they sold 6.4 million tickets. The most frequented movie houses were Baltyk, Wlokniarz, Wisla, Polonia and Tecza. The total number of films screened in Poland as a whole in 1946 was 230. Four out of every five films were foreign productions; only one-fifth was Polish. More than 300 films were shown in the course of 1948. Twenty-two of them were prewar Polish films and six were new Polish films. Out of a total of 273 foreign films, 136 were Soviet, 53 were American, 34 were French and 31 were British. We may assume that a similar proportion held also for Lodz.[29]

Lodz became the undisputed center of Polish film production. Film Polski, the main postwar state film production agency, had its start there, headed by Aleksander Ford. Actually, the beginnings of Film Polski should be attributed to *Czolowka Filmowa*, the Film Unit of General Berling's Polish Army, founded in the Soviet Union in 1943. Among the first wartime filmmakers were Aleksander Ford, his brother Wladyslaw, Jerzy Bossak, Stanislaw Wohl and Adolf Forbert. Officers of the Film Unit arrived in Lodz on January 19, 1945 and settled in the Grand Hotel. Most of Film Polski's locations were on Narutowicza and Targowa streets. The Preparatory Film Course from Kracow merged with the Film Polski Studio in Lodz in 1947. In time, additional filmmakers and other film professionals who had survived the war in Poland, German camps, or the West joined the Studio. Among them were Jerzy Toeplitz and Wanda Jakubowska. The first postwar full-featured film produced in Lodz was *Zakazane Piosenki* (*Forbidden Songs*), which showed the fates of Poles under German occupation and featured a number of songs which soon became popular hits. Another Lodz-produced film dealing with wartime Poland was *Ulica Graniczna* (*Border Street*). Several leading contemporary filmmakers from abroad, such as Georges Sadoul from France and Sergei Obraztsov from the Soviet Union, lectured and taught at the Lodz Film School. In time the Lodz Film School could boast of such prominent filmmakers as Roman Polanski and Andrzej Wajda.[30]

The late 1940s marked an end of an era for Lodz. There was a nearly total exodus of the cultural and intellectual elites and institutions to Warsaw. Most of the writers, artists and academics, even those who later recalled their "Lodz years," with nostalgia, had sensed from the start that Lodz would be only a point of transit. The exit began sometime in mid-1948 and continued for the next year or two. Adolf Rudnicki spoke at a farewell party on the eve of his departure for Warsaw: "Forty people have gathered here to take leave of a city which was for them like a mother. It's not a native town for any of them, it's not beautiful either. In spite of this they love it and it will remain forever one of those few places considered as their homeland."[31] In the opening scene of the Syrena Theater premiere in Warsaw, in December 1948, actors dressed in raincoats and holding suitcases sang:

> Lodz accepted us with tender care,
> but we weren't worth it, since we
> called Piotrkowska Marszalkowska.
> We were strangers and guests.
> How could we live in that good city,
> reminiscing and comparing it,
> each of us who was born here, to
> Main Station Warsaw, Main Station Warsaw.[32]

***

I MET JOZEF POTEGA ON THE RECOMMENDATION OF MARIA LORBER. She was an ex-government official who had left Poland for Israel; he was a retired journalist from Lodz who had moved to Warsaw. We met at the Hotel Forum, where I usually stayed during my visits to Warsaw. Jozef Potega, a teenager during the war, had lived with his family on the outskirts of Lodz. His father decided for some reason that it would be safer to be in the city center when the Russians arrived. Jozef recalled: "At night, between January 17th and 18th, we started to walk toward the center. It was pitch dark. A large group of people marched in formation in the opposite direction. Somebody yelled at us in German: 'Are you crazy? Walking right into the Bolsheviks' jaws!'"

Two or three days later, after the liberation, Jozef accompanied his father to the Natural History Museum in Sienkiewicza Park, where his father had been director before the war. They crossed Piotrkowska Street on their way. "I distinctly recall a big puddle of blood in front of Piotrkowska 96. Later on the Lodz Press House was located in that same building and I worked there as a journalist for seventeen years. Whenever I crossed that spot I always recalled that puddle." Jozef also vividly remembered seeing a lot of German corpses. "Horse carts were carrying away dead Germans from the Park. I saw a German soldier's corpse in the middle of a road. I was told that a Russian tank killed him on the spot, and then rolled over his body. I also saw the corpses of twelve SS soldiers right next to our prewar house on the outskirts of town. There were puddles of blood and pieces of brain nearby."

Jozef's family eventually returned to their prewar home, which had been occupied by the German family of Wilhelm Jerdens of Hamburg. "I found a lot of souvenirs. There were German books, various documents, and even a pair of paper angel wings for Christmas, which I later used in a school performance. Old man Jerdens had fought in the First World War and even earned an Iron Cross. I still have a pitchfork and a *Wehrmacht* helmet which I found in the house."

Jozef entered the sixth grade at a school where his mother taught, and after graduation continued in the Skorupki Gimnazjum on Zeromskiego Street in Baluty. It took him more than an hour each way by tram. Most of the staff had been teachers before the war, and during the first postwar years they even had regular classes in religion. The most popular form of entertainment was cinema. "My first film was Walt Disney's *Snow White*, back in 1936 or 1937. This very same film, dubbed into Polish, was screened after the war in Polonia, on Piotrkowska Street, opposite the Grand Hotel. I saw it twelve times."

Jozef joined the Scouts, the Harcerstwo, in 1949, and when Jacek Kuron organized the "Red" pro-Communist scout movement, he and his friends decided to go underground. They called themselves Zwiazek Bialej Tarczy — "The White Shield Union." "And then, three or four months later they arrested us and brought us to the District UB Office. This was in June 1950. I was seventeen then. The trial took place a few months afterward and I was sentenced to five years in prison. I was then in the tenth grade, and this was the end of my schooling." Potega was completely unaware of the fate of Lodz Jews and the Lodz ghetto during the German occupation. The first time he encountered Jews was when his family rented out two rooms in their suburban house to a Jewish couple for a summer, sometime in 1946 or in 1947. The husband was a journalist at a Lodz newspaper, the *Dziennik*. Years later Potega worked for the *Dziennik* as a journalist. During the Polish October of 1956, Potega joined a student cabaret and it was then that he met Maria Lorber, who supervised publications and performances in Lodz. She wasn't too strict. "It was at Mrs. Lorbers' that I ate Jewish *chulnt* for the first and last time until now," he remarked.[33]

Bozena Piwkowska was born in Lodz to a prosperous family. Her maternal family settled in the city in the mid-19th century. Her grandfather, Karol Hofrychter, owned a textile factory which employed a thousand workers. Bozena was fifteen when the war started. They were evicted from their comfortable apartment on Piotrkowska Street, which became part of a German army barracks, and settled in a modest place on Zeromskiego Street. Bozena recalled the flight of the Germans in January 1945. "I walked with my mother from Zeromskiego Street, in the direction of Kilinskiego, and saw Germans on the run. It reminded me of our own flight back in 1939. I tried to fight off a feeling of *schadenfreude*. It was completely dark. Mothers were looking for and calling their children. Wounded Germans were loaded on trucks. I shall never forget that sight."

She was scared to leave the house for some days after the arrival of the Russians. "I was then a young women of nineteen. Strange things occurred here at that time. Murdered girls were found in the bushes, in the snow." One day, towards the end of January, when she and her sister were walking to their place of work along Pabianicka Street, she noticed a small crowd standing in front of some Polish soldiers. "There were perhaps four of them, dressed in military overcoats. They wore *rogatywki*, Polish four-cornered military caps, although the Polish eagle on top of them was missing its traditional crown. The locals didn't get really close to these soldiers. They just watched them. I was overcome by mixed emotions and by a sense of tragedy. Still, we were completely thrilled that we had survived the war, that the store signs were in Polish, that there was a Polish press, that there were Polish films and Polish theaters."

When their family factory reopened after nationalization, some of the long-time workers suggested that Bozena and her sister work in the factory office. "This was a quite unusual situation, for ex-owners' granddaughters to be welcome there, under the new regime. We worked there for nearly two years." One of the new administrators wanted Bozena to write a false document, which she refused to do. Two longtime workers defended her and told her: "'Miss, we warned that fellow that we will throw him down the stairs if he bothers you again.' From that time on he was all honey. The workers' attitude towards their former employers wasn't always the way the authorities wished. There was absolute solidarity and trust between us." As for social and cultural life in postwar Lodz, Bozena defined it as "a time of temporary euphoria." "Life was exciting. There were lots of small coffee houses. The best theaters performed in Lodz. All this continued until the late forties, until Warsaw grew its feathers again, and then they all returned there. We used to call all those literati and artists *karierysci, Warszawisci* — Warsawian careerists." Bozena's family associated mostly with their own kind, cultured Polish families, prewar intelligentsia. The man she married in

1949 was originally a Warsawian. Most of his family members were killed by the Germans.

Bozena knew about the Lodz Ghetto and even crossed it by tram on occasion. The windows were painted blue, and it was impossible to see anything on the outside. "Only after the war we learned what had happened in the ghetto and in the concentration camps." Her family was friendly with an elderly, assimilated Jew. He was the only survivor in his family. "He never remarried, and lived an ascetic life, like a monk. He did not allow his room to be heated, even during the cold of the winter."[34]

Halina Sander-Janowska was born in Lodz in 1933 to a middle-class family. By Nazi standards she was a first degree *Mischling*. Her mother was Jewish, her father German. They were primarily Polish in a cultural sense. Halina humorously boasted that her mother could quarrel in four languages: Polish, German, Russian and French. She had an older, very attractive sister, Lilka. Before the war they had lived in a comfortable, modern apartment on Narutowicza Street. Most of their prewar neighbors were Germans. During the German occupation Halina and Lilka were taken several times to be examined at the local Nazi Rassenpolitisches-Amt, the Office for Race Policy. "They checked our height, weight, skull shape etc. I was too young to react, but Lilka protested and told our father that she wasn't a guinea pig, and would not return there." Although a Gestapo man once beat their father up, there were no serious or dangerous incidents. Quite soon they were forced to give part of their apartment to Dr. and Frau Selbach, a German couple from the Reich. Luckily, the couple turned out to be "wonderful people," according to Halina. Another new tenant in their house was Heinrich Schuld, who played first violin in the Germanized Lodz Philharmonic. He became quite friendly with the Sanders and adored Halina's mother. He used to visit them, and Mrs. Sander would accompany him at times on her piano.

Halina recalled: "Red Army units entered Lodz on January 19. There was some bombing and the Germans fled. My father never considered leaving. He was happy when the Russians arrived, although during the First World War he had spent some time in Siberia as a POW." Halina's father, who had contacts with the AK, the Polish underground Home Army, was arrested and accused of spying. He was sent to a labor camp in Russia, and died there. There was a constant danger that her older sister, Lilka, would be raped by Russian soldiers. She would escape and run on rooftops, and would hide with friends. Soviet soldiers and officers used to appear from time to time in their apartment. Halina recalled one such 'visit.' "Once a whole group of Russian soldiers appeared in our apartment. They were looking for vodka and for girls. Lilka learned that she should disappear on such occasions and our mother knew very well how to deal with the Russians: she would treat them to vodka, play Russian melodies on the piano and on the accordion. They would sing, reminisce and become sentimental, and then they would leave."

Halina, a teenager in the postwar years, had serious identity problems. She spoke of a split identity. She was partly German, partly Jewish and partly Polish. She attended Polish and Jewish schools at various times, which made things even worse. Pani Eugenia, her home room teacher in a Polish girls' school, in which she enrolled in March 1945, told the class: "Remember girls, if an unfamiliar man on the street attempts to entice you into a building entrance, run as fast as you can. You should know that Jews are kidnapping Polish children these days in order to use their blood for matzah." When Halina was in Jewish schools or institutions "they would drill into us how wonderful the Jews are." Finally, in 1949, she ended up in the Lodz First RTPD, Robotnicze Towarzystwo Przyjaciol Dzieci, Workers' Association of Childrens' Friends school where she felt finally at home. The RTPD schools in Poland had a strong liberal-socialist tradition. Halina's school had many Jewish students, mostly from families who had survived the war in the Soviet Union. "We used to sing Russian songs during the breaks and there was admiration for Communism and for Soviet Russia."[35]

It was a colleague, and a Lodz fan, Padraic Kenney, who told me that Jerzy Urban had lived in postwar Lodz as a teenager. I called at Urban's Warsaw office the next day and arranged for my research assistant to interview him. Urban is one of the richest people in contemporary Poland. He made most of his fortune on the stock market, while his professional life centered on journalism, writing and editing. Urban is most known as the publisher of and moving spirit behind the extremely funny, notoriously critical, mean, sacrilegious, sexist and quite vulgar popular weekly *Nie-No*.

Urban's life story and his personality are highly unusual. He was born in Lodz in 1933 into an affluent and utterly assimilated Jewish family. His father was the editor of a liberal-socialist daily and the family's social milieu, according to Urban, was cosmopolitan and open-minded. Young Jurek was told of his Jewish origin only during the war. The family's correct name had been Urbach, a typical Polish-Jewish surname. A mistake of a clerk in Soviet-occupied Lwow turned it into the Polish-sounding Urban, which for various reasons the family has kept ever since.

Urban lived with his parents during the war on Aryan papers in German-occupied Eastern Galicia. As a boy he heard about Germans killing Jews and at least once witnessed directly the shooting of a young Jewish woman. When asked years later about his feelings at the time, he commented" "I've been quite close to the Holocaust, still, I was on the other side. The

Holocaust, somehow, concerned the others." Asked about his reaction to the Kielce pogrom he replied, "Jews, as I've learned later, had been extremely frightened, but this wasn't part of my life."

Following liberation the Urbans moved to Lublin. Jurek's father had been dispatched to Lodz in early 1945. Jurek and his mother joined him a few weeks later and the family moved back to their comfortable prewar apartment. Urban recalled that in spite of that, it took them some time to adjust: "After our return to Lodz we still stuck to our wartime habit of sleeping in the same room." Still, he was a typical adolescent. Speaking of his teenage friends in postwar Lodz, he remarked sarcastically: "Our erotic yearnings assumed the form of a herd-like behavior. We walked daily, starting at five o'clock, along the *deptak, the promenade,* on Piotrkowska Street, where young people from all over the city would get together. Boys and girls walked for hours in twosomes and threesomes. When a girl agreed to be accompanied to the entrance of her house, that was considered a great success."

Urban's recollections of the schools he attended in postwar Lodz indicate that the percentage of Jewish students was quite high: "If a certain grade contained about thirty students, a third of them were Jews. They didn't admit it. However, they still stuck together. Even my closest friends were of Jewish origin." Urban had been a consistently bad and spiteful student. He was an untiring prankster and a master of practical jokes. He was expelled from several Lodz schools in a row. His behavior improved somewhat when he became active in the ZMP, the communist youth movement. At one time he was in charge of ZMP activities at the Peretz Yiddish School on Kilinskiego Street. "They would conduct their meetings in Yiddish. I protested, since I didn't understand a word. Various Zionist organizations were also active in that school."

As a result of Urban's growing political engagement in the late 1940s, his contacts with Jewish schoolmates weakened. "I became increasingly involved in my political milieu. I would get away from school whenever possible. I was busy with organizational matters until late in the evening. It is at that time that I started drinking and smoking." Jurek's father left Lodz for a better position in Warsaw sometime in 1948. Jurek and his mother joined him two years later. "This was a terrible shock to me. My world collapsed. I lost my high position at the ZMP as well as my whole milieu. I knew nobody in Warsaw. At least for a while I used to consider Lodz as my lucky city and Warsaw as my disaster."[36]

Professor Krystyna Sreniowska came from Lwow, where she was born in 1914. Her father's family was Polonized Germans; her mother's family was Polish. She graduated before the war with a degree in history from

Lwow University. Her husband, Stanislaw, a converted Jew, was a specialist in legal history. During the German occupation they moved from Lwow to Krakow. They took along her husband's widowed mother, who was identified as a Jewess and ended up in Auschwitz. Krystyna recalled: "When they caught my husband's mother he was in such a state. I thought that he would go crazy. He was an only child and adored his mother. He was completely broken." They then moved to Warsaw, and after the uprising of 1944, friends helped them settle in a village near Krakow. A short while after liberation Krystyna and Staszek decided to move to Lodz, as they heard that a university was being founded there.

They arrived in Lodz in March 1945. "The trip from Krakow to Lodz took a whole night, perhaps eight or ten hours; we were on the floor of a freight train. As I had seen Warsaw in ruins, Lodz and its Piotrkowska Street looked like a miracle. Here was a whole city, intact. This was something unusual. Crowds milled around along Piotrkowska. Half of Warsaw was here. There were various cafes, such as Fraszka, full of all kinds of literati. These were mostly outsiders. The local Lodz people were rather provincial, not really intellectuals."

The Sreniowskis stayed for a short while with a Polonized Jewish family who owned a large apartment on Kosciuszko Boulevard. Their daughter had just returned from the Ravensbrueck concentration camp. "They were a wonderful family, and hosted all kinds of people arriving in Lodz. Their place looked like a poor people's *kolkhoz*." Krystyna's mood in those days was rather upbeat. "I felt like embracing people on the street, whether Poles or Jews. There was a lot of goodwill around. We had managed to survive Hitler and I sensed a certain euphoria. Walking along Piotrkowska Street we met friends and acquaintances from occupied Warsaw. We would embrace each other."

Krystyna's husband started working for the Czytelnik Publishing House, and she became a research assistant at Lodz University. At the same time she also taught at an RTPD high school on Jaracza Street. Some of her students were Jewish and they would suddenly disappear in the course of the school year. When she inquired why, she was told that they lived in Lodz temporarily and had to leave. She and her husband lived for a while in the Hotel Monopol, not far from Plac Wolnosci. This was a small and transitory intellectual milieu that had etched itself strongly on Krystyna's memory. She relived it in detail half a century later. "We were allotted one room on a wing of the second floor and it became a kind of paradise for us." The number of tenants increased from day to day. "When we heard that Professor Gasiorowska would be coming a whole crowd showed up in the corridor to greet her." After a while they moved to a spacious room in a modern apartment building, on 60 Kosciuszko Boulevard. The room had only one bed without any linen. Krystyna was in despair. "I cried. And suddenly the door opened and there stood Witek Kula with a blanket and a pillow under his arm. This was sheer happiness." Witold Kula, a historian and economist, had taken part in the Warsaw uprising and had been incarcerated in a German camp. He settled in Lodz in May 1945 and joined Lodz University. He was one of the Polish intellectuals who strongly condemned the Kielce pogrom.

For Professor Sreniowska, the most memorable public event in postwar Lodz was the funeral of a murdered university student, in December 1945. "Thousands of students followed the casket. At the head of the procession marched the Rector, Kotarbinski." This was, according to her, one of the few local protests against the new regime. "Lodz, compared to Krakow and other cities, wasn't particularly oppositionist. *Kuznica*, the leftist journal, was published there. It used to attack the Catholic, Krakow-based *Tygodnik Powszechny*. Numerous academics at Lodz University were leftists, connected with the prewar *Wolna Wszechnica*. Prewar Communists were in seventh heaven. They were naive. For example, such a man as Woroszylski. And even myself and my husband, though we weren't party members, we too were influenced by Communist propaganda: the country would be rebuilt, things will improve. And we weren't an exception. There was a widespread conformism. This acceptance of the regime stemmed from an enormous naivete." Professor Sreniowski was appointed Rector of the Lodz School of Higher Education, but after a while he had to step down. "This was either in 1949 or in 1950. Two sad-looking types, apparently from the Security Office, visited him once and suggested that he cooperate with them. He refused, and then he decided to resign."[37]

Professor Edward Zajicek, a highly intelligent, friendly, and witty man who was in his eighties when I met him, had been part of the film establishment in postwar Lodz. It was great fun to sit with him in the ground floor cafe of the Grand Hotel, sip coffee and listen to his story. During the Warsaw uprising, young Zajicek was living in Praga, that part of Warsaw which had been liberated in September 1944. Shortly thereafter he joined the Polish Army Film Unit, where he worked in an administrative capacity. "Two cities competed then for the location of the postwar Polish film industry, Krakow and Lodz, and Lodz won out. Krakow was extremely crowded, whereas Lodz could offer numerous ex-German houses and apartments in the best midtown area."

Following a short stay in Krakow, Zajicek arrived in Lodz as chief production administrator of what would become Film Polski. He lodged on and off in the Grand Hotel, of which he has very pleasant memories.

"I spent a quarter of my life in Grandka. In the first weeks after liberation, waiters would serve us French champagne and cognac in our rooms. We didn't have to pay for anything, including dinners. It was very lively in the Grand. Everybody who was anybody used to meet there. We met, we drank, we talked. Army officers used to mix with writers, and of course, there were also some good looking young ladies, *za mundurem panny sznurem* — 'young ladies follow uniforms,' as the saying goes."

Prof. Zajicek recalled postwar Lodz as a very busy place. There was a lot of commotion. The cars one spotted on the streets in the first weeks after liberation were mainly military vehicles, among them American Dodges and Willyses. He remembered literary and artistic life in Lodz in those years. "The years 1945, 1946, 1947 were the NEP years, so to speak. Private initiative was still allowed: private stores, private crafts, private jewelers, coffee houses and restaurants. Life was rather modest, but normal. The situation deteriorated with the onset of Stalinism, when the screws were tightened." The exodus to Warsaw started as early as 1948. "A studio for documentary films was founded in Warsaw in 1949. It was headed by Jerzy Bossak, who took me with him to work as his production chief."

While still in Lodz, Zajicek was involved with the production of *Zakazane piosenki (Forbidden Songs)*. Ludwik Starski wrote the script. He first suggested that a short feature be made based on illegal melodies and songs. When it turned out well, it was decided to produce a full-length film, the first of its kind in postwar Poland. Zajicek vividly recalled a heated debate among filmmakers and writers in the Pickwick Club in the Savoy. "Starski, a Jew, was accused of presenting a rather narrow perspective of German occupation in Poland. His witty reaction was: 'I must confess that I observed the whole occupation through the keyhole of a closet, where I was hiding.'" Zajicek recalled that several of the leading people in postwar Poland's film industry were of Jewish origin — Stanislaw Wohl, Artur Brauner, the two Forbert brothers, and of course, the great Aleksander Ford. "I was lucky to be among those who were rebuilding Polish cinematography. I became friendly with many among them. Some of my best friends used to refer to me in a humorous way as 'Jew *honoris causa*.'"[37]

The leading Polish philosopher, Leszek Kolakowski, was a young student at Lodz University during the first postwar years. As a child he had lived with his family in Lodz before the war, and they returned to their prewar apartment in the fall of 1945. There he completed his Matura, began his higher education and joined the PPR. According to Kolakowski there was an intense and interesting social and cultural life in postwar Lodz. "University students used to meet for discussions all the time. Both those who were Party members as well as the others. There were lots of events, official and unofficial." He also recalled the funeral of the murdered female student. "I was in the streets then. It was on the corner of Piotrkowska and, perhaps, Narutowicza. An army unit arrived and started shooting in the air. Then people dispersed."

Among Kolakowski's friends and acquaintances were some Jews, such as Kuba Goldberg and Henryk Flug. Kolakowski knew that there was anti-Semitism in postwar Poland, but in his student circles there was none. Kolakowski spoke as a representative of the Communist Zycie youth organization at the unification conference of the Jewish socialist youth movements, Borochow Yugnt and Dror. Later on he met Marek Edelman and his wife Ala Margolis. It is also in postwar Lodz that Leszek Kolakowski met his future wife, Tamara Tynenson. She came from an assimilated Jewish family. Her father, Dr. Issac Tynenson, a pediatrician, worked for a local Jewish health insurance institution. They spent the war years in the Soviet Union, and returned in 1946 to Lodz, where Tamara studied medicine with Marek Edelman. Her father worked for a number of years for TOZ, the Jewish health and welfare organization. Tamara, too, remembered a lively cultural life in postwar Lodz. "There was an excellent theater, which we attended very often. There were Schiller and Dejmek. There was the Philharmonic, which we attended on Fridays, there were literary evenings, authors' evenings. There was everything we needed. In these first postwar years we wanted to make up whatever was lost and missed during the war. Life was very intense."

When Kolakowski received an Honorary Doctorate from his *alma mater* in Lodz, after the collapse of Communism in Poland, he commented: "I am strongly attached to this city. It is certainly not famous for its beauty. However, just as we become friendly with people notwithstanding their looks (except for erotic relations), we get attached to cities as well. Lodz was from its very start a city of workers and of poverty, and it seems that it has remained such. Still, this is a city towards which I nourish a great deal of sympathy."[39]

Hanna Swida arrived in Lodz in November 1945, shortly after her sixteenth birthday. She graduated there from the Emilia Szaniecka high school for girls, studied at Lodz University, and in time became a Professor of Sociology. In a recent study on Polish youth in the immediate postwar years, partly based on her own Lodz memories and observations, she wrote: "The reaction to the end of the war was a 'rebirth of life.' The early postwar years were a time of tremendous social revival." According to her study, young people, both Poles and Jews, tended to suppress wartime experiences and memories. They mostly lived in the present and for the future.[40]

3

JEWS IN POSTWAR LODZ

CLOSE TO THREE AND A HALF MILLION JEWS LIVED IN POLAND ON THE eve of the Second World War. They constituted 10% of the overall and 30% of the urban population. Only some 380,000 Jews, 10%-11% of the prewar Jewish population, survived the War and the Holocaust. It has been estimated that two-thirds of these survived mostly in the Soviet Union, and one third in camps and in hiding. The Jewish population in Poland in the immediate postwar years was in constant flux. There was an inflow of Jewish returnees from the East and an outflow of Jews to the West. There was also considerable internal relocation. Attempts to resettle and start a new life in Poland were matched by successive waves of emigration. Since not all Jews registered with the Central Committee of Polish Jews (CCPJ), the official representative organization of Polish Jewry, and since there were sometimes "double" registrations as a result of relocation, it has been impossible to establish precise data. In midsummer 1946 the number of Jews living in postwar Poland was at its highest — around 250,000.[1]

More than 200,000 Polish Jews survived the war in the Soviet Union as refugees and deportees. After the war, they, along with other prewar Polish citizens, were allowed to return to Poland. An overwhelming majority took advantage of this opportunity. The first to return were thousands of Jewish soldiers and officers who had entered Poland with General Berling's Army, formed in Russia. Among the Polish-Jewish returnees were also those few who survived in the German-occupied prewar Polish eastern borderlands which had become part of Soviet Russia. The repatriation to Poland was usually conducted in freight train transports. These began as early as 1944 and lasted until the end of July 1946. More than half of these transports disembarked in Lower Silesia, part of the Recovered Lands. Other transports arrived in Upper Silesia and in such major cities as Stettin, Lodz, Kracow and Warsaw.[2]

What was the geographical pattern of Jewish resettlement in postwar Poland? On the whole, Jews settled in large urban centers. This was because of the better economic prospects in the cities and the lack of safety, even outright danger, in the small towns. Even those Jews who initially returned to their original towns meaning to settle there, at least for a while, were forced by harsh reality to move to larger cities. A wish to live "among Jews" exerted its impact as well. At the end of 1945, Jews were dispersed among 235 localities all over Poland. This number shrank considerably during the following years. As for major urban centers in postwar Poland, in midsummer 1946, 30,000 Jews were living in Lodz, 20,000 in Stettin, 13,000 in Kracow and 8,000 in Warsaw. Lower Silesia became an impressive center of Jewish population, which at its peak reached 100,000.[3]

The war and the Holocaust severely affected the gender composition of the Jewish population. The ratio of men to women was reversed. Whereas in 1931 there were 109 Jewish females for every100 males, in mid-1946, the ratio of women to men was 45.7% to 54.3%. The postwar gender composition among Polish Jews was also markedly different from that of the postwar population at large. There were two main reasons for that: the Germans preferred to keep males as a more efficient working force, and among those who escaped eastward in 1939 and survived in the Soviet Union, were more men than women. The age composition of the postwar Jewish population in Poland also differed completely from that of the prewar years. The share of children and the elderly declined sharply and the percentage of those in their twenties and thirties increased. The 10-19 age-group shrank by half, whereas the 30-39 age group doubled in size. At the same time there was a surge in births in the immediate postwar years. Children born in 1946 and early 1947 comprised close to 5% of the total Jewish population. The postwar increase in the birth rate among Jews is particularly amazing when compared with the much lower birth rate among the general Polish population.[4]

Jews began to leave Poland immediately after liberation. Jewish emigration in the first postwar years, within the framework of the Brichah, the Flight and Rescue operation organized and directed by the Zionists, was mostly illegal. Close to 15,000 Jews left Poland as early as July-August 1945. Nearly 33,000 had left by the end of that year. Close to 15,000 left during the first half of 1946. The emigration's peak was, undisputably, in the months following the Kielce pogrom. Thus, 19,000 Jews left Poland in July 1946, 33,000 in August and more than 12,000 in September. Then the flow tapered off. Only 10,000 Jews left Poland throughout 1947. All in all, around 126,000 Jews, assisted by the Brichah, left Poland in the years 1945-1947. Emigration decreased considerably in the years 1947-1949 and a slight reverse trend even became visible. Thus, 5,000 Jews returned to Poland from DP camps in Germany and Austria in 1947. Whereas close to a quarter-million Jews lived in Poland on the eve of the Kielce events, their overall number shrank now to about 100,000. The major centers of Jewish population were still the large cities: 14,000 Jews lived in Lodz, more than 12,000 in Wroclaw, close to 6,000 in Krakow and 5,000 in Warsaw.[5] The possibility of legal emigration of Jews from Poland to the newly established State of Israel was announced in the early fall of 1949. As a result, close to 30,000 Jews left for Israel in the years 1949-1951, and the total Jewish population of Poland shrank in early 1952 to slightly over 70,000.[6]

The economic situation of Polish Jews in the immediate postwar years was precarious. If the Polish population at large suffered from material devastation, the surviving and returning Jews actually had to start from scratch. A considerable part of the prewar Jewish property was nationalized by the new regime. The local Polish population grabbed material goods previously owned by Jews when they were deported and annihilated. Most of it was never returned. At the same time, however, both the Polish government and Jewish welfare organizations abroad assisted Jewish survivors. The CCPJ, the Central Committee of Polish Jews, received the first modest government allotment as early as December 1944. Five million Zlotys followed in April 1945. Financial and other support from Jewish organizations in the U.S.A., England and Palestine also started arriving around that time. Most of the financial and material support was provided in the following years by the JDC, The American Joint Distribution Committee. The JDC's overall assistance to Polish Jews in the years 1944-1949 amounted to 20 million dollars. The Polish authorities seemed to be very interested then in Jewish support from abroad.[7]

Most of the Jewish survivors could not resume their prewar ways of earning a living. Petty commerce and artisanship, a major source of income for Polish Jews before the war, could hardly be practiced on a large scale. Thus, the new postwar circumstances almost completely changed the occupational structure of the working Jewish population. They had to move now into production and administration. Thus, in 1947, more than 46% of Jewish wage earners worked in industry and mining, more than 18% in administration, and only 12% in commerce. Jews, usually barred before the war from state and local offices, were able to occupy now a wide range of positions in the state administration, in academia, in the army and in the security apparatus. Jewish students were accepted by institutions of higher learning. In the immediate postwar period there was still a possibility to set up private workshops, and some Jews returned to traditional prewar Jewish occupations such as tailoring, shoemaking and furriery. In time, however, these and other crafts were organized into cooperatives, encouraged by the new regime[8]

The Jewish cooperative movement in postwar Poland was, at least for a few years, a success story. Whereas in 1946, only slightly over 100 Jewish cooperatives employed more than 2,000 workers, in 1949, there were 220 Jewish cooperatives with 9,000 workers. Numerous Jewish cooperatives were located in such cities as Lodz, Stettin and Wroclaw. Most of the financial backing came from the JDC and the Polish Government. Eventually, however, these cooperatives employed a growing number of non-Jews and were merged with the state cooperative system.[9]

Official Polish attitudes and policies towards Jews were not clearly defined in the immediate postwar years, and at times they were adopted on the run. However, the pro-Communist, and later outright Communist, regime in Poland was on the whole quite accommodating towards the Jewish minority. The positive attitudes and policies were motivated by both ideological and practical considerations. Polish Socialists and Communists always believed in equality, regardless of ethnic, national and religious affiliation. The fact that the world at large became sensitive to Jewish needs in the wake of the Holocaust had its impact on the Polish authorities as well. Individual Polish Jews, and the Jewish community as a whole, were assisted by the authorities in their postwar attempts towards recovery. The existence of a wide range of Jewish organizations and institutions was allowed throughout the second half of the 1940s. Contacts with Jewish organizations in the West, as well as financial and material assistance from abroad, were tolerated. The new regime in Poland, following Soviet foreign policy interests, also supported the establishment of a Jewish State, and allowed semi-legal, and later legal, emigration of Polish Jews, most of whom ended up in Palestine/Israel.[10]

The major Jewish framework in postwar Poland, considered by the authorities as the representative of Jewish interests, and regarded by Jews as an address for their needs and concerns, was the CCPJ, the Central Committee of Polish Jews. It had been established as early as the fall of 1944, and was supervised, as were other Jewish organizations, by the Ministry of Public Administration. The CCPJ was meant, actually, to operate as an intermediary between the state bureaucracy and the Jews. It was also clear from the outset that the Committee was considered by the government a significant and useful means for mobilizing foreign aid for Polish Jews. The CCPJ's support was also used by the new regime against its ideological and political opponents in the West.

The Committee's leadership consisted of representatives of most of the Jewish political parties, and some Jewish organizations active in postwar Poland. Thus, in 1946, the Committee Presidium consisted of 13 Zionists, 6 Communists, 4 Bundists and 2 representatives of The Union of Jewish

Partisans. The Zionists usually formed a majority. Since the Committee leadership represented a coalition of parties with differing ideologies and interests, it could not avoid conflicts and frictions, in most cases resulting in compromises. A basic and ongoing contention was between those who supported the idea of rebuilding Jewish life and a Jewish community in postwar Poland and those who saw emigration to Palestine/Israel their ultimate goal.

The CCPJ ran a network of regional and local committees active in the centers of Jewish population throughout the country. The CCPJ's activities were conducted and supervised by a number of departments, such as the Department of Registration and Statistics, the Department of Culture, the Youth Department and the Department of Health and Social Welfare. The CCPJ Youth Department supported, among others, the *bursy*, boarding centers for young Jews studying in universities and other institutions of higher education. It helped in the establishing and funding of *landsmannschaftn*, hometown societies, quite popular in the immediate postwar period. The Committee also organized and supported Jewish self-defense in times of danger.[11]

Although the Jewish population of postwar Poland was at its highest less than 10% of its prewar size, the number of revived Jewish political parties was nearly the same as before the war. The majority were Zionist-oriented, and enjoyed a wide-ranging support among the Jewish population. The largest Zionist party was Ichud, Unity, close in its leanings to the prewar center-right General Zionists. It had 7,000 — 8,000 members in 1947. On the left of the ideological and political spectrum were the Right and Left Poalei Zion parties, whose membership was 3,000 and 2,000 respectively. They merged in late 1947. The Marxist-Zionist youth-oriented Hashomer Hatzair had 1,500 members. All Zionist parties were affiliated with their respective youth movements, which were very popular among Jewish youth in postwar Poland. Most of them cooperated within the Hehalutz-Pioneer framework.[12]

The socialist Bund, a major political force in prewar Poland, lost most of its social base in the Holocaust. After the war it hoped for a close cooperation with the PPS, the Polish Socialist Party. However, with the increasing influence of the Communists, and the final merger of the PPS with the PPR, the impact of the Bund among Poland's Jews became increasingly marginal. When still active, in 1947, the Bund had 1500 members. The Bund leadership consisted mostly of prewar activists who survived in hiding, in camps or in the Soviet Union. Its youth movement, the Tsukunft, consisted predominantly of youngsters from traditional Bundist families. The Bundists shared with Jewish Communists the belief that there was a future for Jews in Poland, and opposed the Zionist stand on emigration to Palestine/Israel. In the cultural sphere, Bundists traditionally supported Yiddish and opposed Hebrew. They vehemently opposed "train station agitation" conducted by Zionist parties and youth movements among freshly arrived Jewish returnees from Russia. Bundists accused Zionists of deliberately causing a state of panic among Polish Jews, in order to promote flight and emigration. Hopes nurtured by the Bundists in respect to Jewish life in postwar Poland, were crushed by the Kielce pogrom and by the onset of Stalinism.[13]

Besides Communist leaders of Jewish origin, active mostly in the higher ranks of the party, the government and the security apparatus, Jewish Communists with a strong Jewish identity and specifically Jewish interests were represented by the Jewish Fraction of the Polish Communist Party, first the PPR and later the PZPR. It had around 4,000 members in 1946, and their number increased later to 7,000. Many were Jewish industry workers in Lower Silesia. The Fraction's most outspoken leaders were Szymon Zachariasz, Ber Mark and Hersz Smolar. The Fraction was an integral part of the PZPR, as well as of the CCPJ, where the Fraction's leadership had to come to terms with the Zionists. Whereas in the CCPJ and in local Jewish Committees the Fraction exerted a considerable influence, it was not popular with the Jewish population at large. Fraction activists were torn between their inherent belief that the best future for Polish Jews was in Communist Poland, and the practical considerations and policies of the Polish authorities, which supported massive Jewish emigration.[14]

Jewish culture in postwar Poland, in spite of the fact that most of the Jews were on the move, and in spite of the relative instability of life, was lively and impressive. It seemed that the years of suffering, death and exile resulted in an insatiable drive for those aspects of normal life that had been lost in the war. Participation in cultural and entertainment events also let those who had lost their families and friends fill a need "to be together." Although a few Jewish theatrical and entertainment performances already took place during the first months after liberation, Jewish cultural activities picked up steam only when the Jewish returnees from the Soviet Union began to settle in the large cities. Lodz and Wroclaw became major centers of Jewish theater. One of the first public Jewish events took place in liberated Lublin, as early as October 1944. It was a concert of Yiddish songs and recitations by Diana Blumenfeld and Jonas Turkow. A viewer reported: "The hall was bursting at the seams. Diana, with swollen legs, wearing a purple-red dressing gown, started to sing a song in Yiddish. She had hardly uttered the first words, when sobbing was heard all over the place." The first light music teams started performing in Lodz and in Lower Silesia at the end of 1945.

A full-fledged Yiddish theater began to hold performances in Lodz in the summer of 1945. Shalom Aleichem's *Tevye the Milkman* and Jacob Zonshein's *Hershele from Ostropole* were performed in the fall of that year. Ida Kaminska, the first lady of the Yiddish theater, and her husband, the actor Marian Melman, returned from Russia in late December 1946. Their first performances were in the Lodz Jewish Theater, in mid-January 1947. According to a review, "The Jews of Lodz hurried to meet with the adored artistic couple. The narrow hall of the temporary Jewish Theater on 2 Jaracza Street could hardly contain all the admirers of Kaminska's talent." The Jewish Theater of Lower Silesia, in Wroclaw, premiered in November 1947 with Gordin's "Mirele Efros". Ida Kaminska directed it and played the leading role. This would be her most famous performance of the postwar years. She was appointed artistic director of the Jewish Theater in Lodz in the summer of 1948. Both the Lodz and the Wroclaw Jewish theaters went on tours all over Poland.[15] Besides the two official Jewish theaters, Jewish cultural clubs, libraries, drama workshops and choirs existed in all major centers of Jewish population. Moreover, lectures on a wide range of Jewish-related themes, as well as Jewish poetry and prose readings, were quite frequent.[16]

Although a far cry from the massive and multifaceted prewar Jewish press, the postwar Jewish press in Poland was quite lively. More than seventy Jewish newspapers and journals in Polish, Yiddish and Hebrew, were published in the years 1944-1950. Among the most popular were *Dos Naje Lebn* (*New Life*), published by the CCPJ, Hashomer Hatzair's *Mosty* (*Bridges*), and Ichud's *Opinia* (*Opinion*). The mouthpiece of Yiddish writers and poets was the monthly *Yiddishe Schriftn* (*Jewish Writings*). Zydowska Agencja Prasowa, the Jewish Press Agency, run by the CCPJ, served as a significant source of information on Jews and Jewish-related themes both inside and outside of Poland.[17]

Historical documentation of the Holocaust began even before the war had ended. A Jewish Historical Commission was founded in liberated Lublin as early as August 1944. It moved to Lodz in March 1945. The Commission collected various sources and documents concerning the extermination of Jews under Nazi rule. A major activity, from its very inception, was the collection of personal testimonies. Among the initiators and most active members of the Commission were such Polish Jewish historians as Philip Friedman, Isaiah Trunk and Joseph Kermisz. The Holocaust was commemorated by the remnants of Polish Jewry in various ways. The high point was the annual commemoration of the Warsaw

Ghetto Uprising on the site of the ruined Ghetto. The first gathering took place on April 19, 1945, the second anniversary of the Uprising. A monument to commemorate the Warsaw Ghetto fighters, as well as the martyred Jews of Warsaw, was unveiled on the fifth anniversary of the Uprising, in April 1948. The ceremonies were attended by thousands of Polish Jews, representatives of Polish Jewish organizations and youth movements, as well as by Jewish guests from abroad.[18]

The CCPJ and other organizations which assisted Jews in postwar Poland were concerned particularly about the young. Jewish children had suffered different fates during the war. Most of those who survived the war did so either with their families or as orphans and half-orphans in the Soviet Union. Others emerged from their hiding places, and still others were saved by Polish families or in convents. All in all, less than 30,000 Jewish children out of close to a million in prewar Poland survived the war. Only 5,000 children survived in German-occupied Polish lands. Although both children survivors in Poland and returnee children from the Soviet Union suffered during the war, there were differences between them. There were more orphans among the survivors than among the returnees. There were more boys than girls among the returnees. More of the youngest children, those born during the war, were returnees. As a quite large percentage of the survivor children were orphans or had only one parent, and as the economic situation was difficult, there was an urgent need for orphanages, or as they were usually referred to, "Children's Homes." The first Jewish Children's Home was established in liberated Lublin in 1944. Additional Homes were organized by the CCPJ in the spring and summer of 1945 in Lodz, Warsaw and in other centers of Jewish population. Close to a thousand children survivors lived in such Homes in the fall of 1945. By the second half of 1946, thirteen Children's Homes existed all over the country. The CCPJ also supported needy children living with their families or in other frameworks. More than 20,000 Jewish children were aided by the CCJP in mid-1946.[19]

A considerable number of those Jewish children who had passed the war under assumed identities, either with Polish families or in convents, were reclaimed by Jewish organizations. Most active in what was considered then to be a "rescue operation" was the Coordination Committee, consisting of representatives of various Zionist parties. Another "rescue campaign" sponsored by Jewish religious organizations was headed by Isaiah Druker. Druker, a man in his early thirties at the time, and a captain in the Polish Army, ran a highly successful rescue effort almost single-handedly.[20]

Some Jewish children studied in Polish schools; others attended

Jewish institutions. Jewish education in postwar Poland had two sectors: schools run by the CCJP, oriented toward Jewish life in Poland, in which the official language of instruction was Yiddish, and Zionist-oriented schools run by the Hehalutz Pioneer Center, with emphasis on Hebrew and Palestine. These were elementary schools in the main. The first Yiddish and Hebrew schools were established as early as 1945 in Warsaw, Lodz, Krakow, and in a few other cities. A real boost occurred only in 1946, when large numbers of Jewish returnees from the Soviet Union arrived in Poland. Twenty-four Jewish schools, most of them in Lower Silesia, were in existence in mid-1946. Their number was almost doubled in 1947. Close to 3,000 children attended Yiddish schools, 2,000 attended Hebrew schools and more than 1,000 studied in Jewish religious schools. The number of Jewish children ages 7-14 in the school year 1947/1948, has been estimated to be 6,000. Two-thirds attended Jewish schools, and one-third Polish ones. The number of Jewish schools decreased to 33 in 1948.

A major problem in postwar Jewish schools, both Yiddish- or Hebrew-oriented, was language. Most of those children who survived in Poland, especially the youngest, spoke Polish only. Most of those who arrived from Russia spoke primarily Russian. Many of the pupils, whether in a Yiddish or a Hebrew school, had to be taught Yiddish and Hebrew from scratch. According to Dr. Samuel Amarant, head of the Hehalutz Education Department: "The incoming student body was of a highly diversified nature. There were serious problems of communication with children who spoke different languages (Polish, Russian, Ukrainian, Yiddish)." Textbooks and other instructional materials were in short supply. The constant arrival and departure of both students and teachers had a negative impact on stability and normalization. At the same time, however, an atmosphere of closeness and care usually prevailed among the educators and their pupils.[21]

Despite, and perhaps at least partly because of, the relatively positive official attitudes to the Jewish minority, anti-Semitism was quite prevalent in postwar Poland. Its roots were both historical and recent. To traditional anti-Jewish attitudes, fed by religion, economics and nationalism, new elements were added as a result of the war, the Soviet and German occupations and the postwar Communist regime. A central element was the stereotype of the *Zydokomuna*, Judeocommunism, Jewish loyalty to and collaboration with Soviet Russia. Jews were also perceived as a threat by their Polish neighbors, who had appropriated Jewish property during the Holocaust. There were also elements of a psycho-social nature, such as hate stemming from guilt in collaboration in the Nazi extermination of the Jews. Despite the enormous Jewish losses, there was hardly any empathy and compassion toward Jews. They were often perceived as a "threatening other."[22]

Anti-Semitism in postwar Poland ranged from derogatory and offending remarks in public spaces, through physical assaults, and up to full-scale pogroms. Anti-Jewish pogroms occurred in a number of cities. Jews were also taken off trains and killed in nearby fields. Estimates of the overall number of Jews killed in Poland in the immediate postwar years vary significantly. The lowest estimate is 400, the highest — 1500. According to a calculation based on official Polish reports, more than 300 Jews were killed between September 1944 and September 1946. A third of them were murdered in the Kielce Province alone. Certain regions and cities were more dangerous for Jews than others. Thus, according to a report by the Polish Ministry of Public Administration, close to 200 Jews were killed between March and August of 1945, nearly half of them in the Kielce and Lublin Provinces. Only nine Jews were murdered during that period in the Lodz Province. Most of the violent and deadly acts against Jews occurred between March and August 1945, and between February and July 1946. The killings decreased considerably after the summer of 1946.[23]

The apogee of anti-Semitism in postwar Poland was the Kielce pogrom. It resulted in 41 killed and dozens of wounded. The Kielce events in early July of 1946, and their emotional and symbolic impact, were a watershed for Polish Jews. Many of those who still contemplated the possibility of resuming their lives in Poland decided to leave. The sense of collective security among the Jews was severely undermined. The pogrom had its repercussions within Polish society as well. Officially organized meetings in factories and offices condemned the killings and justified the punishment of the perpetrators. However, there were also incidents of popular protest against the verdicts. Among the Jewish reactions to the Kielce pogrom was a countrywide organization of self-defense, mainly in the form of local Defense Commissions, affiliated with and supervised by the CCPJ. A central Special Commission was set up in Warsaw. It supervised a network of local Special Commissions. The central and local Special Commissions maintained ongoing contacts with the regular and secret police. The Jewish self-defense network succeeded in securing some 2,000 weapons. Its people guarded close to 400 Jewish institutions throughout the country. According to a report by the Central Special Commission, it intervened with the authorities in excess of 2,000 instances related to anti-Jewish activities between July 1946 and May 1947.[24]

When Lodz was liberated on January 19, 1945, close to a thousand young Jewish survivors, whom the Germans had kept alive for cleanup operations, were in the area of the former ghetto. Other survivors started arriving from camps and hiding places. By the end of February 1945, more than 5,000 Jews were already living in Lodz. The first post-liberation Jewish public event occurred on February 11th. A thousand Jews participated in a mass meeting in the Stylowy cinema hall. It was chaired by the historian Philip Friedman, a representative of the Central Committee of Polish Jews, established a few months earlier in Lublin. The participants elected a local committee for Jewish affairs, which would shortly become affiliated with the CCPJ. It was headed by Michal Mirski, a veteran Communist, who had arrived in Poland from the Soviet Union with the Polish Army. The Jewish Committee in Lodz was the only Jewish committee in Poland elected by a mass meeting. The membership of other local committees was usually agreed upon by Jewish parties and organizations. The Lodz Committee's Deputy Chairman was Bernard Weiskopf, a lawyer, whose brother, Dr. Daniel Weiskopf, was admired by surviving Lodz Jews for resisting and for wounding Hans Biebow, the chief German administrator of the Lodz Ghetto. The Committee's secretary was also a lawyer, Anatol Wertheim, a communist. Among the initial members of the Lodz Jewish Committee was Feigele Peltel, better known as Vladka Meed, who had acted as liaison for the Warsaw Ghetto underground. She represented the Left Poalei Zion. Another member was Hilary Sztrowajs, a well-to-do Lodz Jew.

The most urgent task of the newly-established Committee was to assist Jews arriving daily in the city. One of its first achievements was the designation by Kazimierz Mijal, the Government representative in Lodz who shortly became its first postwar Mayor, of a thousand apartments for the incoming Jews. Mijal agreed that the Jewish Committee would directly assign those apartments, which could accommodate up to 10,000 people. Thus, Jews who arrived in Lodz during the first months after liberation faced no difficulties in getting settled there. In time it became increasingly difficult for incoming Jews to find dwelling quarters. Numerous individual Jews and Jewish families would move into apartments vacated by Jews who left the city on their way out of Poland.

A Passover Seder was held by the Committee for Jewish soldiers and officers in Tivoli Hall, on March 28. The ritual part was performed by Rabbi Szczekacz and by the head of the Lodz Jewish religious community, Josef Atlas. Among the speakers were Mirski and Wertheim. Stalin and Bierut were toasted enthusiastically. The first Jewish public cultural event in postwar Lodz, a commemoration of the anniversary of I.L. Peretz's death, was held in the Baltyk cinema hall on March 30. [25]

From its very inception the Committee registered all newcomers and assisted them in their attempts to find surviving relatives. Usually, the first place newcomers used to visit, after arriving at the railroad station, was the Committee's offices. One of those incoming Jews was Sara Zyskind, who had resided with her family in prewar Lodz. She was returning from a camp in Germany. "We had to change trains three times in order to get to Lodz, and each train was more crowded than the last. On one leg of our journey we were forced to ride on the train's roof. Early in the morning after our arrival in Lodz, my friends and I were waiting in the courtyard of the Relief Committee office. When a new group of returnees arrived from the train station, we rushed forward to scan their faces. This became our daily routine."

Mirski recalled that "the walls leading to the Committee's Registration Department were covered with hundreds of notes in all languages, mainly in Polish and Yiddish. People were looking for relatives. It was like a map of cities and towns with thousands of names." The first Jewish-Yiddish newpaper in postwar Poland, *Dos Naje Lebn*, New Life, which started publication in April 1945, carried pages of announcements by survivors looking for relatives, as well as announcements of Jews abroad, mostly in the US, searching for surviving relatives.[26]

It is difficult to establish an accurate demographic profile of the Jewish population in postwar Lodz. Many of those who arrived in the city would leave within weeks or months. Others stayed for years. The fluctuation was enormous. Still, some reliable estimates are available. The Jewish population in postwar Lodz was steadily increasing. By July 1945, more than 20,000 Jews had settled there. The number of Jews in Lodz reached 30,000 by the end of the year. At that point in time they constituted 5-6% of the total city population and 40% of the Jewish population in Poland. There were 41,474 Jews registered in the city and province of Lodz at the end of 1945; every second person was a camp survivor. About 10,000 were returnees from the Soviet Union. Close to 7,000 survived on the Aryan side, and the rest were partisans, soldiers, and those who survived in forests and bunkers. The time of the largest concentration of Jews residing in Lodz and in the Lodz Province was apparently in late June 1946, on the eve of the Kielce pogrom.[27]

During the first months after liberation, an overwhelming majority of Jews residing in Lodz were people who survived under German occupation. However, the proportion of those who survived in the Soviet Union increased steadily. Whereas in early 1946, out of about 40,000 Jews who lived in Lodz, less than 12,000 were returnees from the Soviet Union, in mid-1946, out of a total of about 57,000 Jews living in Lodz and in the Lodz Province, more than 26,000 were returnees. By the end of the year more than 30,000 returnees had passed through or remained in Lodz. According to Mirski "the number of returnees was so large that all Srodmiejska street leading to the Committee would be packed with people. Some of them were sitting on the sidewalks. Those who could not find a room would be set up temporarily in a huge empty factory hall on Jakuba Street, in the former Ghetto area. Dom Repatrianta, the Repatriates' House on 16 Jakuba Street, was turned, eventually, into a quite comfortable place with a capacity for 700 people."[28]

How many of those who settled in postwar Lodz were original Lodzer Yidn — Lodz Jews? Only a few thousand of the Lodz Ghetto Jews survived the camps and the death marches. Some of them never returned to their native city, and eventually settled in Israel and in other countries. Thousands of Lodz Jews returned from the Soviet Union and settled, at least for some time, in Lodz, while other Lodz natives settled in other cities. In mid-1947, more than 4,000 prewar Lodz Jews resided in Lodz, whereas 2,000 prewar Lodz Jews lived in Lower Silesia. It seems that a larger proportion of Lodz Jews returned to Lodz than that of Warsaw Jews who returned to Warsaw. The predominant reason was the fact that Lodz remained quite intact, while most of Warsaw was in shambles. On the whole, those few who survived tended, at least initially, to return to their prewar places of residence. There were indications that the Polish government preferred not to turn postwar Warsaw into a significant center of Jewish population.[29]

The age structure of the Jewish population in postwar Lodz was severely affected by the war and the Holocaust. The number of children and the old was disproportionately small. During the first months after liberation 85% of the Jewish population in Lodz were people aged 15 to 45. Only 3% were children under age 7, 4% were children aged 7-14, and less than 8% were people older than 45. However, as a result of the arrival of Jewish returnees from the Soviet Union, among whom there was a considerable number of families, the number of Jewish children increased. In mid-1945 less than a thousand Jewish children resided in Lodz. By January 1946 there were already more than 2,000 children, and by June 1946 — more than 4,500. In spite of the difficult conditions and the unsettled, temporary nature of Jewish life in Poland, babies were being born to Jewish families. In only one year, 500 newborns were delivered in the Jewish Hospital in Lodz, which opened in January 1947. The gender composition of the Jewish population reflected the impact of the War and the Holocaust. Thus, among Jews who settled in Lodz throughout 1945, 55% were male and only 45% were female. There was a great majority of singles. They accounted for nearly 62% of those registered by the Lodz Jewish Committee in 1945.[30]

The significance of Lodz as a Jewish urban center in postwar Poland stemmed not only from the size of its Jewish population at a given point in time, but also from the cumulative number of Jews who had lived there for varying periods of time. Around 63,000 Jews were registered by the Lodz Jewish Committee between February 1945 and February 1947. Since the overall number of Jews who lived in Poland in the early postwar years is estimated at slightly more than 270,000, it seems that every fourth Jew lived at least for some time in Lodz.[31]

Structural changes in Poland's postwar economy, the wartime uprootedness of Jewish survivors both under German occupation and inside the Soviet Union, as well as the temporary nature of Jewish settlement in postwar Lodz, affected the ways in which Jews earned a living. During the first post-liberation year, more than 40% of the Jews residing in Lodz had no profession. Among the approximately 11,500 working-age Jews in mid-1947, close to 4,500 were unemployed. Out of the 7,000 who worked, about one thousand were employed in textile factories, 700 worked in craftsmens' cooperatives, close to 1,200 were independent craftsmen, close to 1,000 worked in various administrative positions, and slightly less than 500 were petty merchants. There were also a few hundred in the free professions, mostly in medicine. The occupational profile of the Jewish population in postwar Lodz makes it sufficiently clear why many among them needed assistance from the CCPJ and other Jewish institutions.[32]

Jewish cooperatives in Lodz were initiated within a few months after liberation. In mid-1946, 18 Jewish cooperatives employed more than 500 craftsmen, such as tailors, shoemakers, carpenters, metal workers and printers. An American Jewish journalist visited a carpenters' cooperative on Jaracza Street at that time. "Twenty-one carpenters were employed there. Only two were from Lodz. Almost all of them were the only survivors of their families; some had been repatriated from Soviet Russia, and some had their death camp numbers tatooed on their wrists." The membership turnover in that cooperative reflected the fluidity of the Jewish population at large. "In the course of the last two months the membership had changed several times. The founders had gone away long ago." Still, the number of Jewish cooperatives in Lodz and their membership kept growing. Twenty-one Jewish cooperatives, eight of them tailors' cooperatives, existed at the end of 1947. Twenty-eight Jewish cooperatives, with 1600 workers, were active in Lodz in 1948.[33]

Most of the Jews who lived in postwar Lodz resided in the midtown area. Jewish institutions and organizations were concentrated in the center of the city as well. In a sense, this was a markedly Jewish urban space, within the much larger and outlying space of Polish Lodz. Whereas Polish Lodz was mostly proletarian and stable, Jewish Lodz was economically and socially diversified and extremely fluid. The parameters of postwar Jewish Lodz were, approximately: Plac Wolnosci, Liberty Square, in the north, Narutowicza Street in the south, Gdanska Street in the west and Kilinskiego Street in the east. The offices of the Jewish Committee, the hub of postwar Jewish Lodz, were located on 32 Srodmiejska Street and occupied three floors. TOZ, the Jewish Health Care Society, was at number 31. Offices of Hashomer Hatzair and its Polish language periodical *Mosty* were at number 4, and a kindergarten run by the Jewish Committee was at number 10. Another "Jewish" street was Zachodnia, which ran parallel to Piotrkowska. The Jewish religious community center was located on 66 Zachodnia Street. The offices of the Poalei Zion party were at number 26, and some quite strange neighbors, such as the Zionist Ichud party and the PPR Section of the Jewish Committee, were at number 20. A craftsmen's cooperative run by the Bund, was at number 42.

A short section of Jaracza Street hosted a variety of Jewish institutions. The Lodz Jewish Theater was at number 2. The Bund cultural center and a Bund craftsmen's cooperative were in the same building. Poalei Zion and its youth movement Dror were located at number 4. The offices of the Poalei Zion–Left party were at number 15, and of the Bund at number 17. Hashomer Hatzair activities in postwar Lodz were held at 49 Kilinskiego Street. Several rooms were used by the youth movement and by a cultural center. Close by was also the editorial office of Hashomer Hatzair's publication, *Mishmar*. The Jewish-Yiddish school named after the writer I.L. Peretz, run by the Lodz Jewish Committee, was also located at 49 Kilinskiego Street.

Narutowicza was one of the most modern and impressive streets in the center of Lodz. Number 32, a huge, stylish and elegant building, planned by the Jewish architect Gustaw Landau-Gutenteger was built before the First World War. After the Second World War it hosted the Society of Jewish Writers, Journalists and Artists. Here too were the editorial offices of *Dos Naje Lebn*. Some of the Jewish writers and journalists, such as David Sfard, Joseph Kermisz, Nachman Blumental and Rachel Auerbach lived in that building. Inside its extensive inner yard were located the CCPJ storage rooms, full of used clothing donated to the Jews of Lodz by American-Jewish organizations.[34]

Lodz was the center of Jewish culture in Poland during the first postwar years. According to Hersz Smolar, one of the communist Jewish leaders, "Lodz became a drawing magnet for the Jewish intelligentsia." The most significant Jewish cultural institutions and organizations, such as the Association of Jewish Writers, Journalists and Artists, and the Central Jewish Historical Commission, were located in this city. The first postwar Jewish newspaper started publication in Lodz. Jewish scholars, writers, and artists settled, at least for a while, in Lodz. Among them were the historians Philip Friedman, Bernard Mark and Joseph Kermisz, the writers Chaim Grade, Binem Heller, Isaac Ianasovich, Shmerke Kaczerginski, Mendel Mann and Joseph Rubinstein, the poets Nachum Bomze, Abraham Sutskever and Rachel Korn, the journalist Leon Leneman, the composer Shaul Berezovski, and the filmmaker Natan Gross. A number of *landsmannschaftn,* Jewish hometown associations, were founded in postwar Lodz. The largest and most active was apparently that of Vilna Jews.[35]

Postwar Lodz was home to a wide range of Jewish periodical publications in Yiddish, Hebrew and Polish, representing various and at times conflicting views and opinions. The first Yiddish typesetting fonts found in Lodz after liberation were unearthed among the ruins of the former ghetto in February 1945. They had previously been used for the printing of the ghetto newspaper. The first issue of *Dos Naje Lebn* was published in Lodz, on April 10. It became the official publication of the CCPJ for the next five years. As early as 1945, its circulation reached 7,000 copies. Its chief editor was Michal Mirski. Initially, the editorial board represented all major ideological and political trends within postwar Polish Jewry. In time, it became the mouthpiece of the Jewish Communists. A Yiddish publishing house, bearing the same name and headed by Mirski, was also established. By early 1947, it had a staff of sixty-three. Besides salaries, paid by the Jewish Committee, the employees received material assistance from time to time. According to a list dated January 1, 1946, the writer and journalist Rachel Auerbach received a dress, a skirt, a blouse, a sweater, a dressing gown and a pair of shoes. Aleksander and Tosia Klugman, a typesetter and his wife, received 12 items each. Chief Editor Mirski got on that occasion a waterproof coat and three pairs of socks.[36]

Jewish cultural events became a common feature in Lodz quite soon after liberation. Here is a sample of events which took place between mid-May and early July 1945:

> Rachel Auerbach read excerpts from her wartime writings at the Committee of Jewish Writers, Journalists and Artists, on May 18.
> The singers Diana Blumenfeld and Dido Epstein performed at the Sala Spiewakow, The Singers' Hall, on May 19th and 20th.
> There was a commemoration of Shalom Aleichem at the Sala Spiewakow on June 3.
> The popular prewar Yiddish film *Mayn Shtetl Belz (My Town of*

Belz) was screened in Wlokniarz, the largest cinema hall in town, on June 16.

Dr. Adolf Berman, the leading leftist-Zionist politician, spoke at the Baltyk cinema hall on June 17, and Chayele Rozental, a young Jewish singer and survivor of the Vilna Ghetto, performed on that day.

A commemoration of Herzl and Bialik took place at the newly opened Hehalutz House on July 2.

A Zionist celebration, with the participation of the hero of the Warsaw Ghetto uprising, Antek Zuckerman, was held on July 8.

Literary evenings with the participation of new arrivals from the Soviet Union drew Jewish literary-minded audiences. One of the first events of this kind was a reception in honor of Bernard Mark, Moshe Grosman, Nachum Bomze, Mendel Mann and Shmerke Kaczerginski in early March 1946. A literary evening dedicated to Soviet Yiddish literature with the participation of close to twenty speakers took place on November 8, 1947.[37]

Polish people, mostly leftist intellectuals and writers, participated in some of the Jewish events. A poetry evening dedicated to Wladyslaw Broniewski, a leading "proletarian" Polish poet who had lived for some part of the war in Jerusalem, was held at the Hashomer Hatzair Cultural Center in early November of 1946. The evening opened with greetings by Binyamin Tene-Tenenbaum, Broniewski's Hebrew translator. Broniewski read some of his Jewish-oriented poetry, such as the poem "The Western Wall." He was most known in the Jewish intellectual circles for his elegiac poem "For Polish Jews." Broniewski told the public about life in the kibbutzim, in Palestine. He also strongly condemned anti-Semitism in postwar Poland: "As a Pole I am ashamed that even today, after the murder of millions of Jews, there is still anti-Semitism in Poland." Leszek Kolakowski, at that time a young philosophy student at Lodz University, recalled participating in an event celebrating the unification of the socialist Zionist youth movements Borochov Yugnt and Dror. There was also a continuous flow of visitors from abroad, mainly from the US and Palestine. Yitshak Gruenbaum, a prominent Zionist leader in prewar Poland who had settled in Palestine, spoke at the Wlokniarz cinema hall. His popularity was such that people bought tickets to the film screened before his speech, so as to secure seats. Another famous visitor was the popular Soviet-Jewish writer and journalist Ilya Ehrenburg. He visited Lodz in the fall of 1947 and spoke to an overflowing Jewish crowd. At a reception hosted by the Organization of Jewish Writers and Journalists, Ehrenburg spoke of the wartime Jewish tragedy and of contemporary anti-Semitism, but he also criticized Jewish generalizations and stereotypes concerning anti-Semites and anti-Semitism.[38]

It was only natural that the commemoration of the Holocaust would be a recurring theme in public Jewish events. The first Jewish commemorative event in postwar Lodz took place on November 1, 1945; it was announced officially as a commemoration day for the victims of Nazi Germany in Poland. According to a report by the Jewish Press Agency, "a mass march, including representatives of the Polish community, all Jewish political and social organizations, and Jewish schoolchildren started at the Lodz Jewish Committee offices on Srodmiejska Street. An Army Honor Guard was waiting for the marchers at the Jewish cemetery." Among those who spoke on that solemn occasion were head of the Lodz Jewish Committee Michal Mirski, and the head of the Jewish congregation, Rabbi Krawiec. Another occasion was the annual memorial for the Lodz Ghetto victims. The Jewish Telegraphic Agency reported that "on September 27, 1947, the Jewish and Polish community of Lodz marked the third anniversary of the liquidation of the Lodz Ghetto." A ceremony to unveil a commemorative plaque took place at the Jewish cemetery. Numerous delegations laid wreaths at the martyrs' tombs. In September 1949, the commemoration ceremony at the cemetery was attended by 2,000 people.[39]

Another highly-attended event was the anniversary of the Warsaw Ghetto Uprising. The fourth anniversary, in April 1947, was celebrated in Lodz at the Polish Army Theater. The first speaker was Mirski. Marek Edelman and Tuvia Borzykowski, both participants in the Warsaw Ghetto Uprising, shared their memories with the audience. The renowned Jewish actress, Ida Kaminska, was one of the performing artists. A fundraising campaign for the erection of a monument to commemorate the Warsaw Ghetto Fighters was initiated in the early fall of 1947. It was widely supported by all Jewish organizations in Lodz. Impressive donations were raised by local Jewish cooperatives.[40]

Postwar Lodz witnessed at least two trials against Nazi perpetrators, that of Rudolf Krampf and that of Hans Biebow. Krampf, a *Volksdeutsche*, worked in Lodz as a printer before the war. After the establishment of the Lodz Ghetto he became one of the chief assistants to Biebow, the Ghetto Administration chief. He was also involved in the organization and functioning of the Chelmno death camp, not far from Lodz. Numerous witnesses appeared in the course of Krampf's trial in December 1945. Among them was fifteen-year-old Shimon Srebnik, whose testimony would open Lantzman's monumental film *Shoah*, decades later. Srebnik told the court how he, together with other Jewish teenagers, had been forced to burn bodies of gassed Jews. When the Red Army advanced in the direction of Chelmno and Lodz, in January 1945, Krampf ordered the shooting of these youngsters. Srebnik, though severely wounded, managed to survive. Krampf also planned to kill the last of the young ghetto Jews, who were supposed to clean the area after the final deportations to Auschwitz. He was sentenced to death.[41]

The trial of Hans Biebow, "the butcher of the Lodz Ghetto," was held in late April 1947. Biebow, a middle-class German merchant born in Bremen who had joined the Nazi Party, was nominated to be head of the Lodz Ghetto administration. He was not only responsible for implementing Nazi policies in respect to the ghetto Jews, but was personally involved in torture, rape and killings. He often used his official position to seize Jewish property and valuables. Biebow traveled from Lodz to Dresden in connection with his business activities, in mid-January 1945, a few days before the arrival of the Red Army. He was identified and picked up by the British, on a request of the Polish legal authorities.

It was the trial of Krampf that led to the identification of Biebow in Germany. He was extradited to Poland in May 1946 and brought to the Sterling Street Prison in Lodz at the end of June. Biebow's trial started in the morning of April 23, 1947, in the Lodz District Court on Dabrowski Square. It provoked wide public interest, and was reported on daily by the general Polish press, as well as by local Lodz newspapers. Numerous Jewish witnesses gave evidence in the trial. Historian Arthur Eisenbach quoted from the extensive documentation collected by the Jewish Historical Commission. Mirski, head of the Lodz Jewish Committee and Chief Editor of *Dos Naje Lebn*, was one of the three aldermen appointed by the court. *Dos Naje Lebn* reported that "a huge Jewish crowd assembled on Wednesday, April 30, inside the courtroom and in front of the loudspeakers installed in the street, to hear the verdict." The final court session was covered by Polish and foreign media. Biebow was found guilty and sentenced to death. His appeal to President Bierut was rejected. He was hanged at dawn, on June 23.[42]

One of the most remarkable achievements of postwar Jewish culture in Poland was the Jewish Theater of Lodz. Most of its actors and staff were returnees from the Soviet Union, who had begun to arrive in Lodz in the spring of 1946. The Theater's opening was officially announced in August. Its first director was Moshe Lipman, who had just returned from Russia with his wife, the actress Natalia Lipman. Among the other artists were Aizik Rotman, Nadia Kareni, Eni Liton and Ketty Efron. They were joined by a few graduates of Mikhoels' Yiddish State Theater Studio in Moscow. Between August and December 1946 the Theater performed eight plays. In January 1947, it premiered with Anski's classical Yiddish play, "The Dibbuk." Altogether eleven productions were staged in the course of the year. They included mainly classical and popular Yiddish plays by such writers and playwrights as Shalom Aleichem, Goldfaden and Gordin. Ticket statistics indicate how popular the Lodz Jewish Theater was. More than 28,000 tickets were sold throughout 1947. In 1948 the Lodz Jewish Theater went on tour in Poland and abroad.[43]

By mid-1948, the renowned Yiddish actress Ida Kaminska, daughter of Ester-Rokhl Kaminska, "the mother of Yiddish theater," had become the art director of the Lodz Jewish Theater. She was assisted in administrative and organizational matters by her husband, the actor Marian Melman. Kaminska was not only an excellent actress, but also a resourceful and energetic director. With the help of Jack Greenbaum of New York and the assistance of the CCPJ, Kaminska renovated the small and modest hall on 2 Jaracza Street. One of the first plays performed in the renovated theater was Kaminska's adaptation of Max Bauman's *Glueckel Hameln Demands Justice*, with Kaminska in the leading role. The gala premiere in November 1948 was attended by the Polish Minister of Culture, the Mayor of Lodz and CCPJ representatives. Leon Schiller, Poland's leading theater director, sent a congratulatory telegram. He had always been an enthusiastic supporter of the Jewish theater in Poland. Kaminska made continuous efforts to get official approval and financial support for the construction of a large modern Jewish theater building in Lodz.[44]

The most popular Yiddish actors in postwar Poland, besides Ida Kaminska, were the comedians Shimon Dzigan and Israel Schumacher. Their paths crossed for the first time in Brodersohn's theater studio in prewar Lodz. Dzigan was raised in the poor Baluty neighborhood. Schumacher was from a middle class family, and he graduated from one of the best high schools in town. They started performing together in the Ararat Revue Theater, which specialized in Jewish folklore, and soon became popular with Jewish audiences. Dzigan and Schumacher were among the throngs of refugees who escaped eastward in the fall of 1939 and eventually found themselves in remote regions of the Soviet Union. They tried to join General Anders' Polish Army, but were accused of desertion and sent to Soviet labor camps. They were released only in August 1946, and shortly thereafter were rearrested. Dzigan and Schumacher managed finally to leave the Soviet Union in the summer of 1947, reaching Warsaw first and settling later in Lodz.

Dzigan and Schumacher's performances in postwar Lodz were a tremendous success. The crowd at their first program, *Abi men zet zikh* (*We Meet Again*) was huge. The reunion between the Yiddish speaking audience and the popular Yiddish comedians after years of suffering and loss was highly emotional. Both audience and actors stood for a few moments facing each other and cried. Dzigan and Schumacher were the highlight of the New Year's Artists' Ball at the Lodz Jewish Theater, on December 31, 1947. Musical arrangements for the Ball were by Shaul Berezovski. Among the performing actors were Sylvia Swen and Ketty Efron. The dancing went on up to the early hours of the morning. Dzigan and Schumacher's subsequent programs, such as *Nu, un vos vayter?* (*So, What's in the Future?*) and *Zingendik un Tantsndik* (*With a Song and a Dance*) were based on prewar themes, on their wartime experiences, and on hopes for the future. Dzigan and Schumacher went on extensive tours to Jewish population centers throughout Poland.[45]

Modest attempts to renew Jewish filmmaking in postwar Poland were initiated in Lodz, the center of Polish film production at that time. This is where Kinor, a Jewish filmmaking cooperative, was founded in the fall of 1946 by the Goskind brothers, the leading producers of Yiddish films in prewar Poland, who had survived the war in the Soviet Union. Kinor functioned under the auspices of the CCPJ, while funding was supplied by the JDC. Facilities and technical support were provided by Film Polski. Most of Kinor's productions were newsreels and short documentaries on Jews and Jewish life in postwar Poland. The first full-length documentary, produced in 1947, was *Mir Lebngeblibene* (*We, The Survivors*) directed by Natan Gross.

The film documented various aspects of Jewish life in Poland in the immediate postwar years. It opened with *el maleh rahamim*, the traditional prayer for the dead, performed by cantor Koussevitski, went on to show the excavation of the Ringelblum archive from under the rubble of the Warsaw Ghetto, and presented scenes from the Lodz Jewish Committee offices, where survivors attempted to find information about their families. A considerable part of the film showed Jewish children and youth in CCPJ Children's Homes and in various Zionist youth movements. Its last part portrayed Jewish culture and entertainment. The film was warmly accepted by Jewish audiences throughout Poland, but its screening for the general Polish public was not allowed. A shorter documentary was filmed in the spring of 1948, documenting the fifth anniversary of the Warsaw Ghetto Uprising. Still another, apparently the last one prepared by Kinor in postwar Poland, was a film about the arrival of the Israeli Legation in Warsaw. Polish-Israeli relations began to deteriorate quite soon, as a result of the Cold War. The film was never screened in Poland. It was smuggled to Israel illegally.[46]

Undzere Kinder (*Our Children*) was the only full-length Jewish feature film produced by Kinor in postwar Poland. The movie's ideas and concepts, its implementation, as well as the film's fate, reflect the vicissitudes and hardships of Jewish/Yiddish filmmaking in Poland. The initial idea was Shaul Goskind's. He decided to make a film that would center on Dzigan and Schumacher, who had just returned from Russia. Time was of the essence: it was quite clear that the two popular comedians would not remain in Poland for long. It was only natural that the film must, in some way, present the tragedy and rebirth of Polish Jewry. Still another problem was postwar Polish politics and propaganda. These constraints resulted in the production of a rather eclectic film, in which various and at times contradicting concepts and stories were pieced together. Goskind first approached Arnold Mostowicz, a Lodz born physician, writer and editor, and survivor of the Lodz Ghetto. Mostowicz could not see how the tragedy of the Holocaust could be combined with the comedy of Dzigan and Schumacher. Finally, the scenario was worked out by a group of people — the film's director Natan Gross, the writer/historian Rachel Auerbach and the two comedians. Auerbach worked at the Jewish Historical Commission and was familiar with numerous war and survival testimonies. Gross was deeply involved in documentary filming, with special emphasis on children and youth. Dzigan and Schumacher would play themselves, Jewish actors — comedians, returning from Soviet Russia and facing the grim realities of post-Holocaust Poland.

Undzere Kinder centers on the comedians' visit to a Jewish Childrens' Home, where they perform in front of the young audience. When late in the evening they walk upstairs to their bedrooms, they peak through keyholes, and are surprised and shocked to witness "stories of survival," flashbacks into what some of the children had undergone during the war. The dramatic and depressing nighttime sequences are in a way "erased" and substituted by the next morning's sunshine and playground scene in which the children are normal again, and even make fun of the comedians. Then comes the "happy end," the departure of the actors, surrounded by marching and singing children. Decades later, when one of the performing children, a survivor from the Vilna Ghetto, was asked about the connection between his acting in the film and his factual past during the war, he remarked: "The filmmaking of *Undzere Kinder* was a happy time in my life and in the lives of the other child actors. This was a new and interesting experience. We did not talk about the past. We lived the present and wanted to return to a normal existence, to have fun." As far as the performers in this film are concerned, there is a mix of professional actors, such as Dzigan and Schumacher, Moshe Lipman, Nusia Gold and Nadia Kareni, and non-professional children-actors from the Helenowek orphanage and from the Hebrew and Yiddish schools in Lodz. The musical adaptation is by Shaul Berezovski, who used the already popular Jewish Partisans' Song for the film's main musical theme. This, along with other songs in the film, was performed by the Hebrew School children's choir, directed by Israel Glantz.[47]

What is the significance, if any, of *Undzere Kinder*? First of all, this was one of the first representations of the Holocaust in postwar cinema, and one of the earliest feature films on the subject. At the same time, however, it does not form a defined and well-thought-through entity. It is rather a montage type of creation, full of contrasts and contradictions: past and present, memories and expectations, grief and hope, tragic loss and comic distractions, adult professionals and amateur children actors. Another set of questions concerns the problem of how to confront the Holocaust: should this be done through reenactment of a traumatic past, as in the bedroom flashback stories of the orphans, or through avoidance of the past and a turn towards a hopeful future, as presented by the playing, working, marching and singing children? Then, there is also the impact and influence of social realism, Soviet-style, prevalent at the time in Russia and in its satellites. One cannot grasp the substance and fate of *Undzere Kinder*, without considering the political context of postwar Poland in general, and the Polish-Jewish context in particular. Even if *Undzere Kinder* is not an impressive achievement in the pure artistic sense, it is significant as an early presentation of the Holocaust. The film was never screened to the public at large in Poland, because of the changing political circumstances. What was, perhaps, permissible when the scenario was being written, became taboo by the time the filming and the editing were completed.[48]

Two Jewish elementary schools existed in postwar Lodz, the Peretz Yiddish school on 49 Kilinskiego Street and the Ghetto Fighters' Hebrew School on 18 Poludniowa Street. The Yiddish school, run by the Lodz Jewish Committee, opened in mid-September 1945 in an apartment on 15 Jaracza Street. Initially, only 45 pupils were taught there by four teachers. One of the teachers was Mendel Mann, a Yiddish writer who had survived the war in Soviet Russia and was serving as head of the Education Department of the Jewish Committee in Lodz. The number of students increased to 180 in the spring of 1946. The school then moved to more spacious quarters, on 49 Kilinskiego Street. This was a large building with an inner court. Two floors were assigned by the Lodz municipality to the Jewish Committee for the school. The number of students soon increased to about 300, and the number of teachers to twelve. At the end of 1946 the number of students in the Peretz school was close to 400, and the number of teachers, twenty. Its principal in the years 1945-1949 was

Michal Helman, a member of the Left Poalei Zion.[49]

The Hebrew school began as a private educational institution in the fall of 1945. This was the first Hebrew school in postwar Poland, and it was run by Hehalutz, the coordinating center of Zionist youth movements. The school was initially located at 72 Wschodnia Street, but it soon moved to larger quarters at 18 Poludniowa Street. A number of former apartments in that building were turned into classrooms. Its founding principal was Baruch Kaplinski. The subsequent principals were Shaul Liberman and Aharon Rashal. More than a hundred children enrolled in the school within the first few days of its opening. The number of students reached 250 in 1946. It was one of the two largest Hebrew schools in Poland at that time. The school's name, The Ghetto Fighters' Hebrew School, was suggested to Kaplinski by Antek Zuckerman. Whereas in the Peretz Yiddish school Hebrew was just one of the subjects of instruction, it was taught intensively in all grades of the Ghetto Fighters' school. The instruction and the general atmosphere of the school were distinctly Zionist and Palestine-oriented. Hundreds of students must have passed through it. Following the emigration of Lodz's Jews to Palestine/Israel and elsewhere, the number of students shrank. By January of 1949 only 153 students attended the school, and it had only twelve teachers.[50]

The Helenowek Jewish Children's Home, usually referred to as Helenowek, was located on the northern outskirts of town, close to an extensive forested area. A wide alley bounded by old chestnut trees led to the main building. A Jewish orphanage run by Chaim Rumkowski, the future "King of the Lodz Ghetto," existed there prior to the war. The orphanage consisted of a number of modern buildings with heating and hot and cold water, which were not too common in prewar Lodz. There were a few small playgrounds for the younger children and a large playground for the older ones. The Helenowek Children's Home also owned a small agricultural farm and an impressive greenhouse. It opened in May 1945, under the auspices of the Lodz Jewish Committee. Maria Feingold was appointed as its director in the fall. She had extensive experience in education before the war. During the war she headed a Polish school and a Polish orphanage in Samarkand, in Soviet Uzbekistan. Among the first children placed in Helenowek by the Lodz Jewish Committee were seven boys, Lodz Ghetto survivors, originally from Germany. They didn't stay for long.

The ages and wartime experiences of the incoming inhabitants of Helenowek varied greatly. Thus, of the ninety children and teenagers who lived in Helenowek in the fall of 1946, twenty-nine were aged 2-6, twenty were aged 7-9 and forty-one were aged 10-18. As for where and how they had survived the war, more than half were returnees from the Soviet

Union, twenty-five survived as Aryans, nine came from camps, seven survived in convents, and two were children-partisans. Most of the school-age children in Helenowek attended the Peretz Yiddish school.[51]

Although the average number of children in Helenowek in the subsequent years fluctuated around one hundred, there was a steady outflow and inflow of residents. Thus, in January 1947, ten children left and twelve arrived. However, in March of that year only six left and twenty-two arrived. Among them were Herszek Grynberg, the future Polish-Jewish writer, and Chaim Preter, one of the children-actors in *Undzere Kinder*. Only a minority were orphans. Most of them were either half-orphans or children with parents who for various reasons had sent them to Helenowek. Out of ninety-eight inhabitants in November 1947, twenty-four were orphans, forty-five had one parent and twenty-nine had both parents. Difficult economic and socio-psychological conditions forced some parents to separate from their children.

Many of the Helenowek children arrived undernourished and sick. Some had serious emotional problems. A psychologist who tested a number of children in Helenowek in early 1946 reported that "Alex, though quite intelligent, is extremely timid, and Stanislaw suffers from rage attacks." Some of the youngest children couldn't talk properly and others suffered from mental disorders. Some were illiterate. The majority, though, improved in time, both physically and mentally. Most of them were successful in school.[52]

Feingold's concept of running the Helenowek Children's Home was to delegate responsibility to its residents and endow them with pride in their achievements. A Children's Council was elected from time to time, and the *Helenowek Chronicle* documented everyday life in the Home. Sven Sonnenberg, one of Helenowek's graduates, remains full of praise for the Home, and particularly for its Director. "Looking back it seems that her personality carried the day. She never raised her voice or used physical discipline. Mrs. Feingold, by the force of her personality, created a unique milieu. The care was superb, the discipline and standards to strive for were demanding. Most of us, her children, kept a very close relationship with her, way into our adult lives, even in retirement and from abroad." Sven also recalled another Helenowek mentor, Ms. Maria Milstein. "Ms. Milstein was a lifelong communist. She was a tall, rather skinny spinster. She never smiled. Her life was absolutely devoted to spreading and solidifying communism. In other aspects she was reasonable and very caring about the children under her supervision." The Helenowek Children's Home became a showpiece of the Lodz Jewish Committee. Besides educational achievements in the Lodz schools, a wide range of arts was taught on the premises. Some of the best Jewish instructors in dance and music were active there. Among them was Sylvia Swen, an experienced dance and rhythmics teacher, Judith Berg and her husband Felek Fibich, who taught Jewish-Yiddish folk-dancing, the orchestra director Frydland, and the choir director Igor Glantz. When *Undzere Kinder* was filmed in 1948, Helenowek was selected as the location for many of the shots. Jewish Committee members and journalists from *Dos Naje Lebn* would often visit the Home. The Helenowek dance group and choir were invited to perform for representatives of various Jewish organizations from all over Poland.[53]

The so-called Bursa was in fact a Jewish youth dormitory. Young Jewish men and women, mostly without families, started arriving in Lodz in the first months after liberation. These were either camp survivors or those who were hiding on "Aryan" papers during the war. Some of the newcomers had served in the Soviet and Polish armies and a few had been partisans. Growing numbers of young people kept coming with the successive waves of Jewish returnees from the Soviet Union. Although officially the Bursa was meant for both working and studying Jewish youth, a pronounced majority of its tenants intended to start higher education. Some had to complete their prewar schooling. Others, who had completed their secondary education before the war, were looking forward to higher education. The age profile of the "Bursants" varied, from the upper teens up to the late twenties. What was common to all was a prevailing urgency to start a new life after years of war, exile and loss. In those difficult times, the Bursa was an ideal place to live and study. It provided both an appropriate physical setting and a friendly, encouraging social environment. The Lodz Bursa, the first of its kind in postwar Poland, was funded by the CCPJ and opened in late March 1946 in the former ghetto area at 15 Franciszkanska Street. The opening ceremony was attended by Lodz mayor Kazimierz Mijal, Lodz Jewish Committee head Michal Mirski, and representatives of various local institutions of higher education. On the average, around 150 people resided on the Bursa premises, but since there was a considerable turnover, hundreds of young Jewish men and women lived there for varying periods of time.[54]

The Bursa, according to its former occupants, was much more than just a dormitory. Rachelka Kaufman wrote years later "We started to live a new life in that house on Franciszkanska 15. Living with that group of people who had survived the horrors of war, and a feeling of togetherness, strengthened us." Adam Broner recalled that "the Bursa was for us, those who survived the wartime catastrophe, a new home and family. It was there that we started a new life and formed longtime friendships." He recalled that the elite at the Bursa were the university students, who showed off their colorful academic caps. Many of those who initially worked in factories and cooperatives eventually decided to study. Among the "Bursants" were future engineers, physicians and professors. Adam Broner shared a room with Kuba Goldberg, who later became a known historian. Another roommate was Lucek Dobroszycki, who would become a leading scholar of the Holocaust and editor of *The Chronicle of the Lodz Ghetto*. People were intensively involved in their studies as well as in social and cultural events. There was a lot of singing and dancing. The Bursa even boasted its own choir, directed by Wlodek Szejnman, a future surgeon. The Bursants rarely returned to their recent past. Pola Calecka wrote years later, "It seems that each one of us, subconsciously, ran away from the nightmarish past." Henryk Fajnhaken remembered heated political discussions, particularly during the first two years of the Bursa. The gamut ran from staunch Communists through socialists and Bundists and up to outright Zionists. He recalled a rather unexpected event: "A group of dedicated Communist girls disappeared one night and went off to Palestine." Memoirs of former Bursants speak of prevailing notions of togetherness and "family." As a matter of fact, some real families started in that crowded dormitory. A few children were born and raised there. One mother recalled "the first child was born. Ours. Halinka had a mother and a father but no other family. However, quite soon she discovered that she had a lot of aunts and uncles."[55]

Jews arriving in Lodz after its liberation encountered various forms of anti-Semitism. Prewar Lodz Jews who survived and returned found their homes occupied by Poles. Some of them managed to recover their apartments by legal action. Others did not. An American-Jewish journalist who visited Lodz shortly after the war found that "the most bitterly disappointed were the repatriates of Lodz who had found their homes intact but nevertheless had to move to the refugee center on Jakuba Street." Some Jewish children who attended Polish schools in postwar Lodz encountered anti-Semitism. Samuel Bak, who had survived the Holocaust in his native Vilna, and who would later become a renowned artist, recalled that he was mocked by his Polish classmates. "My classmates would come up to me, sniff me out and murmur that 'for a regular kike' I smelled not too bad. There was no attempt at physical violence, no pushing, pulling or kicking, but the overt anti-Semitism of a few boys, nonchalantly tolerated by all the others, started to annoy me greatly." He left school and went to study art with a private tutor.[56]

Though Lodz seemed to be safer for Jews than other cities, anti-Semitic moods prevailed among parts of its population. Rumors of all sorts, quite typical of the immediate postwar years, generated anti-Jewish suspicions, fears and accusations. According to a rumor circulated in Lodz in the summer of 1945, every Jew returning from the camps was receiving 30,000 zlotys. A much more ominous rumor spread in town in the spring of 1946, around the Passover Holidays. Mijal, the mayor of Lodz, speaking at the inauguration of the Bursa, mentioned a rumor about supposed kidnappings of Polish children by Jews. Still another rumor spoke of great numbers of Jews being brought in from Soviet Russia. A leaflet circulating in Lodz in the summer of 1946, warned that "the Government planned to send 60,000 Jews to Lodz, in order to take over the industry."[57]

An accusation, prevalent in Lodz as well as all over Poland, was that the Polish security establishment had been permeated by Jews. As a matter of fact, some of the highest positions at the Lodz regional military court, a major instrument of repression, were occupied by Jews. Some Jews were also among the leadership of the Lodz WUPB, the Regional Office of State Security. The fact that some Jews held leading positions in the Security apparatus was widely used by the political opposition to the Communist regime in the immediate postwar years. Anti-Semitic rumors and accusations in Lodz, and in the country as a whole, should also be viewed in their specific postwar context. Poverty and lack of supplies were quite widespread. The Jewish population received material assistance from foreign Jewish organizations, and some Jews received help from their families abroad.[58]

Killings of Jews occurred in Lodz and in the Lodz Province. According to one report, eighteen Jews were murdered in the Lodz Province in January-September 1945. Another report states that fifty-one Jews were murdered in the Lodz Province during the first year after liberation. The same report stated that sixty-four Jews were killed in the Lublin Province and fifty-seven in the Warsaw Province over the same period of time. The fact that there were more killings in provinces with a smaller Jewish population than in the Lodz Province indicates that it was relatively safer for Jews to live in and around Lodz than in other areas. It also seems that most of the killings took place in Lodz Province rather than in the city itself. According to Marek Edelman, a student of Medicine in postwar Lodz, a Jewish female student of Medicine was murdered while traveling from Lodz to Pabianice, where she lived. "During the first few months after liberation, trams between the city and nearby towns didn't run yet, and people traveled by trucks. Two armed Polish youngsters stopped the truck on which that medical student was traveling, ordered her to get off, and killed her on the spot."

Another murder occurred half a year after liberation. Aron Ellenblum, a lonely and sickly cigarette peddler residing on 61 Pilsudskiego Street, was killed in the morning hours of August 25, 1945. Ellenblum's wife and two children had perished in Auschwitz. A survivor of several camps, he returned to his native Lodz shortly after liberation. A Jewish woman residing on 101 Limanowskiego Street was killed by three members of the nationalistic underground in early November 1945. They demanded cash, and since she didn't have any, they shot her. Severely wounded and unconscious, she was brought to a hospital, where she died. Fiszl Barbanel, a barber, was murdered in early December 1945, in the Poniatowski Park. The body was found a few days later. Four members of a religious Zionist kibbutz in Lodz, three men and a woman traveling from Lodz to Krakow, were murdered on their way in early March 1946. They were apparently beaten before being shot. All were camp survivors in their early twenties. Their funeral left from the Mizrachi kibbutz location on Poludniowa Street and was attended by a huge Jewish crowd. Among those who eulogized the victims were representatives of the Lodz Jewish Committee, the Lodz congregation, and Louis Segal of the World Jewish Congress, who was visiting Poland at the time.[59]

The most notorious murder of a Jew in postwar Lodz was that of Feliks "Fishke" Neiman, a Bund activist. He was shot in the afternoon hours of June 24, 1946. When his Bundist friends arrived in his apartment to take him to a Party meeting, they found his bloodied body in the bathtub. The murderers took his gun and his army uniform. Before the war Neiman had been a leading member in Tsukunft, the Bund youth movement. He survived the war in the Soviet Union, and returned to Poland as an officer with Berling's Army. Besides his political activities as a Bundist, he worked as a foreman in a Jewish tailoring cooperative, and studied at Lodz University. Neiman's funeral was attended by thousands, both Jews and Poles. Among them were his fellow Bundists and numerous Jewish cooperatives workers. Representatives of the PPS, PPR and other local Polish organizations paid their tribute as well. Among those who spoke at the cemetery were representatives of the Bund Central Committee, the Polish Army and Lodz University.[60]

The Kielce events, in early July 1946, affected Lodz Jews as they affected Jews all over Poland. The front page of *Dos Naje Lebn* of July 12th, all in black, listed the names of the murdered under the headline "The Martyrs of the Kielce Pogrom." The following pages abounded in gruesome details of what had taken place in Kielce on July 4th. Antek Zuckerman, dispatched by the CCPJ, traveled to Kielce in the wake of the pogrom and discussed with local Polish officials the possibility of moving all Jews from there to Lodz. His most urgent task, though, was to immediately move the wounded victims. Zuckerman traveled with the wounded to Lodz in a special Red Cross train, guarded by an army unit.

He recalled that there was tension in the air. " At every stop, we got out with the soldiers and surrounded the train to protect it. In the morning we arrived in Lodz, where ambulances were waiting for us." The wounded were taken to a local hospital. One of them, Simcha Sokolowski, died in the hospital. His funeral, attended by a large crowd, was organized by the Lodz Jewish Committee. Among official protests against and condemnations of the Kielce pogrom there was also a protest signed by thirty-seven Lodz writers, artists and scholars.

A number of anti-Semitic incidents in Lodz were reported in the second part of July 1946. Grafitti calling for an anti-Jewish pogrom appeared on some walls. There were also rumors about an aborted pogrom planned for mid-July, with the Helenowek Children's Home as a primary target. An incident almost did occur at the Dom Repatriantow Zydowskich, The Jewish Immigrants' House, on 16 Jakuba Street. "A crowd started gathering in front of the House, and anti-Jewish threats were voiced. The police, informed by telephone, appeared immediately, within eight minutes of the call. They arrived in dozens of trucks. The crowd was dispersed on the spot." Some hooligan incidents occurred at Plac Wolnosci. Marek Edelman was attacked on Narutowicza Street.[61]

The Kielce pogrom had a profound impact. Thousands of Jews who had considered settling in Poland for good, or delaying their departure, decided to leave at once. A Jew residing in Lodz described the post-Kielce moods and attitudes: "We, people who lived in the largest Jewish community, i.e. in Lodz, though we sensed that our existence was anchored in quicksand, we didn't allow this sensation to affect our consciousness. We wanted to resume living again as human beings. The Kielce pogrom woke us up from our illusion. One shouldn't stay here even for a moment." Still, Lodz respondents to a sociological survey conducted at the time among Polish Jews mentioned the Kielce pogrom less than Jews from other localities. It is possible that although the Kielce pogrom affected Lodz Jews in one way or another, they felt relatively safer than Jews living in other places. According to Marek Web, who as a child had survived the war in the Soviet Union and lived with his parents in postwar Lodz, "Jews considered it as a relatively safe city. Postwar Poland wasn't a safe place, especially after the Kielce pogrom. Whoever didn't go abroad right away, hurried to Lodz." Indeed, in spite of rumors, threats and fears, pogrom-type events like those in Krakow or Kielce did not occur in Lodz.[62]

Jewish self-defense frameworks were organized in all major locations of Jewish population in Poland in the wake of the Kielce pogrom. They were headed and coordinated by the CKS, CCPJ's Centralna Komisja Specjalna, the Central Special Commission. A network of local Commissions existed for a while in various centers of Jewish population. The first chairman of the Central Special Commission was Antek Zuckerman. A report of the CKS states explicitly that "we had our people in factories, markets, schools and universities." The Special Commission in Lodz included representatives of various Jewish organizations in town. It was headed by Arkadjusz Kahan and Jakob Szpigel. Kahan represented the Bund. Szpigel, a former Labor Union activist, had been a member of the Polish Communist Party before the war. According to Mirski, guards were assigned by the local Special Commission to the offices of the Jewish Committee, as well as to the various Zionist collectives, the kibbutzim, in town. The kibbutzim, according to Mirski, had also their own armed men. Some of the future members of the Haganah, the Jewish military underground in British ruled Palestine, started their training in the ranks of the Special Commission guards. The Lodz Bundists established their own self-defense units. Among the instructors were Marek Edelman and Yosl Zygelbojm, an ex-partisan and son of Artur Zygelbojm, a Bundist leader who had lived during the war in London and had committed suicide as a protest against the world's indifference to the Jewish tragedy.[63]

The Special Commission in Lodz started its activities shortly after the Kielce pogrom. During the next few months it acquired ninety-one weapons of various sorts. In October it had forty guards on its payroll, assigned to various Jewish locations throughout the city. Jewish institutions in Lodz were in possession of weapons and ammunition. Thus, the Bursa had 3 rifles and 1 sub-machine gun, the Helenowek Children's Home had 5 rifles and 3 sub-machine guns, the Poalei Zion collective had 3 rifles and 1 sub-machine gun. Jewish institutions in Lodz had a total of 17 rifles and 11 sub-machine guns. According to a September 1946 report of the Lodz Special Commission, 450 people were organized in several units. "The city has been divided into districts, and various CKS people are in charge of each one of them. Relations with the UB are good, and the Deputy Head of the Special Commission maintains continuous contact with them." The Commission also trained its people in the use of arms. The Lodz Commission report for the latter part of December 1946 stated: "The situation in Lodz is quiet on the whole. ORMO, Voluntary Reserves of the Citizens' Militia and MO, Citizens' Militia, check the streets, Jewish neighborhoods in particular. There were no anti-Jewish events. Due to the determined stand of the security authorities Jews are not afraid of disorders. We have daily contact with the Security Office."[64]

14. A kindergarten run by the Lodz Jewish Committee. Top right: Ewa Frenkel-Przemyslawski. Courtesy of Ewa Frenkel-Przemyslawski.

15. Aleks and Tosia Klugman. Lodz, 1946. Courtesy of the Klugmans.

16. Members of a Jewish leather products cooperative in a 1st of May demonstration in postwar Lodz. Courtesy of Ewa Frenkel-Przemyslawski.

17. Young girls in the Jewish children's home in Helenowek, 1945. Courtesy of the Nitzbergs.

18. Children-partisans in the Jewish children's home in Helenowek. Courtesy of Dziunia Dublin.

19. Marek Edelman at the funeral of the murdered Bundist Fishke Neiman. Lodz, June, 1946. Courtesy of Gazeta Wyborcza.

4

FRIENDS, ACQUAINTANCES, STRANGERS

THE LODZ INTERVIEWEES I WAS MOST INTIMATE WITH WERE MY CLASSMATES from the Hebrew school. Most of them settled in Israel; some live in the US and Canada. I had known vaguely where they survived the war, but only recently did I learn the specifics of their prewar lives and wartime plights.

I knew Rachel Patron back in Lodz as Rachel Rubinow and later, in Israel, as Rachel Rav-Nof. She is a writer and journalist who lives in Boca Raton, Florida, and on one of her frequent visits to Israel we spoke about Lodz. Rachel's story goes back to prewar Bialystok. The opening statement of her life story summed up succinctly her self-perception in the context of the war and the Holocaust. "Given the choice, I would have never been born in Bialystok in the year 1936. Only a few of the Jewish children born that year in our city were still alive in the autumn of 1943. I was one of the lucky ones." The Rubinows were deported from Soviet-occupied Bialystok in a freight train on Saturday, June 21, 1941, one day before Germany attacked Russia. After a short stay in the tundra region at the foot of the Altai Mountains, they were moved to the town of Biysk, not far from Novosibirsk. They lived there until March 1946, when they were allowed to return to Poland. Their homecoming to Bialystok was sad: the bustling Jewish neighborhood of their memories had been wiped out. They left in a matter of weeks and traveled to Lower Silesia, from which Rachel's father illegally crossed the border to Austria. Rachel arrived in Lodz with her mother in the fall of 1946.[1]

Shlomo, or Salek, Pomerantz is a retired music teacher. I met with him shortly after his return from a recent visit to Poland. It had been fifty-five years since he had left Lodz. He had strong impressions of his first return to the city and we spoke about both postwar and contemporary Lodz. Salek and Moniek Pomerantz, my closest friends at the Lodz Hebrew school, along with their sister Hania, were triplets. They were born in Lodz in 1934. Their father owned a cloth store. He was mobilized into the Polish Army as a reservist in September 1939. A few weeks later, already a civilian, he reached Soviet-occupied Lwow. In the meantime, Lodz was occupied by the Germans. The mother, her younger sister and the triplets managed to leave the city and joined him. After a short stay in Lwow, the Pomerantz family was deported to Siberia. Finally they settled in Andizhan, in eastern Uzbekistan. Since daily existence, especially with three young children, was very difficult, the triplets were delivered to a Polish children's home. They could have left Russia with General Anders' Army, but their father was against it, and they were reunited with their family. Shlomo distinctly recalled the end of the war in May 1945 and the celebrations. A year later they traveled from Uzbekistan to Poland, and returned to Lodz.[2]

Richard Lubelsky, Rysiek, a close friend during my Lodz years, was now a retired electronics engineer. He used to come quite often to our apartment on Gdanska Street. After leaving Lodz, we did not see each other for decades, but when I went to the US for graduate studies in the early 1960s and he was livimg in Montreal, I reestablished contact. Almost forty years later Richard recalled that moment: "I was sitting at home, I think it was Sunday afternoon, the telephone rang, and I answered it. The voice at the other end said, 'Is this Richard Lubelsky?' I said, 'Yes.' The voice at the other end said 'and you lived in Lodz?' I said, 'Yes.' The voice at the other end said something like 'do you remember Shimon Redlich?'" Since then we have met in Canada, in the US and in Europe. Richard has never visited Israel. Our last meeting was in September 1999, in Prague, and that's when we spoke about Lodz.

Richard, born in 1934, was an only child. Both his father and grandfather were MDs. Richard, his parents, and a few members of his father's family traveled in the direction of the Russian border in the fall of 1939. They were then deported to Siberia, where they settled in a village named Itatka. Sometime in the late summer of 1941 the Lubelskys traveled south, to Kazakhstan, and settled in Semipalatinsk, on the Irtysh River. Richard's mother worked in a shoe factory and his father joined the Polish Army. Richard's parents separated sometime in the summer of 1943. From then on, Richard lived with his mother. Both branches of the Lubelsky family continued living in Semipalatinsk. Strangely enough, when the repatriation of Polish citizens began after the war, Richard, his mother, and his father's new family left on the same train. When they reached Poland, Richard's father settled in Krakow, and Richard and his mother in Lodz.[3]

Ada Gibraltar and Hanka Rydel were among the prettiest girls at the Lodz Hebrew school. They first met as children in faraway Uzbekistan, then studied in the same school in postwar Lodz. They have maintained their friendship throughout the years that followed, though Ada lives in Israel and Hanka in Canada. They meet at least once a year, when Hanka visits Israel.

Ada, a retired pathologist, was born in 1936 and lived with her family in Warsaw. Her father died during the war in Uzbekistan. He was only twenty-six then, and Ada doesn't remember what he looked like. She does recall, however, that he was very talented. He was good at drawing and sculpting. Her mother hardly spoke about him. Ada had very scant memories of their flight from bombarded Warsaw. They lived for a while in Bialystok, then traveled in a freight train to the Urals. Ada's mother, who had worked as an accountant in Warsaw, became a washerwoman. After a while the family moved to Uzbekistan. It was there that all three fell ill with typhoid at the same time. When her father died Ada was put in a Polish children's home. Things improved when her mother remarried. Gibraltar, an engineer, originally from Zgierz, near Lodz, was twelve years older than Ada's mother. To make a living he worked as a shoemaker. Ada was taken back home, and they stayed in Uzbekistan until 1946. After an arduous journey to Poland, they settled first in Zgierz, and then moved to Lodz.[4]

The first time I met Hanka since our school days in Lodz was in the fall of 1997, when she arrived from Montreal for the Hebrew school reunion in Tel-Aviv. She was still good-looking. I was also pleasantly surprised to learn that she is on the Board of Governors of Ben-Gurion University. We might even have participated in the same events without knowing about each other. I interviewed Hanka at the Tel-Aviv Hilton. Hanka was born in Siedlce, not far from Warsaw. She was three-and-a-half when the war started. Her first distinct memories were from Siberia. Her father, who owned a cloth factory before the war, became a woodcutter. Her mother worked in a foodstore. Hanka quite vividly recalled the Siberian forests. She even saw once a bear near their window. Her family too, like numerous Polish citizens, moved south and settled in Uzbekistan. They were lucky to escape and live together with other relatives, all on her father's side. This was "a clan of fifteen," as she described it. Hanka recalled heat and dirt. She became severely ill with malaria and typhoid. Her father was arrested and accused of being a *spekulant,* a profiteer. When he returned from prison, she hardly recognized him. The Rydels returned to Poland in 1946. Her aunt, the sole survivor of her mother's family, lived at that time in Lodz, and that's why the Rydels decided to settle there.[5]

I wasn't sure at all whether I should interview Heniek Napadow. He was always a down-to-earth kind of person, never too articulate. Short and stocky, with easygoing manners, he didn't seem to be a good candidate for an in-depth interview. To my utter surprise, he turned out to be the most dramatic and colorful of my Hebrew school narrators.

We were sitting in my university office, and his story kept rolling on and on. I was both amazed and moved. It seems that only recently had he begun to verbalize some of the most traumatic events of his early life. What triggered it was his decision to seek therapy at Amcha, the Israeli Association for Assistance to Holocaust Survivors and their Descendants.

Heniek was born in Warsaw, but wasn't sure about the exact date of his birth. When asked about it after the war, at the Koordynacja Children's Home in Lodz, he arbitrarily chose the date of January 1, 1934. He recalled that his grandfather was religious, but his father, a veterinarian, was quite secular. Heniek recalled fragmentary images from his Warsaw childhood, like playing in Ogrod Saski, the Saxonian Garden in the city center. He was also sure that they lived on Ogrodowa, Garden Street. Heniek's memories of the bombardment and the arrival of the Germans were quite clear and detailed. His father and the father's younger brother escaped eastward. Heniek with his mother joined them after a while in Soviet-occupied Bialystok. The following trajectory was most unusual. They were deported first to Magnitogorsk, in Siberia, and later arrived in the Crimea. Then, they moved to the Kuban region, where Heniek's father worked as a veterinarian. Heniek, a boy of 6 or 7, started riding horses. One day Heniek's father was drafted into the Red Army and disappeared from his life. From then on it was only Heniek and his mother. The advance of the Germans forced them to leave Kuban. Heniek's next memory fragments were from areas around the Caspian Sea. Finally they reached Uzbekistan, where they stayed until the war ended. It was in Uzbekistan that Heniek parted with his mother. She delivered him into a children's home, and the relationship between mother and son steadily deteriorated. Heniek and his mother left Uzbekistan for Poland on the same train, but not together, sometime in 1946. The next thing he remembered was living in the Koordynacja Children's Home in Lodz.[6]

Aharon Zalkind, today Eynat, was one grade above me at the Lodz Hebrew school. We met several times after coming to Israel. I clearly recall his visit to the recruits' training camp, where I was stationed after being drafted into the army. Aharon, already a sergeant at that time, was a year ahead of me. He came to visit his younger brother and dropped in to say hello. He also brought me a flannelette used to clean rifles, a very scarce and useful item. Aharon, as it later turned out, made a career in the IDF as a senior officer in the Engineering Corps. After retiring from the army he worked as chief administrator at the Diaspora Museum in Tel-Aviv, and as such, facilitated our 1997 Hebrew school reunion on its premises. He also travels from time to time to Poland as a guide for Israeli youth groups. At age 70 he received his doctorate in History. His thesis was on the Vilna Ghetto administration.

Aharon was the only one of my Hebrew school interviewees who survived the German occupation. He was born in Vilna in 1934. His parents ran a small grocery store on the outskirts of the town. Although significant changes occurred in Vilna starting in the early fall of 1939, for Aharon "real war" started only two years later, in June 1941. Aharon was the only one among my Lodz friends to be interviewed at the Jewish Historical Commission in Lodz. It was only in the early 1990s that he found his 1947 testimony at ZIH, the Jewish Historical Institute in Warsaw. The interviewer had noted that "the blond, blue eyed boy is perceptive, serious, pensive and sad. He conceives the facts related in his testimony almost as an adult. His narration is logical and matter-of-fact. His eyes tear from time to time, as he tells his story."

Shortly after the German occupation of Vilna, Aharon's father was taken away for forced labor, and never returned. Aharon had quite distinct memories of life in the Vilna ghetto, especially of the fearsome roundups. But he also recalled children playing games and having fun. Prodded by the interviewer, the 13-year-old described in detail a number of these ghetto games. When the Vilna ghetto was liquidated, in September 1943, Aharon, with his mother and younger brother, ended up in a nearby labor camp, whose inmates worked for the German army. When the camp was liquidated, the Zalkinds found a hiding place in an attic on the empty campsite, but since there was no food, they had to leave. They wandered for a week or two from village to village in the vicinity of Vilna. And then, one day, they saw a Russian soldier. It was the summer of 1944. They stayed on in Vilna for two years after the liberation and Aharon studied in a local Soviet-Yiddish elementary school. They left Vilna, along with other Polish repatriates, and arrived in Lodz in the late summer of 1946.[7]

Baruch Kaplinski and Binyamin Majerczak were among the very few of our former teachers who showed up at the Hebrew school reunion. Kaplinski was the first principal and Majerczak was our gym teacher. I did not recall Kaplinski at all. The only proof that he somehow touched my life in postwar Lodz was his signature on my second grade report card, dated June 10, 1946. All of us remembered Majerczak. He made a big impression, arriving at school dressed in his Polish Army captain's uniform. He was also a good-looking man. Kaplinski was then in his early thirties and Majerczak in his late twenties. When I met them in Tel Aviv forty years later, they were both retired. Kaplinski was a successful lawyer for many years. Majerczak worked as an electrical engineer. Both were very busy even after retirement. Kaplinski wrote books on the Old Testament and Majerczak did extensive research on Jewish officers in the

Polish armies during the Second World War.

Kaplinski was born in Vilna in 1913 and studied in a Jewish high school. He also got his Polish Matura (matriculation certificate). He studied law at the Vilna University, but did not graduate. Eventually he studied in a Jewish teachers' seminary and worked as teacher and principal in several Jewish schools. In 1939/1940 he was principal of a Jewish school in the town of Eishyshok. After leaving Eishyshok he worked for a while as a store superintendent in Soviet-occupied Vilna. When Vilna was occupied by the Germans, he spent most of his time in hiding. Some Poles helped him. Others denounced him. Eventually, he ended up in a German labor camp, near Danzig. When the Red Army advanced into north-western Poland, Kaplinski was sick with typhoid. He was one of the very few prisoners in his camp who weren't shot by the Germans before their retreat. His memory of the first weeks after liberation was that of hunger and disease. He went through several hospitals and ended up in a Soviet military hospital in Torun. A Jewish Red Army officer and the Jewish hospital director were instrumental in his convalescence. Kaplinski arrived in Lodz at the end of February 1945.[8]

Binyamin Majerczak was born in 1917, in Wloclawek, on the Vistula, and graduated from the local Hebrew high school. Like Kaplinski, he got his Polish Matura. Then he moved to Warsaw, where he studied electrical engineering. Majerczak graduated in 1938, and since he was a staunch Zionist, he made plans for traveling to Palestine. The war, of course, affected his plans. Like many other Polish citizens, Majerczak traveled east, was arrested in Soviet-occupied Lwow and deported to the Soviet interior. He ended up in a labor camp in Yaroslavl, on the upper Volga. Following the Polish-Soviet agreement, in the summer of 1941, Majerczak hoped to join General Anders's army, but wasn't accepted. After a while he was mobilized into General Berling's army, and his military career commenced. He participated in one of the bloodiest battles, in Lenino, and moved west, to the Ukraine. He was then given orders for officer training at a Red Army Armoured Corps academy, which he graduated with distinction in the fall of 1944 before rejoining his Polish unit and participating in a number of battles. When the war ended, he was stationed in Prague. He became seriously ill at the end of 1945, and was moved from hospital to hospital. His younger sister, the only other survivor in his family, helped him to get through his illness. Although they could have emigrated to the US, both decided to opt for Palestine. When I asked him why they decided to settle temporarily in Lodz, his answer was short and to the point: "Lodz was a Jewish center."[9]

One of the few names from Hashomer Hatzair in Lodz that I

remembered throughout the years was that of Fayvl. Only recently I learned that his last name was Podemski. In Israel he had Hebraized it to Podeh. I came across his published memoirs, but I had never met him in person since the Lodz days. I traveled to Herzlia Pituach, an affluent seaside town near Tel-Aviv, to interview him. His wife had passed away a few years earlier, and he was living by himself in a well-kept house by the seashore. He didn't recall me at all from postwar Lodz, which was to be expected: I was then in my early teens, while Fayvl, a native of Lodz and a survivor of the Lodz Ghetto, was in his early twenties.

Prior to the war the Podemskis lived in a Jewish neighborhood in Lodz, on 20 Poludniowa Street. Fayvl's father was co-owner of two bakeries. "I can smell even now the aroma of those rolls and bagels." His father died of jaundice in 1933. Fayvl was a boy of nine at that time. The mother, who became the breadwinner of the family, used to bake and sell cakes. "Business was good, especially in summertime, in Kolumna, near Lodz. We kids had the time of our lives." Fayvl had his first encounter with Hashomer Hatzair at age twelve, when his older brother took him to the local Hashomer Hatzair branch, the *ken*. From then on Hashomer Hatzair was Fayvl's second home. He fondly recalled the Hashomer Hatzair summer camps, especially the last one, in Zakopane, at the foot of the Carpathian Mountains. All this came to a halt in September 1939.

In his memoirs, Fayvl recorded the daily life of the Lodz Ghetto. Despite or perhaps because of the new, oppressive existence in the closed Jewish quarter, Hashomer Hatzair activities became even more meaningful and significant than in the prewar years. The Hashomer Hatzair now became Fayvl's first home. Some of the Jewish youth in the Lodz Ghetto, among them young Fayvl, were given the opportunity to work and spend time in Marysin, a kind of agricultural colony that was adjacent to the ghetto. Various prewar Jewish youth movements resumed their activities in Marysin. The purpose was to give the teenagers a temporary break from the crowded conditions and dreariness of everyday life in the ghetto.

Hunger, roundups and deportations during the next three years stand out in Fayvl's ghetto memories. Despite the harsh conditions, suffering and loss, the youth movement activities continued. There was a strong will for survival. The final deportations occurred in the late summer of 1944. These were the last days of the ghetto. It then turned into a desolated and eerie place. Fayvl was part of the last group of Lodz Jews left in the ghetto — in a labor camp, located at 16 Jakuba Street. It consisted of young Jewish males who were supposed to clean up the area after the last deportation. Fayvl's labor unit was kept together until early January 1945.[10]

Although Matityahu Mintz is twelve years my senior, we both studied history at the Hebrew University at the same time. I was vaguely aware of his past in Hashomer Hatzair. As it turned out, he spent some time at Hashomer Hatzair in postwar Lodz too. We even might have been there at the same time. When I went to interview him he had already retired from Tel-Aviv University. This was a hot summer day, and Matityahu opened the door without his shirt on. We chatted like old friends. I was fascinated by the fact that Matityahu knew Mordechai Anielewicz, the legendary leader of the Warsaw Ghetto Uprising.

Professor Mintz was born in Lublin in 1923 in a traditional, Zionist-oriented family. He never went to a *heder* and excelled in the local Hebrew school. As a young boy he knew Yiddish, Hebrew and Polish. Mintz's father was a coal contractor. During the economic crisis of the early 1930s he lost his work, and the family moved to Warsaw. Matityahu continued his studies at an elementary Hebrew school, and then in a Jewish high school. It was there that he met Anielewicz, three years his senior. Both Anielewicz and Mintz were close to the right-wing Zionist nationalist Betar youth movement. When they met, Anielewicz had already switched from Betar to Hashomer Hatzair. He convinced young Mintz to join him.

Matityahu and some other of his Hashomer Hatzair friends left German-occupied Warsaw in mid-October 1939. After weeks of wandering along Poland's eastern borders he reached Vilna, where he remained until January 1941. Mintz was one of the lucky few to be able to leave the Soviet Union and reach Palestine. His unusual trajectory included Odessa and Moscow. He arrived in Palestine in March 1941. His first home there, where he would stay for the next fourteen years, was Gan-Shmuel, a rather intellectual, left-wing kibbutz of Hashomer Hatzair. In time Mintz became active in the leadership of the youth movement. When Hashomer Hatzair started sending emissaries to postwar Europe, the 25 year-old Mintz, with his knowledge of Polish and his experience with youth, was a natural candidate. He arrived in Poland in the summer of 1948.[11]

After the filming of *Undzere Kinder* in Lodz in 1948, and an attempt to film an additional sequence in Tel-Aviv in 1950 or 1951, many years passed before I again saw Natan Gross. It was only in the spring of 1981 that we met, at the Tel-Aviv Cinemateque. Natan had arranged for a public showing of the film and for a get-together of the "children," now people in their fifties. For Natan they always remained children. It was shortly thereafter that he gave me a video copy of *Undzere Kinder*. A few years later we happened to get involved in yet another "project." I was conducting research on Metropolitan Andrei Sheptytski, head of the Ukrainian Uniate Church in Galicia, who had saved numerous

Jews, mostly children, during the Holocaust. Natan was a member of the Righteous Gentiles Commission at Yad Vashem. We were convinced that Sheptytski, despite his complex relations with Jews and Germans, should be recognized posthumously as a Righteous Gentile. Yad Vashem thought otherwise. Both of us appealed on behalf of the unrecognized "Ukrainian Schindler." I started visiting Natan in his Givatayim apartment and we spent long hours discussing Sheptytski, postwar Lodz and *Undzere Kinder*.

Natan Gross, or Natek to his friends, was born in Krakow to a prosperous Jewish family. They owned two stores which sold expensive porcelain and glassware products in the center of the city. He had two brothers and a sister. Except for his father, who fled eastward with his oldest son and was murdered by the Germans, all survived the Holocaust. His older brother, Jozek, detained by the Soviets, managed to join General Anders' Army and ended up in England. Natan, his younger brother Jerzyk, his sister Klara, and their mother, survived under assumed identities on the "Aryan side." In his wartime memoirs Natan related the saga of his adventures as a Pole. He was very lucky. He had "good looks" and spoke excellent Polish. When living in German-occupied Warsaw, Natan witnessed the Warsaw Ghetto Uprising and its brutal suppression. In order to avoid denunciation, the Grosses had to constantly move from place to place. In the summer of 1944, one day before the Polish Uprising erupted in Warsaw, Natan moved to Otwock, where his younger brother had lived for a while. Natan's mother stayed in Warsaw, and after the tragic end of the Uprising was sent to Auschwitz. Natan's sister, Klara, ended up in the mountain resort of Zakopane, working under an assumed Polish identity as a maid for convalescing German soldiers. She left Poland shortly after liberation. Natan was reunited with his mother in Krakow, in the summer of 1945.

Natan was preoccupied with the documentation of the Holocaust. He worked at the Jewish Historical Commission branch in Krakow. He also recorded his and his family members' fates during the war and became active in the Gordonia Zionist youth movement. He began to translate Hebrew, German and Yiddish poetry into Polish and wrote articles for postwar Jewish newspapers in Poland. He led an extremely active life, at the same time enrolling in a course for filmmakers, offered by the Jagiellonian University. He arrived in Lodz, the film center of postwar Poland, in the summer of 1946.[12]

Shlomo Pomerantz strongly recommended that I meet Wanda Rotenberg. He knew her quite well from postwar Lodz. Wanda, the admired counselor of Shlomo's sister Hania, used to visit their place from time to time, and the Pomerantz family maintained some contact with her later on, in Israel. It was extremely difficult to get an appointment with Wanda. We finally met in her small, neat house in the southern outskirts of Tel-Aviv. She had been living there since her arrival in Israel in 1950.

Wanda was born as Bela Elster in 1924, in Warsaw. Her father was a successful accountant, and had worked for Polish commercial companies. They lived on Mila Street in a distinctly Jewish neighborhood, and Wanda attended a Jewish primary school and later a Jewish high school. Her older sister, Pola, became active in the Left Poalei Zion and she introduced her to the party's youth movement. Later on, when Wanda joined the ZOB, the Jewish Fighters' Organization in the Warsaw Ghetto, her "good looks," i.e. blond hair and blue eyes, enabled her to become a liaison with the Polish underground. She left the ghetto a week before the Uprising, in April 1943, and found refuge with a Polish family. Wanda arrived in Lodz some time before its liberation, and lived there under an assumed Polish identity.[13]

Sara Shner-Nishmit lived in a kibbutz that was given an identical name to that of our Hebrew school in Lodz, apparently by the same person, Antek Zuckerman, one of the founders of Kibbutz Lohamei Hagetaot, the Ghetto Fighters' Kibbutz, in Northern Israel. I went to check its Holocaust Museum holdings for documentation on Jews in postwar Lodz, and to interview Sara.

Sara was born in 1913, in the town of Sejny, in North-Eastern Poland. Living in the Polish-Lithuanian borderland, which until the First World War had been Russian, she spoke Russian, Polish, Lithuanian, and Yiddish. Her father, a graduate of the Warsaw School of Engineering, owned a small estate in interwar Lithuania. When he died in 1931, the family disintegrated, and each of the siblings went their own way. Sara, after a very short stint in the Medical School in Kovno, studied Classics and Education. She recalled being interested from early adolescence in working with children. At age 14 she was already a counselor in a youth movement affiliated with the Poalei Zion. She married in the summer of 1939, but her husband was killed shortly thereafter. Sara worked for a while in the Jewish Teachers Seminary in Vilna. It closed when Lithuania became Soviet, in the summer of 1940. When Germany invaded the Soviet Union, in June 1941, Sara started wandering by foot to the East, but the Germans advanced faster and she ended up in German-occupied Lithuania. For a few months she worked in a labor camp. Eventually, she escaped and joined a Soviet partisan group. She worked there as a nurse in a field hospital. The Red Army arrived in the summer of 1944. Sara then returned to Kovno where she was joined by her mother and sister, who had survived the war in Russia. Within a year, she arrived in Lodz.[14]

For years I was hardly aware of the "others," the Communists, the Bundists, the assimilationists. Only following the Polish-Jewish emigrations of the late 1950s and the late 1960s did I learn about their fates in postwar Poland. When I started to collect documentation on Jews in postwar Lodz, I realized that without their story, my Lodz book would be incomplete. The first Polish- Jewish Communist in postwar Lodz whom I interviewed was Maria Lorber. She used to work for Professor Matityahu Mintz at the Diaspora Research Institute of Tel-Aviv University, and he recommended that I meet with her. Mrs. Lorber, in her late eighties, was living by herself at the time in a senior citizens' high-rise project near Tel-Aviv. We spoke Hebrew interspersed with Polish.

Maria's family was quite well off. One of her grandfathers owned land, and her father had owned a cinema in Warsaw. Her other grandfather had owned a travelling zoo in Russia before the Revolution. Maria was an only child. Her parents lived in Ryki, south-east of Warsaw. After graduating from the local Polish elementary school, Maria studied in a Jewish high school in Warsaw, and it was there that she joined a socialist youth organization. When I asked her for her motivation, her reply was unequivocal: "These were the times of the *numerus clausus* in Polish universities, and Jews got fired from jobs. I wanted to be equal." Maria studied education, history and Polish literature in the Konarski Educational Institute, and psychology in the socialist-oriented Wolna Wszechnica. After graduation she taught in a Jewish elementary school. Most of her friends were young Jewish Communists. In 1936 she married Henryk Lorber, a first cousin and a Communist, but they lived together for three months only. Henryk left for Paris to complete his medical studies, and from there he traveled to Spain as a volunteer in the Civil War. They didn't see each other for 11 years. "I went my way, he went his way. I never married again."

When the Germans arrived Maria was with her family in Ryki. The Germans set fire to a large part of the town, and the Jews were ordered into the local ghetto. Maria remained there until early May 1942, when the ghetto was liquidated. She lost track of her parents during the liquidation and, with other young Jews, was taken to a labor camp in nearby Deblin. From there she was transferred in early July 1944 to another large labor camp affiliated with the Hasag ammunition plant in Czestochowa. For Maria, the war ended on January 16, when Czestochowa was liberated by the Red Army. Like many other survivors, Maria went back to her hometown, to look for her parents. They hadn't survived. Her father had been killed in Treblinka, her mother in Sobibor. When six Jewish survivors were murdered by Poles in Ryki in the summer of 1945, Maria and the few other Jews in town moved to Lodz.[15]

Noah Flug, Henryk to his Polish friends, President of the Auschwitz International Committee and head of the Center of Organizations of Holocaust Survivors in Israel, is a well-known public figure. I interviewed him in his office, at the impressive Zionist Confederation House in Jerusalem. Flug was born in Lodz, in 1925. Both of his grandfathers were Hasidim. His maternal grandfather owned a small textile plant in Pabianice, near Lodz. His paternal grandfather was rather poor, and Flug remembered him studying the Holy Books. Like most of Flug's family, both perished in the Holocaust.

Flug's father earned his living as a textile merchant, and he had a German partner. "That German was not only a business partner, but also a friend. They dealt in *'shmates'*." Although both parents knew Yiddish, with Noah they spoke Polish. He was sent to a private Hebrew elementary school and entered a Hebrew high school before the war. As a youngster he was a member of various Zionist youth organizations, but it was only in the Lodz Ghetto that young Flug became associated with Communist youth. At the same time, he continued his education in the Ghetto high school. When I asked him why he and others were attracted by the illegal Communist youth organization in the Lodz Ghetto, his answer was, "only the Russians could save us."

Flug, with a group of friends from the Communist underground, was deported to Auschwitz in late summer 1944. Eventually he was moved to other camps. His group of friends tried to stick together. Those who survived until winter of 1945 were sent on the death marches, and Flug spent the last two months of the war in Mauthausen and Ebensee. The war ended for him on May 5, 1945. He returned to Lodz a few weeks later.[16]

Aleksander Klugman, a journalist first in postwar Poland and later in Israel, has a pronounced Lodz identity. "I was born in Lodz. This place always was, and remains for me, as Tuwim wrote in one of his poems, my native city." Klugman was born in 1925, and recalled having a large family, most of which lived in the same Jewish neighborhood. His father was an unsuccessful textile merchant. "Three times he opened a textile store, and each time, after a short while, it closed." Then he worked as a wholesale agent and provided textiles to a store owned by Germans. "Their relations with father went far beyond usual business connections. They often visited our house." Aleksander had one brother and three sisters. Two of them, Masha and Dziunia, joined illegal Communist circles even prior to the war. Alek and Hela, the youngest sister, joined Communist groups in the Lodz Ghetto. Alek's friend Jozek, two years his senior, was the child of two members of the Communist party and became a model figure for Alec, introducing him to the Communist youth movement. All of Aleksander's close family were either killed or deported to death camps, and Alek himself was deported from the Lodz Ghetto to Auschwitz in the last transport, at the end of August 1944. There he found some of his Communist friends, and they stuck together. They ended up in the Flossenburg labor camp. Alek returned to Lodz in the summer of 1945.[17]

I met Ewa, one of my most eloquent narrators, by pure chance. I was flying from Tel-Aviv to Warsaw, and the next seat was occupied by Tamar Horowitz, a colleague from Ben-Gurion University. As I started telling her about my Lodz project, she suggested that I meet Ewa Frenkel-Przemyslawski, who used to be her research assistant after emigrating from Poland to Israel. Only days after returning from Poland I was sitting in Ewa's apartment in a Jerusalem senior citzens' Home. Ewa, an extremely warm, engaging and outspoken person, was in her mid-eighties. Frenkel was the last name of her first husband; Przemyslawski of the third.

Although two generations of Ewa's family were Lodz Jews, she herself was born in Dzialoszyce, a small town between Kielce and Krakow. Her family had moved there during the First World War. They returned to Lodz in 1926, when Ewa was six. Her Hasidic, Yiddish-speaking father was a textile merchant, and Ewa was sent to the Beyt Yaakov private religious girls' school. "Mother had sewn me a dark-blue dress with a white collar, and I was very proud of it." The family's financial situation deteriorated as a result of the economic crisis of 1929, and Ewa was forced to leave Beyt Yaakov. She then continued her education in a Polish elementary school.

Ewa, an eager student, had always excelled. When she completed elementary school at age 14, her family was struggling to make ends meet, and she had to find work. "This was a tragedy for me. I so much wanted to continue studying." She couldn't work in a textile plant, since they worked on the Sabbath. Finally, her family rented a grocery kiosk, where Ewa and her father sold cigarettes. It was during that time, the late 1930s, that Ewa started devouring Polish and Russian books. "I read Chekhov, Sholokhov, Pasternak, Tuwim." Some of her older cousins were already Communists at that time, and Ewa became increasingly involved in Communist youth circles. She also participated in Communist demonstrations. "These activities and events were the center of my life, and it seems that this affected my very survival. Otherwise I wouldn't have gone to Russia."

Ewa went with her Communist friends to a three-day youth camp in the early summer of 1939. When Lodz was occupied by the Germans, she traveled with three of them to Soviet-occupied Bialystok, where she volunteered for work in the Soviet interior. One of the volunteers was Israel Frenkel, Ewa's future husband. They arrived in Magnitogorsk, in the Urals, in January 1940. Ewa became pregnant, and they married. Within a few months they moved to Poltava, in the Ukraine, where their daughter was born in February of 1941. Israel was drafted into the Red Army in the summer of that year. Ewa, prompted by a friend, moved to Orsk, in the southern Urals. Her husband in the meantime had been released from the Army and joined his family. In May 1943 he was drafted again, this time into the Polish Kosciuszko Division. For months Ewa didn't know anything about him. Only in March 1944 did she receive an official note about his death in the battle of Lenino, in October 1943. Ewa and little Nadia left Orsk with the assistance of the ZPP, the Union of Polish Patriots, in April 1946. They arrived first in Wroclaw, and then settled in Lodz.[18]

Dziunia Dublin was the youngest ex-Communist I interviewed. I was particularly interested in her story because of Helenowek. The postwar years in the Helenowek Children's Home became a significant component in her biography and memory. She continued meeting people associated with Helenowek throughout her adult life. I met with Dziunia in Kiryat Motzkin, North of Haifa. She served typical Polish-Jewish food and we spoke a mix of Hebrew and Polish. Dziunia was born in Lodz, in 1929, to very young parents: her mother was only 19 and her father was in his early twenties. Her father had 12 siblings and belonged to an affluent family which owned a leather and rubber business. When her paternal grandfather died before Dziunia was born, his children divided the inheritance and went their own ways. One aunt emigrated to America, another to Australia. A few went to Palestine. Dziunia's father and one of his brothers remained in the leather business in Lodz. "The good life ended with the economic crisis. There was a change. We moved to a smaller apartment." Still, they weren't really poor. Dziunia recalled that her father was a socialist and her mother was a semi-professional singer. She sang in the "Hazamir" Jewish choir in Lodz. "When I was about nine she took me along to a charity concert in the Helenowek Children's Home. She was a soloist and they sang Beethoven's Ninth Symphony."

Dziunia went to a Jewish girls' school on Poludniowa Street. In September 1939, she was just about to enter the fifth grade. Dziunia distinctly recalled the arrival of the Germans. "I was utterly scared, though mother kept telling me that I shouldn't worry, and that the Germans were cultured people." Things started changing very quickly. Her father was taken for forced labor and looked miserable when he returned home. In November, he and one of his brothers decided to travel eastward. The plan was that he would come back to bring Dziunia and her mother with him when he was settled. This plan was never carried out. "I ran behind the droshke and waved goodbye. This was the last time I saw my father." For years she didn't know what had happened to him. Only in the mid-1960s, after having immigrated to Israel, did she learn that he was deported to a labor camp in the Urals, where he died of typhoid.

Dziunia and her mother lived in the Lodz Ghetto, Dziunia working in a shoe factory and her mother scrubbing floors in the Judenrat offices. After a while Dziunia, who had joined Hashomer Hatzair before the war, started participating in Hashomer Hatzair activities in the ghetto and in Marysin. I was amazed to hear that Fayvl Podemski was her counselor. He was a most significant person for Dziunia and her teenage friends. Towards the end of 1943, Dziunia left Hashomer Hatzair and joined the Communist Anti-Fascist Youth organization. Dziunia, her mother and a few of her girlfriends were deported to Auschwitz in late August 1944. The girls where subsequently sent to the Stutthof camp, and her mother disappeared during one of Dr. Mengele's selections. Dziunia was sent to an airplane parts production factory in Halbstadt, in the Sudetenland. After a while she became very sick, and was in the hospital barracks when the Russians liberated the camp in early May 1945. In a few weeks, though not fully recuperated, Dziunia joined her girlfriends on their trek home. Dziunia hoped that her father would return from Russia and, like herself, come back to Lodz. After a long journey by foot, on trucks and by train, Dziunia arrived in her hometown in August 1945.[19]

I met Delphine Bechtel, a Paris-based cultural historian of East European Jewry, at ZIH, the Jewish Historical Institute in Warsaw. She told me about Szulim Rozenberg, an ex-Bundist who lived in Lodz after the war and later settled in Paris. He had been active for years in the Paris Medem Center for Yiddish Culture. I also knew that Dr. Ala Margolis-Edelman, the ex-wife of Dr. Marek Edelman, lived in Paris. She, like Marek Edelman, had studied medicine in postwar Lodz. I interviewed Szulim and Ala during a short stay in Paris.

Szulim Rozenberg was born in Warsaw in 1918. His family lived in a house on a narrow alley between Nalewki and Zamenhofa streets, at the very center of prewar Warsaw's crowded Jewish quarter. Rich and poor Jewish families shared the building. Szulim's father was a shoemaker. The whole family, parents and six children, lived in two rooms. The outhouse was in the courtyard. Szulim's family spoke Yiddish, and his older siblings were members in the Bund youth organization, so it was only natural for him to become a Bundist. Besides Yiddish authors like Shalom Aleichem, he also read Zeromski, Reymont and Konopnicka. He worked from an early age: prior to the war, Szulim was employed by a textile wholesale business and would often travel to Lodz. He had clear memories of the onset of the war, the bombardments and the Warsaw Mayor's call to all able-bodied men to leave the capital and move eastward in order to join the Polish Army there. Szulim left Warsaw with a group of friends.

Szulim's trajectory was typical of the wanderings of Jewish refugees at the time. From Malewicz in Belorussia he went to Sarny in Volhynia, and from there to Vilna. In Sarny he met the Polish-Jewish filmmaker Aleksander Forbert and the young Jewish painter Yosl Bergner. When Polish Jews who refused to take on Soviet citizenship were deported, Szulim was sent to the Komi Autonomous Republic, in the Russian North. Later he settled in the Gorki region. Unlike most of my interviewees who were deported to the Soviet interior, Szulim had mostly pleasant memories from his wartime experiences in the Soviet Union. He was apparently a good organizer, easygoing at any type of work, and was mostly in charge of other people. Szulim was socially engaging, accommodating, optimistic, and full of energy. It seems that he liked people, whether Russian, Jewish or Polish, and they liked him. In 1944, Szulim went to Krasnodar, north of the Black Sea, where he stayed until 1946. One of his sisters, who had survived the war in Russia, was already living in Lodz at the time, and Szulim decided to join her.[20]

I met Dr. Ala Edelman-Margolis in a pub on a Sunday morning. The men around us were having their first beers, and it was quite noisy. Two years earlier I had interviewed Marek Edelman in his small and shabby house in Lodz. Now, I was eager to hear Ala's part of the story. Throughout the nearly three hours of our Polish conversation, I could not establish Ala's date of birth. She just refused to reveal it. Assuming that she was 18 or 19 when she started her medical studies in postwar Lodz, she must have been born in the mid- or late 1920s. Her family lived in Lodz, and both parents were physicians. "My father was a handsome man. He was a doctor and worked in a hospital, but had a private practice at home as well. He was active in the Bund, and participated in the 1st of May demonstrations." Her parent's milieu consisted of Poles and assimilated Jews. "They both worked very hard, but they also led an active social life. They would play the piano and dance with their friends." Ala attended an experimental progressive elementary school.

Soon after the arrival of the Germans in Lodz, a German officer, Herr Werner, was assigned to the Margolis's spacious apartment. It turned out that he and Ala's father had been students at Heidelberg at the same time and had known each other. Soon Dr. Margolis was taken to the Radogoszcz camp, and Werner's attempts to have him released were of no avail. "Werner was relentless; he went to the Gestapo and wrote letters to Berlin. He was my mother's mainstay. Some ten days later the Gestapo came and picked him up." Ala and her younger brother Olek were sent by their mother to Warsaw to stay with an aunt. When their mother joined them, they moved to the Warsaw Ghetto. Ala's mother worked in the Jewish Children's Hospital in the Umschlagplatz, and Ala studied in the ghetto's school for nurses. When the deportations started Ala was taken out of the ghetto and moved in with a Polish family. After the Polish Uprising she lived in Grodzisk, near Warsaw, and returned with her mother to Lodz a few weeks after its liberation.[21]

When I returned to Jerusalem from my graduate studies in the US in the late 1960s, I heard that a Polish-Jewish historian, Kuba Goldberg, had arrived from Poland. I met with him once or twice, but since his field was the History of Polish Jews in the early modern era, there were hardly any common research interests between us. After I left Jerusalem for Ben-Gurion University in Beer-Sheva, I did not see him for years. When I started my Lodz project, Goldberg's name popped up in some of my interviews with people who had lived in postwar Lodz. They recalled Kuba as a young student at Lodz University. I met with Professor Goldberg in his Jerusalem apartment. He had retired from the Hebrew University several years earlier. We realized that, although both of us lived in Lodz in the immediate postwar years, the subject of Lodz had never come up in our previous encounters.

Jacob Goldberg, or Kuba to his friends and acquaintances, was born in Lodz in 1924. Both of his grandfathers had successful businesses. Kuba's father was a lumber merchant and maintained business relations with local Germans. "There was a tremendous difference between my grandparents' generation and that of my parents. Whereas my grandparents were religious and spoke Yiddish, my parents spoke mainly Polish, and weren't religious in any sense. My generation spoke Polish only." Kuba studied at the Ignacy Skorupka high school, where almost half of all students were Jewish. "There was no anti-Semitism in our school. There were friendly relations among Polish and Jewish students. These friendships, however, stopped at the school entrance. They never invited each other to their homes."

During his high school studies Kuba joined the semi-legal SOMS, Socjalistyczna Organizacja Mlodziezy Szkolnej — The Socialist Organization of School Youth. Kuba's mother died when he was ten years old and his father remarried. "Everything changed. I went to live with my grandma, and lived there until the war." His father and his stepmother moved to Warsaw. Kuba stayed in Lodz.

Kuba recalled that when Lodz had been occupied, most local Germans behaved nastily toward Jews. Kuba with his grandmother were forced into the Ghetto. In the ghetto he joined Tsukunft, the Bundist youth movement. When his grandmother died Kuba was left alone and was eventually deported. He was interned in several concentration camps. When the war ended, Kuba was seriously ill, and stayed for two months in a hospital in Czechoslovakia. "It was completely natural for me to return to Poland." He arrived in Lodz in midsummer 1945.[22]

Reading a weekend edition of *Haaretz*, I spotted a photo of a handsome young man wearing a World War II pilot's cap. The article told the story of Kazimierz Rutenberg, an ex-pilot in the Polish Air Force. I met him in his modest, neat house in Ramat-Aviv. Rutenberg, although born in Krakow, as a young boy had lived in Sosnowiec, in south-western Poland. His family had roots in Lodz. Since his grandparents lived in Lodz, young Kazik used to travel there for visits. He tried to keep kosher at his grandparents', but aside from that he was hardly religious, and recalled going to the synagogue only when the students from his Polish high school were attending their respective places of worship, on official Polish holidays. He did not go to the synagogue even on Rosh Hashana and Yom Kippur. Kazik had both Polish and Jewish friends, some of them from mixed families.

When war started, Kazik and his mother were visiting friends of the family in Rovno, in northeastern Poland. Following the occupation of Eastern Poland by the Soviets, they were separated from his father, who stayed in Sosnowiec and was eventually gassed in Auschwitz. Kazik and his mother were deported in the summer of 1940 to a labor camp near Tomsk, in Siberia. "We met Poles, Jews, Russians and Ukrainians there. Thousands died, mostly of typhoid." Following the Soviet-Polish agreement, after Germany's invasion of Russia, Rutenberg tried to join General Anders's Army, but was turned down. Subsequently, in 1943, he was mobilized into General Berling's Army. After serving in an anti-tank infantry unit, he was accepted at a pilot's school, becoming a fighter pilot at age twenty. After demobilization he joined his mother, who had survived the war in Russia and settled in Lodz.[23]

Though we had lived in postwar Lodz and in the Helenowek Children's Home at the same time, my friendship with Henryk Grynberg dates only from the 1990s. I didn't recall him from Helenowek, but he remembered me, as "that little guy with the Chinese, slanted eyes." I knew that in the 1960s he had been an actor with the State Jewish Theater in Warsaw, and that he had defected when the company was on tour in the US. During one of my first visits to Poland, in the early 1990s, I went to Krakow with my Polish friends, Ludwik and Jola Czaja. They took me to Kazimierz, the historical Jewish quarter. I was browsing in a local Judaica store and came across a small, slim book with a strange title: *Dziedzictwo* (*Inheritance*). The author's name was Henryk Grynberg. I became totally enthralled, and devoured it on the spot. I'm convinced that this is one of the most powerful texts ever written on the Holocaust.

Dziedzictwo tells the story of Henryk's return after half a century to the area where his family hid out during the war, and where his father was murdered by a Polish neighbor. He had come on a fact-finding mission, and after meeting and talking for many hours with a dozen old local peasants, Grynberg finally managed to establish the identity of the murderer and the site of the burial. A lengthy and dramatic exhumation followed. The diggers recovered some bones, a skull and an old, prewar milk bottle, the kind that Henryk's father, a milkman, always carried with him. It turned out that Jola was familiar with the book and even reviewed it. She also told me that she knew Henryk and had met him several times. I met him myself a few years later in Washington, DC, where he had been working and living after leaving Poland. I invited him to come and meet my Holocaust class at Ben-Gurion University. We watched a film documenting Henryk's quest for his father's end and the exhumation of his remains. With Henryk right there in the classroom, this was a difficult and moving experience for all of us. Next day I invited him to my house for a cup of coffee. We spoke about the war, the Holocaust and postwar Lodz.

Henryk was born in Warsaw in 1936, but lived with his parents in the village of Radoszyna, about 60 kilometers East of the capital. They were the only Jewish family there. His maternal grandparents lived in nearby Dobre, a much larger settlement. His paternal grandparents, and his mother's three sisters, also lived nearby. In fact, all of Henryk's family were small-town and village Jews. They knew everybody and everybody knew them. Henryk's father, Abram Grynberg, owned cows and calves and sold milk and milk products. The tragic history of Henryk's extensive family under German occupation is discussed in his books. Grynberg avoids generalizations and superlatives, dealing mainly with facts and words. Still, his sparing and seemingly pedestrian language conveys in an utterly concise form the drama, terror, and tragedy of those times.

Only a few of the Polish neighbors around Radoszyna and Dobre were ready to help. Most were either indifferent or hostile. Henryk, his younger brother, and their parents, hid together for a while. His brother, who was only a year and a half old, was denounced by a Pole and shot by a German. Around March 1943, Henryk and his mother left for Warsaw, to live there on "Aryan papers." His father preferred to stay on familiar terrain. He continued to wander and hide. As Henryk discovered decades later, his father was eventually murdered by a Polish neighbor out of sheer greed. Henryk and his mother stayed in Warsaw for a few months, and then moved to the Podlasie area, northeast of the city. They lived there under assumed Polish identities. The Russians arrived in their village in the summer of 1944. Henryk and his mother returned to Dobre and lived there for a while. They settled in Lodz in the spring of 1945.[24]

20. The Pomerantz family from Lodz with their Uzbek neighbors. Courtesy of Shlomo Pomerantz.

21. Red Army officers and Polish trainees at the Leningrad Pushkin Military Armored Corps Academy near Rybinsk, 1944. Second row from bottom, first on the left: Binyamin Majerczak. Courtesy of Binyamin Majerczak.

22. Kazik Rutenberg, fighter pilot in General Berling's Army, January 1944. Courtesy of Kazimierz Rutenberg.

5

SURVIVING

JEWISH LIFE IN POSTWAR LODZ CAN BE PROPERLY UNDERSTOOD ONLY when the wartime experiences of those who settled there are examined. Jews who settled in Lodz after its liberation were either Holocaust survivors or returnees from the Soviet Union. Both populations were severely affected by extreme upheavals in their lives. They suffered from dislocation, harsh living conditions, loss and trauma. Still, there was a basic difference. In the vast expanses of wartime Russia, Polish-Jewish refugees and deportees shared the wartime fate of the general Soviet population. Jews in Nazi-occupied Poland were singled out for degradation, isolation and annihilation.

Poland, the historic and demographic center of European Jewry, became the epicenter of the Holocaust. Most victims, both Polish Jews and Jews deported to Poland from other parts of Europe, perished on Polish soil. Ghettoization and annihilation in concentration and death camps were conducted mainly in this part of the continent. Although Nazi anti-Jewish policies were initiated immediately after the invasion of Poland, in early September of 1939, the process of annihilation was gradual, lasting until the spring of 1945. The first two years of German rule in Poland were marked by economic exploitation, acts of terror and ghettoization. The mass murder of Jews began only in the fall of 1941, following the German invasion of the Soviet Union.

Polish Jews shared the fate of the general Polish population in the first weeks of the war. Around 100,000 Jews were mobilized into the Polish Army. Thousands participated in the digging of trenches and in the building of barricades. Both Poles and Jews were killed by the fierce German bombardments of Warsaw and the roads leading eastward. Poland had been divided by Hitler and Stalin in mid-September of 1939. German-occupied Poland included an area incorporated into the German Reich and the Generalgouvernement. The two areas, situated in western and central Poland, were inhabited by more than two million Jews. Between 150,000 and 250,000 Polish Jews fled the Germans in the first months of the war, and ended up in the Soviet-annexed territories of eastern Poland.[1]

The "Heidrich Letter," issued on September 21, 1939, highlighted the initial stage of German anti-Jewish policies. Jews were to be expelled from north-western Poland into the Generalgouvernement, and concentrated in large cities. Jewish councils were to be formed, in order to facilitate the implementation of German instructions. Then, in late November, Jews were ordered to wear arm-bands with a Star of David. This was a first step towards their identification and isolation from the surrounding non-Jewish population. Confiscation of property, roundups for harsh manual labor, and physical assaults on the streets followed. It is estimated that by the end of 1939, 250,000 Jews had already died as a result of shootings, starvation and disease.[2]

Ghettoization began as early as October 1939. The Lodz Ghetto was sealed off in May 1940, the Warsaw Ghetto in November of that year, and the Krakow Ghetto in March 1941. Numerous ghettos were formed throughout eastern Poland, following Hitler's invasion of the Soviet Union. All in all, some 650 ghettos existed in Polish lands at various times. Relocation from small ghettos and the concentration of Jews in larger ghettos, mostly close to railroad stations, occurred throughout 1942. The purpose was to segregate and concentrate the Jewish population so as to enable efficient deportation to the killing sites.

The inhabitants of the ghettos suffered from overcrowding, hunger and epidemics. The most frequent diseases were typhoid and tuberculosis. The rate of death from disease was high. Many starved to death. The ghettos also served as a "showplace" of Jewish misery for Nazi propaganda purposes. Still, there was a strong will to live and to survive. Self-help and various cultural activities, especially in the large ghettos, were quite prevalent. Small study groups and minyanim for prayer met from time to time. Covert political activities took place whenever possible.[3] Although the extreme conditions of life in the ghettos led to numerous deaths, most of the Jewish population was annihilated in the camps. There emerged, in time, a convergence of Jewish and German interests, which postponed for a while the annihilation process. German industrialists and the German army, the Wehrmacht, were interested in utilizing the extremely cheap Jewish labor. Some of the Jewish councils' chairmen believed that working for the Germans was a means for survival.[4]

The two most populated ghettos in Poland were those of Warsaw and Lodz. The Jews of Warsaw formed one third of the capital's population on the eve of the war. The city had also been flooded by Jewish refugees following the incorporation of western Poland into the German Reich. Close to 400,000 Jews were squeezed into the Warsaw Ghetto, which formed less than 3% of the total city area. Poverty, starvation and diseases affected the ghetto from its very start. Over 43,000 people starved to death during its first year. Fifteen thousand died of typhoid in the course of 1941. Some Jews were employed for various periods of time in production shops. The number of workers rose from 34,000 in September 1941 to 95,000 in mid-1942. Such temporary employment, with its meager rewards, could in no way alleviate the fast deterioration of everyday existence. Self-help attempts in the Ghetto were quite impressive. At one point the Jewish Society for Social Welfare aided over 100,000 people. Still, most of the ghetto Jews were starving. The scarcity of food resulted in widespread smuggling, despite the dangers involved. Profiteering created a new class of ghetto *noveau riche* with their restaurants and cafes.[5]

Political life in the Warsaw Ghetto, notwithstanding the prevailing conditions, was varied and dynamic. Almost all the prewar Jewish political parties were active there. The German occupation and Nazi anti-Jewish policies had the effect of bolstering Jewish national identity, which in turn resulted in the appeal of Zionism. After the short-lived Molotov-Ribbentrop pact, Soviet Russia became and was perceived as the chief opponent of Nazi Germany; this increased the popularity and support for leftist organizations among the young. The symbolic apogee of organized Jewish resistance, in Warsaw and elsewhere, was the Warsaw Ghetto Uprising in April-May 1943. Although it was headed mainly by Zionists and Socialists, the Revisionists showed daring and courage as well. Major deportations from the ghetto occurred in the summer of 1942. More than 250,000 Jews were deported to the Treblinka death camp. The ghetto was finally liquidated in the wake of the uprising, in the spring of 1943. Close to 30,000 Jews were in hiding on the Polish side of the city at various times. About 12,000 survived. It has been estimated that Jews on the Aryan side of Warsaw were aided by 70-90 thousand Poles.[6]

The most dynamic parts of the ghettoized Jewish population were the various Jewish youth organizations. The fact that many of the prewar Jewish political and public leaders escaped eastward, along with the extremely harsh conditions of life under German rule, resulted in a completely new and challenging situation. It seems that only organized youth, with its prewar traditions of ideological zeal and strong social bonds, could lead more "normal" and purpose-oriented lives. While the adults attempted to save themselves and their closest families, the young succeeded in creating their own, specific, different world, in which feelings of community, friendship, commitment and self-sacrifice prevailed. Meetings and other activities, with long hours spent together, were replacements of sorts for time with family. Youth organizations became more meaningful than family life. Intimate friendships among the young, in spite of abnormal conditions, added to their vitality. The hub of the

Jewish youth organizations' networks in German-occupied Poland was Warsaw. It was from and to Warsaw that emissaries and liaisons, mostly young, courageous and dedicated young women, traveled in order to maintain contacts. These special qualities were what allowed the young to form an underground.[7]

Whereas in Warsaw some contacts between the Ghetto and the surrounding city were possible, the Lodz Ghetto was almost hermetically sealed off. The total number of its inhabitants over the years was slightly over 200,000. They were crowded into less than 50,000 rooms, mostly in the Baluty neighborhood, the poorest and most dilapidated part of the city. Deportations of Jews from Lodz began already in the first months of 1940. By March, around 70,000 Jews had been taken from the city. Close to 40,000 Jews from smaller towns and other German-occupied countries were resettled in the Lodz Ghetto in the course of 1941-1942. More than 50,000 were taken during the first months of 1942 to the nearby Chelmno extermination camp. Over 40,000 died inside the ghetto of starvation and disease. During the so-called *"shpera"* roundup in the early fall of 1942 close to 16,000 people were deported.[8]

The Lodz Ghetto was the most labor-oriented ghetto in Nazi-occupied Poland. Both Chaim Rumkowski, head of the Jewish Ghetto Council, and Hans Biebow, the German administrator of the Lodz Ghetto, each for his own reasons supported the idea of Jewish labor. Around 50,000 Jews worked in the various production shops in early 1942. Their number increased to 80,000 in the course of that year. The most prevalent shop-work was tailoring, but there were also shoe-making, carpentry and metal works. Although there was some clandestine political activity inside the Lodz Ghetto, it was a far cry from the situation in Warsaw. In Lodz there were no contacts, whatsoever, with any Jewish or Polish underground organizations outside the ghetto. Mordechai Anielewicz of the Hashomer Hatzair, the future commander of the Jewish Fighters' Organization in the Warsaw Ghetto, arrived, apparently, in Lodz sometime in 1940, but did not manage to enter the ghetto. Unlike in Warsaw, complete isolation and a prevailing belief in survival by labor made armed resistance attempts in the Lodz Ghetto impossible.[9]

Still, cultural and educational activities were conducted, and a number of youth organizations existed inside the Ghetto. Rumkowski was particularly interested in education and care for children. He had been involved in the running of the Helenowek Jewish orphanage before the war, and his interest in the young continued during the war. Schools and study groups functioned in the Lodz Ghetto for various periods of time. The Jewish Gimnazjum on Franciszkanska Street was attended by hundreds of students. The most significant achievement, with no parallel in any other ghetto in Poland, was the Marysin Farm. The Ghetto Council was permitted to use the Marysin area for agricultural purposes, and various Zionist youth movements established there their *"hakhsharot"* — pioneering centers, in the spirit of prewar Zionist preparation for settlement in Palestine. Although officially these were "agricultural teams," in practice all youth organizations conducted educational, ideological and scouting activities there. More than twenty Zionist youth groups, consisting of nearly 1,000 members aged 16-24, were active in Marysin in the summer of 1940. The Marysin Farm not only supplied much-needed nutrition to hundreds of Jewish youngsters, it also enabled them to escape, at least for a while, the drab and depressing ghetto existence and to spend time with their peers. Besides youth movement activities, younger children used to arrive for a few hours of nourishment and "clean air." Close to 14,000 children enjoyed Marysin between July 1940 and October 1941. The Marysin Farm, while it existed, was a kind of "children's town," where teachers, instructors and counselors kept the young boys and girls busy and optimistic. This was, of course, just a temporary respite from the ever-deteriorating ghetto life. The Marysin farm closed in the fall of 1942.[10]

One of the most active youth organizations in the Lodz Ghetto was that of the Communist youth. Some were already under the spell of communism before the war. Others joined inside the ghetto. It was particularly after June 1941, following Hitler's invasion of Russia and the heroic struggle of the Russians, that pro-Communist and pro-Soviet moods started affecting Jewish youth. The Communist youth organization functioned in a more clandestine manner than other youth movements. They used to meet only in groups of five. The most typical activities among the Communist youngsters were reading and discussing the classics of Marxism and various Soviet authors. Later on, they were active in efforts to improve working conditions in the production shops. Their slogan was "PP" — pracuj powoli — work slowly — and they organized strikes.[11]

The Lodz Ghetto was the last ghetto in Poland. It remained in existence until the summer of 1944. Slightly over 11,000 people were taken to the Chelmno extermination camp in July 1944. By that time the ghetto population had fallen to less than 70,000. Almost all of the remaining inhabitants of the Ghetto, including Rumkowski and his family, were deported to Auschwitz in August. Many were young men and women, and they were employed in Auschwitz or sent to its satellite camps. It has been estimated that 5,000-7,000 Jews from Lodz survived the German camps. Fewer than 900 Jews survived in the devastated and empty Ghetto area.[12]

The only chance for survival outside the ghettos was either to hide or to live under assumed, Polish identities. A basic prerequisite for living "on the surface" were "good looks," i.e. not looking Jewish. It was also necessary to speak proper Polish. A Yiddish accent was disastrous. Linguistically and culturally assimilated Jews had better chances of survival than others. Women had more chances than men. It was also necessary, of course, to obtain the right identification papers. A most severe hazard on the "Aryan side" were the *szmalcownicy*, the Polish extortionists.[13]

The mass extermination of Polish Jews began in the late summer of 1941. Hundreds of thousands were killed in the East by the *Einsatzgruppen*, following the rapid advance of the German army on the Russian front. The transition from selective to mass murder occurred sometime in August. The decision concerning the Final Solution was taken by Hitler during the last three months of 1941. By the end of that year, about 600,000 Jews had been murdered in the regions occupied by Germany after the invasion of the USSR. The Wansee Conference, in which the logistics of the Final Solution were discussed, convened in January 1942. The following year marked the apex of the process of nearly total murder of European Jewry. The sites of mass murder were mainly the death camps, all of them on Polish soil. Auschwitz, Belzec, Sobibor, and Treblinka started their deadly functions in the course of 1942. Whereas most victims at Auschwitz-Birkenau were Jews deported from all over German-occupied Europe, most of the victims at Belzec, Sobibor and Treblinka were Polish Jews. The total number of Jews killed in Belzec reached 600,000; in Sobibor, 250,000; in Chelmno, 250,000; in Treblinka, more than 800,000. Deportations from Polish ghettos to death and concentration camps took place with the greatest intensity during the second half of 1942. More than a quarter-million Jews were deported from the Warsaw Ghetto to Treblinka in July-September 1942. Only sixty ghettos, out of more than 600, remained in Poland at the end of that year. The Krakow Ghetto was liquidated in March 1943. The Vilna Ghetto ceased to exist in April 1943. The last ghettos in prewar Polish Eastern Galicia were liquidated during the summer of that year. The life of Jews in German-occupied Poland was coming to an end.[14]

The last surviving Polish Jews in the camps were those used as laborers, mainly in German weapons and ammunition plants. Such, for example, were the "Hasag" camps in Czestochowa and Skarzysko-Kamienna. Following the steady westward advance of the Red Army, evacuation of the still functioning camps began in early 1945. Hundreds of thousands of Germany's victims of various nationalities were led in "death marches." Among them were a quarter of a million Jewish camp prisoners. Most of them would die from exhaustion, frost and hunger.[15]

***

OF THOSE POLISH JEWS WHO SURVIVED THE WAR, THE MAJORITY LIVED in the Soviet Union during the war years. Following the German invasion of Poland and its partition between Hitler's Germany and Stalin's Russia, thousands of Jewish men, but also some women and families, escaped from the German occupied part of the country into the Soviet-annexed territories. An official Polish announcement in early September, 1939, called on all able-bodied men to reassemble in the east. Numerous Jews, motivated by their fears of Nazi Germany, joined the exodus. Highways and back roads were clogged by refugees. Heavy German bombardments and strafing took their toll. Terror and panic prevailed along the massive human trek. The Germans were interested in cleansing the new German-Soviet frontier area of Jews, and forced them to move beyond the border, into the Soviet occupied territories.[16]

Between 150,000 and 200,000 Jewish refugees arrived in the Soviet-annexed territories during the fall of 1939. Some settled in small- and medium-sized towns. The majority, however, flowed into large cities. Lwow's Jewish population swelled from 100,000 to 180,000, Vilna's from 50,000 to 80,000, and that of Bialystok from 40,000 to 70,000. A considerable number of refugees came from Warsaw, Lodz and other cities in German-occupied Poland. Because the economic situation in the Soviet-annexed territories deteriorated, and because of the particularly precarious position in which the newcomers found themselves, tens of thousands were eager to accept job opportunities within the USSR. A minority of pro-Communist young Jewish men and women looked forward to the new Soviet way of life. Others just looked for employment. The "volunteers" were sent to the Donbass coal-mining region, to the foundries in the Ural Mountains, and to collective farms in Soviet Ukraine, Kazakhstan and other places. The extremely different ways of life and work inside the Soviet Union and the shortages of basic goods were disappointing. As a result, some volunteers attempted to return to their temporary places of residence in the Soviet-annexed territories.[17]

The only gateway for Jewish refugees from Poland to the free world was Vilna. It became a haven for Jewish individual refugees, as well as for groups and organizations. Nearly all Zionist youth organizations were active there in a semi-legal manner, not only during the Lithuanian phase of 1939-1940, but also during the Soviet phase of 1940-1941. Several

Jewish welfare organizations, such as the JDC and HIAS, maintained offices in Vilna. A few hundred refugees left Vilna for Palestine before the Soviet annexation of Lithuania in the summer of 1940. Surprisingly, for their own reasons and calcuations, the Soviets later allowed a closely-controlled emigration of Polish-Jewish refugees, mainly to Palestine. Some 5,000 Jewish refugees left Soviet Vilna between September 1940 and April 1941.[18]

The Soviet "passportization" campaign in the annexed territories, starting in early 1940, was meant to test the loyalty of the newcomers. At the same time, possibilities opened up for those Jewish refugees who were interested in returning to their families under German occupation. Thousands, weary of the Soviet way of life, and missing their near ones, opted to go back. The majority were apprehensive of losing their Polish citizenship. As a result, the Soviet authorities considered them a disloyal element. Arrests and deportations followed. Jewish deportees were part of the general Soviet deportation campaign, in the course of which hundreds of thousands of Polish citizens were moved to the Soviet interior. The deportations started in early 1940 and continued until June of 1941. Many of the Jewish refugees were deported in June, 1940. Each train consisted of up to fifty freight cars. Each car was packed with up to sixty people. In some cases, as many as 150 people were packed into one car. An average transport consisted of two to three thousand deportees. The total number of deported Jewish refugees, the refugees who opted for labor inside Russia, and Jews who fled the annexed territories following the German invasion is estimated at more than 200,000. An overwhelming majority of the deported Poles originated in the Soviet-annexed territories. Most of the deported Jews were refugees from German-occupied Poland.[19]

The deportation journeys in sealed cars lasted for weeks. The heat was oppressive. Men, women, and children of all ages, the old, the sick and newborn babies were all mixed together. Food and water rations were meager. There was lack of ventilation, toilet conditions were primitive, and people became infested with lice. Diseases, mostly dysentery and scabies, prevailed. The death toll increased over the course of the journey. Up to 10% of the deportees died on the way. The journeys did not always end at a railroad stop. Some deportees continued traveling by cart, truck, barge, and sometimes on foot.[20]

The transports which left the Soviet-annexed territories in June 1940 mostly arrived at points in northern Russia, Siberia and Kazakhstan. Some deportees were brought to urban settlements, to work in industry and construction. Others were brought to collective and state farms. Still others were deposited in unsettled areas and told to build their own dwellings. Relations between Poles and Jews in the Soviet exile varied. There were cases of mutual assistance and other cases of anti-Semitism. Although the conditions of daily existence were harsh everywhere, those in prisons and labor camps had a much lesser chance of survival than the rest. People died from starvation, cold, exhaustion and epidemics. The legal status of the deportees, as well as possibilities for travel and relocation inside Russia, changed drastically in August 1941, in the wake of Hitler's invasion of the USSR, and the Soviet-Polish Agreement. Polish citizens were now officially permitted to leave prisons, camps, and assigned settlements. A mass migration of Polish citizens occurred in the second half of 1941. It was part of a much wider relocation of indigenous Soviet war refugees and evacuees, fleeing eastward from the front. Millions were on the move. The main thrust of the Polish migration was in the direction of the Central Asian Soviet republics. The southern climate was more lenient, and the mobilization centers for the Polish Army, formed in the USSR following the Soviet-Polish Agreement, were located in that area. This second relocation took place under extremely harsh wartime conditions. It resulted in even more deaths than the initial deportation from the annexed territories.[21]

Life in the Soviet South abounded in hardships specific to the region. The hot climate and primitive sanitary conditions caused the spread of contagious diseases. The region was also crowded with Soviet refugees from the German-occupied regions of western Russia. Lack of food and hunger were part of everyday life. Medicines were in short supply. Poles and Polish Jews shared the harsh fate of the overall Soviet population. Those who had managed to bring with them some personal belongings sold them on the black market in order to buy food. Others traded illegally and were often imprisoned for doing so. The Polish Embassy established a network of welfare assistance. Nurseries, schools and orphanages were organized on a wide scale. This meant shelter, a few meals a day and some teaching. The Jewish-Polish refugees received some assistance from Jewish philanthropic organizations abroad, such as the JDC. The most important aid was in the form of food, clothing and medicine. Some parcels arrived from relatives in Palestine. At the end of 1944, as many as 40,000 Jewish families were receiving aid from the JDC. The JDC relief project continued until 1946, saving tens of thousands of Polish-Jewish wartime refugees in Russia from death by starvation. There were also some attempts to initiate cultural activities in centers of Jewish refugee population. A traveling Yiddish theatre troup performed across the Central Asian republics. Among the Jewish artists were the popular prewar comedians Shimon Dzigan and Israel Schumacher. They performed even during their incarceration in Soviet prisons and labor camps. In spite of the harsh wartime conditions and massive relocations, some of the young Zionist refugees managed to maintain contacts. More than the refugee population as a whole, they were known for mutual aid, high morale and an ability to function in the ever-changing and challenging Soviet wartime realities.[22]

A most significant result of the renewal of Soviet-Polish relations in the summer of 1941 was the establishment of a Polish Army in the USSR. It was headed by General Anders, and was referred to as Anders' Army. Thousands of Polish citizens from prisons, camps and assigned settlements started arriving at the centers of mobilization, among them numerous Polish Jews.

Both the Soviets and the Poles, each for their own reasons, attempted to prevent their mobilization. Traditional Polish anti-Semitic attitudes prevailed among the Polish officer corps. This was the reason for the proportionately low percentage of Jews among Anders' Army's evacuees to Persia. Nearly 115,000 Polish citizens, soldiers, and civilians left the USSR in the course of 1942. They were transferred in trains to the port of Krasnovodsk on the Caspian Sea, and from there by ship to the Persian port of Pahlevi. Some 6,000 Jews, about 3,500 soldiers and about 2,500 civilians, left with Anders' Army.[23]

The break in relations between the Soviet Union and the London-based Polish Government in Exile in the spring of 1943 affected the lives and fates of the Polish-Jewish refugees. All Polish activities in Russia were organized and coordinated now by the ZPP — Zwiazek Patriotow Polskich — the pro-Communist Union of Polish Patriots. A nucleus of the future Communist regime in postwar Poland was being groomed by the Soviets for some time. It was based on prewar Polish Communists, many of Jewish origin. First steps toward the establishment of a pro-Soviet Polish military unit, named after the legendary Polish hero, Tadeusz Kosciuszko, were taken in late April,1943. Colonel Zygmunt Berling, shortly to be promoted to the rank of General, was appointed its commander. By July the number of draftees in the newly formed Kosciuszko Division was close to 16,000. The Division left for the front in early September and in mid-October 1943, fought its first major battle against the Germans at Lenino, near Smolensk. By March 1944 the Polish force, designated now as the Polish Army, fighting in close cooperation with the Red Army, consisted of 40,000 soldiers. When it reached the north-eastern territories of prewar Poland, in the summer of 1944, it numbered more than 100,000[24]

There was on the whole no discrimination in the mobilization of Jewish draftees into Berling's Army: every tenth soldier was Jewish. Nearly

20% of the officer corps was Jewish. Among the political officers, Jews comprised almost 40%. These were not only Communists and Communist sympathizers, but also left-wing Zionists. A significant number of Jews, mostly doctors, served in the Army's medical service. Nearly all producers and cameramen in the Army's newsreel team — the Czolowka Filmowa — were Jews. Jewish soldiers excelled on the front. Many died in battles, and many received awards for courage. Jews participated in the battles on the banks of the Vistula and in the capture of Berlin. Jewish soldiers and officers were motivated not only by their obligation as citizens of the newly forming Poland, but also by a desire to take vengeance for their specific losses as Jews. Many hoped to rebuild their lives in postwar Poland. The share of Jews in the Polish Army and their number in the officer corps declined drastically starting in 1945, following the mobilization of Polish draftees in the newly liberated Polish territories. Numerous Jews demobilized in the immediate postwar years. As a consequence, their number among the political officers dropped from 40% to 6%.[25]

The first Jews to return from Russia to Poland were Jewish soldiers and officers of the Berling Army. Their number has been estimated at 13,000-20,000. Several agreements, starting in September 1944, relating to the repatriation of prewar Polish citizens from the USSR to Poland, were signed between the Polish and Soviet governments. The registration of those entitled to repatriation, living at that time in various parts of the Soviet Union, was conducted by the ZPP — the Union of Polish Patriots. Soviet policies in regard to repatriation were generally liberal, and the vast majority of those who opted to return to Poland were given the opportunity to do so. The departure of the first transports took place in a festive atmosphere, with flowers, speeches and music. The first wave of civilian Jewish returnees to Poland, by the end of 1945, consisted of more than 20,000 persons. Most of the Jewish returnees arrived in Poland in the first half of 1946. All in all, more than a quarter of a million Polish Jews survived the war in the Soviet Union. Most of them returned to Poland in the immediate postwar years. Their survival did not result from intentional Soviet policies, but rather from an initial Soviet mistrust, which in turn resulted in their deportation to the Soviet interior. Those who survived the hard times of wartime Russia would form the majority of the Jewish population in postwar Poland.[26]

* * *

CHAPTER FIVE

War: The First Days

BINYAMIN MAJERCZAK, A 22 YEAR OLD ELECTRICAL ENGINEER, LIVED AND worked in Warsaw when the war started on September 1, 1939. "I had a wonderful summer. Then, on August 30, I received my mobilization orders. In the meantime the residents of Warsaw volunteered to dig trenches. Everybody was in high spirits. I recall some of the most popular slogans: 'All of us are equal'; 'We shall fight the Germans'; 'Poland is the motherland of all of its citizens'; 'Poles and Jews are comrades in arms.' The mood changed quite soon, as a result of heavy bombardments." Binyamin called his family who lived in Wloclawek, north-west of Warsaw. His parents advised him to go East. "Father tried to encourage me. 'Perhaps this war won't last long. England and France will intervene, and Hitler will be defeated.' His last words were: 'Son, be brave!' Then we were cut off. I never saw my parents again."[27]

Aleksander Klugman, who lived in Lodz, was 14 on the eve of the war. "The events were sudden, fast and overwhelming. People hardly realized what was happening. Most of them didn't heed the air raid alarms. They gathered in groups, in the courtyards, and watched those tiny planes, high up in the blue skies. They looked like toys, like harmless kites. The worst, though, were the shrieks and wailes of the alarm sirens. I wasn't really scared of the planes. I ran down to the cellar since I couldn't take those shrieks." There was also fear of gas attacks. The Klugmans stayed for a few days in a nearby village. They were terrified one day when, during an air raid in which they hid in the cellar, a strong odor spread through the house. When they finally returned to the kitchen, they realized that the prune jam which Mrs. Klugman had been cooking when the alarm rang had burned. The Klugmans returned to Lodz after it had already been occupied by the Germans. "Although only a few days passed since we left, the house, somehow, wasn't the same anymore. There was a complete change. Something collapsed. It was like an earthquake."[28]

Fayvl Podemski joined Hashomer Hatzair in Lodz when he was 12, three years before the war. "In the early summer of 1939 we were all excited about the approaching summer camp. We anticipated the good time we'll have there." This was the first time that he would travel to Zakopane, the famous Polish resort town at the foot of the Tatra mountains. "And so it happened that just a few weeks before Hitler's soldiers invaded Poland, we climbed the treks in the Carpathians, 'conquered' high peaks, and lived it up. It was like a dream. Then, we were told that a war may be in the offing, but nobody paid any attention to it. Three days later the bad news arrived: our camp would be dismantled, and we would return to Lodz.

It looked like the end of the world." Fayvl vividly recalled his first sight of the Germans. "We lived on Poludniowa Street. I went to the corner of Piotrkowska, and here they were. I was immensely impressed by the order, the discipline, the elegance. They were completely unlike the Polish army. I noted that their cars were marked by consecutive numbers: if one of the passing cars was marked, say, 412, the next one was 413, and so on."[29]

Matityahu Mintz, a year older than Fayvl, was a member of Hashomer Hatzair in Warsaw. He recalled the first days of September 1939, when Warsaw was being bombed day-by-day "Anielewicz, with other senior counselors, left on September 7. The Warsaw *ken* of Hashomer Hatzair was dissolved a day earlier. I was there, at the last roll call. Usually, there were some 600 or 700 youngsters in the Warsaw *ken*, but only 70-100 could make it to the last roll call. It was then and there that the famous Warsaw ken Hashomer Hatzair flag was entrusted to those who would soon leave, and it would finally reach Palestine. When the Germans occupied Warsaw we sensed an immediate change. One didn't know what would come next. People were abducted in the streets. Even a youngster like me was likely to be caught. At times, a German soldier would pity me, saying that I'm only a child, a boy. One day, some 17-18 youngsters from my youth group at Hashomer Hatzair met and decided to leave. This was approximately in mid October. We left Warsaw on October 17, 1939. My parents let me go. They both agreed. My mother cried."[30]

Shlomo, one of the Pomerantz triplets, age five in 1939, had only very fragmentary memories of the early days of the war. He recalled standing on the balcony of their house, watching their father come home wearing an army uniform and a helmet. "He was a real soldier. He had a very short leave from the army, and then went back. Next time we saw him was already in Lwow." Shlomo seemed to remember a parade of German soldiers marching along their street. "A messenger from my father arrived one day and told us that father wants us to join him in Lwow. My mother's younger sister, Itka, joined us, and we started traveling. We traveled in those brown railroad cars, with no seats. We just sat on the floor."[31]

Heniek Napadow had an excellent visual memory for a boy who was five or six at the time. They lived in Warsaw, on Ogrodowa Street. "I definitely recall the bombardments. We ran to the cellar. The only one who stayed upstairs was my grandpa. At one end of our street, at the lower numbers, there were stables, with horses. These stables were bombed. There was a terrible stench of burnt flesh." Heniek also recalled that his father and his father's younger brother were abducted by the Germans for compulsory work. When they returned home, they decided to escape to the East, to Russia. Heniek did not fear the Germans. "I was blond, with light brown eyes, and didn't look Jewish at all." He used to play with a Volksdeutch child. "We used to ask German soldiers for bread, since food was already scarce then, and they would give it to us. These were dark, square loafs." Heniek's father notified them that he would be waiting for them in Bialystok. This was apparently in the late fall of 1939. "I remember an overcrowded train station. Lots of people milled around. A German soldier came by, picked me up, and helped my mother with her valise. Inside the train car he slapped a youngster and forced him to give up his seat to my mother."[32]

Bialystok, where the Rubinows lived before the war, was occupied by the Germans on September 15, 1939. Within a week, following the Soviet-German agreement, it was turned over to the Russians, and remained under Soviet rule until June 1941. Rachel's parents had moved to the most fashionable part of town ten years before she was born. Rala, as she was called then, and her older brother, Vovka, enjoyed an affluent and happy childhood. Rachel, a lifetime later, nostalgically and humorously described what happened to her family. "We lived in the most beautiful and spacious apartment in the city. Word of it reached the ears of an NKVD major, who proceeded to invade our house with his family of nine, leaving us two bedrooms. He also hatched a plot to get rid of us altogether. His solution was Siberia. Taking advantage of the Soviet deportation policy, the major placed us on a priority list. On Saturday, June 21, 1941, at dawn, two NKVD agents dressed in black leather coats burst into our apartment and informed my parents that we were being moved to the 'eastern provinces.' We were driven to the railroad station and ordered onto a train with several hundred detainees from all over the city. The train pulled out. Little did we know that ours would be the last deportation train to leave Bialystok before the arrival of the Germans."[33]

Aharon Zalkind was six when his hometown Vilna, with all of Lithuania, became part of the USSR in the summer of 1940. "We lived quite far from the city center, on Antokolska Street. My parents ran a small grocery store, and we lived in a very modest apartment. My father kept two horses, with which he would bring produce from nearby villages." The Zalkinds had an extended, well-off family in town. They belonged to the poorer branch of the family. In the house they spoke Yiddish, although they knew some Polish and some Lithuanian. "I recall a Sunday. Father didn't go to the store. All of us were in the house. All of a sudden an air-raid alarm rang. The Germans started bombing Vilna. We understood that the German-Russian war had started. My grandma was killed by a bomb, and we stayed for a few days in the countryside." Aharon recalled the mood in their house, as they expected the Germans. "A kind of sadness and gloom was in the air, and worries of what would happen once the Germans would come." He distinctly remembered the first time he saw German soldiers on the street. "I was excited very much by the sight. First appeared the motorcycles, and behind them rolled the tanks. Tankists' heads protruded from the turrets. It impressed me immensely. I remember people watching those tankists and throwing candies at them. Our Polish neighbors seemed very happy. We were rather sad."[34]

The Eastward Trek

NATAN GROSS, FROM KRAKOW, WAS ONE OF THOSE WHO JOINED THE eastward moving masses. "On the fourth day of the war I joined that immense wave of refugees. My father, with my brother Jozek, had left already two days earlier, in the direction of Lwow. I decided to stay at home, with my mother, my sister, Klara, and my younger brother, Jerzyk. People kept asking me, ' Are you still here, a young man like you? What are you waiting for?' The psychological pressure mounted by the day. Then, a few young men from our neighborhood, casual acquaintances, suggested that I join them. We left in the morning. It was early fall, and the weather was excellent. Then came the sudden, deadly, air attacks of those blackcrossed Messerschmidts. This was my first encounter with the atrocities of a war. After a week of adventures, we finally reached the townlet of Zuchowice, not far from Lwow. While resting in a nearby forest we were suddenly surrounded by a group of Polish soldiers, pointing their rifles at us. They suspected that we had deserted the army. We were told later that the Russian army had crossed the eastern Polish border, and that, actually, the war had ended. I decided to return home, to Mama. I wasn't too excited to go back to German-occupied Krakow. Still, I considered it as an obligation to my family."[35]

Binyamin Majerczak, like many other Polish and Jewish young men, left Warsaw in early September 1939, in order to report to the army in eastern Poland. Bombardments dominated his memories of the eastward journey. "German planes incessantly bombed the throngs of refugees. They fired machine guns as well. There was a real massacre on the road. Men, women and children were killed all around me. Human bodies and dead horses lied scattered along the roads. An unbearable stench of burnt flesh was in the air." In Lukow he finally boarded a train, which passed by Biala Podlaska and stopped some 20 kilometers from Brest, since the rails there were in shambles. "The local Poles were very polite. They were

Polish patriots, and knew that we had a common enemy." Binyamin spent the High Holidays of 1939 in Miedzyrzec hosted by a Jewish family. It was also there that he saw for the first time Red Army soldiers. "There were tanks, cavalry and flagbearers. A Soviet officer addressed a Jewish crowd in Yiddish, and told them that they shouldn't worry. The Red Army had come to liberate them." Majerczak then moved to Soviet-occupied Brest. The town was bustling with refugees.[36]

A friend of Szulim Rozenberg's brother came to their house in Warsaw in early September, and told them that many young people were leaving. "So, we too, started talking about going east. The three of us left the house, met two acquaintances on the street, and the five of us started on our way. We walked day and night, and covered close to 500 kilometers in nine days. On some days we walked for twenty-two hours. We wanted to join the Polish Army, supposedly regrouping in the east. By September 17th, we reached a town by the name of Malewicz, in western Belorussia, between Slonim and Baranowicze, and we met Russian soldiers. This made us extremely happy. There were lots of Yiddish-speaking Jews among them. They told us that they had come to liberate us. From Malewicz we went to Sarny, in Volhynia. I met several friends and acquaintances there. Among them were Aleksander Forbert and Yosl Bergner. Since many people proceeded to Vilna, my brother and I decided to go there too. From Vilna we went to Volkovysk, where I stayed for a while."[37]

Ewa was 19 when the war started. Her friends in Lodz in those days were young people affiliated with Communist and left-Zionist circles. She went with some of them to a three-day summer camp in Radogoszcz, on the outskirts of Lodz, in May 1939. "I didn't tell my parents where I was going. This was exactly during the Shavuot holidays, and I told them that I was going to visit a friend. These three days became highly significant in my life. Later, when the war started, some of us traveled eastward, and ended up in Soviet Russia." A few weeks after the occupation of Lodz by the Germans, Ewa and three of her closest communist girlfriends traveled to Soviet-occupied Bialystok. In December, when it became possible to volunteer for work in some regions of the USSR, Ewa and her friends were among the first to register. "The first volunteer groups went to Donbass. It wasn't easy to get accepted. They preferred Communists, and especially those who had been arrested for Communist activities." It was around that time that Ewa started dating Israel Frenkel, an ex-member of the Polish Communist Party, whom she vaguely knew in Lodz. "We were in love then, but it was still platonic." They ended up in a volunteers' transport that left for Magnitogorsk, in the Urals, in January 1940. "There were close to a thousand people in our transport, among them a few hundred from Lodz. I traveled with Israel as a couple."[38]

Matityahu Mintz and his young friends traveled east by train and on foot. They crossed the new German-Soviet border on October 18th, at night, and arrived in Bialystok. They stayed there for a few weeks and were assisted by Hashomer Hatzair. Then they decided to travel south, since it was warmer there, and arrived in Lutsk. "There was an air of adventure. We fantasized. We were quite optimistic in respect to the new Soviet way of life and nourished those unrealistic images." It was only in Lutsk that they woke up to the harsh reality. "It wasn't fun anymore. We had no money left, and I traveled to Lwow to get some from my uncle, who had left Warsaw and was living in Lwow." Mintz was told that there was an active center of Hashomer Hatzair in Vilna, and decided to get there via Grodno. "Hashomer Hatzair people in Grodno arranged for some sleeping facilities. I got a bed without a mattress, and fell asleep immediately. When I woke up at dawn, I saw right near me, on the floor, Mordechai Anielewicz. He apparently knew that I had arrived in Grodno, and wanted to see me. We spoke for a long while, and Anielewicz strongly advised me to travel to Vilna. He also recommended that I read Lenin's 'On Revolution.' We parted, and I boarded a train to Lida, on the Lithuanian border. I finally arrived in the Lithuanian town of Eishyshok. This was December 22, 1939, just before Christmas." Mintz and his Warsaw friends traveled on foot, and arrived in Vilna in late December. He would stay there until January 1941, when he would leave for Palestine. Mintz was sure that Anielewicz, who regarded him as a promising youngster, recommended to Hashomer Hatzair leaders in Vilna that they should take care of him. This is how Mintz explained to me, sixty years later, his unusual chance to leave German- and Soviet-occupied Poland, and join the Jewish Yishuv in Palestine.[39]

Inside Russia

THE JOURNEY FROM THE SOVIET-ANNEXED TERRITORIES TO THE SOVIET interior was recalled by most of my narrators as a traumatic experience. The only exception was Ewa Frenkel, who volunteered to travel to what she had considered "The Soviet Paradise." Ewa was highly excited about her imminent life in Soviet Russia. "We traveled there in cattle cars, but I still nourished that image of a better world."[40]

While in Soviet-occupied Brest, Binyamin Majerczak worked in a welfare agency supporting Jewish refugees. "One evening, at the end of

October, my friend Julek and my 14 year-old brother, Mareczek, arrived unexpectedly. I also urged my parents to join me, but they stayed in Warsaw, ended up in the Warsaw Ghetto, and in April 1943 were deported to Majdanek. "On February 6, 1940, Majerczak watched the Red Army Day celebrations in Brest. "Soviet generals, with their honored guests — German officers with swastikas on their uniforms, arms stretched out in a 'Heil Hitler' salute — occupied a stand overlooking the parade." Majerczak and his younger brother left Brest sometime in March, and traveled to Lwow, where he worked in a plant run by the NKVD. Binyamin and Mareczek were arrested on June 18, 1940. "I begged the NKVD officer in charge to free Mareczek. He finally agreed. Then we embraced, cried, and parted." Majerczak was sure that he was saving his younger brother from Soviet labor camps. "We will meet again, I promised him. Be strong little brother! I never saw Mareczek again. Did I make the right decision? Sixty years have passed, and my conscience is still bothering me."

Majerczak, with other detainees, was taken to the Lwow railroad station and loaded on a freight train. "This was an endless journey. We lost the sense of time for days and weeks. One day I actually collapsed, and couldn't eat. I lived on dirty water. At one of the small, provincial railroad stations, somewhere in Soviet Ukraine, a local woman handed him a slice of freshly baked dark bread, and encouraged him to eat it. "This was the breaking point. I ate it within seconds, and bought some more food for the rest of the journey. The dirt and the stench in our car were terrible. We didn't wash for weeks. Lice were all over us." The journey ended somewhere along the Volga, at the huge "Volgostroi" project.[41]

The Rubinows were put on a freight train in their native Bialystok. Decades later Rachel described their journey, using her wry, sarcastic sense of humour: "We would have been happy if ours were a cattle car. As it turned out, 64 of us were crammed into a car that had previously unloaded coal. Lying on top of bundles and suitcases we resembled listless Cinderellas, our faces and clothing covered with black soot, our throats gagging on noxious fumes." As they approached Minsk, they heard heavy bombardment. The Germans had invaded Russia. Rachel recalled, or perhaps repeated stories told by her parents, about that coal train. "We had equal numbers of Poles and Jews. There were many rich people whose property the Soviets had confiscated. There were also priests and rabbis, Zionists and Freemasons, musicians and actors, university professors and lowly teachers — everyone the Communists had branded 'intelligentsia.' Unexpectedly, some people appeared at the Minsk station, carrying slices of bread, boiled potatoes, pieces of cheese, a few cookies. They ran along the train, handing us what they had." After about two weeks the transport arrived in an abandoned prisoners' camp, at the foot of the Altai Mountains.[42]

Heniek Napadow and his mother reached a remote place on the new Soviet border. "We ended up in a huge shack with many families. The Russians refused to let us cross to the other side." He recalled being driven on a wheelcart by a Pole or a Ukrainian, apparently during an earlier portion of their journey,. They were stopped by German soldiers. "They pointed at us with their fingers and kept asking 'Jude? Jude?' My mother and another woman who traveled with us just moved their heads, indicating that they weren't Jewish." There was yet another image deeply inscribed in the young boy's mind. "I am not sure at all where this took place, whether it was near the border or not, but I kept it for years in my memory. I remembered a place with a barrel full of lime and some Germans standing nearby. There was this old, bearded Jew. The Germans kept pushing his head into that barrel, down and up, several times. And there was laughter." Finally they crossed the border and arrived in Bialystok, where Heniek's father waited for them.[43]

Ewa and Israel arrived in Magnitogorsk in January 1940. "They welcomed us with banners, music and speeches. The temperature was minus 40 centigrade. Some of the new arrivals couldn't take it and returned to Bialystok." Magnitogorsk — Magnetic Mountain City — was conceived by the Soviets as a utopian experiment, an earthly socialist paradise. It was not only a center of modern Soviet industry, it was perceived in Soviet Russia and in Communist circles abroad as a euphoric symbol of the new, enlightened, socialist society. "I was quite excited. Israel literally wept with joy. He was a man of ideals, full of enthusiasm." Ewa was appointed as an assistant to a glazier, a *stekolshchik*. "We worked at a nearly-completed building construction. I carried large plates of glass." In less than two weeks, on the way to the library, Ewa slipped on the frozen ground and fractured her hand. Israel, who also worked in construction, developed a lung infection, and was sent to a sanatorium. Ewa, unable to work, was sent to study how to work a concrete mixer. The course lasted for a few months and she was already seven months pregnant. So they didn't send her to work. Ewa and Israel married in Zags, a Soviet Civil Marriage office. "A Jewish wedding didn't even come to my mind." When I asked Ewa how she reacted to the difficulties of daily life in Magnitogorsk, her answer was, "I took it with a grain of salt, I was laughing things off."

Israel and Ewa decided to leave Magnitogorsk and join some of Israel's friends in Chelyabinsk, in Western Siberia. When they arrived at the local railroad station, somebody told them that there was a shortage of workers at a large textile plant in Poltava, South-East of Kiev. Since Israel used to work in a textile factory in Lodz, they decided to try their luck in Poltava. There Ewa gave birth to a baby girl, whom she named Nadia after Nadezhda Krupskaya, Lenin's wife. This was in February 1941. Israel was drafted into the Red Army soon after the German invasion, in June. Ewa decided then to join two of her girlfriends and travel to Nizhni-Tagil. In two weeks they continued to Orsk, in the Southern Urals. Ewa and little Nadia would stay there throughout the war. Israel, between his release from the Red Army, in February 1942, and his mobilization into the Polish Kosciuszko Division, in the spring of 1943, lived with his young wife and their baby daughter. This was actually the only time that they lived together as a family. Israel Frenkel was killed in the Battle of Lenino, in October 1943, but the sad news reached Ewa only months later. Ewa started working in one of the Orsk restaurants, first washing dishes and later as cashier. When I asked her about recollections from her Orsk years, she casually remarked "There were many terrible things, but it was also fun." Ewa and Nadia traveled to Poland in the spring of 1946.[44]

Majerczak spent fourteen months in the Gulag. He lived and worked in labor camps which were part of the Volgostroi project, in the upper Volga region. In the first camp he felled trees for the construction of a dam and was appointed "brigadir," in charge of a workers' team. "Our shack housed twelve brigades, a total of 300 prisoners. They used to count us early in the morning, before leaving for work. The commander warned us, 'one step out of line, and you'll be shot without warning.'" Food rations were individual. They depended on the 'norm,' i.e. the number of trees cut down by each prisoner. "I became friendly with Ivan, a veteran "brigadir." He was Russian, a criminal prisoner, a thief, and a wonderful guy. He offered valuable practical advice to me and to my team." In November 1940 Majerczak was transferred to a larger camp, also part of the Volgostroi. "All commands in that camp were broadcast by a net of loudspeakers, installed all over the place. Each day we woke up to the tune of the popular Soviet song 'Shiroka strana moya rodnaya' — 'Oh My Spacious Native Land.' Most of the camp population was political prisoners. Among them were Party secretaries, old Bolsheviks, scientists, writers and engineers. The attraction of the new camp was Neli, a young, beautiful, blond Moscow actress. She used to perform and sing Russian folk songs. The men devoured her with their eyes."

Majerczak's work in this camp consisted of digging for building foundations in the frozen, stone-like soil. "It was already winter, and the extremely low temperature was dangerous and threatening. Urinating and defecating during working hours became a serious problem." Still, Majerczak was lucky. Since he was an electrical engineer, he started working as an electrician, and life improved considerably. "I did some work in the nearby camp for women prisoners, and they pampered me there. I was something special for them, an *'inostranets,'* a foreigner. They called me 'Binya.'" His new work provided an opportunity to improve his Russian, and he started reading Russian classics in the camp library. In time he made new friends, among them a 50 year-old Soviet Jew, Boris Davidovich, who could speak Yiddish. "He treated me like a son." In early 1941, Majerczak received a postcard from his younger brother. This would be the last sign of life from Mareczek.

Life was rather peaceful until the spring of 1941. "Sometime in April, at night, I was called to check the electrical equipment at the cement factory, and erroneously caused a short circuit of the main line. An enormous flame blinded me completely. I sensed a terrible pain in my face and chest. My cloths were on fire." Long weeks of recuperation in the camp hospital followed that unfortunate incident. Majerczak's chances for survival were quite slim. "It was Marusia, a nurse, who, actually, saved my life. She would take care of me and feed me like a baby. She was wonderful." Following the incident Majerczak was accused of sabotage and interrogated for long hours by the NKVD. He didn't believe that he would ever survive the Gulag. The interrogations stopped after the German invasion, in June 1941. Then there was another accident, this time at work with lumber blocks. Part of Majerczak's face was deformed, and he spent weeks in the camp hospital. It was again Marusia who took care of him. "The attitude towards Polish prisoners changed, starting in August 1941. We weren't taken to work anymore. Our food ratios improved considerably. And then, during one morning roll call, the camp commander announced that an agreement had been signed between the Soviet and Polish governments, and that the Polish prisoners would soon be released. I bade farewell to Marusia, my 'angel in white'. When we embraced with Boris Davidovich, he whispered 'remember, you are no Pole, you are a Jew, my son. When the war ends go to Palestine'."

After his release Majerczak traveled to nearby Rybinsk, then to Yaroslavl and to Ivanovo. On a train he met a Jew from his native Wloclawek, who convinced him to join Anders' Polish Army. However, after hearing about anti-Semitism in its ranks, Majerczak gave up the idea and decided to travel to Ordzhonikidze, formerly Vladikavkaz, between the Black and the Caspian Sea. There was a sentimental connection with this Russian town in Majerczak's family. One of his great grandfathers had served there in the Tsar's army. "When I arrived in Ordzhonikidze I walked into the railroad station waiting room. There was this old piano in the middle of the room. I started playing some popular Russian tunes, and a crowd gathered around me in a matter of minutes." This was the beginning of an unexpected short-lived 'musical career' at the local Railroad Workers' Club.

Majerczak found soon work as an electrician in a local factory and led a relatively comfortable life. Unfortuntely, he became sick with malaria, and was lucky again. This time it was a nurse by the name of Nina. She took good care of him, and fell in love with "Vinya." After leaving the hospital Majerczak worked as an electrician in a "myasokombinat" — a meat distribution center. From then on, he was never hungry, and even traded some meat, illegally, on the black market. "I made good money, and people got to know me. In my few free evenings I used to visit Nina, as well as Wanda, a beauty of Polish origin, who played the guitar and sang Russian romantic songs." After a while Majerczak met Evgenia Vasil'evna, a Russian army doctor with a rank of captain, and moved in with her. By the summer of 1942, as the front line got closer, he had to leave his comfortable and adventurous love life in Ordzhonikidze, and traveled to Krasnovodsk. On the way there was another romance, with Anna. "Even now, sixty years later, I'm still moved when I remember Anna. We were together for two weeks, first on a refugee train to Baku, then on a Caspian Sea ferry and in the sands of Krasnovodsk."

Majerczak traveled from Krasnovodsk to Samarkand, in Uzbekistan, where he enrolled in a local college to study Agricultural Machinery. "I fondly recall my Russian and Uzbek friends, my teachers and my instructors." He left the college after a few months, and started working as an electrician in a refrigeration plant. Here too, he became the darling of the female workers, and had an affair with the plant's beauty, Vera. It seems that Majerczak's age, good looks, and the wartime scarcity of men worked consistently in his favor. "In April 1943, people started talking about the Polish Kosciuszko Division." Following a dream about his mother, and recalling his father's last words, Binyamin decided that his place should be in the ranks of those who fight the Germans. He joined the Kosciuszko Division in early May.[45]

Szulim Rozenberg was deported to the Komi Autonomous Republic in the Russian North-East, notorious for its labor camps. Even after his release, in the fall of 1941, he decided to stay in that area. The story he told me sounded much more upbeat then those of other interviewees. "There was a group of Russian engineers there, in charge of felling trees, and I was appointed their boss. This was a wonderful job. We had everything: food, clothing, everything we needed." After a while Szulim traveled to Gorki, where his brother's family had settled. He quickly found work in a supply firm. "I felt very good there. The local people 'adopted' me, so to speak. I was sent often on "*komandirovki*" (working trips) all over, and even got to Moscow a couple of times. I have very pleasant memories of those times." From Gorki Szulim traveled to Krasnodar, sometime in 1944, where another brother, Menashe, had settled. On the way he visited Moscow and went to the offices of the ZPP — The Union of Polish Patriots. "Walking down the stairs I saw Ida Kaminska. I had seen her in the theater, in Warsaw, many times. Kaminska knew Ksil, one of my brothers. She told me that they had been together for some time, in Kirgizstan, and gave me his address." Szulim mantained ongoing contacts with his brothers and sisters, dispersed all over Russia, and tried to assist them as much as he could. When I wondered about his resourcefulness and endless energy, he commented, "One had to believe people and trust them. I wasn't scared of anything. I could easily adjust to new conditions and circumstances. I had excellent relations with everybody. People helped me and I helped them." Szulim worked in Krasnodar as a supervisor in an NKVD supply base, and stayed there until 1946.[46]

Rela Rubinow had only fragmentary memories of her first months in the Altai region. "October greeted us with snowflakes. The mud froze, and quite soon we were covered by a blanket of snow. Towards the end of October 1941, we were told that we were free, and could go anywhere we wished. Soon trucks appeared at the camp, and formed a convoy, which would deliver us to Biysk."

Biysk was located some 300 kilometers south of Novosibirsk. The Rubinows would stay there until their return to Poland, in March 1946. Rachel's story was both about the extremely harsh conditions of existence and about basic human kindness. "A miracle happened to us in Biysk. We stepped into the post office, and met an old Russian lady there. Learning the extent of our misery, she invited us to stay with her. Afanasyevna Prokhorova led us to her hut, where we met the other members of her family: her daughters-in-law, Dasha and Sasha, and her two girls, Shura and Valya. The women were married to Prokhorova's two sons, Grisha and Misha, who were 'fighting the fascists.'"

Rachel's most prevailing wartime memories were of freezing and hunger. "One time, returning from school in the dark, I was buried under a pile of snow and might have died, if it hadn't been for a passing Kirgiz tribesman. My strongest memory of wartime is hunger. For the rest of my life I'll remember that at age six and seven, day and night, I dreamed about eating another slice of bread. The only question on my mind in 1943 was: are we going to die by freezing or starving? At 63 degrees below zero cows and chickens froze; the school, the hospital and the library were closed. We could no longer use the outhouse. The only good news was that the Russians in Stalingrad 'defeated the disgusting fascists.'" Still, Rela nourished for decades some good and inspiring memories of the Siberian landscape. "Spring brought the most beautiful sunflowers one may ever see. A pure, distilled concentrate of yellow, with a budding center of black. Coming on the heels of white snow, I'd framed in my mind an eternal image of sunflowers sprouting out of piles of snow." Another prevailing memory was of their landlady, the Russian woman. "There is an old Jewish legend about thirty-six saintly men alive in every generation. To this day I believe that our Afanasyevna — a woman — was a Thirty-Sixer, that rare person of absolute and utter goodness."[47]

Heniek Napadow vaguely recalled that from Bialystok they were deported to Magnitogorsk. "It was deadly cold there. We lived in a gray, dilapidated shack, with many small rooms, a family in each one of them. Older kids would wage wars, with some iron tools. These were Russians, Tatars and Poles. We would also follow trains loaded with coal, pick up small pieces, and bring them home. Snow would cover up our shack completely. There were those small openings on the roof, through which people got out to clean the access to the door."

Heniek couldn't tell me when and how his family ended up in Soviet Kuban, between the Azov and Black Sea. He was there with his mother and father. In the village, where they lived with a cossack family, Heniek's father, a veterinarian, was in charge of cows and horses. "He would go out with a huge herd, perhaps 300 horses and many cows. At some point in time I learned how to ride a horse, and would accompany him. We would clean the horses in the Kuban River, near the village. The horses were kept inside the village, in large corrals, like in the cowboy movies." That part of Heniek's story indeed sounded to me like a western. He told me how, at the age of 6 or 7, he learned to ride horses. "I would climb one of those logs which made up the corral, and put one leg on a horse's back. Then his back would quiver. These were wild horses, untrained. When the horse started jumping, I would grab the log. I would repeat it time and again, until the Russian youngsters taught me how to ride. Spending time with the horses, riding horses, all that felt so good. It was both a sensation of fear and of freedom." Heniek recalled a dangerous and frightening event. "One day I walked to the Kuban River. I was sure I knew how to swim. Usually, people would throw me into the water and I, somehow, managed to stay on the surface. But on that particular occassion I was all alone. I stepped into the river and it pulled me in. I was in the water up to my neck and started gagging. I was terrified, and started beating around furiously with my hands and legs. Finally, somehow, I got out of the water. I never told about it to anybody."

Sometimes Heniek and his father would leave for weeks, for the pastures. This is when he felt closest to his father. "I would sleep near him, we had our own place, just the two of us. Father had a beautiful black horse, "Diavol" — Devil. He was the only person who could ride him. Diavol wouldn't let anybody go near him, except father. He would stand up on his back legs, and it looked as if he was going to tear them to pieces. I never dared to get close to him." Heniek described what seemed as serene and idyllic scenes. "I recall horse races down to the river, where the horses were washed and cleaned. Those of us who made it first would get a prize, some apples. We would then feed the horses and return with them to the village."

Heniek got his earliest sex education in that Kuban Cossack village. "Our neighbors had a daughter. She was, perhaps, 12 or 13. She was always nicely dressed, and urged me time and again to show her my birdie. I told her 'no, you show me first.' And so it went on and on. One day she was standing behind a window, and kept nudging me. Since I was a Jewish smartaleck, I put a finger in my pocket, and pushed it out the fly. And then she pulled up her skirt and showed me her pussy." Heniek also recalled a terrible beating he got from his father. "There was that black dog who would bark at us kids, and bare his teeth. One of the older boys told me to get a needle, break it and stick it into a piece of bread. The dog died a very painful death. Somebody told about it to my father, and he called me in. I was scared, and hid under the bed. He pulled me out and beat me up mercilessly." Still, Heniek summed up his memories of Kuban: "This was a most beautiful and pleasant part of my childhood. I remember those green hills, and the river." One day Heniek's father was called up for service in the Red Army, and disappeared from his life.[48]

In the Soviet South

SHLOMO'S MEMORIES OF THE JOURNEY TO LWOW AND FROM LWOW to Siberia were very scant. What he remembered quite well was life in Uzbekistan. They probably arrived there sometime in the fall of 1941; the triplets, the parents and aunt Itka. "We lived in the town of Andizhan, in a small mud-made hut. We were received quite well by the Uzbeks. They were very friendly. We had a relatively good life there. Father got a job in a 'myasokombinat' — a meat packing plant — and we were never short of meat. My father even used to help other people." Still, it wasn't easy to take care of the triplets, especially for Shlomo's young mother. This must have been the reason why little Salek, Moniek and Hania stayed for a while in a Polish children's home. The Pomerantz triplets returned to their family when the children's home was being evacuated to Teheran, with Anders' Army. "The situation at home wasn't easy. We were lucky that aunt Itka helped out all the time. She was like a second mother." Shlomo recalled daily broadcasts about the advancing Red Army. He was already a boy of 11 at that time. "I listened to the radio announcing the end of the war. People went out into the streets, and they were celebrating. "The Pomerantzs left Andizhan for Poland sometime in the spring of 1946.[49]

Hanka's memories of Uzbekistan were less cheerful. Her family left Siberia sometime in late 1941. "My grandpa, a very wise man, told us that we would be going to warm lands. We started our journey as part of an 'eshelon,' a train transport. Whole families were traveling together. We slept in bunks, one on top of the other. Babies, traveling with their families on the upper bunk, used to wet us at night. In the middle of our train car was a stove. My mother stumbled once and fell on top of it. She completely burned one of her hands. Her crying and sobbing were terrible. I recall myself sitting there and crying." Hanka's mother was taken off the train for treatment, and Hanka wasn't sure that she would return. "I kept crying, terribly, and asked father, 'Daddy, will I ever see Mother again?' I had this fear of abandonment."

Hanka's family arrived in Katta-Kurgan, in southern Uzbekistan, in early 1942. "I recall that after getting off the train, people were sitting and lying around at the local railroad station. Mother wrapped a quilt around me. And then we moved into a room in a primitive clay-house. There were seven or eight people in that room. During summer the heat and the smells were unbearable. People became sick with typhoid and malaria. There were also those huge, yellow scorpions. I was bit once. It hurt and burned terribly. An Uzbek woman healed me with a mixture of scorpion poison. "Sometime later Hanka contracted typhoid and malaria at the same time. "They took me to the hospital. I recall a doctor with one glass eye. He told us that I wouldn't survive. Whenever I talk about it I feel like crying. I was terribly ill then. The nurse told the doctor that my temperature was 42 degrees celcius, and I understood it, since by that time I knew Russian quite well. One day grandpa came, and assured me that I would get better. I was sure that he was lying, to cheer me up. My mother used to come from time to time and bring pomegranate juice. She kept repeating 'drink it, it's rich in iron, it will save you.' And, indeed, somehow I survived."

To make a living, Hanka's father and uncle used to buy all kinds of stolen goods from returning soldiers and resell them on the black market. "The police caught father one day, and he got a terrible beating. Then they took him to prison in nearby Samarkand. We weren't sure we would ever see him again. These weren't normal times. Mother decided that she would travel to Samarkand and see what could be done. And she succeeded in getting him out. I clearly recall his return. I was sitting in the courtyard with some Uzbek kids. My mother stepped into the courtyard with that man. He was thin and emaciated, like a person returning from a camp. He stretched out his hands and called me Khanele, Khanele, come to me. I got very scared, and didn't want to go near him. He looked so terrible."

Hanka also recalled how her father tried to evade mobilization. "The Russians were searching for men, and my father hid somewhere in the Muslim cemetery. Once they came and asked me about my father. They even gave me a piece of chocolate. I repeated time and again '*Ia ne znaiu*' — I don't know.' Actually, I used to bring him food to that cemetery. Mother thought that it would be easier for a child, that nobody would suspect me. I would disappear suddenly, in the middle of a game, and run to the cemetery." Hanka and her family left Uzbekistan for Poland in 1946.[50]

Ada, too, had traumatic memories from the southward journey and from Uzbekistan. "When we reached Fergana a pot of boiling hot soup burned my hand, and as my father was taking care of me, our only small, yellow valise was stolen. Father decided to stay in Fergana in order to find the thief. Mother and I traveled further, to Katta-Kurgan. Three days later he appeared, with the valise." Ada recalled the difficult conditions, particularly the lack of food. "From time to time father would return home with a piece of meat which mother cooked for hours. I could hardly swallow it." The three of them got sick with typhoid. The first one was her father. "He was taken to a hospital, quite far from where we lived. Then mother and I got sick as well, and we were taken to that hospital. Mother told me later that Uzbek women used to bring us food to the hospital. We wouldn't have survived without their help. In the meantime father was released, and returned home. He was still very weak, and there was nobody to take care of him. Then he fell ill with dysentery, and that finished him off." When Ada and her mother were released from the hospital they walked around with shaven heads, weak and hungry. Ada's mother decided to put her in a ZPP children's home. All that happened, as far as Ada could recall, sometime in 1942.

Ada's life changed following her mother's remarriage. Her stepfather, Mr. Gibraltar, an engineer from Zgierz near Lodz, was 12 years older than her mother and suffered from multiple sclerosis. He had arrived in Russia with his wife, who shortly thereafter died of pneumonia. Gibraltar met Ada's mother when Ada was in the children's home. When the children were evacuated to Teheran, Ada returned to her family. She had to get used to her new father. "He dragged one leg as a result of his illness. Otherwise, he was a very cultured and good-looking man. He had studied engineering in Grenoble before the war and spoke French. Still, at least in the beginning, his presence disturbed me." The Gibraltars and their friends led quite an active social life. "They used to meet and play bridge. There were flirtations and love affairs, music, dances, and funerals." Ada attended a Polish school run by the ZPP, and soon became a "star performer." "School children and teachers would meet from time to time in one of the parks. They called it Krasnaya Ploshchad, Red Square. I would recite Russian poems and sing Russian songs."

Since Gibraltar couldn't work in Uzbekistan as an engineer, he became a shoemaker. "He made the best shoes in town. All those Russian women whose husbands were away in the army would come to him and order high-heeled shoes. Mother worked at that time as a mailwoman. Still, we went hungry at times. Mother would walk for kilometers to get us that terrible, watersoaked, purple coloured, inedible cornbread. One day, apparently in 1945, a letter arrived, addressed to my [step]father. It turned out that his two sisters had survived the war, and were living in their prewar family house, in Zgierz. Father decided that if we would return to Poland it would be to Zgierz." The Gibraltars traveled to Poland in the spring of 1946.[51]

Rysiek Lubelsky's family, initially deported to Siberia and released following the Soviet-Polish agreement, settled in Semipalatinsk, in Kazakhstan. Richard's most vivid memory of that part of his life was the separation of his parents. "This must have happened sometime in 1943. My father had someone else, and my parents were, eventually, divorced. It wasn't a friendly or amicable divorce. My mother was sick. She was in the hospital when it all happened. When she left the hospital and found out that my father had someone else, she asked him, 'What am I supposed to do now?' His answer, according to her, was, 'The Irtysh river is not too far away.' My mother was very embittered by father's behavior, and filled me with hatred towards him and his family." Richard also recalled that both his father and his paternal grandfather served as doctors in the Polish Army. "They were both Polish officers, and they wore those square top caps, with one corner pointing towards the front. As army doctors they had certain privileges. My father remarried, right there, in Semipalatinsk, and had a child with his new wife. That child, born in 1944, was my half brother; we shared a father."[52]

The most dramatic and traumatic story from the Soviet South was that of Heniek Napadow. His mother delivered him into a Polish children's home in Bukhara, and the relations between mother and son steadily deteriorated. "I hardly spent any time with her anymore. Most of the children in that children's home were Polish. There were very few Jewish kids there." A lasting and most powerful memory from those times was a sensation of hunger. "I was constantly hungry. We were always on the lookout for food. We would steal vegetables from the fields, which was extremely dangerous. We would climb the roofs of Uzbek houses and steal dried apricots. We would catch turtles, break their shells, boil and eat them. Sometime I even ate grass. I recall an incident when some Uzbeks tried to rob us on our way to school. They chased us with dogs, sticks and axes." There were some pleasant memories, too. "I was a blond, good-looking boy. An Uzbek woman, the wife of the village chairman, used to sit in the inner patio of their house. She would call me and sit me beside her, near her baby. She would then wet her fingers with saliva, and smooth out my hair and my eyebrows. Then she would give me some rice." Heniek recalled making friends with some Jewish boys in the childrens' home. "There was this little boy, Adam Shor, Kajtek, whose mother worked in the children's home, and she would get him some additional food. We were jealous. I was eight at that time and Kajtek was five or six. We became friends, and I defended him. I always defended smaller boys."

Since Heniek's mother lived and worked some 15 kilometers from the children's home, he would run away from time-to-time to visit her, and since he didn't have money to buy a train ticket, he would travel hidden between trainwheels. "Once I reached her place when she was at work. There was a mulberry tree there, in the courtyard. I climbed that tree and started eating berries. Suddenly an adult Uzbek approached me. At first he spoke nicely. Then he caught me from behind and dragged me into a nearby half-ruined house, and raped me. I resisted, of course, but he was much stronger. He almost strangled me. I was close to fainting. I didn't tell my mother about it, and as a matter of fact, I didn't tell it to anybody. For years I was scared to reveal what had happened. I didn't trust people. But I lived with it for years."

Another traumatic moment was when Heniek's mother went into a rage, and nearly killed him. "I came to her hut, and kept asking her for food. She locked the door, grabbed an ax and tried to kill me. She started chasing me around the table. There was murder and madness in her eyes. The door was locked, but I, somehow, managed to break out of it. Since then I never went to see her. There was no contact whatsoever. In time I tried to understand that moment, that terrifying event. It was, perhaps, my constant nagging for food, when she herself didn't have any. She apparently didn't know what to do with me, and she went crazy."[53]

Returning to Poland

BINYAMIN MAJERCZAK AND KAZIK RUTENBERG SURVIVED THE WAR IN THE Soviet Union, and returned to Poland with the Polish Army. Majerczak volunteered in Samarkand for the Kosciuszko Division. He was sent to the Seltsy military base, on the Oka River, south-east of Moscow, where the Division was being organized. First he served as deputy company commander in charge of education and culture, but soon was sent to an officers' course. Majerczak recalled the swearing-in ceremony of the newly established Kosciuszko Division. "This was a very impressive affair. We marched to the tunes of a military band. On the stand were General Berling, Wanda Wasilewska and a few Red Army generals. As I marched in front of my unit, saluted and passed the stand, I thought of my father. I wished he could see me."

The first major battle in which Majerczak fought was the battle of Lenino, in October 1943. "This was just before Yom Kippur. A Jewish sergeant who had served as Rabbi in Lancut, along with some Jewish soldiers, recited 'Kol Nidre' at the front line, not far from the Germans." The Division stayed in the vicinity of Smolensk until early spring 1944, and then advanced westward, towards Poland. It was around that time that Majerczak was sent for training in the Leningrad Pushkin Military Armored Corps Academy, stationed near Rybinsk. This was exactly the area where he had been a prisoner in the Volgostroi labor camps three years earlier. On the way to Rybinsk, he and a few other soldiers from his unit passed liberated Kiev. "This was a beautiful city. We walked along the Kreshchatik Boulevard in our new Polish uniforms, and made an impression. Two local women whose husbands were in the army invited us to sleep over in their two room cellar apartment. We ate and drank. Then my Polish friends went to sleep in one room and I stayed with the two women in the other. I wasn't bored at all that night."

While at the Military Academy, Majerczak fell in love with Nina. "I went one evening to a dancing place in Rybinsk. There were lots of women there. Since there were hardly any men, they danced with each other. Our group of Polish officers made a big impression. I spotted a young, pretty woman sitting in a corner. I introduced myself, and asked her to dance with me. We danced throughout that whole evening. It was love at first sight. Nina Yakovlevna was a nurse in a military hospital. Even now, sixty years later, I'm still moved when I recall that wonderful girl." Their parting, before Majerczak went back to the front, was difficult for both.

Nina, apparently, hoped to see him again. "I didn't return to Nina, of course. I never saw her again."

When Majerczak returned to his company it was stationed in the area of Lublin. He was appointed to head a platoon under a Russian company commander, Major Andrei Ivanovich Rykov. "I admired this man. He was both an excellent teacher and a father figure to me. He used to call me '*synok*' — sonny. Rykov was 45 then and I was 27. Before his mobilization he was a high school principal in a provincial Soviet town." Majerczak's company crossed Poland and reached Poznan, near the prewar Polish-German border. "The local population was thrilled to see Polish tanks and soldiers. There were flowers and kisses. Kids climbed our tanks." In mid-March 1945, Majerczak was on his way to Berlin, and then, to his utter disappointment, his unit was moved back toward the river Nyse, and then fought the Germans in the area of Nisko. In one of the battles, already on German soil, Majerczak's unit suffered heavy losses. Out of 21 tanks, 12 were destroyed. Major Rykov was killed by a direct hit. "This was a tremendous loss to all of us, and to me in particular. All these years I have kept a small photo with his dedication." Majerczak himself was slightly wounded and spent a few days in a field hospital. "The war was over."[54]

Following a short stint in an anti-tank infantry unit of General Berling's army, Kazik Rutenberg was accepted to a Red Army Air Force training school. He had always dreamed of being a pilot. Following a short and intensive course, he became a fighter pilot at age twenty. He flew a Soviet-made YAK-9, named after its planner, Aleksandr Yakovlev. At first his unit did some air photography, but quite soon they took part in air battles over Poland and Germany. He flew missions in the battles of Warsaw and Berlin. Kazik recalled a tragic story concerning another Jewish pilot, Olek, from Kazik's hometown, Sosnowiec. "Somebody notified Olek that his parents had been killed by the Germans. From that day on Olek chased death. He attacked where he was told to and where he wasn't. He was shot down somewhere over the Baltic Sea." When, after the war, Kazik arrived in Sosnowiec, he was told that Olek's family did survive, but that their son was still missing. "It's very difficult for me to speak about it, even today."

When the war ended Kazik was 21 and did not plan a military career. He wanted to study. At that time he was stationed at an air base not far from Warsaw, and his commanding officers advised him not to demobilize. In order to leave the army he first approached a Soviet general in charge of the Polish pilots, who, in turn, referred him to a high-ranking Polish officer in Warsaw. It turned out that this officer was a Jew from Bielsko Biala, whom Kazik had met in a Zionist summer camp before the war. The man intervened, and Kazik was demobilized in the early spring of 1946. Since his mother, who returned in the meantime from Russia, and some of his relatives, lived in Lodz, he decided to settle and study there.[55]

In the Ghettos

A FEW WEEKS AFTER THE ARRIVAL OF THE GERMANS IN VILNA, AHARON'S father was taken for what had been announced as compulsory labor, and he never returned. He had been shot in the Ponar Forest. Since Aharon preserved only a very vague memory of his father, and since no photos of him survived, Aharon doesn't actually know how his father looked. "No pictures of my father or of his side of the family remained. All that branch of our family just disappeared."

Aharon recalled the day on which they moved into the Vilna Ghetto. "We were guarded by German and Lithuanian policemen. It was a very hot day, and still people overdressed. We were allowed to take with us only as much as we could wear and carry. My five-year-old brother carried a pillow. After a while I couldn't carry my bundle anymore, so I just left it in the middle of the street. This was in early September 1941." The first roundup, that of Yom Kippur, was clearly inscribed in Aharon's memory. "People panicked. They were running around like madmen. A truck was parked in the middle of the street. Germans and Lithuanians packed it with women and children. I ran home. Although I was shivering, I held my breath, and tried to be calm. Mother was at work. Then a German and a Lithuanian wanted to take me and my brother, since we didn't have the right papers. We were scared and we started crying. I knew and understood quite well what all this meant. Our aunt begged and cried and gave the Lithuanian some money, and they let us go."

Aharon's memories of the ghetto centered on both fearsome and tragic moments as well as on more normal scenes. "There was a school for a while. I also recall distinctly reading books in Yiddish. I'm about eight years old then, and I devour books." He also recalled having fun and playing games. "We would play war and ghetto. There was a group of kids dressed in rags — these were the Jews. Another group held sticks in their hands: rifles. These were the Germans. At other times we played market. We, the boys, sold and bought cigarettes and candies. The girls traded in bread and rolls. The older boys played policemen and chased us around. There was also a "*lapanke*," a roundup game. My little brother and I would hide, and two other boys would catch us and yell "*verfluchter Jude*."[56]

A number of my interviewees lived in the Lodz Ghetto during the war. Aleksander Klugman was one of them. His most intense memory from the ghetto was hunger. "I could never recall what we actually ate there, but I do recall that whatever it was it was scarce. This was the first time in my life that I had the sensation of hunger. I never imagined that it could be so annoying. One of our biggest daily problems was how to escape that sensation. One way out was to imagine all kinds of food. Another was talking about it."

Aleksander's most cherished memory of those dreary ghetto years was his friendship with Jozek. "He was two years older, but he always treated younger boys as equals. "Jozek's faher was a Communist, and so was his mother. "There were many pictures on their walls. One of them was a portrait of an old Jew with a gray beard. When I asked Jozek whether this was his grandpa, he replied, smiling, 'This is the father of us all.' It was a portrait of Karl Marx." Jozek turned young Aleksander into an admirer of Soviet Russia. "I walked around intoxicated with that idea, and with the hope for a rosy future in that paradise on earth."

The final deportations from Lodz Ghetto started in early summer 1944. "Everything became obvious in a few days. The transports were going to Auschwitz." Among the deported were most of Klugman's immediate family. "Mother perished in Auschwitz, right after her arrival. Hela and Dziunia were sent to the Stutthoff camp. Dziunia died of typhoid in that camp. Hela drowned in the Baltic Sea during an evacuation of camp inmates. This was in April 1945, right before liberation." Aleksander, himself, with a few of his friends from the underground Communist youth organization, were deported in late August 1944. "I saw some of my friends at the Radogoszcz railroad station. We didn't even dare to stare at each other. There was a feeling of helplessness."[57]

Noah Flug was very active in the Communist youth organization in the Lodz Ghetto. He joined it when he was 14; when the ghetto was liquidated, he was18. Ghetto life and the youth organization had in fact become synonymous with his adolescence. For some time he headed the labor committee in one of the largest production shops in the ghetto, and was one of the leaders of the youth organization. "We established the Anti-Fascist Youth Organization, as it was called, when the Soviet Union joined the war against Hitler. Our reasoning went like this: it was only the Russians who could save us. The Western allies kept postponing the Second Front. There was also utter disappointment with the prewar Jewish leadership. Most of them ran away. Moreover, only a Jewish leftist organization had a chance of getting assistance from pro-Communist Poles outside the ghetto in order to fight the Germans. The rightist Polish underground was anti-Semitic."

Among Flug's closest friends in the Communist youth organization in the Lodz Ghetto were Dawid Sierakowiak, Lucjan Dobroszycki and Aleksander Klugman. Sierakowiak didn't survive. His ghetto diary would become in time one of the most significant intimate personal documents of the Holocaust. Dobroszycki would become a historian after the war, and the most eminent student of the Lodz Ghetto. "At its peak," according to Flug, "the Communist organization in the Lodz Ghetto numbered some 1,500 members, out of which close to 1,000 were youngsters. Only about 100 of them survived."

Flug spoke of three principal activities in which the Communist youth organization was involved. "We struggled for an improvement in labor conditions, for higher payments and for better food. There were strikes and sit-ins. We did some sabotage in our places of work, like working slowly and turning out low quality products. We also held all kinds of cultural and educational activities. We disseminated information concerning the situation at the fronts. There was another effort to organize armed resistance, but it didn't materialize. We dreamed of capturing Nazi criminals when the front would get closer, and delivering them to the Russians." Flug was very disappointed that so little had been written about the Communist youth organization in the Lodz Ghetto.[58]

The Hashomer Hatzair youth movement in the Lodz Ghetto remained the most meaningful and cheerful part of Fayvl's wartime memories. Before the ghetto was sealed off, and in spite of the German occupation, the youngsters of Hashomer Hatzair led a very dynamic social life. "My group consisted of ten youngsters. We used to meet very often. These encounters made our life easier. There were moments, and even hours, when we completely forgot the outside world. We would talk, sing and dance. We would reminisce about our last summer camp in the mountains. We also used to sleep over at one of our friends' apartments. Those nights remain deeply imprinted in my memory." Once inside the ghetto, life became more bleak and the get-togethers more difficult. But then, when the Marysin agricultural youth colony was established, an exciting social life was resumed.

According to Fayvl, "Marysin was a state within a state. It was a 'youth island.' Life was different there." A kind of commune was established by Hashomer Hatzair in Marysin. "This was a good and healthy life, in spite of the barbed wires. We would work the land, sow and plant. During meals we would sit around the tables and sing. In the evenings there were lectures, readings and discussions. All that made us forget atrocities which we had witnessed just a few days earlier." The Marysin respite came to an end in early 1941. "It was very difficult now to get used to family life again. We missed our friends, our commune. The realities we had to face back home were extremely tragic." Still, they didn't give up and continued meeting in small, cold rooms. "We would start wih a 'hora' to warm up. And in the middle of a discussion, we would get up and run along the walls, to keep from freezing." In spite of the cold and the hunger, Hashomer Hatzair meetings and activities continued. They even were able to celebrate Bialik's and Herzl's birthdays in the summer of 1943, and the Jewish New Year in the early fall of that year. The Hashomer Hatzair continued functioning in the Lodz Ghetto until the last deportations.[59]

Dziunia Dublin, a few years younger than Fayvl, remembered him quite well from the Ghetto and from Marysin. He was her counselor. "He saved us, and made us believe in the future. He was very significant in my and in my girlfriends' lives. He told us that the youth organization would be our response and resistance to Hitler, so that we could live like human beings." Eventually, though, Dziunia switched from Hashomer Hatzair to the Communist Anti-Fascist Youth Organization. Roza, an older girl whom she adored, convinced her that Communism was a more proper ideology than Zionism. "I got all excited about the October Revolution and about Stalin. I also read about the French Revolution and kept writing its slogans with a stick in the snow. We would meet in groups of five, sing revolutionary songs and talk about the Revolution, which would solve the Jewish problem much better than Zionism."[60]

In the Camps

ALEKS KLUGMAN ARRIVED AT THE AUSCHWITZ RAMP IN A TIGHTLY PACKED freight train which had left Radogoszcz two days earlier. His was one of the last deportation trains from Lodz. None of his deported friends were around. "I felt lost. Completely. The boys who were with me when we started out had disappeared. The camp was huge, and I didn't know how to look for them." Luckily, he found some of them in a day or two. A Soviet prisoner, a former Red Army General, advised them to get out of Auschwitz if they could. Pretending to be electricians, they were moved to another camp inside Germany. Their job there was to dig holes for electricity poles.

It is in that camp that Klugman encountered his "good German." Jurek, one of Klugman's friends, brought a huge loaf of bread one day. "The boys stared at that loaf of bread like hypnotized. Some of them touched it to make sure that they were not dreaming. And then Jurek told us how he got it. While walking around the kitchen and looking for food, as usual, Jurek was told to unload a truckful of carrots. He stuck a few into his pocket. When the SS man in charge noticed it, Jurek, of course, expected the worst. Instead, the SS man asked him whether he was hungry. He told Jurek to wait and returned with that big loaf of bread. Since then the man, whom we nicknamed Hans, used to bring us all kinds of food. The rumor about the 'good German' spread around the camp, and since we were worried about that, we tried to convince him that he should hit us from time to time, in order not to raise any suspicions among his colleagues and superiors. He refused. Hans also brought Jurek German newspapers so that we would learn about the approaching front. He also repeated all kinds of rumors circulating among the guards. Hans was less and less cautious. The catastrophe occurred earlier than we expected. One of the SS men denounced him, and we never saw him again."

Klugman and some of his friends were in the Flossenburg camp in Germany in the early spring of 1945. The cannon barrage at the front became louder by the day, and the camp guards started pouring kerosene on the buildings. Aleks and his friends decided to run away. They hid in a nearby forest and shortly afterward were liberated by the Americans. Klugman was sure that his surviving relatives would return to Lodz, and he decided to get there as soon as he could. "I became part of an immense human wave rolling over German soil. The weather was beautiful. All the highways, even side roads, were filled by multinational crowds. The French, the Dutch and the Belgians marched from East to West. Poles, Czechs and Russians moved from West to East."

On his way to Lodz, Klugman nearly got imprisoned again. He wore a used German army uniform when he reached Jelenia Gora, and looked suspicious to some Red Army soldiers. He told the investigating NKVD officer that he was Jewish and had been a member of a Communist youth group in the Lodz Ghetto. He even tried to use circumcision as an argument, to no avail. Then another Soviet officer, a Jew who knew some Yiddish, came to his rescue. First, he demanded that Klugman respond to him in Yiddish, and then asked him whether he could recite the Shma Israel prayer. Klugman learned once again how human fate could change in seconds. He arrived in Lodz in July 1945.[61]

Noah Flug was deported to Auschwitz on the last train from Radogoszcz, on August 30, 1944. Luckily, he stayed there only a few weeks, and was moved to the Gross-Rosen camp in Lower Silesia. From there he and other inmates were force-marched, in the winter of 1945, to the Ebensee camp within the Mauthausen camp complex, at the foot of the Austrian Alps. "This was a huge camp. There were close to 20,000 prisoners there, among them some 2,000 Jews. There were five of us from the Communist youth organization in the Lodz Ghetto. We helped each other as much as we could. At one point, when I was completely emaciated and my weight went down to 30 kilograms, I was thrown in with the corpses. My friends came at night, looked for me, and hoisted me out of that heap of bodies. I was in the Jewish block most of the time and at work we met some Polish prisoners from Lodz, Communists. We became friendly, and they told us that the Germans intended to lock us up in one of the camp's underground tunnels and blow it up. Just before the morning roll call our Polish friends brought five corpses into the Jewish block, and smuggled the five of us into their block. They saved our lives."

The first units of the US Army reached Ebensee on May 6. "On that day, after the SS left the camp, and even before the Americans arrived, we caught all those Kapos and murderers, and there was a field court, organized by the international prisoners' underground. Fifty-two people were executed. Among them were two Jews." Flug told me that throughout all that terrible time in the camps he and his friends from the Lodz Ghetto kept promising each other "if we survive, we shall meet in Lodz after the war." Flug, dressed in an ex-German airman's uniform, arrived in the Lodz Fabryczna railroad station in the early summer of 1945.[62]

Dziunia and her mother arrived in Auschwitz in late August 1944. She recalled the moment of their parting. "Mengele looked at my mother, and his finger pointed to the left. I wanted to yell 'Mama,' but no sound came out. I wanted to run to her, but my legs froze. That was the last time I saw my mother." In November Dziunia was sent to an airplane parts factory in the Halbstadt labor camp, in Sudetenland. She worked with a few girls there from the Anti-Fascist Youth organization in the Lodz Ghetto. They stayed together as much as they could. Dziunia remembered the constant sensation of hunger. "We used to share whatever we had to eat. We put a cup in the middle, and those who managed to get a potato deposited it there, and then we shared it among us."

After a while Dziunia got very sick with rickets and stayed in the hospital barracks for three months. She was still there when the camp was liberated by the Russians, in early May 1945. "A Russian officer arrived on a motorcycle. He entered the hospital barracks and told us 'girls, you are free now.' He spoke Yiddish." He also advised them to always tell Russian soldiers that they were sick with tuberculosis, to prevent molestation and rape. "Next day they took us to a hospital where we stayed for a few weeks." Though not fully recuperated, Dziunia and the other girls from Lodz decided that they would start their journey back to Poland.

Dziunia knew that her mother had been gassed, but she was sure that her father survived in Russia. "Sewek, a Jewish boy from Lodz, brought me a coat and shoes, and I ran away from the hospital. We traveled mostly in coal trains, and there were all kinds of adventures. At the first stop mice ate my bread." At one point she unknowingly traveled with a group of young hoodlums and thieves, but managed to escape. Then, she trusted a Russian soldier, a stranger, who promised to help her, and hid her under his coat. She was lucky that a Jewish officer came by, and told the soldier to get his hands off her. Some of the Lodz girls, who had decided that they would travel to Soviet Lwow where they would study and enjoy life in the Communist paradise, convinced Dziunia to join them. On one of the trains Dziunia met a group of Polish nuns, who after listening to her story advised her to return to Lodz where she would be most likely reunited with her father. "I traveled with those nuns to Czestochowa, and then proceeded to Lodz." Dziunia arrived in Lodz in August 1945. [63]

On the Aryan Side

NATAN GROSS, ALA MARGOLIS-EDELMAN AND HENRYK GRYNBERG survived at least part of the Nazi occupation on the "Aryan side." Natan, after a failed attempt to join his father and older brother in the Soviet-annexed territories, returned to Krakow. The spacious Gross apartment in the city center had been requisitioned by the Germans, and they moved to the suburb of Czyzyny. Then, they were forced to move to other places in the vicinity of Krakow, where they lived for more than a year. Finally, in September 1942, they had to settle in the Krakow Ghetto. They were four at the time: Natan, Natan's mother, his older sister Klara and his younger brother Jerzyk. They already knew when they entered the ghetto that in order to survive they would have to get out and live on the 'Aryan side.' Sometime in the winter of 1942/43, they took off their armbands and dragged themselves through the snow-covered city. "During the next four months, with the assistance of our Polish friends, we moved from house to house. All in all, we changed locations fourteen times. This happened in a city where lots of people knew us, and could denounce us to the Germans. We couldn't stay in Krakow anymore. We decided to move to Warsaw, where we had some relatives."

The Grosses arrived in Warsaw in early April 1943. Soon Natan witnessed the Warsaw Ghetto uprising. "I saw a German motorized gun on Krasinski Square, firing at the ghetto. A day or two passed, and rumors about the ghetto uprising assumed enormous proportions. Some Poles praised the courage of the ghetto fighters." At the same time, however, Natan witnessed also complete indifference. "It was Easter. Krasinski Square was overcrowded. People were celebrating and having fun. There was a lot of music. Adults and children went up and down swings and merry-go-rounds while the nearby ghetto went up in flames. I saw all of it, and my heart bled."

Although in Warsaw, like in Krakow, they had to change places, they felt more confident. "This was a big city and we were complete strangers. Still, there was the danger of blackmail." The four Grosses lived mostly in different locations. "I do not recall a time during our stay in Warsaw when we didn't look for a place for one of us, at least. We were constantly on the lookout for rooms and apartments." In spite of the dangers involved, Natan, whenever he could, would welcome other Jews to share his place of residence. "Acquaintances as well as strangers used to stay overnight. This was our manner of resistance. We decided that our door would always be open. I even wrote my friends in Krakow that they should give our address to people who had decided to come to Warsaw."

Besides the dangerous moments and the continuing struggle for survival, there were also more "normal" ways of spending time. Much of it was devoted to reading and writing. "Poetry, that of Lesmian in particular, saved me in a way. This might have been pure escapism from reality into a world of fantasy and beauty." Playing bridge was another way to make time pass and evade fear and worries. There were also endless conversations and arguments." Once, Natan and some of his Jewish friends even dared to go to a theater performance. Natan associated with Jews living on "Aryan papers," as well as with Poles. For some time he even distributed illegal newspapers for the Polish underground.

Natan left Warsaw in August 1944, a day before the outbreak of the Polish Uprising, to join his younger brother Jerzyk in Otwock. Their mother was apprehended by the Germans after the suppression of the Uprising, and deported to Auschwitz. Natan could never forgive himself for leaving his mother in Warsaw. "I saved myself, while mother went through the hell of the Uprising, the Pruszkow camp and Auschwitz." Luckily, she survived. Otwock, south-east of Warsaw, was liberated by the Russians within days. "When I saw the first Russian soldier, I ran towards him and greeted him in Russian. I had prepared myself for this moment for a long time. I had studied Russian, and read Pushkin and Lermontov. When I told him, in Russian, that I was Jewish, he wasn't excited at all, and asked me rather suspiciously, how come I survived. This soldier's response was like a stab in my heart."

Natan stayed in Otwock until January 1945, when the Russians finally liberated Warsaw. "I went to Warsaw just a few days after its liberation. It looked like one huge heap of rubble. I walked around in this ghost city, hardly recognizing the streets. Then, after the liberation of Krakow, I returned to my hometown. It was nice and clean, but, somehow, sad and boring. It was Krakow without Jews. I started working at the Jewish Historical Commission, recording survivors' testimonies, as well as my own wartime memoirs. I resumed contact with my 'Aryan' friends, who had known me under my assumed Polish identity, and I revealed my true identity to them. It turned out that they had suspected all along that I was Jewish, but never told me about it. Their noble behavior restored my trust in men."[64]

Ala Margolis, a teenager at the time, lived in the Warsaw Ghetto on 6 Gesia Street. "This was a crowded, small apartment. Besides my mother and me, there were Marek Edelman, Velvl Rozowski and his wife Ryfka, who was also known as Stasia, and Dr. Adina Szwajger. I was the youngest. I didn't know then that Velvl and Marek were members of ZOB, the Jewish Fighters' Organization. Once, it was January 1943, after some shooting during a roundup I saw Marek and Velvl cleaning their guns. I figured out what had happened."

Ala was moved out of the ghetto sometime in April 1943, before the ghetto uprising. "My mother had many friends on the Aryan side. Mama's friends put me up with a family of architects in Ursynow. They were told that my name was Alicja Zacharczyk and that I was the daughter of a Polish officer who had been sent to a POW camp. They treated me like a daughter." Ala vividly recalled an incident that almost ended tragically. She and her good friend Zosia, also on Aryan papers, were approached by two Polish policemen. "We were marched along Swietokrzyska, straight to the police station. I felt like a rabbit caught in a trap." Ala gave a ring to the girl who was scrubbing the floor at the police station, and begged her to find a Polish friend of the family. The policemen let her go, and luckily, she found him. "He was on time, and paid 10,000 zlotys for us. When we ran to the streetcar the girl caught up with us. She was almost out of breath, and in her outstretched hand she held the ring. She handed it to me and ran away."

Ala stayed with the Polish family until the end of the Uprising. She was then moved out of town to nearby Grodzisk, where she lived in the same house with Marek Edelman and Antek Zuckerman. "Marek was a Bundist and Antek a Zionist. Still, they were great friends. "Ala's mother, after leaving the ghetto, lived also on the Aryan side. She was disguised as a nurse, and worked for Stefania Sepolowska, a known Polish writer and social activist. After the Polish Uprising Ala's mother was interned in Pruszkow, near Warsaw, and returned to Lodz after its liberation in January 1945. Ala joined her.[65]

Henryk's father arranged for "Aryan documents" for his wife and son, but did not want to join them. This was apparently in March 1943. "He said he could not go to Warsaw. He would not be able to pretend that he was somebody else." The moment of parting remained inscribed in Henryk's memory for decades. "He was unshaven, almost completely black. His trousers were partly unbuttoned, and a piece of his underwear was sticking out. When we started to walk away, he called, 'Well, won't you say goodbye to me, Son?' I turned back, took leave of him, and never saw him again."

When little Henryk arrived in Warsaw after long months of hiding in and around his village, everything was different. "Uncle Aron took me to a small cafe, and ordered me cocoa and a crescent roll, for these things still existed. We went out into beautiful, paved streets, filled with the clanging of tram bells." Henryk was taught Polish prayers and how to cross himself. Around Easter time, Henryk's mother took him from Praga, where they were living, to the other side of the Vistula, seemingly to go to church. Instead, however, she showed him an enormous fire. "The fire had been burning for several days now, and smoke could be seen even from the Praga side of the river, but Mother wanted me to see it from nearby. 'Look at it closely,' she said. And remember, that's where our aunts and uncles and your small cousins lived. You wouldn't have liked to be there, would you? So, remember once again, no one must know that you're a Jew, ever!'"

One day, walking in front of his mother, so that if one of them would be identified as a Jew, the other could escape, Henryk got lost in the crowd. "I called 'Mama' and started running in circles because I didn't know where to go. I ran in all directions and started to cry. Then I noticed people stopping and staring at me, so I stopped crying." A man asked him whether he remembered his address, but Henryk, even if he did remember it, wouldn't tell him. Instead, he asked the man to lead him to a familiar marketplace, and that's how he got back to his mother. For some reason they had to leave that place, and had nowhere to stay. "A warm May rain was drizzling. We rode in a tram — first one, than another. We had nowhere to go, so we rode back and forth. Finally, we got out near the bridge, and Mother said that we would have to go to the Vistula, because there was no other solution left. But I didn't want to go to the Vistula. I was frightened. I begged her to go for just one more ride on the tram." In the end somebody hid them for a short while, and then they left Warsaw. They moved to a village in Podlasie, a rural area north-east of the city, and stayed there until the liberation. They lived that entire time under assumed, Polish identities. Henryk started to believe he had actually become a Christian. He kept repeating, "I don't want to be a Jew anymore." The Red Army arrived in their village sometime in the summer of 1944. Then they went back to Dobre and stayed there for a while, but life wasn't secure, especially for Jews. Some of the very few local survivors decided to settle in Lodz, and Henryk, with his mother, followed them. They arrived in Lodz in the spring of 1945.[66]

6

THE ZIONISTS

ZIONIST ACTIVITIES IN THE LIBERATED REGIONS OF POLAND BEGAN AS early as the end of 1944. Most of the surviving leaders of prewar Zionist parties and youth movements arrived in Lublin in late 1944 and early 1945. Among them were Dr. Emil Sommerstein of the General Zionists, Dr. Adolf Berman of the Poalei Zion-Left, Rabbi David Kahane of Mizrachi, Abba Kovner of Hashomer Hatzair and Antek Zuckerman of Dror. Various Zionist ideologies and stands were voiced and discussed. All agreed that postwar Zionist activities in Poland should focus on emigration to Palestine. There were, however, varying opinions on organizational and structural matters.

Zuckerman maintained that a unified Zionist structure was needed in the wake of the Holocaust. He also strongly urged the merger of the Dror and Hashomer Hatzair youth movements. In a letter written shortly after the end of the war, Zuckerman expressed his preference for a united Socialist-Zionist movement: "We are all very worried about the schism in Eretz Israel and want to see a united Socialist force." The letter spoke of "the unification of the Labor Movement." The first efforts to establish a joint Dror/Hashomer Hatzair youth movement took place in Warsaw, in a deserted building at 38 Poznanski Street, in February 1945, a few weeks after the city's liberation. Then, in March, Zuckerman settled a group of young Jewish survivors from Czestochowa in that building. This was actually the first Zionist collective in postwar Poland. A second such collective was founded by Dror and Hashomer Hatzair in Lodz in April 1945. These collectives served as early models for the numerous Zionist collectives, the kibbutzim, that would be organized in Poland in the following years. The first Zionist seminar, in postwar Poland, a sort of teach-in, took place in Lodz in the summer of 1945. The attempt to merge Dror with Hashomer Hatzair was short-lived. Meir Yaari and Yaakov Chazan, the two powerful leaders of Hashomer Hatzair in Palestine, were unequivocal in their opposition. Thus, instead of fostering a common and unified effort by two powerful youth movements in post-Holocaust Poland, they started competing for potential members among the survivors and the returnees from the Soviet Union.[1]

The Zionists in postwar Poland, despite ideological differences and fierce competition, had one goal in common: to gain popularity with the Jewish masses and to affect their decisions in respect to the future. There was a tendency among Polish Jews, both those returning to their prewar locales and those settling in other towns and cities, to try to rebuild their lives in Poland. In time, however, economic difficulties and widespread anti-Semitism convinced the majority that they needed to look elsewhere for a solution. The Zionists, with their ever-widening organizational structures, their financial resources, and the semi-legal approval of the Polish authorities for the crossing of borders, gained massive support. It was not so much pure ideology as the specific confluence of Zionist aims and the practical interests of the Jewish population that made the Zionists more attractive and influential than the Jewish Communists, who were opposed to emigration. The ever-growing infrastructure of Zionist collectives, schools and children's homes was far superior to the alternatives offered by the Communist-run Jewish committees. Jewish returnees from the Soviet Union, most of whom arrived in Poland in 1946, when anti-Semitism was at its peak, were particularly likely to accept Zionist assistance.[2]

Zionist organizations and youth movements were highly effective in their attempts to influence young survivors and returnees. Sara Zyskind, a survivor of the camps who returned to her native Lodz after liberation, recalled how she and her traumatized, depressed roommates were approached by a woman who somehow got their address and urged them to leave Poland. The woman, apparently a Zionist activist, told the young women that they should "cross out their past, leave this place, and begin a new life" in Eretz Israel. Zionist activists used their influence with Jewish youth to reach their families and convince them to emigrate to Palestine/Israel. The Zionists remained in close proximity to the Jewish committees and other non-Zionist Jewish institutions. A Lodz survivor recalled that "it sufficed to step into a Jewish restaurant or to move around the Jewish Committee in order to find a way to the Zionists."[3]

In spite of the efforts for unification of so prominent a figure as Antek Zuckerman, the Zionist movement in postwar Poland, though a tiny fraction of its prewar size, was marked by divisiveness and fragmentation. There was constant competition among the collectives and youth organizations. People representing various collectives and youth movements were sent to the destination sites of returnee transport trains, and sometimes as far as the Soviet-Polish border, to "recruit" new arrivals. Zuckerman wrote in his memoirs: "Our people would stand at the railroad stations and, when they saw young people coming, would take them along. That was very important for the young people who arrived, since they immediately had a house, a bed, and food. In Lodz you found apartments, organized groups, clubs. You could come in, get warm, have a drink." The person in charge of a Hashomer Hatzair collective in Krakow complained in a letter to his superiors in Lodz that "there is wild and ugly competition among the kibbutzim." Zionist "recruitment" tactics among returnees from Russia had an impressive effect on the number and size of the kibbutzim. Whereas in early April 1946 Dror collectives throughout Poland could boast of only one thousand members, by late June membership reached 4,000. There were close to three thousand people in the collectives of Hashomer Hatzair at that time, and the total number of members in all Zionist collectives in Poland reached 15,000.[4]

At the core of the Zionist movement in postwar Poland were the collectives, the kibbutzim. They were modeled on the prewar *kibbutzei hachshara* — training collectives of young Zionists who groomed themselves for aliya, settlement and communal life in Palestine. There was, however, a basic difference between the prewar *hachsharot* and the postwar kibbutzim. Whereas before the war, the members of the training collectives went through a gradual process of learning and preparation, the postwar situation forced the kibbutzim to deal primarily in matters of daily life and border crossing. There was also a severe lack of trained personnel. People acquired necessary skills on the run. Instructors and youth leaders in the various Zionist movements were either people who had some prewar Zionist experience or those who had joined the movements shortly after liberation. As far as wartime fates were concerned, there were those Zionists who survived under German occupation and those who returned from the Soviet Union. It seems that the leading figures of the Zionist organizations were people who had been active in Jewish resistance in Nazi-occupied Poland and ex-partisans, such as Antek Zuckerman, Zivia Lubetkin and Abba Kovner. Zuckerman recalled in his memoirs the formative period of the postwar kibbutzim. "We brought all those who knocked at our gates into the Movement and we built collectives. We called every collective, which in fact was nothing but a soup kitchen, a kibbutz; but in that framework, people preserved a sense of self-respect."[5]

Why did young people join those postwar *kibbutzei aliya* — immigration kibbutzim — by the thousands? Their motivation was both practical and psychological. A Zionist collective offered not only a roof, a bed and a meal. It was a substitute for lost families and friends and gave a new meaning and purpose to life. A young man who lost his whole family in the Holocaust and joined a Hashomer Hatzair collective wrote in the collective's broadsheet "Why did I join the kibbutz? I became aware of the fact that my life is worthless. I'm alone, without a family, homeless. The kibbutz impressed me from the first day. I looked at those happy young faces. They were singing and dancing. I envied them. Their enthusiasm seized me. I was no longer helpless and estranged." Even youngsters who had families joined Zionist collectives. A fifteen-year old girl who lived with her family in Lodz joined a local kibbutz almost by chance. "While walking we encountered Jewish youngsters dancing the Hora near one of the houses. It turned out that a kibbutz was being established there. I got all excited. I returned home and told them, 'I'm joining the kibbutz.' They said, 'No!' Still, I joined."[6]

By one estimate, close to two hundred Zionist collectives formed in Poland between 1945 and 1946. Forty-three kibbutzim of the Dror Borokhov Youth Movement alone, with 4,000 members, were established during the first six months following liberation. Close to 11,000 members lived in various collectives in mid-1946.[7] The most effective ideological and cultural work was conducted by the various Zionist youth movements in a series of seminars. These seminars would be held either in Poland or in Germany, and were led mostly by emissaries from Palestine. Seven seminars were conducted by Hashomer Hatzair between November 1945 and October 1946. One of the most outstanding and influential emissaries who arrived from Palestine in 1947 to head an international Dror seminar in Indersdorf, Bavaria, was Yitshak Tabenkin, the charismatic leader of Hakibbutz Hameuhad in Palestine. This and similar seminars organized by the various youth movements shaped the young postwar Zionist leadership.[8]

Lodz was the most significant Zionist center in postwar Poland. The leading Zionist institutions were established in Lodz in the first months after liberation, and numerous Zionist seminars and conferences were held there in the immediate postwar years. Antek Zuckerman wrote in mid-1945: "Lodz became a Movement center as well as a Jewish center, since Warsaw was devastated, and there weren't any intact houses there. In Lodz, however, the houses remained standing. There was no problem forming one or twenty kibbutzim there, as long as there were young people. You could do anything in Lodz." Shalom Cholawski, a Hashomer Hatzair man and ex-partisan from Belorussia who arrived in Lodz in the summer of 1945, recalled that several Zionist youth movements, such as Dror, Hashomer Hatzair, Gordonia, and Hanoar Hatzioni were already active there at the time. In Lodz he met Zuckerman, who convinced him to establish a center for Jewish ex-partisans and demobilized Jewish soldiers. The center opened on 3 Srodmiejska Street, and soon became very popular. The purpose was to prepare its members for emigration to Palestine/Israel.

Hehalutz (Pioneer), an umbrella group of several Zionist-Socialist youth movements, which mainly dealt in matters of education and culture, was formally launched in November 1945 in Warsaw, but actually functioned in subsequent years in Lodz. The Hehalutz supported and coordinated Zionist Hebrew schools throughout Poland.[9]

The most impressive Zionist public event in postwar Lodz was a mass demonstration on the occasion of a visit by the Anglo-American Committee. The Anglo-American Committee of Enquiry Regarding the Problems of European Jews and Palestine had been appointed in November 1945, and some of its members arrived on a fact-finding mission to Poland in early February 1946. The Central Committee of Polish Jews discussed a CCPJ memorandum to be presented to the Anglo-American Committee; however, the Bund and the Communists opposed the inclusion of a Zionist-backed demand for a Jewish State in Palestine. The final version spoke of the need to revoke the British White Paper so as to enable free Jewish immigration and independent Jewish existence in Palestine. Members of the Anglo-American Committee arrived in Lodz on February 9th and lodged at the Grand Hotel. A mass meeting of Lodz Jews was convened in the Wlokniarz Cinema Hall on February 10th. Those who could not get inside the hall filled the nearby Zawadska Street. The meeting was chaired by Jewish Committee Chairman Michal Mirski, who read out to the public the text of the memorandum. Against the wishes of Mirski, a demonstration formed outside and the crowd began to march. It turned out, however, that the guests were not in the hotel. In late afternoon of the same day representatives of demobilized Jewish soldiers met at the Lodz Jewish Committee, and decided to urge all demobilized Jewish soldiers in Lodz to take part in a demonstration planned for the next day. According to a Public Security Office report, some 14,000 people marched on February 11th along Piotrkowska Street to the Grand Hotel. Among them were close to 1,000 demobilized soldiers in uniform. The Jewish Press Agency reported that "numerous banners in Polish, English, Yiddish and Hebrew were carried by the marchers. Piotrkowska Street was blocked completely. All traffic stopped." The members of the Anglo-American Committee appeared on a hotel balcony and greeted the crowds. According to the Jewish Press Agency "Later on the Anglo-American Committee hosted a delegation of the Lodz Jewish Committee headed by Mirski. Mirski declared that the Lodz Jewish Committee supports the general Jewish stands, as expressed in the CCPJ memorandum. Members of the Anglo-American Committee inquired about the situation of Jews in Lodz and about anti-Semitism."[10]

An emissary of the Haganah to Poland recalled the pro-Zionist mood in the days preceding the proclamation of the State of Israel. "The Poland-Israel Friendship Association convened a mass meeting in Warsaw, in the huge Roma Hall. It was attended by government ministers, party leaders and public figures."

Zionist sentiments in Lodz were manifest in public on the occasion of the UN decision in November 1947, and the proclamation of Israel in May 1948. A festive celebration following the UN decision was convened by the Lodz Jewish Committee at the Polish Army Theater in early December 1947. The Lodz Jewish Committee convened another mass meeting of the various Jewish parties and organizations on May 20, 1948. It was chaired by Mirski, and featured speakers such as the Mayor of Lodz, Eugeniusz Stawinski and representatives of the PPR and the PPS. At its close, both the Polish national anthem and the Zionist Hatikva were sung. Mirski, the number one Jewish Communist in postwar Lodz, joined the crowd. Years later, he recalled that "certain Communists and Bundists were shocked by the singing of Hatikva. I hadn't been a Zionist then and I'm not one today. I did, however, grasp that Hatikva was no longer a political Zionist song; it had become the national and official anthem of a state."[11]

Both "Brichah," the Zionist Flight and Rescue organization in postwar Europe, and the "Haganah," the major Zionist military underground in Palestine, were active in Lodz. According to a Polish Security Office report, Brichah activities, including preparation of false Polish passports, were being carried out in Lodz as early as the fall of 1945. Throughout 1946, the year of the greatest flight of Polish Jews, Lodz served as the overall center for Brichah in Poland. Meetings and consultations of its leading activists were held there. By that time, the core leadership of the organization consisted of emissaries from Palestine. Zvi Melnitzer, known by his pseudonym Alexander, was the dominant Brichah operative. He had been a student of Zuckerman before the war. Alexander, of the Hakibbutz Hameuchad movement in Palestine, with which the Dror youth organization in Poland was affiliated, was a Polish Jew with Aryan looks who spoke excellent Polish. He survived the war in Russia, reached Palestine, and returned to Poland as an emissary. This made him attractive and acceptable to all. Alexander met with various Polish officials, mainly of the UB, the Polish Security Office. When Israel Galili, head of the National Command of the Haganah, and Yigal Alon, Head of the Palmach, came on a fact-finding mission to Poland in early 1947, Alexander was their host and guardian. Zuckerman recalled Alexander as the "boss of the borders," and the most successful Brichah emissary in Poland. The organizational skills of the Brichah people, and their success in escorting tens of thousands of Jews past Poland's borders, increased the popularity of Zionism.[12]

The most eminent emissary of the Haganah to Poland was the Polish-born Yitshak Palgi (Ignac Polakiewicz) a member of Ein Shemer, a Hashomer Hatzair kibbutz in Palestine. He arrived in Poland in November 1947. Officially, he was an educator and youth leader for Hashomer Hatzair. His real function was to organize and train people, first for the illegal Haganah, and later for the newly formed Israeli army. He divided his time between the Lodz branch of Hashomer Hatzair and a military training camp in Bolkow, in Lower Silesia. Mobilization centers for the Haganah were set up in various Polish cities. The Lodz mobilization center opened officially in June 1948, with representatives from Hashomer Hatzair, Poalei Zion, Ichud and the Bund. More than 550 volunteers were registered by the Lodz Committee in the summer of 1948. Of these, nearly half were affiliated with Hashomer Hatzair and Poalei Zion; there were also a few members of the Bund and the PPR. Palgi recalled that the Haganah office, located at the Hashomer Hatzair headquarters in Lodz, eventually became the main mobilization center for the Haganah in Poland. The first group of Bolkow trainees included about thirty people from various youth movements. All in all, some 1,500 people were trained there and dispatched to Palestine/Israel over the course of 1948. Among them were former partisans, demobilized soldiers and university students. The total number of Jewish volunteers from Poland for the Haganah and the Israeli Army is estimated to have reached 7,000.[13]

Among the most active Zionist youth organizations in Lodz were Dror, Hashomer Hatzair and Gordonia. Dror was affiliated with the Poalei Zion-Left Party and was located on 18 and 20 Poludniowa Street. It ran several kibbutzim and a youth organization. The first postwar Dror collective in Poland was established in Lodz, in October, 1945. Bela Elster — Rotenberg, whose wartime underground pseudonym was Wanda, recalled: "We decided to turn our group of people, whom we referred to jokingly as 'the kolkhoz,' into a nucleus of a *kibbutz hachshara*. We rented a spacious apartment on 25 Narutowicza Street. Our first steps were quite difficult. Nobody knew how a kibbutz functions." Within a short period of time, however, the kibbutz already had some ninety members. They were mostly aged 17 to 25, but there were also some older adults, including a few writers, composers and painters. A children's collective with some sixty youngsters was established as well. These two collectives soon became models for Dror collectives all over Poland. The Lodz collectives also served as a meeting point for personnel and youth leaders arriving from other cities. A Dror seminar, with the participation of sixty-one youth leaders and activists, convened in Lodz in May 1946. The lecturers included emissaries from Palestine. They discussed the situation of the Jewish Yishuv, Zionism, the Workers' Movement, and the Kibbutz Movement in Palestine. There were also presentations and discussions on the Holocaust by Dr. Adolf Berman, head of the Poalei Zion–Left, Bela Elster and the historians Ber Mark and Nachman Blumenthal. Moshe Grosman, a Polish-Jewish writer who had returned from Russia, spoke about Jewish literature. Dorka Sternberg, a young instructor at a Dror kibbutz on Wolczanska Street, recalled working day and night with Jewish youngsters and the enormous enthusiasm among her fellow instructors. "The skies were the limit. This must have been our reaction to things we went through. Everything was future-oriented. We hardly thought about our tragic past."[14]

The "Hanhaga Harashit," the Headquarters of Hashomer Hatzair in postwar Poland, was located in Lodz on Narutowicza Street. All Hashomer Hatzair activities throughout the country were coordinated there. According to reports sent to the Headquarters, Hashomer Hatzair membership fluctuated between 700 and 2,000 in the course of 1946. The turnover of the Jewish population in Poland in 1946 was at its highest, since this was the peak year of Jewish repatriation from Russia and emigration in the wake of the Kielce pogrom. An education department was established in early 1947. Its members included Mishka Lewin and Moshe Shmutter, both originally from Vilna, who had just returned from the Soviet Union. The department was in charge of organizing training courses for youth leaders. An overwhelming majority of candidates for these courses were returnees from the Soviet Union. A three-week seminar for Hashomer Hatzair activists was held in Lodz in February-March 1947, with forty-three representatives of Hashomer Hatzair collectives from various locations. Among the subjects discussed were: "The Kibbutz Movement in Palestine," "Jewish History and Zionism" and "Political Economics." One of the organizers reported that "there was an unforgettable evening around a traditional Hashomer Hatzair bonfire. People reminisced about their times in Russia and under Nazi occupation." Another seminar convened in Lodz was attended by fifty-five people, ages 17 to 27, eighteen of whom were women. Among the lecturers were Shayke Weiner and Israel "Julek" Barzilai, both members of Hashomer Hatzair kibbutzim in Palestine. Mishka Lewin discussed "Political Economics and Historical Materialism" and the writer Mates Olicki spoke about "The Great Writers of Yiddish Literature."[15]

Lodz could boast of one of the most successful branches of Hashomer Hatzair in postwar Poland. It was established in 1946 and all the indoor activities took place in three crowded rooms on 49 Kilinskiego Street. The Lodz branch, the Lodz *ken* of Hashomer Hatzair, began with sixty members, and reached close to a hundred by the fall of 1948. It was third-largest of the 17 Hashomer Hatzair branches active in Poland at the time, after the Stettin and the Walbrzych *branches*. Most members of Hashomer Hatzair in Lodz attended the local Yiddish and Hebrew schools, though some studied in Polish schools. The basic unit of the educational and training programs, as in other Zionist youth organizations, was the *kvutsa*, the youth group. The youngest were usually boys and girls aged 11-14; the intermediate groups were aged 15-16 and the oldest 16 and older. As for subjects and themes of discussion by age levels, at the Lodz *ken* the schedule for December 1947 expected the oldest group to discuss the political situation in Palestine; the intermediate to discuss Soviet policies and prepare a Hanukkah celebration; and the youngest to learn about Zionism, build a sleigh and light Hanukkah candles. The November 1947 schedule for the oldest group included discussions of books by Shalom Aleichem, I.L. Peretz, Jack London, Emile Zola, Victor Hugo and Herman Hesse.

The most effective occasions for the instruction and training of the young were the annual summer and winter camps, usually set in the mountains. For the participants this meant getting away from drab city life and living with their peers for several weeks. One participant wrote back home: "We are on our way from the mountaintop. Some of us talk, others pick flowers. The view is magnificent. From far away we see the camp and our flag at the top of the mast." Some of the parents, however, were quite worried by the rigors of the outdoor and indoor activities. One protective mother complained to a camp leader: "I couldn't compose myself after reading my daughter's letter. What shocked me most was that they have only one hour for singing and only two hours of rest during the day. And that, after such a long day of hard labor."[16]

Youth leaders from Hashomer Hatzair sought to spread the word about their movement in the various schools in Lodz. Fayvl Podemski was sent to the Yiddish School. Others were sent to the local Hebrew school and to Polish schools. Youth leaders also attempted to establish contacts with the families of their young trainees. The purpose of all of this was to convince parents to take the opportunity to emigrate with their children to Palestine. Fayvl Podemski and Moshe Shmutter were sent to Jewish families in Lodz. A high priority of the movement was to ensure that Jewish families emigrate to Israel as soon as possible, and that their sons and daughters join Hashomer Hatzair kibbutzim in Israel following immigration. The emigration campaign intensified when official permission for Jews to emigrate to Israel was granted in 1949. A letter by a Hashomer Hatzair activist, dated December 1, 1949, stated: "The purpose of our work these days is to get the parents' commitment to deliver their children to *Aliyat Hanoar* as soon as they arrive in Israel. But first of all we urge the parents to submit their own emigration papers. Tragic situations occur when parents do not want to emigrate to Israel and don't give their permission for their children to do so."[17]

A high point in the short-lived postwar history of Hashomer Hatzair in Poland was the visit of Meir Yaari, the movement's founding father and admired ideological leader, in January 1947. The Hashomer Hatzair bi-weekly *Mosty* (Bridges) reported: "The announcement of Meir Yaari's speech aroused unusual interest among Lodz Jews. The large hall of Teatr Powszechny was packed to the brim. Yaari's speech centered on both Zionism and Socialism. He praised the Soviet Union and postwar Poland." Arriving from a World Zionist conference in Basel, where he had been relatively ignored, Yaari must have been elated by the welcome extended to him not only within his own movement but also by the Polish authorities. He met with a number of high-ranking Polish officials, including Poland's President, Boleslaw Bierut. As for Yaari's attitude toward Hashomer Hatzair in postwar Poland, there was a discrepancy between the praise and encouragement he expressed in public during his visit and the doubts he voiced after his return to Palestine. In a farewell message displayed in Hashomer Hatzair branches throughout Poland, Yaari wrote "I'm still under the impression of the Warsaw Ghetto and the catastrophe. My heart is with you, the remnants of our great Movement. I shall never forget your tremendous effort to reconstruct the Movement after the catastrophe." In Palestine he commented: "Our Movement in Poland is rather simplistic. The human material is primitive. These are returnees from the Soviet Union and orphans, who were trained in great haste. Still, this material could be reshaped."[18]

The Gordonia youth movement in postwar Poland, like Hashomer Hatzair, had its headquarters in Lodz. The first Gordonia collective was established in a three-room apartment on 46 Piotrkowska Street, in mid-1945. At first it accepted both members of Dror and of Hanoar Hatzioni. Later, following the arrival of emissaries from Palestine, when the collective moved to 43 Wolczanska Street, it became strictly Gordonian. One of the collective's members recalled the Piotrkowska Street apartment. "It was filled with bunk beds. There were highly emotional encounters. People cried and embraced. It was unbelievable. We were lucky to be Gordonians once again. There were no fathers, no mothers, no sisters and no brothers, but we had a hospitable place." Out of the 125 Gordonia collective members in the spring of 1946, seventy-one were aged 17 to 25, twenty-two were aged 14-17 and the rest were under fourteen.

Gordonia activists would daily go to the local train station and to the Lodz Jewish Committee offices to seek old friends and convince unknown returnees to join their movement. Gordonia seminars and conferences, which brought together representatives of the movement from all over Poland, were held in Lodz. Gordonia published its youth bulletin *Slowo Mlodych* (*The Young People's Word*) in Lodz. Baruch Kaplinski and Natan Gross were among its editors. Gross was also a popular lecturer at various Gordonia events. A major Gordonia public event was the visit of Pinhas Lubianikier-Lavon, the founder of Gordonia, who arrived from Palestine in mid-1946. He lectured in the Wlokniarz Cinema on "The Struggle of the Jewish Workers in Palestine for a Jewish State."

The Gordonia youth movement branch in Lodz was located in four rooms on 3 Wieckowskiego Street. A summary of its activities for 1948 reported: "Its nearly fifty branch members are aged 12-18 and attend various schools. They live with their families in Lodz. Meetings of the various groups at the *ken* convene between 5pm and 8pm. The reading room has a piano, a radio and a small library. Discussions, which take place three times a week, deal with such subjects as History, Sociology, Jewish History and Zionism. Various events such as singing, dancing and drama performances are organized quite often. The young are trained in the spirit of Socialist Zionism and prepared for productive and pioneering work in Israel."[19]

Emissaries from various Zionist parties and youth movements in Palestine/Israel played a significant role in the short-lived rebirth of Zionism in postwar Poland. The first emissary, Isar Ben-Zvi, a member of kibbutz Maale Hachamisha, affiliated with Mapai–the Labor Party– and with the Gordonia youth movement, arrived in Poland in the early fall of 1945. Shayke Weiner, from Ein Hashofet, a kibbutz affiliated with Hashomer Hatzair, arrived in November. Israel "Julek" Barzilai, of the Hashomer Hatzair-affiliated kibbutz Negba, who would be the first Israeli envoy to Poland, spent three months as an emissary in mid-1946. Additional emissaries connected with various youth movements followed. These were mostly people born in Poland and fluent in Polish, who had belonged to Zionist youth organizations in interwar Poland before leaving for Palestine. Contacts between the various Zionist parties and youth movements in Poland and those in Palestine were already well established by the end of 1945. The emissaries assisted local Zionist activists in organizational, ideological, cultural and educational matters. They were instrumental in the organization and implementation of Brichah, the massive semi-legal border crossing from Poland to points west and south, the final destination being Palestine/Israel. The assistance of the emissaries was a mixed blessing. On the one hand, they had experience in practical matters and brought with them the spirit of Eretz Israel and of the kibbutz movement; on the other, however, they introduced into the various Zionist organizations in postwar Poland the inner politics, splits and conflicts rampant within the Zionist movement in Palestine.[20]

Among the last emissaries to reach Poland, immediately before or soon after the establishment of Israel in May 1948, were Moshe Chizhik, "Kalif", from Kibbutz Eylon and Matityahu Mintz from Kibbutz Gan-Shmuel, both affiliated with Hashomer Hatzair. As did many other emissaries, they spent at least some time in Lodz. The correspondence between Lodz and the Hashomer Hatzair Center in Kibbutz Merhavya, in Israel, reflected some of the problems facing Palestinian emissaries at that time. A letter sent from Merhavya to Lodz in late October 1948, addressed to Chizhik and Mintz, spoke of inadequate educational values within the Hashomer Hatzair branches in Poland and the danger of assimilation. "There exist temptations for Jewish youth. Postwar Poland enables them to reach the highest rungs of the social and political ladder." The letter also criticized the rather low numbers of Hashomer Hatzair youth in the local branches. There was also mention of the insufficient efforts made within Polish schools in order to recruit Jewish youngsters into the movement. The exchange of letters with Kalif, who was joined on his Polish mission by his wife and daughter, indicates that there were problems and complaints of a personal nature as well.[21]

The Zionists considered the raising and education of Jewish children who survived the war and the Holocaust in a Jewish, Zionist, and Palestine-oriented spirit to be a task of the highest priority. They were particularly concerned with Jewish children who had lived among Poles during the war and were losing their Jewish identity. Finding and returning them to the Jewish fold was considered an act of redemption. Jewish children saved by Polish families, as well as those who survived in convents and monasteries, were sought out as early as the second half of 1944. The redemption of Jewish children by individual Zionist activists and by various Zionist organizations continued throughout 1945. According to a report sent from Poland to Palestine in March 1946, "1,200 children live with non-Jewish families; between 1,500-2,000 children live in various convents." The first groups of redeemed children were placed by the various Zionist organizations in Zionist children collectives–children's kibbutzim. In the summer of 1946, there were close to 900 children in these collectives. The largest were located in Lodz, Bytom and Pietrolesie. A Palestinian emissary to Dror recalled: "When I arrived in Poland, I encountered children and youth kibbutzim of the various movements. Dror ran two wonderful kibbutzim. These children were mostly orphans."²²

Besides lonely child survivors, a considerable number of half- orphans and children who couldn't stay with their families ended up in Zionist collectives. There was an ongoing rivalry for Jewish children between the Communist-oriented CCPJ and the Zionists. Activists of the various Zionist youth movements attempted to convince children placed in CCPJ institutions to desert them, join Zionist collectives and leave for Palestine/Israel. It was reported to the CCPJ in early August 1945 that "thirty children from a CCPJ children's home in Chorzow, near Katowice, disappeared and traveled in an unknown direction, apparently to Italy." Hashomer Hatzair youth leaders in Lodz used to come to the Lodz Jewish Committee public kitchen in order to talk to Jewish youngsters and convince them to join their collective. A Palestinian emissary recalled: "Children and babies used to arrive from Russia in the framework of children's homes, with their nurses. These children were meant to reach the anti-Zionist CCPJ's children's homes. Following some arguments, we usually managed to convince the Jewish nurses to join us. We loaded them, with the children, on trucks, and they were deposited at our children's homes."²³

Koordynacja (Coordination) an umbrella committee of most Zionist youth movements, aimed at redeeming Jewish children in postwar Poland and taking care of child returnees from Russia, was established in early 1946. Koordynacja directed Jewish children to various Zionist collectives and opened children's homes of its own. Close to a thousand children lived for various periods of time in Koordynacja homes up to April 1948. More than half were returnees from the Soviet Union, close to 200 were redeemed from Polish families and convents, sixty-three were ghetto survivors and six survived the camps. Financial resources needed for the redemption of Jewish children from Christian families and for maintaining children's homes were supplied by Jewish organizations abroad, such as the JDC, the World Jewish Congress and the Jewish Agency.²⁴

The Koordynacja offices in Lodz were located on 17/18 Zawadska Street. The first Koordynacja children's homes in postwar Poland were opened in Lodz: one for small children, up to age 6, at 88 Piotrkowska Street, and another for children aged 7-13 on 18 Narutowicza Street. A woman who arrived as a young girl at the Narutowicza Street home recalled: "there was a closed and locked courtyard with an armed guard at the entrance. All the windows were closed. There was a fear of anti-Semitic incidents, especially following the Kielce pogrom. Most of the children who arrived from Polish homes didn't want to be Jewish. Some tried to run away." The Narutowicza Street children's home was headed by Khasya Bilicka of Hashomer Hatzair, a very efficient and talented prewar educator. It opened in March 1946 with twelve children, and within a week or two their number reached forty. The Piotrkowska Street children's home was run by Hela Leneman.[25]

* * *

FAYVL PODEMSKI WAS ONE OF THOSE WHO SURVIVED IN THE DESERTED Lodz Ghetto and was still there in January 1945. "About 850 people remained in the labor camp on 16 Jakuba Street. Then, something exceptional happened in the evening hours of January 15th. We heard the buzzing of approaching planes and shortly thereafter — a number of extremely powerful explosions. The planes dropped illumination bombs. The skies above turned into a huge projector. Everybody ran to the courtyard. People became ecstatic." A few days later the first Red Army units entered Lodz. Fayvl recalled their arrival. "We walked along the pavement on Brzezinska Street and faced the oncoming soldiers. There were fifteen or twenty abreast. They filled up the street to the brim. It felt as if millions were marching. People were shouting and yelling. I was in seventh heaven." There were two incidents, however, that marred Fayvl's elation. When people started talking to the marching Red Army soldiers, Fayvl kept repeating "ya Evrei," — I'm a Jew — and then one of the soldiers, a Jew, advised him in Yiddish to shut up. Fayvl was shocked. "I was sure that the whole world was waiting for me after those five horrible years in the ghetto, and he tells me to shut up." A few days later Fayvl was approached on a street by two Russian soldiers. One of them told him to take off his good leather boots. When Fayvl started arguing, he was told to choose between his life and his boots. "The street was covered with snow, and I begged them to follow me to the entrance of my house. There I took off my boots, and that was it."

Fayvl became active in Jewish and Zionist affairs a few weeks after liberation. He was elected to the Lodz Jewish Committee in February 1945, and was, apparently, its youngest member. He was twenty at the time. Fayvl met Antek Zuckerman either in March or in April 1945. Antek arrived unexpectedly one evening in Fayvl's apartment on Poludniowa Street. "We sat and talked late into the night. He was interested mainly in the Lodz Jewish Committee and in its most influential members. I told him about Mirski." Antek asked Fayvl to find a location in the city center, in the proximity of the Jewish Committee, for Zionist activities. With the help of Andrzej, a Polish door-keeper on Poludniowa Street whom Fayvl bribed with vodka, a number of empty, post-German apartments were located. This was, apparently, how Poludniowa turned into a Jewish and Zionist street in postwar-Lodz. Fayvl was also instrumental in securing the rooms on 49 Kilinskiego Street for Hashomer Hatzair. He was active in the Hashomer Hatzair Lodz branch from its very start, and served as the first postwar head of the Lodz *ken*.[26]

Baruch Kaplinski arrived in Lodz from the camps less than two months after the liberation. On a street he met a young man from his hometown who told him that his mother had survived and was living in Lodz. "I went crazy and ran to the Jewish Committee. Running up the steps I saw my mother. I wanted to kiss her, but she pushed me away. She thought that a stranger was molesting her. Only when I uttered the word 'Mama,' did she identify me. The two of us stood there, speechless, embracing each other." Antek Zuckerman, whom Kaplinski knew in prewar Vilna, convinced him to establish a Hebrew school in Lodz and become its first principal. "I rented a five-room apartment on Pilsudskiego Street, renamed Wschodnia Street, and advertised that a Hebrew school would open soon. Within days we were flooded with parents and children. The children were seven and eight years old, some of them older." Kaplinski recalled that the school was quite "elastic," it expanded and shrank continuously. Pupils were arriving and departing. "One day we had two hundred children and in a few weeks their number would shrink to fifty or sixty. All this was due to the Flight and Rescue operation. But even those who stayed with us for a few months only turned from little goyim to Jews. They started speaking Hebrew. We had some excellent teachers. The school was assisted by a school committee. These were very devoted people. Most of them were members of local Zionist parties. I recall one of them, Hilary Sztrowajs, a clever, witty businessman. Every week or two he would bring me an envelope stuffed with money. Still, most of our expenses were covered by Hehalutz." Kaplinski served as principal of the Hebrew school for one year only. He was then appointed head of Aliyat Hanoar, Youth Aliya in Poland, but his interest in and assistance for the Hebrew school continued until he left Poland for Israel, in the fall of 1948.[27]

Bela Elster, known better by her underground pseudonym Wanda, was living in Lodz under an assumed Polish identity during the last few months before liberation. Since her family and many of her friends perished in Warsaw, Wanda was reluctant to return there. She did go, however, to look for her older sister Pola, an activist in the Left Poalei Zion both before the war and in wartime Warsaw. "Immediately after liberation I hired a man with a cart and we drove to Zoliborz, where Pola's last hiding place was located. I knew that Pola, Eliyahu Erlich and Hersz Berlinski had stayed in that bunker. But all were dead, shot by the Germans just before the liberation of Warsaw. I was the first person who found their bodies. I dug the soil with my bare hands and covered their heads. Later on a funeral was held, and they were buried in the Warsaw Jewish Cemetery.

Whereas Warsaw represented for Wanda death and loss, she perceived postwar Lodz as a place of rebirth and life. "I fell in love with Lodz. There were people around me. I had many friends at the Left Poalei Zion. Lodz was for me a kind of cure and therapy, after Warsaw. I was amazed how those simple Jews had the strength and willpower to stand up again on their feet. The city was bustling with life. There were the Zionist youth movements, the Zionist parties. Regardless of the differing opinions, there was a sense of a common purpose." Wanda's dream was to study medicine, and she had been accepted, but Party leaders and activists convinced her that postwar priorities and obligations were different. That's how Wanda became active in the Dror youth movement. "The movement was my home. That was the worthiest, the most dynamic and the most significant period in my life. We were like one big family. The young boys and girls loved and trusted me, and I felt good with them, like an older sister, like a mother." Most of those youngsters survived the war in the Soviet Union. Among them was the future writer and artist Marek Halter. "Marek was a very attractive boy. I loved him like a son. We were very close. He was very talented. His drawings and paintings were up on all the walls." Halter, who settled in Paris, later would come and chat with Wanda in her Israel home for hours, whenever he visited the country. "Then, he became famous. He stopped coming and stopped calling."[28]

Sara Nishmit arrived in Lodz in December 1945 from Kovno, in Soviet Lithuania. "My first impression of Lodz was that it was an ugly city. One couldn't see the skies through the smoke." Soon after her arrival she was arrested by the local police, informed apparently in advance by Soviet security. Sara had been previously active in the illegal Zionist Brichah in Kovno. Antek Zuckerman, who had good contacts with Polish Security, intervened and she was released. She met with him and with Zivia Lubetkin. She also met with Zvi Melnitzer. Sara intended to leave soon for Palestine. However, Leybele Goldberg — Aryeh Sarid — from Kibbutz Yagur, one of the first emissaries from Palestine, convinced her to give up her plans. Sara started working for the Koordynacja and assisted in redeeming Jewish children from Polish families and Catholic convents and setting them up in Jewish children's homes. Soon additional children started arriving from Russia. "We were short of experienced youth leaders and educators. They didn't know Hebrew, and spoke mostly Polish. Then, following the waves of returnees from Russia, Russian was heard all over. We sent the older kids to the Lodz Hebrew school."

Sara recalled some remarkable stories from the children's homes. "A girl of 13 or 14 arrived at our children's home in Lodz. Her name was Marysia. She had stayed with a Polish family and become a real anti-Semite. Shortly before her group left for Palestine, Marysia wrote a letter to her Polish saviors and I opened it. I wanted to be sure that the girl didn't reveal any information concerning the illegal crossing of borders. She wrote that she would be traveling with the Yids to Palestine, but would never abandon Catholic religion, and would always remember what her Polish mother had taught her." Numerous Polish families were ready to give up Jewish children for money, but some didn't want to part with them. Sara recalled an amazing story: "Frania, a single, poor Polish woman from Lwow, saw a German army truck with Jewish children stop in the market place one day. The children were apparently driven to a camp. The Germans announced that whoever would hand over ten marks, could take a child. Most of the children were 'purchased' in that manner. Only two boys were left. Frania begged the Germans to wait, ran to her house and brought the money. She took care of the two Jewish boys until the Red Army arrived in Lwow, and then, as a former Polish citizen, moved with the boys to Poland. She came to the Jewish Committee in Warsaw and announced that she was willing to return the boys on one condition — that she could join them wherever they go. The three of them were then sent to a Dror kibbutz in Lower Silesia, where Frania worked as a cook. Frania and her two Jewish sons eventually left Poland with the Brichah and arrived in Palestine."

Sara also recalled some Jewish partisan-boys. "There were only a few partisan-boys in the Koordynacja children's homes. They were quite different from the others. Their personalities were shaped by life in the forests. They were independent, stubborn and quite cynical. They couldn't accept authority and used to mock their instructors and teachers."[29]

Natan Gross, after completing a course for film directors in Krakow, was sent to Lodz to assist in the first full-length feature film made in Poland after the war. While he was at the Lodz Fabryczna train station, on his way back to Krakow, he was approached by Shaul Goskind, a prewar producer of Yiddish films, who had returned from Russia and headed a film cooperative. Goskind hoped to produce his first postwar feature film in Yiddish, with the participation of Dzigan and Schumacher, who had acted in some of his prewar productions. Goskind assumed that after returning from Russia the actors would not choose to settle in Poland, and wanted to use the opportunity of their temporary stay in Lodz for making a film with them. He convinced Gross to be the director. "Goskind got hold of me right there, at the train station, and begged me to work with him. Although I wanted to return to Krakow to continue my Zionist activity there and hardly knew any Yiddish, still, this proposition was very attractive. I would become immediately a full-fledged film director." Although Gross at first couldn't see how Holocaust survival could be combined with Yiddish comedy, Goskind somehow forced him into it. "Finally, I suggested a framework and wrote an outline for the film. The concept was mine. Then, all of us, Goskind, Rachel Auerbach, Dzigan, Schumacher and myself, worked on the scenario. We worked under tremendous pressure because of the approaching departure of Dzigan and Schumacher. *Undzere Kinder* was shot in the summer and fall of 1948. The editing took another few months. All this was done with the cooperation of Film Polski. I actually improved my poor Yiddish on the run, while producing the film."

Besides his work on *Undzere Kinder* and the production of documentaries on Jewish life in postwar Poland, Gross continued his literary and Zionist work. He published Polish translations of Hebrew and Yiddish poetry, wrote articles for various Zionist periodicals, lectured on Zionism and was active at the Lodz branch of the Gordonia youth movement. "I was the editor of *Slowo Mlodych* (*The Young People's World*) the Polish language Gordonia periodical, and my own writings filled up to 60% of its contents. I wrote articles and stories, conducted interviews and translated poems. As for the Gordonia *ken*, I used to come there very often. I would sit with the youngsters and sing Hebrew songs. I was very involved with them." During his Lodz years Gross kept up his contacts with Polish filmmakers. He often met with such future prominent film directors as Wojciech Has and Jerzy Kawalerowicz. He was regularly involved in both the Jewish-Zionist and in general Polish culture. "I worked very intensively, as if I wanted to regain those lost wartime years. On top of the daily professional filmmaking, which took up most of my time, I never stopped writing and translating. I could do it under any circumstances."[30]

Captain Binyamin Majerczak, who survived the war in the Soviet Union and fought in the Polish Army, arrived in Lodz in September 1946. He quickly got involved in various Jewish and Zionist activities. "As captain in the Army and veteran of battles against the Germans I was offered various attractive positions in the new pro-Communist system, but I refused. I was a Zionist and intended to emigrate to Palestine. Although I sympathized with Hashomer Hatzair before the war, I could not accept their pro-Soviet stand, after all I had gone through in Russia. I joined Left Poalei Zion and Dror. I identified with their struggle in Palestine and admired Tabenkin." For a while Majerczak was active in the Brichah, but as an experienced officer he was mostly needed in Jewish efforts for self-defense. He became a member of the KS, the Special Commission for Jewish self-defense in Lodz. Majerczak also taught part-time at both the Yiddish school and the Zionist Hebrew School. He taught gym and physics. "I used to come there fully dressed in my army uniform and that made a big impression on the children. The older girls used to look at me in a special way. The students kept asking me about the war, and how many Germans had I killed. Until then they heard only about ghettos and camps, and here was a young Jewish officer who had fought the Nazis. Whatever I did for those kids was done with great love."

Majerczak was also active in training Jewish volunteers for the Haganah. "I went from place to place and taught them how to hold weapons and how to fire them. They were only five or six years younger than me. This was an extremely dynamic period in my life." Alongside his extensive Zionist activities, Majerczak led an active social life. "I found time for entertainment and romance as well. I decided to enjoy pleasures that the war had deprived me of. I had great fun and was, apparently, in demand." It was in Lodz that Majerczak met his future wife, Fela. "This was either in late 1947 or early 1948. As I was sitting and playing cards with some friends a young woman entered the room. She was really beautiful and had a royal air about her. I was very impressed. Fela must have been the best-looking girl in Lodz in those days. We met once or twice. At first it was just a flirt, but then we fell in love with each other. From a flirt it turned into a great love. Fela moved into my place and we remained together for close to sixty years." Binyamin and Fela left Lodz for Israel in the fall of 1948.[31]

Matityahu Mintz arrived in Poland from Israel in the summer of 1948, as a Hashomer Hatzair emissary. A senior and more experienced emissary, Moshe Chizhik, nicknamed Kalif, whom Mintz had known in Palestine, was already in Poland at that time. Mintz considered himself Kalif's protégé. "He was like a father to me, in a certain sense." Young Mintz had mixed feelings about his mission to post-Holocaust Poland; most of his family hadn't survived. The Polish language and culture, in which he was well-steeped before the war, presented some problems as well. "After reaching Palestine, I stopped speaking Polish. That was, apparently, an emotional reaction." Mintz flew from Haifa to Prague and after a short stay traveled by train to Poland. "I got off at Koluszki, near Lodz. Hashomer Hatzair people waited for me there. One of them was an old-time friend from Vilna, Mishka Lewin, who had survived the war in Russia and had served as an officer in the Red Army." Mintz knew that he had been recommended by Mishka Lewin for work with Jewish youth.

"They brought me to a Hashomer Hatzair collective, and within a few days Mishka took me along to their summer camps in Lower Silesia. These were boys and girls aged 14-17, and the spoken language was Polish. I couldn't speak Polish at first. I understood everything, but I couldn't speak it. Then, in a few days, gradually, I started speaking Polish to such an extent that I could speak in front of large groups of up to 200 people. I never thought I could sing, but when I had to teach them Hebrew songs I did it quite well. Mishka told me I was a great success. The youngsters' attitude towards me was close to admiration." Yohanan Fine, one of Mintz's trainees, described him in his memoirs half a century later as "a young man with an extremely impressive appearance and erudition." Both Mintz and his trainee, who became close friends in time, recalled a confrontation between Mintz and a Communist-Jewish activist, which took place in Wroclaw, in the spring of 1949. According to Fine, "Matityahu's appearance and rethoric were highly impressive. He refuted that fellow's arguments one by one." When I asked Mintz to look back in time and evaluate his postwar Polish experience he confided in me: "Everybody has some glamorous moments in his life. That year in Poland was the most glamorous time of my life."[32]

Aharon Zalkind traveled in the late summer of 1946 from his native Vilna to Lodz with his mother, his mother's sister and his younger brother. "We were now a family of four, the three of us and my aunt Zelda, my 'second mother.' At first we lived in the courtyard of the Jewish community center. This was hardly a room. One had to bend down when entering that small space. We slept on mattresses, right on the floor. Then we moved to a one-room apartment on Lutomierska Street, near the Baluty area, which we shared with another family. There was no running water there." Aharon's mother and aunt started selling cloth in Zielony Rynek, the Green Market, but their meager profit wasn't sufficient to keep the boys at home. They were soon put in the Koordynacja children's home. This was in the early fall of 1946. "I recall that we would walk from the Koordynacja children's home to Piotrkowska Street, to the Grand Hotel. There was a coffee shop at the entrance, with those delicious cakes. We could only dream about them. Around that time I became an ardent Zionist. I started attending the Hebrew school and the *ken* of Hashomer Hatzair. Every few months another group of Koordynacja children were sent to Palestine. Each time when our turn came mother begged them to leave us in Lodz." A year later Aharon and his younger brother returned home. "Life became more cheerful. We started entertaining friends." Aharon had good memories from the Hebrew school. "We studied Hebrew, the Bible and Zionist songs. During the long recess we played in the courtyard. We had lots of celebrations, like Tu Bishvat and Hanukkah." The Hebrew school was closed down at the end of 1949, and after the winter break Aharon started attending a Polish high-school.[33]

Rachel Rubinow arrived in Lodz with her mother in the fall of 1946. Her father was in Austria at the time. Since he had been a longtime member of Poalei Zion, the party promised to arrange for an apartment for his wife and daughter. What actually happened was that Rala was put into a children's home affiliated with Poalei Zion, on Wolczanska Street. "Most of the other children were bona-fide orphans whose parents died in the Holocaust or in Soviet labor camps. The orphanage was a transient place. There were constant comings and goings." Rala stayed there for two years. She recalled two incidents, both connected with the Jewish High Holidays. "On the day of Yom Kippur our instructors took off. This didn't surprise me at all. What did shock me, however, was that many of the children also disappeared. That night on the eve of Yom Kippur, there were only about a dozen children left." Stefan, the only instructor who stayed with them, prepared a surprise for the few lonely children. "Stefan emerged from the kitchen with a steaming pot and placed it on the table. A gasp of disbelief escaped from our lips, as we saw the contents: steaming, plump sausages; a product so rare and expensive that most of us had never tasted it before." The other incident happened on the morning of Yom Kippur. Rala had second-thoughts about the sausages and decided to repent and fast. She recalled the chanting of prayers she had heard a few days earlier on Rosh Hashana. She knew that there was a Jewish prayer place nearby and tried to get in. "I tried to push my way into the prayer-room. Suddenly, a hand caught me by the collar." The man demanded a 'bilyet', a ticket, and refused to let her in. When she told him that she was from the children's home on Wolczanska Street, he made some nasty remarks about 'those Labor Zionists who don't believe in God.' 'I'm not a Labor Zionist, I'm a child', she responded angrily. When, finally, the rabbi intervened and invited her in, it was too late. "I was too angry. I ran towards the staircase, opened the door without looking back and took the steps down two at a time. I ran for two blocks, before I stopped to catch my breath."

When Rala arrived in Lodz the school year had already started. She enrolled first in the Yiddish school, but within a few weeks transferred to the Hebrew school. "I recall a room full of children, our future friends. There was Ada Gibraltar, Salek and Moniek Pomerantz, Shimon Redlich, Josef Spokojny, Rysiek Lubelsky, and Heniek Napadow. The teacher's name was Melamed." Of her Lodz classmates Rala recalled particularly Heniek Napadow. "Heniek would often escort us outside the school and save us from those Polish hooligans." Her prevailing memories from postwar Lodz were associated with anti-Semitism. "The way from the children's home to school was rather long and quite dangerous. I was then 11 years old, small, with braids — *tsepalach* — and a dark complexion. I decided that it would be safest for me to walk face down, not looking at the hooligans, and, perhaps, prevent them from staring at me. Those Polish boys would stand there and try to catch us, the Jewish kids from the orphanage on their way to school. They would shout at us '*Zydzi*'–Yids. First, I tried to look down at the sidewalk, then I said I'm a gypsy. But they would repeat '*Zydowka, Zydowka* — Jewess. It didn't do any good. They would say 'Hitler killed the Gypsies, you are a Jew-girl.' I recall that once they actually beat me up. They particularly enjoyed grabbing my school bag and emptying it on the sidewalk. They would grab my kerchief and the two red braid ribbons I wore. Fights among children weren't completely new to me. I had some experience from Siberia. I knew that the really dangerous stuff was being beaten up on one's face. So, I tried to protect my face, and ran away as fast as I could. Every morning when I got up and packed my schoolbag I wondered whether my walk to school would be peaceful or dangerous. Usually, the way back after school was safer, since we would walk together and Heniek would protect us. On one occasion a few Polish teenagers, they must have been aged 14 or 15, circled around us and started pushing. It was like a human chain. Heniek Napadow saw this and in a second lifted his Finnish clasp-knife and boom, he struck into that living chain. I saw blood. These boys never attacked us again." Rachel recalled some adult anti-Semites as well. "I was walking on the street with my schoolbag, as usual. A woman, she must have been around 40 years old, looked at me and exclaimed 'those dirty Jews. What are you doing here? I thought Hitler had killed you all!' I never heard such words in wartime Russia. I would never forget that scene. This incident shaped my image of the Poles forever."

Rachel's memories of the Hebrew school were vivid and cheerful. "There were about a dozen kids in our grade. We were like a family. We had this feeling of togetherness. We knew that all of us would end up in Eretz Israel, in Israel. I recall distinctly that around the proclamation of the State of Israel, in May 1948, we decided that in ten years, all of us would meet in Tel-Aviv, on the steps of the Habimah Theater. We started reading and writing Hebrew; we even spoke some. We sang Hebrew songs and danced the Hora. Our talks were always future-oriented. We spoke about things we would do once we get to Israel." For Rachel, the Hebrew school replaced, in a way, a family. "The kids at school were my family."[34]

Hanka left Soviet Uzbekistan for Poland sometime in 1946. Her mother heard that her younger sister Hela had survived the war on Aryan papers, and that she was living with her husband and son in Lodz. "There were many Jewish returnees on our train and after it crossed the Soviet-Polish border we were attacked by the AK, the Polish Home Army. We were terribly scared. They told us to get off the train. They threatened to kill us and called us nasty names. Finally, the AK people set fire to one of the train cars, took some property, and the train continued its westward journey. This was a terrible and fearful event." Hanka and her mother got off the train in Lodz and Hanka's father traveled to Siedlce, their hometown, near Warsaw. Hanka's mother decided that she would never return to the place where none of their family had survived. "When we arrived at my aunt's place she wasn't home. She was at her cloth shop on Piotrkowska Street. A neighbor let us into my aunt's apartment that consisted of just one room, and ran to fetch her. We were looking out the window into the courtyard. And suddenly, *ciocia* Hela, Aunt Hela, a beautiful woman, younger than my mother, ran across the courtyard. Mom started screaming from up above and Aunt Hela from down below. In a second she rushed into the room. And, of course, Mom started asking her about the family, and Aunt Hela told her that everybody perished in Majdanek and Treblinka. Mother screamed that this wasn't possible, and both started crying. I just sat there on a bed and cried." Hanka felt guilty for years for not consoling her mother at that moment. "I almost couldn't relate to it. The whole thing was too powerful for a kid to grasp. I also didn't recall these people; it was an abstract matter for me."

Hanka's parents rented a room on Gdanska Street, which they shared with another couple. Then Hanka's mother bought a sewing machine and hired a Polish woman to sew scarves, which Hanka's father would take to stores and markets to sell. "Father used to return home with packets of money. And then we moved into a two-room apartment on Narutowicza Street. It had an inlaid floor and a toilet with running water. We even hired a maid." Hanka remembered how they reacted to the Kielce pogrom. This was still when they lived on Gdanska Street. "We lived there on the ground floor. We locked the door, shut the windows, and pulled down the shutters. We didn't go out for two, three days. I was terribly scared, and kept asking my mother 'would they come to kill us?'" Hanka started attending the third grade at the Yiddish school on Kilinskiego Street. "This was the first time I went to a normal school. We studied Yiddish, Hebrew, Polish and Russian. I recall some anti-Zionist incidents." In 1948, after the proclamation of Israel, Hanka switched to the Hebrew school. She also joined the Gordonia youth movement. "I have wonderful memories from Gordonia. They prepared us for kibbutz life in Israel. Gordonia, with its special spirit, was like a second home."[35]

Ada traveled with her mother and stepfather from Uzbekistan to

Poland in the spring of 1946. They first settled in Zgierz, near Lodz, and lived with her stepfather's family. "He had two sisters. One of them converted and was married to a Christian. That man had saved her and her sister during the war." Ada attended a Polish school and had very pleasant memories from there. "I used to sing the Christian songs with them every morning. I even told my parents that I would like to go with the girls for the Holy Communion. That's when they decided to leave Zgierz and move to Lodz." Ada started attending the Lodz Hebrew School in September 1947. "We lived on Zawadska Street. There were three families in that apartment. Each family occupied one room. Living conditions were quite crowded." Still, the Gibraltars had a piano and Ada took piano lessons. She also liked to sing and had a pleasant voice, becoming a soloist in the Hebrew school choir. Ada recalled that her mother was active at the school PTA and that her parents had Zionist contacts. "When Barzilai, the first Israeli ambassador, arrived in Lodz, I was asked to present him with flowers at the train station."[36]

Shlomo Pomerantz returned with his family to Lodz in the summer of 1946. The journey from Uzbekistan to Poland lasted more than two months. "We traveled in a freight train, similar to that which had taken us into Russia a few years earlier. The train stopped every few hours and people got off to heat up some food. Once our train moved and my father was left behind. We panicked, but he boarded another train and caught up with us." In Lodz, their family of six moved into a one-room apartment on Nowotki Street. "We divided up that single room into two or three smaller spaces by hanging some curtains. The toilet was downstairs in the courtyard. Walking down during those dark and cold winter nights was a nightmare."

Shlomo attended the Lodz Hebrew School from the fall of 1946 until it closed down in late 1949. "I have very pleasant memories from our school. I had many friends and our teachers took good care of us. I recall Rashal, big and tall, and Liberman, who was always smoking. I liked Glantz the most. He was a wonderful person. He loved children. I also recall another teacher, Melamed, whom we nicknamed Krupka, after a character in the comics. We used to make fun of him, but he was a good teacher." Shlomo had Jewish friends only. "There were numerous incidents with Polish youngsters. I recall a humiliating event. A Polish girl, somewhat older than myself, smacked me right in the face. Her male friends appeared in an instant, and I had to run. On another occasion two older Polish boys pushed me into a house entrance, but I managed to escape. Still, on other occasions I hit the Poles. There were mornings when I was scared to walk to school and calculated which streets would be safest." Shlomo and his brother Moshe were members of Hashomer Hatzair. "It was great fun. We used to travel to summer camps. Father initially disproved, and used to repeat in Russian *'mal'chiki, vy nikuda ne poydete'* — kids, you won't go anywhere — but he would usually give in." [37]

Heniek arrived in Lodz sometime in 1946. His earliest memories of postwar Lodz were from the Koordynacja children's home, on 18 Narutowicza Street. His mother started working at the other Koordynacja home, the one for small children. There was hardly any contact between them. Heniek attended the Hebrew school, but did not remember any details. What he did recall very well were his fights with Polish youngsters. He even told me about an incident in which I was involved, which I didn't recall at all. "We walked together and two goyim started in with you. I told them to stop, and they asked me why I defend a Jew-boy." Heniek was blond and blue-eyed; I was dark, with a typical Jewish face. "Then they pushed you, and I started hitting them. When I started hitting I never knew how to stop. My first thought was always to avenge the Jews. I don't know how I got this idea, but it was always there. I was taking revenge for the Jews who were kicked around by the goyim. I hit one of those boys on his head with a lead toy gun, which I always carried around. He fell down. I think he fainted. And then we fled. There were many events like this. I would hit and hit, and wouldn't have minded finishing them off. On one occasion some Poles attacked smaller kids from the Koordynacja. I started fighting them. I jumped on one of them from behind, grabbed his neck and started squeezing. I nearly strangled him. I used to walk around with a truncheon, the kind used by the Gestapo. I hid it inside my coat. I was actually looking for fights, for revenge. It was like an inner-voice that told me to fight. I couldn't understand why the ghetto Jews didn't fight."

Heniek remembered our friendship in postwar Lodz. He used to visit quite often our ground floor apartment on Gdanska Street. "I recall your family. All of you lived together. For me it was very strange that you lived with your family, that some people have families. For me this wasn't normal." Heniek had serious problems with the instructors in the Koordynacja children's home. "At one time they didn't allow us to go to youth movement meetings in the evenings. I, of course, didn't pay any attention to that. Some kid snitched on me, and an instructor slapped me in the face. This happened in the office, and a soup dish was on his table. I grabbed that dish and threw it right to his face. Then he grabbed me, threw me on a bed and pushed his knee on my stomach. I nearly fainted. He and another fellow forced me into a cellar full of coals and they locked me in. I broke the lock and got out."

Heniek also recalled his success with girls. "I must have been 14 or 15 at that time. I used to go out with both Jewish and Polish girls. I would meet Polish girls on the street and start in with them. Once I met a girl named Izabela and walked with her into a church. I wouldn't tell the Polish girls that I was Jewish. I also used to sit with a girl on a park bench and we would discuss books that we had read. I was reading a lot at that time. There were days when I read a book a day. I was forbidden to read at night, since I had an eye problem. So, I would use a flashlight and read books under the blanket." Heniek was a bad student at school, but he was good in music. At one time he even took piano lessons. He also sang in the Hebrew school choir and was one of the child-actors in *Undzere Kinder*. "I recall the scenes shot in the Helenowek Children's Home. I remember blond Lidia, Schumacher's daughter. I tried to start up with her. I would talk with her and we would walk on the edge of the forest. It didn't last long."

Heniek couldn't forget his father. "I used to think about him quite often. One day, as I walked on the street, I saw a man resembling my father riding a motorcyle. I was sure it was him. I started running after that motorcycle and screaming 'Father, Father,' and of course it wasn't him. I kept believing that one day he would show up." When the last batch of Koordynacja children left for Palestine, sometime in 1949, Heniek moved in with his mother. "One day mother brought a man back with her and wanted to introduce him to me. I was mad and started smashing things. Since then mother, apparently, gave up the idea of living with a man. She must have also had guilt feelings, and I would exploit them. I would steal money from her and buy all kinds of stupid things. She would never complain or punish me."[38]

Richard and his mother arrived in Lodz in the late spring of 1946. He attended the Yiddish school for only a few days, and was enrolled in the Hebrew school. Although he studied there for close to three years, his memories of the school were extremely poor. "Of course, I met you in that school and we became friends. That is, probably, the most pleasant memory of those times." I tried to elicit from him the reasons for his suppressed memories. "I can't verbalize anything about those years, those events, that part of my life. I can't say that these were particularly unhappy or terrible years. Certainly, they were better than what we came from. My memory of things until 1949, when we left Poland, is hazy to the extreme. It's just something I can't explain." Richard did recall, however, his visits to his father's family in Krakow. "Just some flashbacks. I remember going to the zoo with my stepbrother who was ten years younger. I remember running around the streets of Krakow on a *hulajnoga*, a scooter."

Richard had some memories of the Helenowek Children's Home. "My mother thought, probably, that I would have a better life there than being with her." When I prodded him, he did recall that his mother used to have a male friend. "I believe his first name was Mietek; his second name was definitely Marchacz. I remember him as a very good friend of my mother. Whether they lived together or not — I'm not sure." Richard had a good recollection of his visits to our apartment. "I remember coming to your house. I remember your dog putting his paws on my shoulders, and being as tall as I am." We wondered together why Richard's Lodz memories were so scant. I suggested that the rest of us, who left Lodz for Israel, maintained some continuity between the Jewish and Zionist elements of our Lodz years and our lives in Israel. Richard agreed. "You stayed with the same people throughout. There was Hebrew; there was Israel. In my case, there was discontinuity. From my life in the Soviet Union to my second life in Poland, to a third life in France, to a fourth life in Canada."[39]

23. Helena Leneman with a child at the Koordynacja children's home on 88 Piotrkowska Street in Lodz. Courtesy of Helena Leneman.

24. At the Koordynacja children's home on 88 Piotrkowska Street in Lodz.

25. A Dror kibbutz in postwar Lodz. Courtesy of the Lohamei Hagetaot Archive.

26. Lodz Hebrew school teachers on a summer vacation. Center front: Binyamin Majerczak. Second row from right to left, first: Saul Liberman. Standing, from left to right, first: Israel (Igor) Glantz, second: Melamed.

27. Arkadiusz Kahan, as officer in the Polish Navy. Courtesy of Vivian Kahan.

7

THE OTHERS

WHEN SPEAKING OF JEWISH COMMUNISTS IN POSTWAR POLAND IT is necessary to differentiate between Communists of Jewish origin, functioning in various sectors of the Party and the State apparatus, and Jewish Communists active in the Jewish milieu. Devoted and experienced prewar Polish-Jewish Communists were indispensable to the regime during its first postwar years. Some of them, like Jakub Berman, Hilary Minc and Roman Zambrowski, occupied its highest ranks. Then there were the numerous younger Jews, the new recruits, who were considered to be loyal and were offered excellent opportunities for social promotion. For reasons stemming from postwar Polish mono-ethnicity and prevailing anti-Semitic attitudes, upwardly mobile Jews were expected to Polonize. This meant, usually, changing names and severing contacts with Jewish life. A large proportion of young Jewish men found non-Jewish spouses. All this meant, of course, further assimilation. Most of them followed this path willingly, and were quite enthusiastic about their future. A Jew could now become a high-ranking Party or Security official or a senior army officer. Jewish intellectuals and scholars took part in the cultural and academic life of postwar Poland, and young Jewish men and women enrolled in the universities. Quite naturally, therefore, Jewish administrators, professionals and students tended to concentrate in large urban centers such as Warsaw, Krakow and Lodz.[1]

Whereas Zionist-oriented Jews joined kibbutzim and Zionist parties, the political framework of Communist-oriented "Jewish" Jews was the Frakcja, the Jewish Fraction of the PPR. Most of the leaders and activists of the Fraction had survived the war in the Soviet Union and looked forward to the reconstruction of Jewish social, cultural and economic life in Communist Poland. They were convinced that in spite of the Holocaust and the tendency of survivors to leave, there was still an option for Jews to rebuild their lives in the country. The Fraction was under the direct supervision of the Party Central Committee; its leaders included Szymon Zachariasz, Bernard Mark, Grzegorz Smolar, and Michal Mirski. Zachariasz, a prewar member of the KPP Central Committee, was now a member of the PPR Central Committee and its referee for Jewish affairs. Fraction activists were represented at the Central Committee of Polish Jews (CCPJ) and they were members of the local Jewish committees. The Kielce pogrom in mid-1946 had a negative effect on the efforts of the

Jewish Communists to have Jews remain in Poland. The situation started changing, however, in the following months. With the Communist victory in the general elections and the stabilization of Jewish life, the Fraction gained influence in Jewish politics. Its leaders and activists sought to limit the impact of their non-Communist partners in the CCPJ and in the various Jewish structures.[2]

The ideals and objectives of the Jewish Communists, as well as the obstacles which the Fraction faced, are reflected in the official correspondence, press articles, and reports of Fraction meetings and conferences. As early as May 1945, a Fraction letter to the Party Central Committee complained of lack of representation in the KRN, the Polish National Council. It criticized the membership of Dr. Adolf Berman, the younger brother of Jakub Berman and the leader of the Left Poalei Zion in the Council. In early August 1945, Fraction activists criticized Polish Prime Minister Edward Osobka-Morawski for supporting Jewish emigration from Poland. At a national conference of Jewish Party activists in early October 1945, Mirski criticized the Zionists for not being interested in the reconstruction of Jewish life in postwar Poland and for supporting Jewish emigration. In an article published in *Folks-Shtime* in early 1946, he derided the Zionists for presenting Poland as a "Jewish cemetery" and for spreading the idea of a Jewish exodus from Europe and from Poland. The Communist-Jewish press turned particularly vociferous in its attacks against Jewish emigration in the summer and fall of 1946, in the wake of the post-Kielce emigration. Life became more stable the following year for those Jews who remained in Poland. Mirski, in his closing remarks at a Fraction conference in the fall of 1947, expressed optimism in respect to the stabilization and the growing impact of the Fraction on Jewish life. At that time, however, only about 100,000 out of the quarter of a million Jews who had resided in Poland in the early summer of 1946 were still there. The Zionists had won the battle for emigration and *aliyah*. In their policies and arguments vis-à-vis the survivors and the returnees from the Soviet Union, the Zionists could point to the negative traits of postwar Poland and enlist Zionist financial resources and organizational skills. The regime's support for emigration and for the establishment of a Jewish state in Palestine conflicted with the ideology of Jewish Communists. This, in turn, at least for the first postwar years, resulted in their grudging compromise with the Zionists.[3]

The uneasy coexistence and continuous conflicts between the Frakcja and the Zionist parties took place on two levels, within the Central Committee of Polish Jews and within the local Jewish committees. Although in 1944-1946 the Communists already had a foothold in the CCPJ, it was dominated at the time mainly by Zionists. However, the influence of Communists in certain local Jewish committees was visible from the very start. Thus, while Lodz had a relatively modest number of Jewish Party members, the two leading positions in the Lodz Jewish Committee were occupied by Michal Mirski, an old-time Communist, and by Anatol Wertheim, who had been a member of a Soviet partisan unit in Belorussia. Both were also members of the CCPJ.

The impact of the Communists in the local Jewish committees increased only in mid-1946. Whereas the main Zionist objective always remained emigration to Palestine/Israel, Fraction activists in the local committees strove for a revival of Jewish life in Poland. They played a decisive role in the initiation and functioning of various Jewish economic, social, cultural and educational activities. The number of Frakcja members increased in early 1947, mostly as a result of the election campaign. The second half of 1948 was marked by a more outspoken and aggressive stand of the Fraction toward the Zionists. This was facilitated by the increasingly hostile official Polish policies toward Israel and Zionism emanating from Moscow. Polish-Jewish Communists also used the campaign against "rightist-nationalist elements" within Poland for their specific purposes on the Jewish street. The reorganization of the local Jewish committees in early 1949 resulted in the final domination of the Communists. In a report presented in April 1949, Anatol Wertheim, secretary of the Lodz Jewish Committee, vehemently criticized Zionist-oriented teachers at the local Yiddish school who, in his words, "sought to instill in the children a sense of patriotism in respect to two homelands — Israel and Poland, forgetting that two homelands actually means no homeland at all." A conference of representatives of local Jewish committees and Jewish organizations convened in February 1949 in Warsaw. Out of the 267 participants, only sixty-one were Zionists. The overwhelming majority were either members of the PZPR or representatives of various Jewish institutions supporting Communist stands.[4]

The earliest meetings and discussions of Bund activists in liberated Poland took place in Lublin, in late 1944 and early 1945. Among the participants were Michael Szuldenfrei and Leo Finkelstein, who had survived the war in the Soviet Union, and Leon Feiner, Salo Fiszgrund and Bernard Goldstein, who had survived in German-occupied Warsaw. The undisputed leaders of the Bund in interwar Poland, Henryk Erlich and Viktor Alter, did not survive the war: Erlich had committed suicide in a Soviet prison and Alter was executed on Stalin's orders. Their tragic fate increased the negative attitude among Bundists toward Soviet Russia. Still, most of the surviving Bund activists initially believed in the reconstruction of Jewish life in postwar Poland. The Bund was represented both on the CCPJ and in local Jewish committees. Lodz was the most significant site of Bund activities in the immediate postwar years: the Bund Central Committee was located in Lodz. The first postwar national Bund conference convened in Lodz in mid-June 1945. The first postwar meeting of Tsukunft, the Bund youth organization, took place in Lodz in July, and a conference of Tsukunft youth leaders was held there in October.

Hundreds of Bundists and Bund supporters convened in Lodz for the celebration of the 48th anniversary of the Bund organization. A meeting in commemoration of Artur Zygelbojm, the Bund leader who had committed suicide in London to protest the world's indifference to the Jewish tragedy under the Nazis, was organized by the Bund in Lodz in May 1946. Among the speakers was Polish poet Wladyslaw Broniewski. He told the audience that he had spent some time with Viktor Alter in a Soviet prison cell. All rose to their feet to honor and mourn Alter and Erlich. The number of Bundists in Lodz increased following the arrival of Jewish returnees from Russia. It has been estimated that close to a thousand old-time Bundists were among them. Many settled in Lodz. The Lodz branch of the Bund, which consisted of 250 members in 1946, grew to 400 members in 1947. The local Bund committee was headed by Gershon Fogel, and one of its members was Marek Edelman.

Although the Bund and the Jewish Communist Frakcja did not see eye to eye on numerous issues, they were united in their opposition to Jewish emigration from Poland. Whereas the Zionists used the Kielce events to advocate Jewish emigration, the Bund attempted to convince both its members and the Jewish population at large not to leave Poland. A national Bund convention in Wroclaw in early 1947 strongly condemned "Zionist emigrational propaganda." Organized emigration of Jews to Palestine/Israel was at the core of the conflict between the Bund and the Zionists. The Bund accused the Zionists of deliberately causing a state of panic among Polish Jews in order to encourage their exodus from the country. Following the January 1947 elections and the victory of the Communist-dominated Democratic Bloc, Bund activists, especially its representatives at the CCPJ, increasingly identified with the Communists. A joint Committee of the Bund and the Frakcja was established in the spring of 1948. These were, actually, the first steps toward a fusion with the Communists. Numerous Bundists, apprehensive of the increasing Stalinization and the approaching end of the Bund's political existence in Poland, opted for emigration.[5]

***

Michal Mirski was a leading Polish Jewish Communist active in the Jewish milieu in postwar Poland and the most prominent Jewish Communist in postwar Lodz. He was a leading member of the Jewish Fraction, a member of the CCPJ and Chairman of the Lodz Jewish Committee. Mirski was born as Hersz Tabacznik in 1905, in the Volhynian town of Kovel in Russia, which would become part of Poland in the interwar years. As a student in the local Russian Gimnazia, young Tabacznik was already an avid reader of Russian literature and spoke Russian better than Polish. He also knew Yiddish. During the Soviet-Polish War he joined the Red Army, lived for a few months in Bolshevik Russia, and returned to Kovel in 1921. For the next few years he became interested and involved in Jewish education. When he attended Jewish teachers' courses in Warsaw, in the early 1920s, he met his future wife, the Warsaw-born Klara Fichman. They grew closer when both were appointed as teachers in a Yiddish Socialist-oriented school in the small town of Skidel, near Grodno. They married there in 1926, when he was 21 and she 25. According to Klara, Mirski was energetic, ingenious and impetuous. Their only child, Maja, was born a year later. Tabacznik's enchantment with Communism recurred around that time. He even considered for some time settling in the Soviet Union. He joined the Polish Communist Party, the KPP, and started using the pseudonyms Michal and Mirski.[6]

Michal and Klara left Skidel, taught for a while in Jewish schools in Czestochowa and finally settled in Warsaw in 1929. During the next decade Mirski became increasingly involved in Communist activities. He worked for a number of years at the Jewish Committee of the Warsaw KPP and was a member of the editorial board of the Yiddish Communist journal *Tsum Kamf*. Like other Communist activists in interwar Poland, Mirski was under constant police surveillance. He was arrested in November 1936, and interned for a year in the infamous Bereza Kartuska prison camp. After returning to Warsaw he was followed closely by the police. Mirski's life took a significant and fateful turn in September 1939, shortly after the outbreak of the war. Like many others he left Warsaw and traveled east to his native Kovel, where his mother, brothers and sister were still living. Following the Soviet occupation of Kovel, Mirski was appointed to a post in the local Education Inspectorate. An attractive Polish-Jewish Party activist named Halina, with whom Mirski had an extramarital affair in Warsaw, lived and worked in Kovel at that time. Klara and Maja arrived there shortly thereafter. Klara's impression was that her marriage was fast reaching a breaking point. Mirski was appointed to a senior position on the editorial board of the Polish language Communist newspaper in Lwow, where he planned to reunite with Halina. What paradoxically saved the marriage was the Nazi-Soviet war. Halina, who stayed in Nazi-occupied Poland, was murdered in Lwow, while Mirski and his family, though separately, were evacuated to the Soviet interior. Halina's shadow would follow Klara for many years.[7]

Mirski ended up as a village school principal in the Stalingrad District and was joined there by his wife and daughter. As the front neared Stalingrad, Mirski and his family, as *zapadniki,* former Polish citizens, were forced to leave the front zone and traveled to the Urals. They settled in a village in the Chelyabinsk District, where Mirski's mother and sisters had been living for some time. Life was extremely difficult. They often starved. A change for the better occurred only in 1943, when the ZPP, the pro-Soviet Union of Polish Patriots was founded. Mirski renewed his contacts with veteran Polish Communists at the ZPP and was appointed supervisor of Polish Communist-oriented schools in several districts, which again caused the parting of the family. Tabacznik-Mirski joined Berling's Polish Army in the spring of 1944. It was apparently then that he started officially using the name Michal Mirski. Like numerous Polish Jews who joined Berling's Army, he was appointed an officer in the Army's Political Department. He thrived as Regimental Instructor. Mirski traveled with his unit westward and reached Zhitomir, in liberated Soviet Ukraine, in the summer of 1944. Soon his Regiment crossed the Soviet-Polish border, and was stationed in Rzeszow, in southeast Poland. It was then that Mirski became fully aware of the tragic fate of Polish Jews. "After a few days in town I was amazed not to have met a single Jew. Suddenly the term Extermination materialized. It simply meant that the Jews had disappeared."[8]

Mirski joined the reestablished Polish Communist Party, the PPR. During a visit in late 1944 to liberated Lublin, still in uniform, he met with Jakub Berman. Mirski recalled that meeting: "When I arrived in Lublin to take care of a certain matter at the PPR Central Committee, I met with Jakub Berman. Among other things, he pointed out to me that Jewish Party activists asked him to transfer me to them. He also added that it would be desirable to strengthen the Communist-Jewish sector, since its work was very important. I had mixed feelings. While I was attracted by the Jewish milieu, I couldn't tear myself apart from my Regiment." It seems, however, that the choice wasn't his. In early February 1945 Mirski was notified by the Army's Political Department that he should report to the PKWN Propaganda Department in Lublin, where he was told that he was being delegated to work in the Jewish sector. He arrived in Lodz in early February 1945.[9]

According to Mirski, he "was delegated by the Central Committee of Polish Jews to form a temporary Jewish Committee in Lodz." A day or two after his arrival in the city he met with a number of Lodz Ghetto survivors representing various Jewish political parties. They decided to convene a meeting of all the Jews then residing in Lodz, in order to elect a Jewish Committee. The meeting convened on February 11th and Mirski was elected head of the Committee. He would hold this position for the next four years. Within a few weeks, Mirski also became chief editor of *Dos Naje Lebn*, the first Jewish-Yiddish newspaper in liberated Poland, printed and published in Lodz. As a devoted Communist, Mirski attempted to minimize the role of the Zionists both in the Lodz Jewish Committee and in the newspaper. When *Folks-Shtime*, the Yiddish language organ of the PPR, began publication in Lodz in 1946, Mirski became its Chief Editor.[10]

In March 1945, Mirski traveled to Lublin, where Klara and their 18-year-old daughter were staying temporarily, and brought them to Lodz.

Mirski told them that "following a request of Jewish PPR activists I have been delegated by the Party Central Committee to work among Jews. I'm already residing in Lodz, the largest center of Jewish population. There I chair the Jewish Committee." Klara distinctly recalled her encounter with Lodz, after a short stay in her ruined native Warsaw. "I suddenly saw a normal, intact city. Our apartment on 27 Sienkiewicza Street was beautiful. In spite of the enormous tragedy which I faced in Poland I was selfishly happy. I had Michal and Majka near me, and the War was over." The first postwar years in Lodz were, apparently, the happiest time in Klara's life. She worked at the Jewish Historical Commission and became absorbed in interviewing Holocaust survivors. Her beloved and adored daughter got married, and the Mirskis' first granddaughter was born.

Although Mirski was totally involved in his public and political functions, he could also be empathic and emotional at times. Years later he recalled the arrival of thousands of Jewish returnees from the Soviet Union. "It was a late Saturday afternoon, the end of a very busy and tiresome day at the Committee. A woman with a small child was ushered into my room by one of the clerks. There was no room anymore at the Jakuba Street hostel. The woman had neither relatives nor friends in town. She had just arrived from the Soviet Union, where she had lost her husband. We were about to lock up the Committee offices and she would have to go out into the streets. I thought for a moment and told the clerk to send her to my home address." The woman and her daughter stayed at the Mirskis for a few weeks.

When in 1949 *Folks-Shtime* moved to Warsaw, Mirski relocated to the capital, where he also joined the Editorial Board of *Nowe Drogi* (*New Ways*), the leading ideological Party publication. He was replaced as head of the Lodz Jewish Committee by Maria Feingold, director of the Helenowek Children's Home. The move to Warsaw must have been a significant step in Mirski's career. Klara, however, missed Lodz. "I was sorry to leave Lodz. I wish we'd never left it. For Michal, Lodz had become too provincial. He never looked back."[11]

Mirski's Communist convictions affected his attitudes toward the Jewish population's future in Poland and towards Zionism. As early as August 1945, he expressed his criticism of Zionist "manipulations" of Jewish youth. It wasn't uncommon for Zionist activists to try to convince boys and girls at the CCPJ's childrens' homes to leave illegally for Palestine. A case in point was the CCPJ childrens' home in Chorzow, near Katowice, from which a group of thirty children had disappeared. Another group of eighteen children disappeared from the CCPJ's childrens' home in Bielsko Biala. Mirski accused the chairman of the Jewish Committee in Katowice of conspiring with the Zionists and demanded an unequivocal condemnation. Mirski, like other Communist Jewish activists, was aware of the somewhat impossible situation in which they found themselves visa-vis the Zionists on the one hand and the regime on the other. During a meeting of the Communist Fraction in May 1945, he stated: "In respect to emigration we are in a rather difficult position. Our Government cannot relate to this problem in a negative manner. We, however, as Party members active in the Jewish milieu, must spread our conviction as Polish citizens in respect to the country's reconstruction and to our obligation to stay here and take part in it." In April 1949, Mirski attacked Adolf Berman, leader of the Left Poalei Zion. "In your newspapers there has not been a single article against the abandonment of Europe and Poland [by Jews]. We, Marxists, cannot accept *aliyah*."[12]

Michal and Klara Mirski were staunch Stalinists in Lodz as well as during their first years in Warsaw. Klara considered Jewish writers, historians and intellectuals who left Poland as opportunists and traitors. "The Historical Commission turned into a train station. People were grabbing their luggage, boarding trains and disappearing. They became strangers to me." She couldn't comprehend how Dr. Philip Friedman, initiator of the Jewish Historical Commision in Poland and a leading historian of the Holocaust, could leave for the US. The Yiddish writer Shmerke Kaczerginski left for Paris and settled in Argentina. Klara detested particularly the young Vilna poet-partisan Abraham Sutskever. "He had been the darling of the Soviet authorities. Now, like a snake, he used to slip into the room where I worked with Kaczerginski. He would walk around and sniff like a cat. He was secretive, withdrawn and hateful in his own, special way. He, too, intended to travel West. I considered him a traitor and abhorred him. Shortly afterward he left for Palestine, where he started attacking the Soviet Union."[13]

In 1947/48, when the Soviet Union and Poland supported the establishment of a Jewish state, Mirski's anti-Zionist criticism was somewhat muted. The onset of full-blown Stalinism in Poland in 1949-1953 resulted in his most vicious attacks against Zionism and Israel. Mirski's article "Zionism as a Tool of American Imperialism," published in the January 1953 issue of *Nowe Drogi,* backed Soviet accusations in regard to the "Doctors' Plot" in Moscow and the trial of Slansky in Prague. Stalin's death, destalinization, and Khrushchev's anti-Stalinist speech in February 1956 affected Mirski's ideological and political attitudes. In a lengthy speech at a meeting of the Polish Writers' Union, he expiated his past mistakes. The events of March 1968 and the subsequent anti-Semitic campaign in Poland forced the Mirskis to emigrate. Unlike most of his Communist colleagues who had been working in the Jewish sector and emigrated to Israel, Mirski preferred to settle in Denmark. Although he now regretted his past adoration of Stalin and Stalinist Russia, he still identified with Communism and considered himself Polish. In his correspondence with Adolf Berman, who had earlier emigrated to Israel, Mirski was mostly defensive. As for his identity, he stated unequivocally:

"I am a political emigrant and my home is Poland."[14]

***

MARIA LORBER ARRIVED IN LODZ IN JUNE 1945. SHE HAD FLED HER native Ryki, where six Jewish camp survivors were murdered by Polish nationalists. In Lodz, she stayed for a time with a married friend with whom she had been in a camp in Czestochowa. One day she met Prof. Lipska-Librachowa, her former Professor of Education from Warsaw, who took her to the Lodz Party School where she met another prewar Communist acquaintance. Upon her recommendation, Maria took a job at Film Polski, and began to advance there quite fast. It was around that time that she joined the PPR. She also changed her former last name, Loberbaum, to Lorber. Eventually, she held an important position in the censorship. When I asked Maria to compare the prewar years with the postwar situation, her immediate response was: "The principal difference was a sensation of freedom. It was a time of freedom, of hope for a better future, of reconstruction. I believed that the world would be completely different. I might have been naïve, but I still believe in man. I am not sorry for having been a Communist. The Party taught me to love people and not to kill them." In spite of her Communist milieu and her dedication to the Party, Maria maintained close relations with her Jewish aunts and even used to invite her Polish Communist friends for *gefilte fish*. "I was living between two worlds."[15]

Ewa and her five year-old daughter left Russia in April 1946. They arrived first in Wroclaw, where Ewa had a few friends. She then left little Nadia with the friends and traveled to Lodz in the hope of finding survivors from her family. "Wroclaw was in ruins. The streets were already dark at 5 p.m. Lodz was full of life. Many Jews were walking the streets. There was a tremendous difference. I met a friend from Orsk, an older man with three adult daughters, and he invited me on the spot to stay with them. Friendships have always been significant in my life. I have been lucky in this sense." Ewa went to look for her prewar house, on Polnocna Street, bordering on the ghetto area, but the building wasn't there anymore. She proceeded then to her grandmother's home on the same street. "The doorkeeper recognized me and I recognized him. He told me that nobody had survived. I walked the streets and cried. I realized then that I was completely alone in the world." One of Ewa's Wroclaw friends brought Nadia to Lodz, and Ewa was lucky once more: still another friend gave her money to rent a room. Although Ewa joined the PPR and met some of her prewar Communist friends, the man who helped her most in finding work was a Poalei Zion contact, Kagan, a member of the Lodz Jewish

Committee. She started working in a Jewish kindergarten. At the same time she met Maria Feingold, director of the Helenowek Children's Home. "When we met in postwar Lodz, she must have been in her late thirties. She had been in charge of a Polish orphanage in Samarkand before her return to Poland."

Ewa remarried sometime in 1947. Her second husband, Leon Zisman, eight years her senior, was a sickly survivor of Mauthausen. He had lost his first wife and a son in Auschwitz. Ewa gave birth to her second daughter Miriam in early 1949. Nadia was eight at that time. Leon died within half a year. When I asked Ewa whether she loved him, she unhesitatingly replied: "It was love at first sight. We were extremely happy together." Ewa's friends and parents of the children in the Jewish kindergarten she ran offered help. "Falkowska arrived right after the funeral and took me and my two daughters to a summer camp. At that time, in the summer of 1947, she headed both the children's home in Helenowek and the Jewish Committee's Education Department. I used to consult with her very often. She was motherly and authoritative at the same time. I've stayed in touch with her for many years." Nadia started attending the Lodz Yiddish School on 49 Kilinskiego Street. She recalled: "The classes were conducted in Yiddish. We were taught about Jewish holidays and the story of little Moses in the cradle. We didn't study on Saturdays and studied instead on Sundays. It wasn't pleasant to travel with a school bag on a tram on Sundays. People made nasty remarks. So, I decided to walk all the way to school, and was always late." When, towards the end of the interview, I asked Ewa how she recalled postwar Lodz, she didn't hesitate. "When I returned from Russia to Poland I hoped that Communism there would be different. Nadia's father died at Lenino, a soldier in the Polish Army, and I felt that I belonged there, that we had made a contribution to the new Poland."[16]

Henryk Flug returned from the camps to his native Lodz in June 1945. He went straight to the Jewish Committee to look for relatives. The only one who had survived was an uncle, and Flug moved into his apartment. The uncle, an engineer, advised him to resume studies as soon as possible. Flug also established contact with the surviving members of the Communist youth organization from the Lodz Ghetto. They lived then in a collective. Most of them, like Flug, decided to complete their high school requirements. There were special classes for people whose education had been interrupted by the war. "I was treated very well there. They knew that I had been through the ghetto and the camps. Our homeroom teacher was Professor Skwarczynski, a philologist, who would later serve as Rector of Lodz University. He was very friendly and supported me all the way." Flug got his high school diploma within a year and enrolled in the Lodz Polytechnic. He also joined the PPR and became very active in the Party. Most of his friends were young, educated, Communist-oriented

Poles. "We intended to study and to build the new Poland. Hitler lost and we had won. We saw the red flag at the top of the Reichstag. Poland had been liberated and we expected it to be different. "Flug also told me how he got involved in Party work. "My friends spread the word about my activities in the German camps and one day I was invited by the Party boss in Lodz, Loga-Sowinski. He told me that the Party was in dire need of people like me and suggested that I become number two in the Lodz ZWM, the Communist youth organization."

Flug got married within a few months of his return to Lodz. "I met a friend of mine, Dorotka Tugentraich, who had belonged to our Communist youth organization in the Lodz Ghetto. Dorotka's mother and part of their family had survived and our wedding was arranged in her family's apartment. There was a *chupah*, with the Lodzer Rebbe's son officiating. It was a happy Jewish wedding." Flug met Leszek Kolakowski sometime in 1946. "I met him when I started studying Economics at Lodz University. One of our courses was Logic, taught by Kotarbinski, and Leszek was his assistant. Besides that, we were both active in the University Students' Organization. Kolakowski was ideologically more leftist than myself, more Stalinist. We used to meet at 48 Piotrkowska Street where Kolakowski used to speak. We have remained friends for years."[17]

Aleks Klugman returned from Germany to Poland in the summer of 1945. He boarded a freight train in Jelenia Gora and traveled for three days and nights. "The train stopped in the middle of a field. I was told that it will not proceed any further and that we were only three kilometers away from Lodz Kaliska, the Kaliska Station. I was so excited that I almost ran those last three kilometers. Only when I reached the station, I realized that although I had finally returned to my hometown, I didn't have a home anymore and had no idea where to go." Somebody advised him to go to the Jewish Committee. There he learned that some of his friends from the Communist youth organization in the Lodz Ghetto had survived and were living in a collective on 1go Maja Street, May 1st Street. Klugman joined them. Most of these young Jewish Communists were soon appointed to various positions in the Party. Aleks met Tosia, a friend from the ghetto, and they moved as a couple to the Bursa, the Jewish youth dormitory. "We felt like one big family there." Aleks decided to learn printing and was directed to the printing shop of *Dos Naje Lebn*. "My mentor was Solomon Halter, a master of the craft, a scion of a family of Jewish printers reaching back to Guttenberg. He was the father of the future writer and artist Marek Halter." Klugman's son was born in April 1947 and became the darling of the Bursa.[18]

Sixteen year-old Dziunia arrived at the Lodz Kaliska Station in the end of August 1945. "I was alone and penniless. I walked the streets. I was terribly hungry. Then I stopped in front of a food store. A woman steps out of that store and asks me '*amchu*' (one of us) and I say, 'Yes.' 'I had a niece your age in the Lodz Ghetto. She didn't return. She probably perished in the camps.' Then I asked her, 'What's her name?' and she said Rutka, so and so. And then I told her, 'She will arrive soon. We were in the same camp and she's alive.' The woman was overwhelmed. She immediately gave me some sugar and a few rolls and told me to go to the Jewish Committee." Dziunia was assigned a lodging at the Dom Repatrianta on Jakuba Street, where she was given just a mattress. "I sat up on that mattress and started crying. I felt offended and degraded, like a stray dog. I was completely shattered. And then somebody called out 'Dziunia!'" It turned out that some of her camp friends, who had previously traveled to Lwow, were disappointed there and came to Lodz. These girls were serving in the Polish Army and took Dziunia along. This was the first time that Dziunia could eat as much as she wanted, and she got sick. She was taken to a military hospital, where she stayed for three weeks. "When I woke up in my hospital bed, I saw a sign above it, 'Private Diziunia Liberman.' There was no end to my joy and pride." After leaving the hospital Dziunia was sent by the Lodz Jewish Committee to Helenowek.

Dziunia had very good memories of her two years in Helenowek. "The first director was a woman who didn't get along well with the kids and then Mrs. Feingold arrived. She was excellent. Some of our instructors were people who had worked with Korczak, like Lunia Gold and Pola Barenholc. They were dedicated to Korczak's system of education and attempted to give us back our lost childhood. There was also a tremendous urge to continue our schooling. First, they taught us at Helenowek, and then, after some exams, we were accepted at the RTPD school in Lodz. The ideological and political line was Communist, but still, some of the children were affected by Zionist ideas. A whole group, headed by Pani Goldmanowa, disappeared one night."

Dziunia recalled that the first arrivals in Helenowek were camp survivors, those who emerged from hiding places and those who had been living with Polish families. In time, Jewish returnee children from Russia started showing up. "Among them were some children partisans. They were dressed in fitted Soviet army uniforms. They taught us Russian songs and we used to march and sing those songs. I became friendly with two of them, Isak and Marian. They even gave me a photo in which they were dressed in those Red Army uniforms."

In time, Dziunia, who was one of the most active and creative youngsters in Helenowek — she used to write and recite poems — drew very close to Mrs. Feingold-Falkowska. "Falkowska liked me very much. She was childless and decided to adopt me. She was then living with the film producer Aleksander Ford. Theirs was a big, beautiful apartment on Narutowicza Street. Natan Gross had a room there. He used to invite me to his room, to read out what he had written and ask for my opinion. I was flattered, of course. Gross also gave me a slim volume of poetry which he had translated from Hebrew to Polish. The place was frequented by the intellectual elite, people like Adam Schaff and Professor Muszkat." Dziunia, however, didn't feel at home there, and after a few months decided to return to Helenowek. After graduating high school in 1948, she began studies in the Lodz Pedagogical Institute and moved to the Bursa. "First we lived six or seven girls to a room, but when it became possible to move to smaller 'couple rooms' on the upper floor, I moved there with my boyfriend. We married when I was eight months pregnant. We just went to register in the appropriate office. I even didn't know that a Jewish wedding could be arranged at that time in Lodz, and I didn't really care." Dziunia was a member of ZWM, the Communist youth organization. "We used to travel to nearby villages to spread Communism among the peasants. I adored Stalin. I wholeheartedly believed that my future was in Poland."[19]

Szulim Rozenberg arrived in Lodz in March 1946. He intended to join his sister there. He learned upon arrival, however, that she had moved to Lower Silesia. Szulim stayed with her for a few weeks and then decided to settle in Lodz. He worked in the Registration Department of the Lodz Jewish Committee and was active in the Bund.

"When I came to the Bund Center, on 17 Jaracza Street, I met some of my former Warsaw friends. We used to sit there for hours and tell our wartime stories. Within a year Szulim married a Bialystok woman who had returned from the Soviet Union. They were not at all interested in a Jewish wedding, but his sisters insisted. The *chupah* and the party took place in Wroclaw, where Szulim's sisters were living at the time. Szulim recalled various cultural events in postwar Lodz. "I enjoyed Oistrach's performance in the former Poznanski Palace and used to go to concerts of the Lodz Philharmonic. I went to the first performance of Dzigan and Schumacher. Both the artists and the audience cried. Molly Picon, the great Jewish American actress, performed in the largest auditorium in town. People were laughing and crying at the same time. They didn't let her get off the stage."

When we discussed Jewish life in postwar Lodz, Szulim repeated several times that people hoped for a "new beginning." "They wanted to start a new life. There were lectures and literary evenings. There was a lot of educational and social activity. We used to meet on Friday evenings in the Bund Center. About 100-150 people arrived regularly. Marek Edelman used to come from time to time. We knew each other as teenagers, in prewar Warsaw. One of my best friends was Arkadiusz Kahan, who had survived the war in the Soviet Union. He stayed in Lodz for about two years, went to America and became Professor of Economics at the University of Chicago."

Szulim's plans to stay in Poland were shattered by the Kielce pogrom. A close friend, Fiszke Neiman, had been murdered in Lodz two weeks earlier. "Fiszke survived the war in the Soviet Union. There he joined the

Polish Army and ended up in Berlin. He was a talented and ambitious young man. He started studying medicine at Lodz University and at the same time was very active in the Bund youth organization. We lived on the same street, in adjoining houses. One evening we decided to meet next morning in Fiszke's apartment. When we arrived there the door was half open. We stepped in and looked for him. We found him, shot dead, in the bathtub. As a result of various anti-Semitic events my Bundist friends started considering the possibility of leaving Poland. Communist pressure on the Polish Bund to detach itself from the Bund in the West increased. All this had a strong effect on us. The idea of leaving Poland was increasingly discussed in Bundist circles. Bundist groups started leaving Poland in August 1948." Szulim, too, left Lodz around that time.

Szulim's reminiscences about Arkadiusz Kahan rang a bell. It suddenly dawned on me that I've seen that name on some of the archival documents concerning Jewish self-defense in postwar Lodz. As a result of a few telephone calls to veteran Bundists in Israel and Australia and to Kahan's daughter in Los Angeles, I could piece together basic biographical details concerning Kahan. Arkadiusz, or Avreml to his friends, was born in 1920 in Vilna. His father was a Bundist. When Avreml came of age he, too, joined the Bund. Before the Second World War, he studied History at the Stefan Batory University in Vilna. Following Vilna's occupation by the Soviets, Arkadiusz lived for a while in Minsk and then traveled to Moscow. While there he signed a petition demanding the release of imprisoned Bundist leaders. As a result, he was arrested and sent to a camp in the Soviet North. He was released in the fall of 1941, following the Polish-Soviet agreement, and traveled to Uzbekistan. In a short while he became fluent in the Uzbek language and even knew parts of the Koran by heart. Some of his family and friends maintained that Arkadiusz served in the Red Army. In 1945, he enlisted in General Berling's Polish Army, where he attained the rank of captain. When Arkadiusz arrived in the Bund Center in Lodz in early 1946, he donned the impressive uniform of a Polish Navy officer. He was at the time the editor of a Navy newspaper. Following demobilization, Arkadiusz became intensely active in the Lodz Bund. He used to lecture at the Bund youth movement's summer camps and edited the Tsukunft newspaper. For some time, Kahan headed the Lodz Komisja Specjalna — the Special Committee in charge of Jewish self-defense.

Kahan's Bundist friends recalled him with great respect, love and admiration. Kahan was a tall, attractive and highly intelligent man. The Lodz apartment which he shared with Bono Wiener and other young Bundists was known as a popular social venue. They used to discuss ideology and politics and sing Yiddish songs. It was apparently there that he met his future wife, Pearl. She had previously been the girlfriend of Fiszke Neiman. When Bundist activists started leaving Poland, Arkadiusz joined a group which illegally crossed the border to Czechoslovakia. There were seven of them: Bono and Pinche Wiener, Avreml Zheleznikov, Simche Binem, Hillel Kempinski, Pearl and Arkadiusz. This was in September 1948. Kempinski, whom I met in the 1960's in New York, was then in charge of the Bund Archives. Students and scholars of East Europen Jewry who used the Archives recall him as a somewhat eccentric but always helpful old bachelor who spoke a special dialect of Yiddishized English.[20]

Ala Margolis arrived in Lodz a few weeks after liberation. She joined her mother, who had reclaimed their spacious prewar apartment. According to Ala, Marek Edelman settled in Lodz mainly because of her. Marek was then 26 and Ala 18. Ala's mother did not approve of their relation at first, but some time later agreed that they could move together into Ala's grandmother's house on Mostowa Street. Ala's friend Aniela, also a first year medical student, moved in with them. They used to study for exams together. "Aniela and myself were very serious students, but Marek was rather lazy and we tried to convince him to take things seriously. He used to lie for hours on the sofa, and although he didn't really prepare for exams, he somehow passed them." Marek Edelman also recalled those days in postwar Lodz. "The war was over, but I didn't consider its ending a victory. For me it was a lost war. I lay down and slept, for days and weeks. People told me that I must do something. Initially I considered studying Economics, but Ala enrolled me in medical studies, so I went there, though I wasn't interested in the least. When we returned home from the University I would go to bed and lay for hours facing the wall. Some time later I understood that as a doctor I could save human lives, like I did at the Umschlagplatz in the Warsaw Ghetto." Whereas Marek was quite active in the Bund, Ala was completely apolitical. "I remember how Leszek Kolakowski used to lecture about Marxism on Piotrkowska Street. I intended to go there, but Marek forbade me to do so. I'm indebted to him for not letting me join the Party."

Marek's moods, apparently, alternated. At times he was depressed and apathetic. At other times he was humorous and even frivolous. Ala recalled: "We were young and we weren't depressed at all. A new, different life had started. We took a trip out of town once and Marek arranged for a competition — who would reach first a certain tree. All of us started running, but Marek remained standing, laughing at us. On another occasion we went dancing, but since Marek didn't know how to dance, he just started jumping, and all of us joined him."[21]

Kuba Goldberg arrived in Lodz in July 1945. "It was only natural for me to return to Poland, to Lodz. The city looked very familiar, it hadn't changed, except for the ghetto area. I went to our prewar house, where some people were living in our apartment. I didn't have the energy to claim it. I also went to my grandma's prewar house and the doorkeeper was very welcoming. He let me stay with him for some time. He also told me that nobody of my family had shown up. That meant that I was the only survivor. Of course I was sad, but somehow, I had to face it."

Kuba didn't marry in the immediate postwar years and was convinced that life for lonely Jewish men was more difficult than for couples. What seems to have kept him going was his strong will to continue his studies. "I definitely knew that I wanted to study. I was interested in History, Jewish History in particular. After completing my interrupted high school education, I enrolled at Lodz University in the fall of 1947. I was successful in my studies and was quite soon appointed as an assistant." Kuba was also active in a Socialist student organization and used to have arguments with Communist students. He recalled such political theorists as Adam Schaff and Jan Strzelecki. Kuba also knew Leszek Kolakowski. After the merger of the PPS with the PPR and with the increasing power of the Communists, Kuba was squeezed out of his social and political student activities. All that time he was living in the Bursa, which he perceived as his home.

It wasn't easy for Kuba to bridge the gap between his Jewish and Polish identities. "We would argue about Polish and Jewish suffering and loss during the war and the occupation. My Polish colleagues tried to convince me that the Polish tragedy was worse than that of the Jews. I was astounded: my entire family had vanished. Numerous Jews, who either survived the German occupation or returned from Russia, left Poland. However, most of the young Jews steeped in Polish culture, like myself, didn't leave." Professor Goldberg was proud of the fact that he had never considered Polonizing his name. "I never concealed my roots. I didn't change my name to Zlotogorski or Zlotoryjski. I've always remained Jakub Goldberg. Among my Jewish friends and colleagues who were steeped in Polish culture I was a Jew *par excellence,* since I was interested in Jewish matters." Kuba was friendly with Marek Edelman and Ala Margolis. He recalled that Ala wanted Marek to be less active in the Bund, so that he could devote his time to studying medicine. "She, actually, made him complete his studies."

Although the Kielce pogrom shocked Kuba, the conclusion he drew from it differed from that of the Zionists. "The Kielce tragedy increased my conviction that only the type of government which existed at that time in Poland could overcome anti-Semitism. Following the emergence of the State of Israel, a new exodus of Polish Jews began. I never considered leaving Poland. For me this was unthinkable." When Goldberg the historian was asked decades later about the negative Jewish and Israeli attitudes toward Poles, he expressed his belief that "Poland should be examined not only as a country where Jews had perished, but also as a country where Jews had lived for centuries, and where religious tolerance had functioned on a larger scale than in any other place."[22]

Kazik Rutenberg visited Lodz a number of times when he was still in the Polish Air Force. He went to the Jewish Committee to look for survivors from his family, and after demobilization settled in Lodz. He lived there with his mother, who in the meantime had returned from Russia. "It was a six-room apartment on Kilinskiego Street. Each family occupied one room. One of the families was that of Dr. Redlich. He lived there with his wife and his 11- or 12-year-old son. Mothers used to come to him with their children for consultations." Kazik, who did not complete his high school education before the war, joined a preparatory course for the Lodz Polytechnic. "Some of them were demobilized soldiers, like myself; others were ex-partisans, ghetto survivors and people who had returned from Siberia." It was in that course that Kazik met his future wife, when he was 22 and she was 17. Ada and her mother had survived the war in the Soviet Union. She recalled that she hardly knew Polish then and spoke mostly Russian. Before she met Kazik, Ada was a member of Hashomer Hatzair for a while. Her mother was in charge of the Hashomer Hatzair culture club in Lodz. "We were about to leave for Palestine with my uncle. However, since his daughter got sick, our departure was postponed several times and, finally, we returned our passports and stayed." Even Kazik, who never considered leaving Poland, had some contacts with the Zionists. He was asked to instruct a group of Haganah volunteers in topography. "Although I was keenly aware of being Jewish, I considered myself Polish as well, and that's how I defined myself. I never hid my Jewish roots. I considered myself a Pole of Jewish origin. I expected and hoped that the new regime would, in time, eliminate anti-Semitism."

Kazik fully internalized the Jewish tragedy and loss. "I didn't suppress anything. When we first learned about Majdanek, and saw those strangely dressed people in the striped clothes, I started to grasp what had happened. I remember crying on two occasions while flying my fighter plane. The first time was when we flew over the Soviet-Polish border. I was happy to leave Russia. The second time was when we escorted the victory parade over liberated Warsaw in January 1945. Before returning to the air base, we flew very low over the city. There was that huge area, completely devastated, with one lonely church amid the ruins. I burst out crying. I later learned that this was the site of the Warsaw Ghetto and that the church had served converted Jews, forced into the Ghetto."[23]

Henryk Grynberg arrived in Lodz with his mother in April 1945. His first impressions render quite well the essence of the city at that time: "The low gray buildings stood even and undamaged, all covered with prewar grime. The streetcar windows had been painted blue, but that only lent them a certain charm. Goods from American and English 'Care' packages filled the shop windows. The streets and gutters were overflowing and pulsed with life." Henryk recalled the excitement in post-liberation Lodz. "In the last days of April, people massed on Plac Wolnosci, Liberty Square, where loudspeakers relayed communiqués from the front. Newspaper boys ran around the streets shouting 'Berlin has fallen, Hitler's in hell!'

There were grand parades of soldiers and youths, parade after parade — on the first of May, the third of May, the ninth of May."

Henryk and his mother moved into a room in an apartment occupied by a family they used to know in Dobre. They'd been making a living buying and selling textiles. Henryk's mother joined in. Henryk, with his best friend Izak, roamed the streets and played with other kids in the courtyard. "I was happy. For the first time I was allowed to play with children and didn't have to be constantly careful." It was also the first time that Henryk could identify himself as a Jew. "More and more people were coming to Lodz, where it was easier to start life over. And most of those who came were Jews. Izak and I would walk the streets, staring at everyone passing by. Whenever we saw a thin, pale person with large sad eyes, we'd step in front of him and ask '*amkhu — one of us?*' If they didn't know that Hebrew word, we'd excuse ourselves, and run off. But sometimes a person would stop and cry, 'Yes, *amkhu!*' We'd feel great joy. We kept searching the streets. It had become our passion." Yet, during the first few months, Henryk pretended at times to be Polish. In the Polish school which he attended and in the municipal summer camp, he was Henryk Krzyzanowski, using his assumed wartime Polish surname.

Henryk recalled some Jewish cultural events in Lodz. The first postwar screening of the sentimental prewar Yiddish film *Mayn Shtetl Belz* (*My Town of Belz*) etched itself distinctly in his memory. "All of them wanted to get into the hall. They broke down the doors, all the mirrors, railings and windows. The lobby was so packed I couldn't breathe. When the well-known song came on — 'Oh Belz, my beloved Belz' — terrible cries burst from everyone, a great collective groan and cry of pain."

A medical checkup in late 1945 revealed some lung problems. Henryk didn't attend school for a few weeks and then was dispatched to the Helenowek Children's Home, where he stayed for the next three years. For decades he remembered the exact date of his arrival: January 26, 1946. He ceased being a "street boy" and was placed in a well-structured educational and social framework. Although he'd been reading books before Helenowek, it was there that he became an avid reader. "There was a good children's library there, and one had to order the most popular books weeks in advance. There were book games, from which I learned a lot. There was also music, singing and dancing. I joined the dancing group." Henryk was sent to a sanatorium in the spring of 1946, and when he returned to Helenowek in the summer, the place had changed considerably following the arrival of returnee children from the Soviet Union. "Helenowek was invaded by Asians. They were running around barefoot, without shirts, just in their '*trusiki*' — slips — those savages, and they spoke Russian. The heads of those boys and girls were shaved." Henryk was sent to a convalescents' sanatorium, in the mountains, in October 1946. He went there with a friend, Chaim Preter, who survived the war in Russia and had been placed by his mother in Helenowek. Henryk would return to school, this time to the Peretz Yiddish school on 49 Kilinskiego Street, only in March 1947.

The Helenowek years must have been a significant formative period in Henryk's life. It is there that he expressed in writing for the first time his thoughts and emotions concerning the wartime fate of the Jews. Following a field trip into a flowering meadow with his favorite teacher, Pani Pola Barenholc, who remarked something about those who did not live to see that beautiful spring day, Henryk wrote a short essay about those who did not make it. "My page was included in the children's wall broadsheet. Children would read the broadsheet, look in my direction and some of them would nod their heads, but nobody uttered as much as a word." In an interview conducted half a century later, Grynberg, the writer, recalled that "neither at school nor in the Helenowek Children's Home did we talk about our worst experiences. We never discussed our dreadful past. We did know that somebody doesn't have a father and somebody else doesn't have a mother, but we never inquired how these things happened. We didn't talk or think about the past. Only the present mattered." Henryk once joined a group of "Russian" youngsters and, with them, was caught stealing vegetables from the Helenowek greenhouse. Pani Maria, an educator whom Henryk respected highly, scolded him and expressed her disappointment. "After the stealing incident my mother took me back home." That was October 1949.

Henryk was very attached to his mother. It is with her that he had shared his most dangerous and dreadful times. She remarried in Lodz. Uszer, Henryk's stepfather, came from Dobre and had known Henryk's family. He was a survivor of the Warsaw Ghetto, Mauthausen and Treblinka. Uszer had lost his first wife and their two children. In prewar Warsaw Uszer had leaned towards Communism. "When Uszer married my mother, the cantor himself said the Kiddush, since Uszer didn't know such things. All Uszer said was 'Amen'." In his highly emotional, elegiac memoir about his deceased mother, Grynberg relived his love and adoration for her. He used the diminutive, endearing Yiddish *Mamesi*, which he apparently had never used in her lifetime. "I'll never forget your flowered cloche-gown when you arrived to visit me in Helenowek. It was my birthday. You brought a jar of strawberries in sour cream, which we ate sitting on the grass, in the shade of apple trees. I can assure you that never in my life had I tasted anything like those strawberries and never have I been happier than in those moments."

Henryk attended the Yiddish school on Kilinskiego Street for five years. This was an unusual experience for young Henryk, who had been previously instructed to think and act like a Polish boy. "On Sunday mornings, with schoolbags on our backs, we used to run along the cleanly swept streets to the amazed looks of passersby and tram conductors."

Henryk remembered some of his teachers, especially Mr. Helman, the History teacher, whom he presented later as a tragicomic figure in one of his autobiographical novels. The school was usually overcrowded. "It was difficult to walk the corridors. The kids used to sing and dance during the recesses. These were mostly Zionist songs. And they kept dancing the Hora." The school started changing around 1948/1949. Numerous students left for Israel. "My best friends disappeared, as did the Zionist youth movement uniforms. Classes became increasingly smaller. They stopped teaching us Hebrew altogether and most of the subjects now were taught in Polish. Those students who stayed on came mostly from assimilated and Communist families. There were also a few *shlemazls* like myself." Although Henryk's family planned to leave Poland at one time, his stepfather was arrested for illegal trading at an inopportune moment. By the time he was returned to the family, their emigration papers had expired.

Henryk, who would later join the Warsaw Jewish State Theater, started his acting career in postwar Lodz. He was assigned his first role, that of a Jewish youngster, in Kruczkowski's "Germans," at the Teatr Powszechny. He was thirteen at the time. "Some women fainted as I told the audience, 'They killed everybody, mother, grandpa and little Esterke. Only I've survived.'" He was also selected to play a Jewish boy-smuggler in Aleksander Ford's *Border Street*. Henryk participated in Gross's *Unzere Kinder* as well. Although, as he recalled, there was very little discussion about the Holocaust among Jewish children, the issues and themes of Henryk's future writings started budding already in those first postwar years. Grynberg, whose books would depict wartime Jewish tragedy and suffering, admitted years later that "as a survivor of the Holocaust, I consider bearing witness my most important moral duty."[24]

28. Young Bundists. Lodz, 1946. From left to right: Hersz Mokotow, Szulim Rozenberg, Tesia Mokotow, Fiszke Neiman. Courtesy of Szulim Rozenberg.

29. Celebration in honour of the State of Israel. Lodz, May 1948. Standing: Michal Mirski. Sitting, third from right: Binyamin Majerczak. Courtesy of Binyamin Majerczak.

EPILOGUE

THE YEARS 1949-1950, THE PERIOD OF THE GROWING STALINIZATION OF Poland, marked the end of Jewish life as it had been during the immediate postwar years. The change in the previously supportive Soviet-bloc attitudes and policies toward Israel, and the increasing Soviet attacks against Jewish nationalism and Zionism, directly affected Jewish life in Poland. A gradual, yet decisive, suppression of all Zionist and non-Communist Jewish structures ensued. The Jewish Fraction of the Communist Party was effectively and extensively used for this purpose. The Zionists and the Bundists were gradually squeezed out of the Central Committee of Polish Jews and the local Jewish committees. Increasing controls and restrictions preceded the final liquidation of the Zionist parties and Zionist youth movements. A Ministry of Public Security directive concerning the celebrations of the First of May and the Proclamation of Israel Day in May 1949 stated that "no public gatherings, demonstrations and the flying of white and blue banners are allowed. Events celebrating the Proclamation of Israel are to take place exclusively inside the locations of Zionist organizations and with the participation of their members only. As for the First of May celebrations, all Jewish organizations participating in public demonstrations must march under the slogans of the PZPR. Zionist slogans and white and blue banners are prohibited." And indeed, for the first time in the postwar years Jewish organizations did not march separately in the First of May celebrations.[1]

In early July of 1949, the Ministry of Public Administration issued a directive prohibiting Zionist summer camps, particularly those of Hashomer Hatzair. Still, some Hashomer Hatzair camps were organized. The last Hashomer Hatzair summer camp, with the participation of close to a hundred campers, took place that summer in Dziwnow on the Baltic Sea. A Hashomer Hatzair circular mailed to all of its branches in early August 1949 stated, "Our Movement in postwar Poland has never faced such difficulties and obstacles in organizing summer camps." A few Dror and Gordonia summer camps took place in a nearly clandestine manner. The various Zionist youth movements convened their last pre-emigration meetings in the fall of 1949. One of the last Hashomer Hatzair meetings was held in Wroclaw. Criticism and attacks against the Zionists by Jewish Communists became increasingly frequent. Even outright provocations were used for this purpose. During a meeting of representatives of Jewish committees in Lodz in the fall of 1949, Mirski and Zachariasz accused Zionist members of a local Jewish cooperative of posting anti-Communist slogans on the walls. Hebrew schools came under increasing criticism. Already in early 1948, a report concerning the Hebrew school in Swidnica, near Walbrzych, stated that "the school educates the students in the spirit of a separate Jewish people, aiming at their upbringing as citizens of a Jewish state." Sometimes, pretexts of a purely administrative nature, such as the fact that some Hebrew schools functioned in converted apartments instead of official public spaces, were used for their termination. Jewish Fraction activists, including Communist principals of CCPJ schools, forced the closure of some Hebrew schools during the school year of 1948/1949. The few remaining Hebrew schools were shut down in the fall of 1949. All Zionist newspapers and periodicals were also forced to close at that time.[2]

Arrests and interrogations of some Zionist activists preceded the liquidation of the Zionist parties. Three members of the Left Poalei Zion were arrested in Lodz in early March 1949. Following appeals to the Government by Poalei Zion leaders, they were released within a few weeks. There were also arrests of Brichah activists. One of them, Mordechai Mittelman, was sentenced to two and a half years in prison. The decision to terminate all Zionist parties and organizations was made in the fall of 1949.The Ministry of Public Administration designated specific deadlines: it would begin in December 1949 and end in February 1950. The Poalei Zion Central Committee, which convened in mid-November 1949, agreed to shut down the Committee and all of its branches by November 25. The last Hashomer Hatzair council convened in early December 1949. The opening appeal to the participants spoke of Hashomer Hatzair's achievements in Poland during the five postwar years, and of the future in Israel. The Chief Command of Hashomer Hatzair in Poland issued its last appeal on December 19, 1949: "Following the decision of the authorities concerning the liquidation of the Zionist organizations, our Movement concludes its activities in Poland. Our journey towards a new life and our dreams are being accomplished by aliya. We shall soon meet in trains and on ships, on our way to Israel."[3]

The closure of all Zionist organizations in Lodz followed suit. The Ministry of Public Administration recommended on November 2, 1949, the immediate closure of the headquarters of Keren Hakayemet, the Jewish National Fund, and of Keren Hayesod, the Palestine Foundation Fund, both located in Lodz. The Lodz office of Hashomer Hatzair closed on December 23. Some of its files were transferred to the Lodz Municipality, and 150 books were sent to the Jewish Historical Institute in Warsaw. Hehalutz closed on the same day and transferred 34 items to the Lodz Municipality.

The Ichud offices closed on December 12, 1949. The Liquidation Report stated that "7 desks, 10 chairs, 12 benches, 2 chandeliers, and 1 blackboard were donated to the children's home in Helenowek."[4]

Significant and far-reaching changes concerning Jewish non-Zionist and CCPJ-controlled institutions occurred in 1949 and 1950. As early as June 1949, Zachariasz, following the Party line, proposed that all Jewish institutions in Poland be nationalized. At a meeting of the PZPR Central Committee Secretariat on August 4, 1949, a decision was taken to nationalize all Jewish institutions which had hitherto functioned under the auspices of local Jewish committees, such as schools, children's homes and student dormitories. CCPJ-controlled Jewish schools, including the Peretz School in Lodz, were nationalized over the next few months. Instruction in Hebrew, Yiddish and other Jewish subjects in these schools was gradually restricted. The Jewish Theatre under the directorship of Ida Kaminska became the State Jewish Theatre in January 1950. The process of nationalization was completed by the spring of 1950. The TKZ — The Jewish Cultural Society, until then one of the remaining Jewish institutions, now merged with the CCPJ and became the TSKZ — the Cultural and Social Jewish Society — fully controlled by Jewish Communists and by the regime.[5]

A report by the Lodz Jewish Committee submitted in early 1950 and signed by Maria Feingold, who had replaced Mirski as Committee Chairman, reflected the new situation. "The Committee has ceased representing the *wachlarz,* the 'party fan' (i.e. the multi-party representation which had been common in the previous years). It has turned into the representative of the Jewish working masses (i.e. of the Communist party). We reinforced our struggle with the remnants of the Jewish reaction and Jewish nationalism. This struggle, expressing political vigilance, has been and is being greatly supported by the Lodz Committee of the PZPR." As for specific Jewish institutions in the city, Feingold pointed out that the Peretz School "is still being haunted by the remnants of nationalism — the heritage of such people as Kagan and Helman. The fluctuation of pupils (close to seventy children had arrived from the Hebrew school on January 1, 1950) raises difficulties in the stabilization of our educational influence." In other words, the children from the Hebrew School, which had just been shut down, had a deleterious ideological effect on the student body of the CCPJ-controlled Peretz School. Feingold's report also spoke of the nationalization of all Jewish educational and welfare institutions in the city.[6]

The period marked by the liquidation of all Zionist organizations and by the far-reaching changes in the remaining Jewish structures also saw the final wave of postwar Jewish emigration from Poland. A Government announcement published in early September 1949 spoke of the option for Jews to emigrate to Israel. According to Zionist estimates, close to 40,000 Jews applied for emigration papers. Close to 30,000 actually left for Israel between the fall of 1949 and the summer of 1951. Among them were 5,000 Jews from Lodz. The Jewish population of Poland had now shrunk to 70,000. A Polish-Jewish sociologist who in 1950 submitted her doctoral dissertation on postwar Polish Jewry to the Warsaw University Institute of Sociology remarked: "Those Jews who are most prone to maintaining the traditionally separate character of Jewish institutions are leaving for Israel. Zionist activists are leaving; Zionist political parties are being disbanded; the Zionist press, so active in the period immediately following the war, is practically extinct. Only a small fraction of the Jewish community chooses to remain in Poland."[7]

***

MATITYAHU MINTZ, THE HASHOMER HATZAIR EMISSARY FROM ISRAEL, would extend his Polish visa from time to time. The police officer in charge of visa extensions in Lodz was Marko Tomasz. Marko would extend Mintz's visa for a few months at a time, and it looked like a mere formality. However, when Mintz arrived in Marko's office at the end of May 1949, he was granted only a short extension. Marko told him that he must leave Poland by July 15. "I started organizing some of the summer camps, but I had to leave." In the early 1970s, a man stepped into Prof. Mintz's Tel-Aviv University office and introduced himself as Shlomo Strauss-Marko. The two recognized each other instantly. "I took out my old passport with his signature and showed it to him. The man was stunned. And then he told me out of the blue 'they wanted to implicate you in the Slansky Trial and I saved you by not extending your visa."[8]

Towards the end of 1949, Fayvl Podemski's uncle was told by his Communist friends that the UB was interested in Fayvl's whereabouts. Fayvl consulted immediately with Moshe Chizhik, the Hashomer Hatzair emissary, and the next morning they traveled together to the Israeli Legation in Warsaw. Fayvl was told that he must leave. "I understood the gravity of the situation. Some Zionist activists were being arrested. My papers were arranged within days, and I was on my way to Italy. Following a short stay in Venice, I boarded a ship sailing for Israel. It must have been early 1950. When I left Lodz it was snowing; when I arrived in Italy it was snowing, and when we arrived in Israel it was snowing there as well."

Fayvl had stayed in the devastated Lodz Ghetto after its liquidation. Like a few hundred other young Jewish men, he was forced by the Germans to search the empty houses for Jewish property. Fayvl used that opportunity to find and hide Hashomer Hatzair materials, such as wartime letters, diaries and reports. After liberation and the arrival of the Israeli diplomats, Fayvl brought this invaluable documentation to the Israeli Legation in Warsaw. It was eventually deposited at the Hashomer Hatzair Archives in Israel.[9]

Natan Gross filmed the arrival of the Israeli Legation and made short documentary sequences on its activities in postwar Poland. When the film was ready, it was already too late to receive official approval to take it out of the country. The first step was to smuggle it out of the Film Polski Studios. "I approached Piotr, the guard at the gate, and proposed to replace him for a few minutes while he goes to buy a bottle of vodka to celebrate the completion of our film. A taxi was waiting nearby, and in a short while we were at the Israeli Legation. The film was then forwarded to Israel by diplomatic mail." Natan, his wife and his infant son left Poland in late December, 1949. Natan was concerned about his private papers, which included his memoirs of the War and Holocaust years. "When our baggage was opened for inspection there was a sudden electricity cut, caused apparently by the heavy snowfall. The custom officials were quite tired, and they just passed us through. I was relieved. My papers were safe now." The Grosses traveled to Israel from Venice on the "Galila," and arrived at the Haifa port on January 11, 1950.[10]

Hanka's family left Lodz in September 1950. They first traveled by train to Gdansk or Gdynia on the Baltic Sea and boarded a small Israeli ship. "The voyage to Haifa lasted for two weeks and everybody was sick." Hanka lived in Israel for a few years. In 1955, she met Romek Hornstein, a Jewish survivor who was living in Canada. They were married in 1956. Since then Hanka has been living in Montreal. When I asked her about her perception of the Lodz years, she told me that it was an optimistic period in her past. She kept repeating, "Those were the first normal years of my life." She had no memories whatsoever of the prewar years. "In Russia I'd had no idea that a different kind of life was possible. Postwar Lodz was, actually, the beginning of my life."[11]

Following the closure of the Lodz Hebrew School in late 1949, Aharon began attending a Polish school. "This was a total change. All my classmates were Polish. There were no more Jewish friends. After classes we went for a swim. We used to jump naked into the pool. I recall my embarrassment. I didn't want them to see that I'm Jewish. There were no more Zionist youth movements and I became, in a way, Polonized. My mother, of course, spoke Yiddish at home, but I started to despise that language. I became an admirer of Polish literature and Polish culture. I read a lot of Polish books. I owe my good Polish to that short period in my life." All this lasted until August 1950, when Aharon's family left for Israel.[12]

When I interviewed Richard in my hotel room in Prague, he broke down and cried twice. The first time was when he told me how his great uncle David from New York, a successful photographer and portraitist, had contacted his mother when they were living in Lodz. "I think I owe him the life that I now have. He got us into France. He supported us in Paris while we stayed there, and eventually he managed to get us immigration papers to Canada. He got us on the road to a new life." The second time was when Richard recalled meeting with his father after decades of estrangement. "My mind was quite poisoned against my father by my mother."

Richard's wife, Marika, a Holocaust survivor, tried for years to convince him to establish contact with his father. When she went for a visit to her native Hungary in the late 1970s, she stopped in Frankfurt herself to meet with him. As a result, Richard met finally with his father in New York. "We had a marvelous time."[13]

Ada Gibraltar continued her high school education in a Polish school. Her stepfather, who had worked in Lodz for the Keren Kayemet, The Jewish National Fund, until it closed, moved to Warsaw, where he accepted a position at the Israeli Legation. Gibraltar was denied emigration papers several times. He died of cancer in 1953. Ada studied in a Warsaw high school for two years and graduated in 1954. I wondered about her transition from a Jewish, Zionist-oriented life at our Lodz Hebrew School and the Gordonia youth movement into a Polish milieu. "When people are 15 or 16, they are quite immersed in themselves. They attempt to be like all the others. My best friends now were some Polish girls. I even went out for a few months with Michal, a Pole." Ada completed two years of medical school in Warsaw and emigrated to Israel in 1957.[14]

Ewa's second husband Leon died in mid-1949. Her older daughter Nadia was eight and her infant daughter Miriam was six months old. Nadia recalled that things started changing at that time. "People were making choices in their lives, deciding about their future, defining their identities. And children could sense it. I remember that people were emigrating to Israel. On my way to school, I noticed that some stores were being closed. The notices on the doors usually announced 'closed for renovation.' But those stores never reopened." Some of Ewa's friends left for Israel, but she wasn't offended or hurt. She just accepted the fact that they had made their choice. Ewa with her two daughters moved to Warsaw in 1954 and continued her studies in education at the Party Institute for Social Studies.

That year she also met Abraham Przemyslawski, who would become her third husband. "He lived in Lodz at that time and I lived in Warsaw. It was very romantic. Like a novel." At the Institute, Ewa renewed her contact with Feingold-Falkowska, who worked there as a pedagogical secretary. "I used to consult with her a lot during those years. I would cry and ask her whether I should leave Poland." Ewa emigrated to Israel in 1959.[15]

Henryk Flug left Lodz for Warsaw in 1948. "Many of my Polish and Jewish friends moved to Warsaw around that time." Flug was appointed Deputy Editor of *Sztandar Mlodych,* the Party youth newspaper. After a while, he was sent to study at the Higher Party School and after graduation, in the mid-fifties, he was offered the position of Regional Party Secretary in Bialystok. The mid-fifties in Poland were a time of internal Party conflicts between hardliners and liberals. Flug was supposed to increase the number of liberals in the Bialystok Region. However, an incident that occurred eight months after his arrival had a dramatic effect on his life. "The top Party functionaries of the Communist Party of Belorussia and of the Bialystok Region in Poland met in Puszcza Bialowieska. I was the only Jew at that meeting. The Soviet representatives started complaining to their Polish comrades that 'a clique of Jewish cosmopolitans is gaining control over the Polish Communist Party. We should not allow this to happen.' This was the breaking point for me. I returned to Warsaw and told Dorotka that we must leave Poland." Flug left the Party. Following a number of futile attempts to get official approval, the Flugs left Poland for Israel in early 1958.[16]

Kuba Goldberg, after completing his Ph.D. in history, lectured at Lodz University. He stayed in Lodz until 1967 and emigrated to Israel before the March 1968 anti-Semitic events. "Anti-Jewish moods in Lodz were more prominent than elsewhere. These moods were felt at the University as well. Some of my Warsaw friends accused me of panicking. I had been convinced that anti-Semitism was on the rise. I sensed that they would not allow me to be Polish anymore. That's why we left in 1967. Numerous Lodz University historians had been active in the 1968 events. The younger generation there is completely unaware of the disgrace of their academic mentors. Anti-Jewish incidents in Lodz, even before 1968, differed from those in other places. Whereas in other cities people were forced to go to anti-Zionist meetings and rallies and were rather passive, in Lodz they initiated those acts." Still, in an interview published in Poland in 2002, Goldberg maintained: "I am part of the Polish school of history. I live abroad, but I do not consider myself a foreigner in Poland."[17]

CONCLUDING REMARKS

THE ARRIVAL OF JEWS IN POSTWAR LODZ TOOK PLACE WITHIN THE WIDER context of the return of Jewish survivors to cities and towns throughout postwar Europe. Jews were returning to countries and societies, especially in Central and Eastern Europe, which had suffered major demographic, political and social upheavals, and were trying to rebuild their lives. The return of Jews to locations where thriving communities with a vibrant Jewish life had been eradicated was mostly a sad and traumatic affair. Still, there were attempts to revive, at least partly, that which had been lost.

Jewish life in Lodz was affected by the circumstances that shaped Jewish life in all of Poland during the immediate postwar years. Some Jews considered their stay in Poland a transitory stage in an attempt to rebuild their shattered lives elsewhere. Others hoped to reestablish themselves among their prewar neighbors. For Jews in Poland widespread anti-Semitism, and particularly the Kielce pogrom, had a decisive effect. Nevertheless, even after the events in Kielce, some Jews still hoped to make Poland their home.

The survivors shared feelings of loss and dislocation. Most, however, did not allow these deep-seated emotions to overwhelm their daily lives. Whether in their truncated families or within various social, political and ideological frameworks, they managed to cope with the difficulties of daily life and nurtured hopes for the future. They married and had children, even in the most unusual circumstances. The Lodz Bursa — the crowded Jewish dormitory — was not only a place to live and study in, but also a place to start families.

Although all Jews living in postwar Poland for varying periods of time were, in a sense, survivors, some of them had lived under direct Nazi occupation while others survived the war in the Soviet Union. Both groups had suffered immensely. Nonetheless, more of the returnees from Russia survived with their families than was the case for the survivors of Nazi occupation. And whereas Jewish deportees and refugees in the Soviet Union had shared the travails of war with the Soviet population at large, Jews under German rule were singled out for total annihilation. The accounts of returnees from Soviet Russia fill a significant gap in the historiography of Jewish survival. Listening to the stories of the returnees, I grasped the enormity of their wartime trajectories, in both the geographical and cultural sense. Ewa's wartime journey took her from Lodz to Soviet-occupied Bialystok, then to Magnitogorsk, to Poltava in Soviet Ukraine, to Orsk in the Southern Urals, and then back to Lodz. Szulim Rozenberg traveled from Warsaw to Soviet-occupied Vilna, then to the Komi Autonomous Republic in the Soviet North, to the Gorki region and to Krasnodar, north of the Black Sea, from where he traveled to Lodz. Majerczak traveled from Warsaw to Soviet-occupied Lwow, was deported to the Volgostroi labor camps on the Upper Volga, lived for some time in Ordzhonikidze and in Krasnovodsk, from where he traveled to Samarkand in Uzbekistan. There he joined Berling's Polish Army and returned to Poland as an officer.

The postwar population of Lodz, although severely diminished and different in ethnic composition, was steadily growing. Lodz was also becoming the largest Jewish urban center in Poland, particularly as a result of the flow of Jewish returnees from Russia. An overwhelming majority of those who settled in or passed through Lodz in the postwar years were not native sons, *Lodzer Yidn*. They originated from throughout Poland, and some of them even founded *landsmannshaftn,* hometown societies of their own. Many Jews were attracted to the city because they already had a relative, friend or acquaintance there. A sort of snowball effect took place. Loneliness and anti-Semitism were also factors in a prevailing quest for "togetherness." Like other centers of Jewish population in postwar Poland, Lodz served as a transitory venue. Still, more Jews lived there for various periods of time than in any other Polish city. In fact, every fourth Jew in postwar Poland lived for weeks, months and sometimes for years in that city, and found that it was safer for Jews than were other Polish cities.

Postwar Polish and Jewish Lodz were permeated, if in different ways, by a sense of vitality, intensity and even euphoria. As Warsaw was in ruins, Lodz effectively became the center of Polish culture, arts and entertainment. It was a significant center of Jewish life as well. Hope for the future was more common among the ideologically-inclined and among the young: people became immersed in their personal and social rehabilitation; young Jewish men and women focused on rebuilding their shattered lives. They resumed their interrupted education. In spite of differing and conflicting ideologies, there was something the young Jewish Communists and the young Zionists had in common: both were intensely future-oriented. The former were convinced that there was a future for Jews in postwar Poland. The latter believed in rebuilding their lives in Palestine and in Israel. As for older Jews and their families, their Palestine/Israel-oriented response was a result of a wish to live among Jews, in a Jewish state and the impact of the organizational abilities and financial resources of the Zionists. Some

Jews decided to leave Poland as a result of the growing Stalinization of the country.

People did not just help themselves. They also helped others. They were willing to share their crowded apartments and rooms with relatives, friends and even complete strangers. Perhaps the extreme conditions of life in Nazi-occupied Poland, in the ghettos and camps, as well as in war-ravaged Russia, changed their peacetime habits and attitudes. When I asked old, sick Helena Leneman, who as a young woman had been in charge of a Koordynacja children's home in Lodz, what motivated her, she replied: "We had lost everything, and they were orphans. Somebody had to replace their missing parents." Tsipora Nahir, in her mid-seventies when interviewed, and a youngster of fifteen and sixteen in postwar Lodz, confided: "Hashomer Hatzair gave me back my youth, the ability to laugh, to fool around, to fall in love, and to be normal again." Professor Matityahu Mintz, now in his eighties, never forgot the euphoria of working with Zionist youngsters in postwar Poland.

Following Warsaw's reconstruction and revival in the late forties, most of the out-of-town intellectuals, writers and artists left Lodz for the capital. So did significant institutions. Lodz, which had always been a distinctly proletarian city, became now increasingly provincial. Although thousands of Jews still remained there after the 1949-1951 emigration, and despite the few remaining Communist Jewish frameworks in the city, the vibrant and variegated Jewish life of the immediate postwar years was gone. Even Communist Jewish institutions, like the Jewish Historical Commission, and Communist Jewish leaders such as Michal Mirski, moved to Warsaw. As a result of the ensuing emigration of Polish Jews in the late fifties and in the late sixties, Lodz became almost *Judenrein*. Even the memory of things Jewish faded away.

BIOGRAPHICAL NOTES

Dublin, Dziunia, formerly Liberman (1929-). Lived in Lodz, attended a Jewish girls' school and joined Hashomer Hatzair. She participated in illegal Hashomer Hatzair activities in the Lodz Ghetto and later on joined the communist youth organization. She was deported to Auschwitz in August 1944, then transferred to the Stutthof camp and ended up in Halbstadt, where she was liberated in May 1945. She returned to Lodz in August 1945, served for a short while in the Polish Army and lived for two years in the Helenowek Children's Home. After graduating a Polish high school Dziunia studied Education. She joined first the ZWM, the Communist youth organization and in 1950 became a member of the Communist Party. She moved from Lodz to Wroclaw where she worked as an editor at the Ossolineum Institute. Dziunia left Poland for Israel in 1957.

Edelman, Marek, (1919-2009). Lived in prewar Warsaw and was active there in the Bund youth movement. Edelman was one of the leaders of the Warsaw Ghetto Uprising in 1943 and participated in the Warsaw Uprising in 1944. After the war he settled in Lodz and married Alina Margolis. Edelman studied medicine at Lodz University and was active in the Bund. He became in time a leading cardiologist. Edelman stayed in Lodz until 2007. He died in Warsaw and was buried in the Warsaw Jewish Cemetery.

Eynat, Aharon, formerly Zalkind (1934-). Lived in prewar Vilna and in the Vilna Ghetto. His father was murdered in Ponary. Aharon survived with his mother and younger brother. He studied for two years in a Soviet-Jewish school in Vilna and settled with his family in Lodz in 1946. There he attended the Hebrew Ghetto Fighters' School and was a member of Hashomer Hatzair. Following the closing of the Hebrew School in 1949, Aharon studied in a local Polish high school. He emigrated from Poland to Israel in 1950.

Flug, Noah, Henryk, (1925-). Lived in Lodz. He studied in Hebrew schools in prewar Lodz and in the Lodz Ghetto high school. Flug was active in the Communist youth organization in the Lodz Ghetto. He was deported to Auschwitz in 1944 and subsequently interned in a number of camps. He returned to Lodz in 1945, completed his high school education and studied at the Lodz Polytechnic. Flug also became a leader in the local ZWM, the Communist youth organization. He moved to Warsaw in 1948 and attended the Higher Party School. After graduation, he was appointed Party Secretary in Bialystok. Flug left Poland with his family in 1958 and settled in Israel.

Frenkel-Przemyslawski, Ewa (1920-). Lived with her family in Lodz. She studied there first in a Jewish religious school for girls and then in a Polish elementary school. Ewa joined pro-communist youth circles in prewar Lodz. Following the German occupation of the city, she traveled to Soviet-occupied Bialystok and volunteered for work in the Soviet interior. She arrived in Magnitogorsk, where she married Israel Frenkel, a fellow volunteer from Lodz. She lived for a while in Poltava, Ukraine, and ended up in Orsk, in the Southern Urals. Israel died in the Battle of Lenino. Ewa returned to Poland with her five year-old daughter, Nadia, in 1946 and settled in Lodz, where she worked as a kindergarten teacher. She remarried in 1947. Her second husband died within a few months. Ewa moved to Warsaw in 1954 and studied Education at the Party Institute for Social Studies. She married Abraham Przemyslawski. Ewa emigrated to Israel in 1959.

Goldberg, Jacob, Jakub, Kuba (1924-). Lived in Lodz and studied in the Ignacy Skorupka Polish high school. He also joined a Polish socialist youth organization. In the Lodz Ghetto he joined Tsukunft, the Bundist youth organization. Following his deportation from the ghetto he was interned in several concentration camps. Goldberg returned to Lodz in 1945 and completed his secondary education. He attended Lodz University, earned a doctorate, and taught history at the University. He left Lodz in 1967 and settled in Israel.

Gross, Natan, Natek (1919-2005). Lived in Krakow and studied at the local Hebrew high school, from which he graduated in 1938. He lived intermittently in the Krakow Ghetto in the years 1941-1942, and then, under an assumed Polish identity, first in Krakow and then in Warsaw. He left Warsaw for Otwock in the summer of 1944. After liberation, Gross returned to Krakow where he worked for the Jewish Historical Commission and studied filmmaking. He arrived in Lodz in 1946, and became a successful film director. Among the films he directed in Lodz were the Yiddish documentary *Mir Lebengeblibene* (*We, The Survivors*) and *Undzere Kinder* (*Our Children*). Gross left Poland in 1949 and settled in Israel.

BIOGRAPHICAL NOTES   217

Grynberg, Henryk (1936-). Lived with his parents in the village of Radoszyna, east of Warsaw. Part of their extended family lived in nearby Dobre. Henryk and his family were hiding in the vicinity under German occupation. Henryk and his mother left in 1943 for Warsaw, where they lived under assumed identities. Henryk's father stayed around Radoszyna and was murdered by a Polish neighbor. Henryk and his mother left Warsaw and lived under assumed identities in a village North-East of Warsaw. After liberation, they settled in Dobre and then moved to Lodz. Henryk lived for several years in the Helenowek Children's Home and studied at the Yiddish School in Lodz. Later on he studied journalism in Warsaw and became an actor in the State Jewish Theatre. He defected while the company was touring the USA in 1967.

Hornstein, Hanka, formerly Rydel (1936-). Lived with her parents in Siedlce, near Warsaw. Shortly after the German occupation Hanka's family moved to the Soviet-occupied territories in eastern Poland and was deported to Siberia. They left Siberia in late 1941 and settled in Uzbekistan. Hanka's family left Uzbekistan in 1946 and settled in Lodz, where Hanka attended the Hebrew School and was a member of the Gordonia youth movement. Hanka's family left Poland in 1950 and settled in Israel. Hanka married Romek Hornstein, a Holocaust survivor from Canada, in 1956, and settled in Montreal.

Horowitz, Ada, formerly Gibraltar (1936-). Lived with her parents in Warsaw. After the German occupation the family traveled to Soviet-occupied Bialystok and was deported to the Urals. From there they traveled to Uzbekistan, where her father died. Ada lived for a while in a Polish children's home. When Ada's mother remarried, Ada returned to her family. They were repatriated to Poland in 1946, lived first in Zgierz and then settled in Lodz. Ada studied at the Ghetto Fighters' Hebrew School and joined the Gordonia Zionist youth movement. Following the closing of the Hebrew school, Ada studied in a local Polish high school. Ada's stepfather died in 1953. After moving to Warsaw, she completed her secondary education in 1954 and studied medicine. Ada and her mother left Poland and settled in Israel in 1957.

Kaplinski, Baruch (1913- 2008). Lived in Vilna, studied in a Jewish high school and also received the Polish Matriculation Certificate, the *Matura*. He studied in a Jewish Teachers' Seminary and taught in Jewish schools prior to World War II. When Vilna was occupied by the Germans,

Kaplinski went into hiding. He was eventually caught and deported to labor camps. Kaplinski arrived in Lodz in February 1945, and became active in the local Zionist movement. He was the first principal of the Hebrew Ghetto Fighters' School. Within a year he was appointed head of the Aliyat Hanoar — Youth Aliya in Poland. Kaplinski emigrated to Israel in the fall of 1948.

Klugman, Aleksander, Alek, (1925-). Lived in Lodz. He joined the underground communist youth organization in the Lodz Ghetto. Klugman was deported to Auschwitz in August 1944 and ended up in the Flossenburg camp in Germany. He returned to Lodz in July 1945. He was the only survivor in his family. In Lodz, he learned printing and worked as a printer for the Yiddish newspaper *Dos Naje Lebn*. Later he became a journalist. Klugman left Poland for Israel in 1957.

Lorber, Maria, (1914-2005). Lived in Ryki and then in Warsaw. After graduating from a Polish elementary school, she studied in a Jewish high school. She studied in the Konarski Educational Institute and in Wolna Wszechnica in Warsaw. She also taught at a Jewish elementary school. Following the German occupation, Maria lived in the Ryki Ghetto and when it was liquidated in 1942, she was interred in several labor camps. After liberation, she lived for a few months in Ryki and then settled in Lodz. She worked there at Film Polski and joined the Communist Party. Later on she held a senior position at the local censorship bureau. Maria left Poland in the late 1960s and settled in Israel.

Lubelsky, Richard, (1934-). Lived in Radomsko. His family traveled to Soviet occupied Eastern Poland in the fall of 1939 and was deported to Siberia. The Lubelskys traveled to Kazakhstan in late 1941 and settled in Semipalatinsk. Richard's parents separated there in 1943. Richard and his mother left for Poland in 1946 and settled in Lodz. Richard then lived in the Helenowek Children's Home. He attended the Ghetto Fighters' Hebrew School. Richard and his mother left Lodz for Paris in 1949 and they settled in Montreal, Canada in 1951.

Majerczak, Binyamin, (1917- 2005). Lived in Wloclawek and graduated from the local Hebrew high school. He studied electrical engineering in Warsaw. He traveled to Soviet-occupied Brest in the fall of 1939, and ended up in Lwow. He was arrested there in June 1940 and deported to a labor camp, part of the Volgostroi project on the upper Volga. He was released in the fall of 1941, and traveled to Ordzhonikidze. where he worked as an electrician. Majerczak left Ordzhonikidze in the summer of 1942 and settled in Samarkand, Uzbekistan. He joined the Polish Kosciuszko Division in May 1943, and participated in the Battle of Lenino in October 1943. After graduating as an officer from a Soviet Armored Corps Academy, Majerczak fought in a number of battles in Poland and Germany. He arrived in Lodz in the fall of 1946, and was active there in the Zionist movement. He also taught at the local Hebrew and Yiddish schools. He left for Israel in the fall of 1948.

Margolis-Edelman, Alina, Ala, (1922- 2008). Lived in Lodz. She was sent by her mother to relatives in Warsaw in the fall of 1939. Ala lived in the Warsaw Ghetto, studied nursing and worked as a nurse. She participated in the Warsaw Ghetto Uprising and in the Warsaw Uprising. Later on she lived in Grodzisk and returned with her mother to Lodz a few weeks after the liberation of the city. In Lodz, Ala studied medicine, became a pediatrician and worked in a children's clinic. She married Marek Edelman in 1951. Following the March 1968 events in Poland, she left with her two children for Paris. Alina Edelman-Margolis was active for years in various medical organizations in France and abroad. She died in Paris and was buried in the ecumenical cemetery in Bagneux.

Meridor, Ivri, formerly Heniek Napadow (1934-). Lived in Warsaw. He traveled to Soviet occupied Bialystok in the fall of 1939, was deported to Magnitogorsk and lived for a while in the Kuban region. His father was drafted into the Red Army, and he never returned. Heniek and his mother ended up in Uzbekistan, where he was put into a children's home. Heniek arrived in Lodz in 1946. He lived in the Koordynacja Children's Home, studied at the Hebrew School and joined Hashomer Hatzair. He left Poland for Israel in 1950.

Mintz, Matityahu, (1923-). Lived in Lublin and moved with his family to Warsaw in 1932. He studied there in a Jewish high school and joined Hashomer Hatzair. Mordechai Anielewicz, the future leader of the Warsaw Ghetto uprising was Mintz's counselor in the Warsaw branch of the movement. Mintz left German-occupied Warsaw in October 1939. He reached Vilna in December 1939 and remained there until January 1941, when he traveled to Palestine. There he joined kibbutz Gan-Shmuel and was active in Hashomer Hatzair. He was sent in 1948 to Poland as an emissary to the Hashomer Hatzair youth movement. Mintz returned to Israel in the summer of 1949.

Patron, Rachel, Rela, formerly, Rubinow, Rav-Nof (1936-). Lived in Bialystok. Her family was deported to the Soviet interior in June 1941. After living a few months in the Altai region, they moved to the city of Biysk. They lived there until their return to Poland in 1946. Rachel arrived in Lodz in the fall of 1946. She lived in a Zionist children's home and studied in the Ghetto Fighters' Hebrew School. She left Poland in 1948, lived a few months in a DP camp in Marseille and arrived in Israel in the early fall of 1949.

Podeh, Fayvl, formerly Podemski (1924-). Lived in Lodz. He joined Hashomer Hatzair in 1933, and became a youth counselor. Fayvl was active in Hashomer Hatzair in the Lodz Ghetto. He was among the few survivors of the Lodz Ghetto liberated there in January 1945. He was elected to the Lodz Jewish Committee in February 1945. He also served as the first head of the Hashomer Hatzair branch in postwar Lodz. Fayvl arrived in Israel in early 1950.

Pomerantz, Shlomo, (1934-). Lived in Lodz. He traveled with his family to Soviet-occupied Lwow in the fall of 1939. They were deported to Siberia and later settled in Uzbekistan. The Pomerantzs returned to Lodz in 1946. Shlomo attended the Ghetto Fighters' Hebrew School and joined the Hashomer Hatzair youth movement. Following the closing of the Hebrew School in late 1949, Shlomo studied at the Peretz Yiddish School. The Pomerantzs emigrated from Poland to Israel in late 1950.

Rotenberg, Wanda, formerly Bela Elster (1924-2008). Lived in Warsaw and studied in Jewish schools. Her older sister, Pola Elster of the Poalei Zion Left, introduced her to the party's youth organization. Wanda joined the Jewish Fighting Organization (the ZOB) in the Warsaw Ghetto and acted as a liaison with the Polish underground. After the war she lived in Lodz and was active in the Dror youth organization. Wanda settled in Israel in 1950.

Rozenberg, Szulim, (1918-). Lived in Warsaw and joined the Bund. He traveled to the Soviet-occupied territories of Eastern Poland and was deported to the Komi Autonomous Republic in Northern USSR. Later he settled in the Gorki region. He moved to Krasnodar in 1944, and returned to Poland in 1946. He worked for the Lodz Jewish Committee and was active in the Bund. Szulim Rozenberg left Lodz in 1948 and settled in Paris.

Rutenberg, Kaimierz, Kazik, (1924-). Lived in Sosnowiec. He was with his mother in Rovno when the Soviet Union annexed Eastern Poland. They were deported to Siberia. Kazik joined General Berling's Polish Army in 1943, and became a fighter pilot. He was demobilized in 1946 and settled in Lodz, where he completed his secondary education and studied engineering. He settled in Israel in 1957.

Nishmit-Shner, Sarah, Sonia, formerly Dusznicki (1913-2008). Lived in Lithuania and was active as a youth counselor. She studied Classics and Education. Sarah taught for some time at the Jewish Teachers' Seminary in Vilna. Following the German invasion she joined a Soviet partisan unit and worked as a field nurse. She arrived in Lodz in 1945, and was active in the Koordynacja. Sarah married Zvi Shner; both settled in Israel and were among the founders of the Ghetto Fighters' kibbutz.

NOTES

1. MY LODZ MEMORIES

1. Shlomo Avineri, "A Jewish Boy from Poland," *Ma'ariv,* January 11, 1985.
2. Yehudit Hendel, quoted in J. Kugelmass, "The Rites of the Tribe: The Meaning of Poland for American Jewish Tourists," *YIVO Annual* 21 (1993): 396-7.
3. Eva Hoffman, *Exit into History: A Journey Through the New Eastern Europe.* (Penguin Books, 1993), ix.
4. Audio recording of the reunion of the Ghetto Fighters' Hebrew School in Lodz, Tel-Aviv, September 16, 1997.
5. *Ibid.*
6. A. Kurnatowski, ed., *Profesorowie i docenci wydzialow medycznych Uniwersytetu Lodzkiego i Akademii Medycznej w Lodzi, 1945-1964* (Lodz: Wyd. Uniwersytetu Medycznego w Lodzi, 2003), 220.
7. *Biuletyn Wydzialu Statystycznego Zarzadu Miejskiego w Lodzi, Rok I, nr. 32, 23. IX, 1948:* 10. Archiwum Panstwowe w Lodzi (APL), Zarzad Miejski w Lodzi, Wydzial Statystyczny. Frekwencja w kinoteatrach Lodzkich, 1947: 8.
8. Fayvl Podeh (Podemski), interview by author, Herzliyah, August, 2002.
9. Prof. Moshe Lewin, telephone interview by author, March 2002.
10. Beniek Miznmacher, interview by author, Tel-Aviv, December, 2002.
11. Pinchas Zajonc, telephone interview by author, April, 2006.
12. Ziporah Hurwitz (Rosenstein), interview by author, Gal'on, April 2006. See also Zipora Rosenstein-Hurwitz, "From Majdanek to Freedom — Against All Odds," *Yalkut Moreshet* 83 (2007): 175-181.
13. Prof. Moshe Lewin, telephone interview by author March 2002.
14. Zeev (Vovke) Klachko, interview by author, Ra'anana, May, 2006.
15. Henryk Grynberg, *Zycie ideologiczne. Zycie osobiste.* (Warsaw: Panstwowy Instytut Wydawniczy, 1992), 51-55.
16. *Yediot Aharonot,* April 29, 1981.

2. POSTWAR LODZ

1. Hans Roos, *A History of Modern Poland* (New York: Alfred A. Knopf, 1966) 209-235; Krystyna Kersten, *The Establishment of Communist Rule in Poland, 1943-1948* (Berkeley- Los Angeles- Oxford: University of California Press 1991) 163-167, 222-223; Jan T. Gross, *Fear: Antisemitism in Poland After Auschwitz. An Essay in Historical Interpretation* (Princeton and Oxford: Princeton University Press, 2006), 3-30; Andrzej Paczkowski, *Zdobycie wladzy, 1945-1947* (Warsaw: Wydawnictwo szkolne i pedagogiczne, 1993), 21-45. On varying estimates of the number of Poles killed during the war see also: *Dzieje Najnowsze,* 26(2), (1994) and Michael Steinlauf, *Bondage to the Dead: Poland and the Memory of the Holocaust,* (Syracuse, NY: Syracuse University Press, 1997.)

2. Eugeniusz Mironowicz, *Polityka narodowosciowa PRL*. (Bialystok: Wydanie Bialostockiego Towarzystwa Historycznego, 2000); Leszek Olejnik, *Polityka narodowosciowa Polski w latach 1944-1960* (Lodz: Wydawnictwo Uniwersytetu Lodzkiego, 2003).
3. Ludwik Mroczka, "Dynamika rozwoju i struktura spoleczno-zawodowa glownych grup etnicznych w Lodzi w latach 1918-1939," in *Polacy-Niemcy-Zydzi w Lodzi w XIX-XX w: Sasiedzi dalecy i bliscy*, ed. Pawel Samus (Lodz: Ibidem, 1997), 99-117.
4. Pawel Samus, "Lodz - mala ojczyzna Polakow, Niemcow, Zydow." in *Polacy-Niemcy-Zydzi w Lodzi*, ed. Pawel Samus, *ibid*., 118-161; Andrea Loew, Juden im Ghetto Litzmannstadt: Lebensbedingungen, Selbstwahrnehmung, Verhalten (Goettingen: Wallstein Verlag 2006), 63-65.
5. S.L. Shneiderman, *Between Fear and Hope*, (New York: Arco Publishing Company, 1947), 155.
6. Michal Unger, *Lodz: The Last Ghetto in Poland* (in Hebrew), (Jerusalem: Yad Vashem), 2005.
7. Joanna Michlic, "Lodz in the Post-Communist Era: In Search of a New Identity," (Center for European Studies, Harvard University, Program on Eastern and Central Europe. Working Paper Series # 65 (2006).
8. Ludwik Mroczka, "Dynamika rozwoju," op. cit.; Pawel Samus, "Lodz - mala ojczyzna," op. cit.; Gordon J. Horwitz. *Ghettostadt: Lodz and the Making of a Nazi City*, (Cambridge, MA and London: The Belknap Press of Harvard University Press), 2008; Leszek Olejnik, "Lodz wielonarodowa w pierwszych latach po II Wojnie Swiatowej," *Rocznik Lodzki*, XLV (1998): 185-210; Leszek Olejnik, Spolecznosc zydowska w Lodzi w latach 1945-1950, zarys problemu," *Acta Universitatis Lodziensis*, Folia Historica 60 (1997): 125-129; Archiwum Panstwowe w Lodzi. Zarzad Miejski w Lodzi. Wydzial statystyczny, ZM, sygn. 28.
9. Ryszard Rosin, "Szkice z dziejow Lodzi — 1945 rok," *Kronika Miasta Lodzi*, zeszyt 1 (2000): 115-129.
10. Janusz Kozlowski, ed., *Gorace dni, gorace lata. Wydawnictwo Lodzkie* (Lodz: 1976), 51-52.
11. Padraic Kenney, *Rebuilding Poland: Workers and Communists, 1945-1950* (Ithaca and London: Cornell University Press 1997), 74.
12. Antony Beevor and Luba Vinogradova, eds., *A Writer at War: Vasily Grossman with the Red Army, 1941-1945* (New York: Pantheon Books, 2005), 315.
13. *Gorace dni*: 34, 55, 77, 142.
14. *Ibid*.: 26, 46, 175.
15. Michael Checinski, *Poland: Communism, Nationalism, Anti-Semitism* (New York: Karz-Kohl Publishing, 1982), 156-157.
16. Krzysztof Lesiakowski, *Mieczyslaw Moczar, "Mietek": biografia polityczna*. (Warsaw: Rytm, 1998), 95-130.
17. Lukasz Kaminski, "Lodzkie protesty mlodziezy, 1945-1946," *Kronika Miasta Lodzi* zeszyt 1-2 (1997): 176-185; Tomasz Rostworowski. *Zaraz po wojnie: wspomnienia duszpasterza (1945-1956)* (Paris: Editions Spotkania, 1986), 27-31.
18. Padraic Kenney, *Rebuilding Poland: Workers and Communists, 1945-1950*, (Ithica and London: Cornell University Press, 1997), 90.
19. *Ibid,*: 104, 134; Krzysztof Lesiakowski, "Nastroje mieszkancow Lodzi i wojewodztwa Lodzkiego w latach 1945-1948," *Acta Universitatis Lodziensis*,

Folia Historica 71 (2001): 133.
20. Padraic Kenney, *Rebuilding Poland*, 107-115; Lukasz Kaminski, *Polacy wobec nowej rzeczywistosci, 1944-1948: Formy pozainstytucjalnego zywiolowego oporu spolecznego* Torun: Wydawnictwo Adam Marszalek, 2000), 68-71; Krzysztof Lesiakowski, "Nastroje," *Acta Universitatis Lodziensis*, Folia Historica 71 (2001): 125-127.
21. *Tranzytem przez Lodz*. (Lodz: Wydawnictwo Lodzkie. 1964), 94, 96; Adolf Rudnicki. *Niebieskie kartki. Slepe miasto tych lat* (Warsaw: Czytelnik, 1958), 197.
22. Glowny Urzad Statystyczny Rzeczypospolitej Polskiej, "Rocznik statystyczny 1946 r," (Warsaw: Glowny Urzad Statystyczny Rzeczypospolitej Polskiej, 1947), Vol XI: 174.
23. *Tranzytem przez Lodz*, op. cit., 18, 41, 66, 69, 172, 178.
24. Krystyna Sreniowska, "Warcholy w akcji: Sprawa Marii Tyrankiewiczowny," *Tygiel Kultury*, Lodz, 4-5 (1998): 96-97; *Tranzytem przez Lodz*, 13, 19, 21, 40, 43-71, 175-176.
25. *Tranzytem przez Lodz*, 24, 29, 66; Marci Shore, *Caviar and Ashes: A Warsaw Generation's Life and Death in Marxism, 1918-1968*, (New Haven: Yale University Press, 2006), 260-261, 283.
26. *Tranzytem przez Lodz*, 21, 239-270.
27. Erwin Axer, "Schiller w Lodzi," *Tygiel Kultury*, Lodz, 7-9 (104-106), (2004), 110-130.
28. Andrzej Lapicki. *Po pierwsze, zachowac dystans. Proszynski i S-ka*, (Warsaw: 1999), 60.
29. *Biuletyn Wydzialu Statystycznego Zarzadu Miejskiego w Lodzi*, Rok 1. nr. 32, 23. IX (1948): 10; Wydzial Statystyczny, *Archiwum Panstwowe w Lodzi. Zarzad Miejski w Lodzi*, (Lodz: Wydzial Statystyczny, Frekwencja w kinoteatrach Lodzkich, 1947 r.), 8. ; Glowny Urzad Statystyczny Rzeczypospolitej Polskiej, *Rocznik Statystyczny 1946 r*, (Warsaw: Glowny Urzad Statystyczny Rzeczypospolitej Polskiej, 1947 r.), Rok XI: 176; Glowny Urzad Statystyczny Rzeczypospolitej Polskiej, *Rocznik Statystyczny, 1949 r*. (Warsaw: Glowny Urzad Statystyczny Rzeczypospolitej Polskiej, 1950), Rok XII: 227.
30. Edward Zajicek, "Nad Oka," Film, 41 (1788), October 9, 1983: 3-5; Edward Zajicek, "Na rubiezach Grand Hotelu: Jak powstawala filmowa Lodz," *Odglosy* (Lodz), January 16, 1988, 1, 3.
31. *Tranzytem przez Lodz*, 93-94.
32. *Tranzytem przez Lodz*, 25.
33. Jozef Potega, interview by author, Warsaw, June 18, 2003.
34. Bozena Piwkowska, interview by author, Lodz, June 23, 2003.
35. Anita Janowska, *Krzyzowka*, (Wroclaw: Siedmiorog, 1997); Anita Janowska, interview by author, Warsaw, June 19, 2003.
36. Jerzy Urban, *Jajakobyly*. Spowiedz zycia Jerzego Urbana.Spowiadali i zapisali Przemyslaw Cwiklinski, Piotr Gadzinowski (Warsaw: "BGW"); Lawrence Wechsler, "The Troll's Tale: Jerzy Urban," in *Vermeer in Bosnia: A Reader* (New York: Pantheon Books, 2004) 151-181; Jerzy Urban, interview by Ewa Kozminska-Frejlak, Warsaw, August 2009. See also an interview with Jerzy Urban by Ewa Kozminska-Frejlak published in *Midrasz*, January-February 2010:5-14.
37. Prof. Krystyna Sreniowska, interview by author, Lodz, July 1, 2002; Krystyna Sreniowska, "Hotel Monopol," *Tygiel Kultury*, Lodz, 7-9(1999): 49-53.

38. Prof. Edward Zajicek, interview by author, Lodz, June 24, 2003.
39. Prof. Leszek Kolakowski and Dr. Tamara Kolakowska, telephone interview by author, January 16, 2004; *Honoris Causa: Ksiega pamiatkowa dla uczczenia aktu nadania profesorowi Leszkowi Kolakowskiemu honorowego doktoratu Uniwersytetu Lodzkiego* (Lodz: Wydawnictwo Lodzkie. Wydawnictwo Uniwersytetu Lodzkiego, 1994), 15.
40. Hanna Swida-Ziemba, *Urwany lot. Pokolenie inteligenckiej mlodziezy powojennej w swietle listow i pamietnikow z lat 1945-1948.* (Krakow: Wydawnictwo Literackie, 2003).

3. JEWS IN POSTWAR LODZ

1. David Engel, *Between Liberation and Flight: Holocaust Survivors in Poland and the Struggle for Leadership, 1944-1946* (in Hebrew) (Tel Aviv: Am Oved Publishers), 1996), 15 ; Israel Gutman, *The Jews in Poland After World War II* (in Hebrew), (Jerusalem: The Zalman Shazar Center,1985), 12; Leszek Olejnik, *Polityka narodowosciowa Polski w latach 1944-1960,* (Lodz: Wydawnictwo Uniwersytetu Lodzkiego, 2003), 344-351; Lucjan Dobroszycki, "Restoring Jewish Life in Postwar Poland," *Soviet Jewish Affairs* 3 (1973): 59-60. Bozena Szaynok, *Ludnosc Zydowska na Dolnym Slasku, 1945-1950)* Wroclaw: Wydawnictwo Uniwersytetu Wroclawskiego, 2000), 7; David Engel, *Between Liberation and Flight,* 155.
2. David Engel, *Between Liberation and Flight,* 40; Yosef Litvak, *Polish-Jewish Refugees in the USSR, 1939-1946* (in Hebrew), (Tel Aviv: Hakibbutz Hameuchad Publishing House, 1988), 358; Jozef Adelson, "W Polsce zwanej Ludowa," in *Najnowsze dzieje Zydow w Polsce (w zarysie do 1950 roku),* ed. Jerzy Tomaszewski (Warsaw: Wydawnictwo Naukowe PWN, 1993), 387, 388, 391, 397.
3. Bozena Szaynok, *Ludnosc zydowska na Dolnym Slasku,* 54, 59; Jozef Adelson, "W Polsce zwanej Ludowa," 399; Michal Grynberg, "Problemy zatrudnienia ludnosci zydowskiej w Polsce w pierwszych latach po II Wojnie Swiatowej," *Biuletyn Zydowskiego Instytutu Historycznego w Polsce* 1-2(137-138) (1986): 101.
4. Irena Hurwic-Nowakowska, *A Social Analysis of Postwar Polish Jewry* (Jerusalem: The Zalman Shazar Center for Jewish History, 1986), 35-36; Israel Gutman, *The Jews in Poland After World War II,* 14; Leszek Olejnik, "Lodz jako centrum spolecznosci zydowskiej w Polsce (1945-1949)." Pawel Samus and Wieslaw Pus, eds., *Fenomen getta lodzkiego, 1940-1944* (Lodz: Wydawnictwo Uniwersytetu Lodzkiego, 2006), 407.
5. Yehuda Bauer, *Flight and Rescue: Brichah.* (New York: Random House, 1970), 119; Bozena Szaynok, *Ludnosc zydowska na Dolnym Slasku,* 110-117.
6. Israel Gutman, *The Jews in Poland After World War II,* 60; Jan T. Gross, *Fear,* 39-51.
7. Lucjan Dobroszycki, "Restoring Jewish Life in Postwar Poland," 63; Jozef Adelson, "W Polsce zwanej Ludowa," 451; David Engel, *Between Liberation and Flight,* 58-59, 84-85; Israel Gutman, *The Jews in Poland After World War II,* 61; David Engel, "The Reconstruction of Jewish Communal Institutions in Postwar Poland: The Origins of the Central Committee of Polish Jews, 1944-1945," *East European Politics and Societies* 10 (Winter 1996): 102-105.
8. Israel Gutman, *The Jews in Poland After World War II,* 61-63; Irena Hurwic-

Nowakowska, *A Social Analysis of Postwar Polish Jewry*, 38-45; Michal Grynberg, "Problemy zatrudnienia ludnosci zydowskiej w Polsce w pierwszych latach po II Wojnie Swiatowej," 100-107.

9. Israel Gutman, *The Jews in Poland After World War II*, 64-65; Michal Grynberg, *Zydowska spoldzielczosc pracy w Polsce w latach 1945-1949*, (Warsaw: PWN, 1986), 167-171.

10. Israel Gutman, *The Jews in Poland After World War II*, 87-91; Lucjan Dobroszycki, "Restoring Jewish Life in Postwar Poland," 60-61; Maciej Pisarski, "Emigracja Zydow z Polski w latach 1945-1951," *Studia z dziejow kultury Zydow w Polsce po 1945 roku*, ed. Jerzy Tomaszewski, (Warsaw: TRIO, 1997), 29-30.

11. Jozef Adelson, "W Polsce zwanej Ludowa," 426-428; Lucjan Dobroszycki, "Restoring Jewish Life in Postwar Poland," 61-63; David Engel, "The Reconstruction of Jewish Communal Institutions in Postwar Poland," 100-102; Bozena Szaynok, *Ludnosc zydowska na Dolnym Slasku*, 9, 64, 73-74, 77, 82-83; August Grabski, *Zydowski ruch kombatancki w Polsce w latach 1944-1949* (Warsaw: TRIO, 2002), 20-25.

12. Natalia Aleksiun, *Dakad dalej? Ruch sjonistyczny w Polsce (1944-1950)* (Warsaw: TRIO, 2002); Jozef Adelson, "W Polsce zwanej Ludowa," 433-447; Alina Cala and Helena Datner-Spiewak, eds. *Dzieje Zydow w Polsce, 1944-1948* (Warsaw: Zydowski Instytut Historyczny, 1997), 76-86.

13. Jozef Adelson, "W Polsce zwanej Ludowa," 434-439; Bozena Szaynok, *Ludnosc zydowska na Dolnym Slasku*, 172-175; Natalia Aleksiun, "Where Was there a Future for Polish Jewry? Bundist and Zionist Polemics in Post-World War II Poland," Jack Jacobs, ed., *Jewish Politics in Eastern Europe: The Bund at 100* (New York: University Press), 227-242. Bozena Szaynok, "Bund i Komunisci zydowscy w Polsce po 1945 roku," *Midrasz* July-August (1998): 57-64.

14. Jeff Schatz, *The Generation: The Rise and Fall of the Jewish Communists of Poland*, (Berkeley-Los Angeles-Oxford: University of California Press, 1991); Bozena Szaynok, *Ludnosc zydowska na Dolnym Slasku*, 175-177; Krystyna Kersten, "Rok pierwszy," *Midrasz* July-August (1998): 26-29; Maciej Pisarski, "Na zydowskiej ulicy: szkic do dziejow zydowskiej frakcji PPR i zespolu PZPR przy CKZP, 1945-1951," *Biuletyn BZIH* 2 (1997): 35-48.

15. Szczepan Gasowski, *Panstwowy Teatr Zydowski im. Ester Rachel Kaminskiej: przeszlosc i terazniejszosc*, (Warsaw: PWN, 1995), 100-111.

16. Irena Hurwic-Nowakowska, *A Social Analysis of Postwar Polish Jewry*, 47; Bozena Szaynok, *Ludnosc zydowska na Dolnym Slasku*, 76-77.

17. Jozef Adelson, "W Polsce zwanej Ludowa," 470-471.

18. Jozef Adelson, "W Polsce zwanej Ludowa," 471; Israel Gutman, *The Jews in Poland After World War II*, 72-74; Natalia Aleksiun, "Rescuing a Memory and Constructing a History of Polish Jewry: Jews in Poland, 1944-1950" Jews in Russia and Eastern Europe, 1-2 (2005): 5-27.

19. Irena Kowalska, "Kartoteka TOZ z lat 1946-1947," *Biuletyn ZIH* 3\95-2\96(175-178) (July 1995-June 1996): 97-106; *ZAP Bulletin* 99\109 (November 12, 1945).

20. Israel Gutman, *The Jews in Poland After World War II*, 79; Nachum Bogner, *At the Mercy of Strangers: The Rescue of Jewish Children with Assumed Identities in Poland* (in Hebrew) (Jerusalem: Yad Vashem, 2000), 226-294.

21. Israel Gutman, *The Jews in Poland After World War II*, 67-68; Israel Bialostocki,

"Rehabilitation of the Jewish Community in Poland After the Holocaust, 1944-1950" (Ph.D. diss., The Hebrew University of Jerusalem, 1990), 153-156; *Bozena Szaynok, Ludnosc zydowska na Dolnym Slasku,* 74-76, 123-126; Helena Datner-Spiewak, "Instytucje opieki nad dzieckiem i szkoly powszechne Centralnego Komitetu Zydow Polskich w latach 1945-1946," *Biuletyn ZIH* 1,3(117, 119), (1981): 44-47; Helena Datner, "Szkoly Centralnego Komitetu Zydow w Polsce w latach 1944-1949," *Biuletyn ZIH* 1-3 (169-171) (1994): 104-108; S. Amarant, "Hebrajskie zaklady wychowawcze w Polsce." *Mosty* 2(7), 13.

22. Jan T. Gross, *Fear: Anti-Semitism in Poland After Auschwitz. An Essay in Historical Interpretation,* (Princeton and Oxford: Princeton University Press, 2006), 192-243, 247-248, 255-260; Joanna Beata Michlic, *Poland's Threatening Other: The Image of the Jew from 1880 to the Present,* (Lincoln and London: University of Nebraska Press, 2006), 216-217.

23. Lucjan Dobroszycki, "Restoring Jewish Life in Postwar Poland," 66; Jan Tomasz Gross, *Upiorna dekada: trzy eseje o stereotypach na temat Zydow, Polakow, Niemcow i Komunistow, 1939-1948* (Krakow: Universitas, 1998), 96-97; Jan T. Gross, *Fear,* 35; Marek Jan Chodakiewicz, *After the Holocaust: Polish-Jewish Conflict in the Wake of World War II,* (New York: East European Monographs, 2003), 221; David Engel, "Patterns of Anti-Jewish Violence in Poland, 1944-1946, *Yad Vashem Studies* XXVI (1998): 43-85.

24. Bozena Szaynok, Pogrom Zydow w Kielcach 4 Lipca, 1946 (Warsaw: Bellona, 1992); Jan T. Gross, *Fear,* 81-166; Israel Gutman, *The Jews in Poland After World War II,* 34-39; Jan Tomasz Gross, *Upiorna dekada,* 94-95; Jan T. Gross, "In the Aftermath of the Kielce Pogrom: The Special Commission of the Central Committee of Jews of Poland," *Gal-Ed* XV-XVI (1997) 119-136.

25. Michal Unger, *Lodz: The Last Ghetto in Poland* (in Hebrew) (Jerusalem: Yad Vashem, 2005), 542; *Lodz and Lodz District* (in Hebrew) [what is this? Missing data]. Pinkas Hakehillot, *Poland.* Vol. 1 (Jerusalem: Yad Vashem, 1976), 38; Report by A. Wertheim, ZIH Archive S 330/5, 7; *ZAP Bulletin* 23/33 (April 4, 1945) 2-3; A. Siedlecki, "How the Jewish Community in Lodz was Resurrected," *Bleter far geshikhte* 24 (1986): 200-204; Michal Grynberg, "Lodz, 1945," *Folks-Sztyme* 5 (1974). Michal Mirski, Vegn lodzer yiddishn komitet, Yad Vashem Archive 037/25, 4-10, 17-18; *ZAP Bulletin* (April 4, 1945).

26. Sara Zyskind, *Stolen Years.* (Minneapolis: Lerner Publications Company, 1981), 267-270; Michal Mirski, *ibid.,* 21.

27. Leszek Olejnik, "Mniejszosci narodowe w Lodzi w latach 1945-1950," *Kronika Miasta Lodzi* 1/2 (1999): 194-195; Leszek Olejnik, "Spolecznosc zydowska w Lodzi w latach 1945-1950: zarys problemu," *AUL* Folia Historica 60 (1997: 126-127); Leszek Olejnik, "Lodz jako centrum spolecznosci zydowskiej w Polsce (1945-1949)," in Fenomen getta lodzkiego, 1940-1944, eds., Pawel Samus and Wieslaw Pus (Lodz: Wydawnictwo Uniwersytetu Lodzkiego, 2006), 410; Israel Bialostocki, *Rehabilitation of the Jewish Community in Poland After the Holocaust, 1944-1950,* 6; *ZAP Bulletin* 39/49 (June 22, 1945), 1; Israel Gutman, *The Jews in Poland After World War II,* 26.

28. David Engel, *Between Liberation and Flight,* 228 ft. 66; *ZAP Bulletin* 15/263, (February 20, 1947): 5; Glowny Urzad Statystyczny, "Rocznik statystyczny," 167. Michal Mirski, "Vegn lodzher yiddishn komitet," 20.

29. Michal Unger, *Lodz: The Last Ghetto in Poland,* 557; *ZAP Bulletin* (June 27,

1947) 3; Irena Hurwic-Nowakowska, *A Social Analysis of Postwar Polish Jewry*, 33-34. David Engel, " Warsaw as a Jewish Metropolis? Aborted Reconstruction in the Aftermath of the Holocaust." Paper presented at Warsaw-the History of a Jewish Metropolis, the UCL IJS Summer Conference, London, 22-25 June 2010.

30. Israel Gutman, *The Jews in Poland After World War II*, 14; Helena Datner-Spiewak, "Instytucje opieki nad dzieckiem i szkoly powszechne Centralnego Komitetu Zydow w Polsce w latach 1944-1949," 37; *ZAP Bulletin* 39\49 (June 22, 1945): 1; Israel Bialostocki, *Rehabilitation of the Jewish Community in Poland After the Holocaust, 1944-1950*, 21, 134; *ZAP Bulletin* 13\389 (February 3, 1948): 4; Lucjan Dobroszycki, *Survivors of the Holocaust in Poland: A Portrait Based on Jewish Community Records, 1944-1947* (Amonk, NY: M.E. Sharpe, Amonk, 1994), 14.

31. *ZAP Bulletin* 15/263 (February 20, 1947): 1; *Opinia* (Lodz) 12(25), February 20, 1947, 2.

32. Israel Bialostocki, *Rehabilitation of the Jewish Community in Poland After the Holocaust, 1944-1950*, 23; CCPJ Productivization Department Report, ZIH Archive.

33. S.L. Shneiderman, *Between Fear and Hope* (New York: Arco Publishing Company, 1947), 182-183; Michal Grynberg, "Zydowska spoldzielczosc pracy w Polsce w latach 1945-1949",169; CCPJ Report, April 23, 1949, ZIH Archive S/330/5, 11.

34. Polska Agencja Prasowa, "Lodz urzedowa, spoleczna, przemyslowo-handlowa, 1947" (Lodz: Polska Agencja Prasowa PAP, 1947); Ryszard Bonislawski, walking interview by author, Lodz, June 22, 2003.

35. Hersz Smolar. *At the Last Stand. With the Last Hope* (in Yiddish) (Tel-Aviv: Y.L. Peretz Publishing House, 1982), 37. Leszek Olejnik, "Mniejszosci narodowe w Lodzi w latach 1945-1950," 199; Shlomo Strauss-Marko *The History of the Jewish People in Poland after the War* (in Hebrew). Self-publication (Tel-Aviv, 1988), 211-248; Anna Lipphardt, "Forgotten Memory. The Jews of Vilne in the Diaspora," *Osteuropa. Impulses for Jewish Modernity in East European Tradition* (Berlin) (2008): 187-198.

36. Israel Bialostocki, *Rehabilitation of the Jewish Community in Poland After the Holocaust*, 63, 144-146; Jozef Korzeniowski, 'Dos Naje Lebn' — pierwsza gazeta zydowska w PRL," *ZIH* (119) (1981): 52-61; ZIH Archive, 303/VIII/370 (Jan. 17, 1947).

37. *ZAP Bulletins* (May-July, 1945); *ZAP Bulletin* 27/147 (March 11, 1946), 3; Collection of Posters from Lodz, Yad Vashem Archive, M49/199.

38. Shlomo Strauss-Marko, *The History of the Jewish People in Poland after the War*, 259-262; Prof. Leszek Kolakowski and Dr. Tamara Kolakowska, telephone interview by author, January 16, 2004; Aleksander Klugman, "Jak feniks z popiolow," *Kronika Miasta Lodzi* 2 (2007): 107-108; Mordechai Altshuler et al. eds., *Soviet Jews Write to Ilya Ehrenburg,1943-1966*, (Jerusalem: The Hebrew University and Yad Vashem, 1993), 68-69, 102; Yad Yaari Archive, 1-2, 63(5).

39. *ZAP Bulletin* 95/105 (November 3, 1945): 2-3, 96/344 (October 1, 1947): 2, 71/551 (September 7, 1949), 1.

40. *ZAP Bulletin* 37/285 (April 22, 1947): 11, 122/370 (December 12, 1947): 3, 124/373 (December 18, 1947): 2, 92/340 (September 17, 1947): 3.

41. *ZAP Bulletin* 133/24 (December 19, 1945): 1-2.

42. Jacek Pietrzak, "Hans Biebow-portret oprawcy," in *Fenomen getta lodzkiego*,

1940-1944, eds. Pawel Samus and Wieslaw Pus, 200-203; *Dos Naje Lebn,* April 28, 1947, and May 5, 1947; *Opinia* 17(3) (May 5, 1947): 4.

43. Leszek Olejnik, Z dziejow teatru zydowskiego w Lodzi po IIej wojnie swiatowej," in *Lodzkie sceny zydowskie: studia i materially,* ed. Malgorzata Leyko (Lodz: Wydawnictwo Uniwersytetu Lodzkiego, 2000), 144-147.

44. Malgorzata Leyko, "Ida Kaminska i Lodzki Teatr Zydowski," in *Lodzkie sceny zydowskie,* ed. Malgorzata Leyko, 161-165; Ida Kaminska, *My Life, My Theatre* (New York and London: Macmillan & Collier, 1973) 212, 216-218; *ZAP Bulletin* 96/471 (November 26, 1948): 1; *ZAP Bulletin* 64/312 (July 9, 1947): 1.

45. Michal Unger, *Lodz: The Last Ghetto in Poland,* 46; Pawel Spodenkiewicz, *Zaginiona dzielnica: Lodz zydowska — ludzie i miejsca* (Lodz: Lodzka Ksiegarnia Niezalezna, 1999), 96-98; Shimon Dzigan, *The Impact of Jewish Humour* (in Yiddish) (Tel-Aviv: The Public Committee for the Celebation of the 40th Anniversary of Shimon Dzigan's Acting in the Yiddish Theatre, 1974), 262-267, 280-295; Israel Gutman, *The Jews in Poland After World War II,* 69; Lidia Ofir (Schumacher) and Natan Gross in Israeli TV documentary *In the Land of the Jews,* 2003; Collection of Posters, Yad Vashem Archive.

46. J. Hoberman, *Bridge of Light: Yiddish Film Between Two Worlds* (Philadelphia: Temple University ,1995), 327-329; Natan Gross, "The Jewish Film in Poland After World War II, 1945-1950," (in Hebrew), *Kolnoa* 2 (May, 1974): 63-69; Natan Gross, *Przygody Grymka w ziemi swietej* (Krakow: Rabid, 2006), 42-47.

47. Pawel Spodenkiewicz, *Zaginiona dzielnica,* 98; Natan Gross, interview by author, Givataim, February 21, 2002; Lila Holzman, interview by author, Ramat-Gan, October 25, 2006; Hagai Hitron, "A Rare Glimpse of a Destroyed World," *Haaretz,* September 20, 2006.

48. Sharon Pucker Rivo, "The Beginning of Holocaust Cinema: Contextualizing *Undzere Kinder* (Poland, 1948)" (presentation at the Annual Conference of the Association of Jewish Studies, Boston, 1994); Lawrence L. Langer, *Preempting the Holocaust* (New Haven and London: Yale University Press, 1998), 157-165; Gabriel N. Finder, "The Place of Child Survivors in Jewish Collective Memory after the Holocaust: The Case of *Undzere Kinder*," in *Nuturing the Nation: Displaced Cildren in Europe and the USSR, 1918-1953,* ed. Nick Baron (Leiden: Brill).

49. *ZAP Bulletin* 55/430 (June 30, 1948): 2-3; Michal Mirski, Vegn Lodzer Yiddishn Komitet. Yad Vashem Archive, 037/25, 32; Report by Michal Helman, ZIH Archive, 303/IX/1277; Report by Anatol Wertheim, ZIH Archive, s/330/5, 19-22; Helena Datner-Spiewak, "Instytucje opieki nad dzieckiem i szkoly powszechne Centralnego Komitetu Zydow Plskich w latach 1945-1946," 44-47; Helena Datner, "Szkoly Centralnego Komitetu Zydow w Polsce w latach 1944-1949," 105-108.

50. Leszek Olejnik, "Lodz jako centrum spolecznosci zydowskiej w Polsce (1945-1949), 417; Helena Datner, "Szkoly Centralnego Komitetu Zydow w Polsce w latach 1944-1949," 114; Baruch Kaplinski, interview by author, Tel-Aviv, March 5, 2002; *ZAP Bulletin* 104/114 (November 23, 1945): 2; Report on "The Ghetto Fighters'" school [January 31, 1949], [the preceding brackets are part of the style] Archiwum Akt Nowych, 472/1949 (Warsaw: Education Ministry).

51. Maria Falkowska, "Dzieci z Helenowka," in *Losy zydowskie, swiadectwo zywych,* Vol. 2, ed. Marian Turski (Warsaw, 1999), 31-33; Michal Mirski, *Vegn Lodzer Yiddishn Komitet,* 29-31; Report on the Children's Home in Helenowek, ZIH Ar- chive, CCPJ Education Department Collection, 303/IX/1126, 1-2.

52. Report for 1947, ZIH Archive, CCPJ Education Department Collection, 303/IX/1127, 8, 11, 17 and 303/IX/135, 13.
53. Maria Falkowska, "Dzieci z Helenowka," 42-51; Sven Sonnenberg, *A Two Stop Journey to Hell* (Montreal: The Canadian Foundation of Polish-Jewish Heritage, 2001), http://polish-jewish-heritag.org/Ksiazka_Svena_Sonnenberg.htm (April 2, 2009).
54. *ZAP Bulletin* 34/154 (April 1, 1946): 2; Aleksander Klugman, "Jak Feniks z popiolow (2): Bursa nowej nadziei," *Kronika Miasta Lodzi* 3/2006: 87-92.
55. Collection of memoirs of former "Bursants," in the possesion of the author, received from Mr. Aleksander Klugman.
56. S.L. Shneiderman, *Between Fear and Hope*, 176-177; Samuel Bak, *Painted in Words*, 398.
57. *ZAP Bulletin* (August 6, 1945): 3; *ZAP Bulletin* 35/155 (April 3, 1946): 1; Bernard D. Weinryb, "Poland," in *The Jews in the Soviet Satellites*, eds. Peter Meyer et al. (Syracuse, NY: Syracuse University Press, 1953), 251.
58. Janusz Wrobel, "W cieniu Holokaustu: odrodzenie spolecznosci zydowskiej w Lodzkiem po II Wojnie Swiatowej," *Biuletyn IPN* 11(58) (November 2005): 31-32.
59. Natalia Aleksiun, "The Situation of the Jews in Poland as Seen by Soviet Security Forces in 1945," *Jews in Eastern Europe* 3(37) (Winter 1998): 62; Israel Gutman, *The Jews in Poland After World War II*, 144; *ZAP Bulletin* 66/76 (August 27, 1945): 1; *ZAP Bulletin* 98/108 (November 9, 1945): 1; *ZAP Bulletin* 111/112 (December 10, 1945): 1; *ZAP Bulletin* 25/145 (March 4, 1946): 1; *Dos Naje Lebn*, March 13, 1946. Joanna Szczesna, "Powszechna rzecz zabijanie. Rozmowa z Markiem Edelmanem," *Gazeta Swiateczna*, January 19, 2008.
60. *ZAP Bulletin* 68/178 (June 26, 1946): 3; *ZAP Bulletin* 70/180 (July 11946): 2; *Dos Naje Lebn*, June 28, 1946; J. S. Hertz, *The History of the Jewish Labor Bund in Lodz* (in Yiddish) (New York: Unser Tsait, 1958), 470.
61. *Dos Naje Lebn* July 12, 1946; Yitzhak Zuckerman ("Antek"), *A Surplus of Memory: Chronicle of the Warsaw Ghetto Uprising* (Berkeley, Los Angeles, Oxford: University of California Press, 1993), 662-664; *ZAP Bulletin* 82/192 (July 27, 1946): 3; *ZAP Bulletin* 86/186 (July 12, 1946): 2.
62. David Engel, *Between Liberation and Flight*, 130-131; Irena Hurwic-Nowakowska, *A Social Analysis of Postwar Polish Jewry*, 32-33; Teresa Toranska. *Jestesmy: rozstania '68* (Warsaw: Swiat Ksiazki, 2008), 14.
63. Jan Tomasz Gross, *Upiorna dekada*, 94-96; Michal Mirski, *Vegn Lodzer Yiddishn Komitet*, 35-36; J. S. Hertz, *The History of the Jewish Labor Bund in Lodz*, 466; Jan T. Gross, "In the Aftermath of the Kielce Pogrom: The Special Commission of the Central Committee of Jews in Poland," *Gal-Ed* XV-XVI (1997): 119-136; Jan Tomasz Gross, *Upiorna dekada. Wydanie nowe,poprawione i rozszerzone* (Krakow; Wydawnictwo Austeria, 2007), 75-93.
64. Special Committee Collection, ZIH Archive, 303/XVIII/53 and 303/XVIII/25.

4. FRIENDS, ACQUAINTANCES, STRANGERS

1. Rachel Patron, interview by author, Omer, Israel, November 2000. Rachel Patron, "Flowers in the Snow," a memoir, in the possesion of the author.
2. Shlomo Pomerantz, interview by author, Tel-Aviv, July 7, 2005.

3. Richard Lubelsky, interview by author, Prague, September, 1999.
4. Ada Horowitz, interview by author, Tel-Aviv, May, 2005.
5. Hanka Hornstein, interview by author, Tel-Aviv, June 2005.
6. Ivri Meridor (Heniek Napadow), interview by author, Beer-Sheva, May, 2005.
7. Aharon Eynat (Zalkind), interview by author, March 9, 2005. Testimony for the Jewish Central Historical Committe, Lodz, November 17, 1947, ZIH Archive Warsaw, 301/3619.
8. Baruch Kaplinski, interview by author, Tel-Aviv, March 5, 2001.
9. Binyamin Majerczak, interview by author, Tel-Aviv, March 4, 2002.
10. Fayvl Podeh (Podemski), interview by author, Herzliya, February 20, 2002; Fayvl Podeh (Podemski), *Memories from the Lodz Ghetto* (in Hebrew) (Ra'anana: Docustory Publishers, 2004); Fayvl Podeh (Podemski), "The Ken of Hashomer Hatzair in the Lodz Ghetto" (in Hebrew), *Yalkut Moreshet* Kaf Het (1979): 7-36; Fayvl Podeh (Podemski), "The Liquidation of the Ghetto" (in Hebrew), *Yalkut Moreshet* Nun Het (1994): 157-177.
11. Prof. Matityahu Mintz, interview by author, Herzliya, August 19, 2003.
12. Natan Gross, interview by author, Giv'atayim, February 21, 2002; Natan Gross, *Who Are You Mr. Grymek?* (in Hebrew), (Tel-Aviv: Moreshet, 1986).
13. Wanda Rotenberg, interview by author, Tel-Aviv, July 17, 2005; Shulamit Kesari, "A Heroic Story" (in Hebrew), *Shiur Hofshi* (Israeli Teachers' Association) (March 2003): 6-8. Obituary by Uri Dromi, *Haaretz,* January 16, 2008.
14. Sarah Shner-Nishmit, interview by, author, Lohamei Hagetaot, August 12, 2003; Sarah Shner-Nishmit, *I Did Not Acquire Peace* (in Hebrew) (Tel Aviv: Hakibbutz Hameuhad Publishing House, 1988).
15. Maria Lorber, interview by author, Neve Ef'al, April 4, 2002.
16. Noah Flug, interview by author, Jerusalem, February 17, 2003; Noah Flug's testimony, Yad Vashem Archive 03/4069.
17. Aleksander Klugman, interview by author, Tel-Aviv, March 4, 2002; Aleksander Klugman, "Lodzkie impresje," *Midrasz* (July-August 2001): 6-7; Aleksander Klugman, "Strzepy zyciorysu," *Tygiel Kultury,* Lodz, (2004): 5-106.
18. Ewa Frenkel-Przemyslawski, interview by author, Jerusalem, November 23, 2005.
19. Dziunia Liberman (Lublin), interview by author, Kiryat Motzkin, June 7, 2005.
20. Szulim Rozenberg, interview by author, Paris, September 26, 2004; Szulim Rozenberg, "Lodz zydowska po wojnie," *Midrasz* (July-August, 2001): 24-25; Szulim Rozenberg, "Memories from Postwar Lodz" (presentation at the Medem Library, Paris, June 9, 2001).
21. Dr. Alina Margolis-Edelman, interview by author, Paris, September 26, 2004; Alina Margolis-Edelman, "Ala from the Primer," *Polin* 11 (1998): 94-111.
22. Prof. Jacob Goldberg, interview by author, Jerusalem, February 9, 2004; "Na zajecia niose mape Polski Jagiellonow," *Nowe Ksiazki* 6 (2002): 4-8.
23. Kazimierz Rutenberg, interview by author, Tel-Aviv, September 17, 2003; Yossi Elgazi, "My Grandpa's Fighter Plane," *Haaretz,* April 25, 2003.
24. Henryk Grynberg, interview by author, Omer, December 18, 2002; Henryk Grynberg, *The Jewish War and The Victory* (Evanston, IL: Northwestern University Press, 2001); Jolanta Brach-Czaina, "Kompleks," *Tygodnik Powszechny* 8(23-27), (February 20, 1994); Joanna B. Michlic, "Bearing Witness: Henryk Grynberg's Path from Child Survivor to Artist," *Polin* 20 (2008): 324-332.

5. SURVIVING

1. Nora Lewin, *The Holocaust: The Destruction of European Jewry, 1933-1945* (New York: Shocken Books, 1973), 150, 170; It seems that the often quoted number of 300,000 Polish-Jewish refugees from German-occupied Poland in the Soviet annexed territories has been exaggerated.
2. Israel Gutman, "The Jews in Poland," *Encyclopedia of the Holocaust,* ed. Israel Gutman (New York: Macmillan, 1989), Vol. 3, 1155-1176.
3. Israel Gutman, "The Jews in Poland," 1164-1165; Teresa Prekerowa, "Wojna i okupacja," in *Najnowsze dzieje Zydow w Polsce (w zarysie do 1950 roku),* ed. Jerzy Tomaszewski (Warsaw: Wydawnictwo Naukowe PWN, 1993), 283, 331, 316, 317; Saul Friedlaender. *The Years of Extermination: Nazi Germany and the Jews, 1939-1945* (New York: Harper Collins, 2007), 38.
4. Israel Gutman, "The Jews in Poland," 1170-1171; Saul Friedlander, *The Years of Extermination, 246.*
5. Nora Lewin, *The Holocaust,* 167, 207, 216; Lucy S. Dawidowicz, *The War Against the Jews, 1939-1945* (New York: Holt, Rinehart and Winston, 1975), 246; Saul Friedlander, *The Years of Extermination,* 148-149; Teresa Prekerowa, *Wojna i okupacja,* 285.
6. Teresa Prekerowa, *Wojna i okupacja,* 298-300, 323, 336-340; Israel Gutman, *The Jews of Warsaw, 1939-1945: Ghetto, Underground, Revolt* (Indiana: Indiana University Press, 1982); Gunnar S. Paulsson *Secret City: The Hidden Jews of Warsaw, 1940-1945* (New Haven and London: Yale University Press, 2002).
7. Israel Gutman, *The Jews of Warsaw,* 132-144; Israel Gutman, "Youth Movements in the Underground and the Resistance in the Ghettos," *Jewish Resistance During the Holocaust* (in Hebrew) (Jerusalem: Yad Vashem, 1970), 206-224.
8. Shmuel Krakowski, "Lodz," *Holocaust Encyclopedia* (in Hebrew) (Tel-Aviv: Yad Vashem and Sifriat Hapoalim, 1990), 612-621.
9. Michal Unger, *Lodz: The Last Ghetto in Poland* (in Hebrew) (Jerusalem: Yad Vashem, 2005), 326-334, 402.
10. *Ibid.,* 212-216, 403-415; Gordon J. Horwitz, *Ghettostadt: Lodz and the Making of a Nazi City* (Cambridge, MA and London: The Belknap Press of Harvard University Press, 2008), 255-256.
11. Michal Unger, *Lodz: The Last Ghetto in Poland,* 424-433.
12. *Ibid.,* 557; Shmuel Krakowski, "Lodz," 620; Andrea Loew, Juden im Ghetto Litzmannstadt: Lebensbedingungen, Selbstvahrnehmung, Verhalten (Goettingen: Wallstein Verlag 2006), 485-491.
13. Teresa Prekerowa, *Wojna i okupacja,* 352-355; Joanna Nalewajko-Kulikow, *Strategie przetrwania: Zydzi po aryjskiej stronie Warszawy* (Warsaw: Neriton, 2004; Nechama Tec, "Hiding and Passing on the Aryan Side: A Gendered Comparison," in *Contested Memories: Poles and Jews during the Holocaust and Its Aftermath,* ed. Joshua D. Zimmerman New Brunswick, NJ and London: Rutgers University Press, 2003), 193-211.
14. "Proceedings of the Fourth Yad Vashem International Historical Conference: The Nazi Concentration Camps" (in Hebrew), Jerusalem, 20-24 January 1980; Saul Friedlander, *The Years of Extermination,* 188, 207-209, 272, 280-281, 286, 529, 531; Teresa Prekerowa, *Wojna i okupacja,* 323-332; Israel Gutman, "Varsha,"

Holocaust Encyclopedia in (Hebrew) (Tel-Aviv: Yad Vashem and Sifriat Poalim Publishing House, 1990), Vol. 2, 470-475.
15. Saul Friedlander, *The Years of Extermination*, 648-649.
16. Dov Levin, *The Lesser of Two Evils: Eastern European Jewry Under Soviet Rule, 1939-1941* (Philadelphia and Jerusalem: The Jewish Publication Society,1995), 179-180; Maciej Siekierski, "The Jews in Soviet-Occupied Eastern Poland at the End of 1939: Numbers and Distribution," in *Jews in Eastern Poland and the USSR, 1939-46*, eds. Norman Davies and Antony Polonsky (New York: St. Martin's Press, 1991), 110-113.
17. Shimon Redlich, "The Jews in the Soviet Annexed Territories, 1939-41," *Soviet Jewish Affairs* 1 (1971): 83; Maciej Siekierski, "The Jews in Soviet-Occupied Eastern Poland at the End of 1939," 115; Keith Sword, *Deportation and Exile: Poles in the Soviet Union, 1939-1948*, (New York: St. Martin's Press: New York, 1994), 11-12; Dov Levin, *The Lesser of Two Evils*, 198-217.
18. Dov Levin, *The Lesser of Two Evils*, 198-217.
19. *Ibid.*, 191-197; Keith Sword, *Deportation and Exile*, 13-19, 26-27; Maciej Siekierski and Feliks Tych, eds., *Widzialem aniola smierci: losy deportowanych Zydow polskich w ZSRR w latach II wojny swiatowej* (Warsaw: Rosner i Wspolnicy, 2006), 16-17. Personal communications from Prof. Antony Polonsky and Prof. Mordechai Altshuler, see Stanislaw Ciesielski, "Masowe deportacje z ziem wschodnich II Rzeczypospolitej w latach 1940-1941 i losy deportowanych uwagi o stanie badan." See also Mordechai Altshuler, "The Distress of Jews in the Soviet Union in the Wake of the Molotov-Ribbentrop Pact," *Yad Vashem Studies* 36/2 (2008): 73-114.
20. Irena Grudzinska-Gross and Jan Tomasz Gross, eds., *War Through Children's Eyes: The Soviet Occupation of Poland and the Deportations, 1939-1941* (Stanford, CA: Hoover Institution Press, 1981), xxiii; Keith Sword, *Deportation and Exile*, 19-24; Yosef Litvak, "Jewish Refugees from Poland in the USSR, 1939-1946," in *Bitter Legacy: Confronting the Holocaust in the USSR*, ed. Zvi Gitelman (Bloomington and Indianapolis: Indiana University Press, 1997), 130-131.
21. Yosef Litvak, "Jewish Refugees from Poland in the USSR, 1939-1946," 134-135; Keith Sword, *Deportation and Exile*, 42-47; Maciej Siekierski and Feliks Tych, eds., *Widzialem aniola smierci*, 18-19; see also Rebecca Manley, *To the Tashkent Station: Evacuation and Survival in the Soviet Union at War* (Ithaca and London: Cornell University Press, 2009).
22. Irena Grudzinska-Gross and Jan Tomasz Gross, eds., *War Through Children's Eyes*, xxiv-xxvi; Yosef Litvak, "Jewish Refugees from Poland in the USSR, 1939-1946," 134-135, 143-144; Dov Levin, *The Lesser of Two Evils*, 303; Maciej Siekierski and Feliks Tych, eds., *Widzialem aniola smierci, passim*.
23. Ryszard Terlecki, "The Jewish Issue in the Polish Army in the USSR and the Near East, 1941-1944," in *Jews in Eastern Poland and the USSR, 1939-46*, eds. Norman Davies and Antony Polonsky, 161-164; Shimon Redlich, "Jews in General Anders' Army in the Soviet Union, 1941-42," *Soviet Jewish Affairs* 2 (1971): 90-98; Israel Gutman, "Jews in General Anders' Army in the Soviet Union," *Yad Vashem Studies* 12 (1977): 231-296.
24. Klemens Nussbaum, "Jews in the Kosciuszko Division and First Polish Army," in *Jews in Eastern Poland and the USSR, 1939-46*, eds. Norman Davies and Antony Polonsky, 183-186.

25. *Ibid.*, 183-208; Wlodzimierz Rozenbaum, "The Road to New Poland: Jewish Communists in the Soviet Union, 1939-46," in *Jews in Eastern Poland and the USSR, 1939-46*, eds. Norman Davies and Antony Polonsky, 220-221.
26. Yosef Litvak, "Polish-Jewish Refugees Repatriated from the Soviet Union at the End of the Second World War and Afterwards," in *Jews in Eastern Poland and the USSR, 1939-46*, eds. Norman Davies and Antony Polonsky, 230-234; Yosef Litvak. *Polish-Jewish Refugees in the USSR, 1939-1946* (in Hebrew) (Tel Aviv: Ghetto Fighters' House, 1988), 358; Jozef Adelson, "W Polsce zwanej ludowa," in *Najnowsze dzieje Zydow w Polsce*, ed. Jerzy Tomaszewski(Warsaw: PWN, 1993), 387; Keith Sword, *Deportation and Exile*, 193, 195; Yosef Litwak, "Jewish Refugees from Poland in the USSR, 1939-1946," 148.
27. Binyamin Majerczak, interview by author, Tel-Aviv, March 4, 2002; Binyamin Meirtchak. *I Love You. Grandpa Beniek* (published posthumously by the family, Tel-Aviv, 2007), 31-34.
28. Aleksander Klugman, interview by author, Tel-Aviv, March 4, 2002; Aleksander Klugman, "Strzepy zyciorysu," *Tygiel Kultury*, Lodz, (2004): 7-9.
29. Fayvl Podeh, interview by author, Herzliya, February 20, 2002; Fayvl Podeh (Podemski), *Memories from the Lodz Ghetto* (in Hebrew) Ra'anana: Docustory, 2004), 39-40.
30. Matityahu Mintz, interview by author, Herzliya, August 19, 2003.
31. Shlomo Pomerantz, interview by author, Tel-Aviv, July 7, 2005.
32. Ivri Meridor (Heniek Napadow), interview by author, Beer-Sheva, May, 2005.
33. Rachel Patron. *Flowers in the Snow*. An unpublished memoir.
34. Aharon Eynat (Zalkind), interview by author, Tel-Aviv, March 9, 2005; testimony, the ZIH Archive, Warsaw, 301/3619.
35. Natan Gross, interview by author, Giv'atayim, February 21, 2002; Natan Gross, *Who Are You Mr. Grymek?* (in Hebrew) (Tel-Aviv: Moreshet, 1986), 9-14.
36. Binyamin Majerczak, interview by author; Binyamin Meirtchak, *I Love You Granpa Beniek*, 34-39.
37. Szulim Rozenberg, interview by author, Paris, Septenber 26, 2004.
38. Ewa Frenkel-Przemyslawski, interview by author, Jerusalem, November 23, 2005.
39. Matityahu Mintz, interview by author.
40. Ewa Frenkel-Przemyslawski, interview by author.
41. Binyamin Majerczak, interview by author; Binyamin Meirtchak, *I Love You. Grandpa Beniek*, 39-52.
42. Rachel Patron, interview by author, Omer, November, 2000.
43. Ivri Meridor (Heniek Napadow), interview by author.
44. Stephen Kotkin, *Magnetic Mountain: Stalinism as a Civilization* (Berkeley-Los Angeles-London: University of California Press, 1995; Ewa Frenkel-Przemyslawski, interview by author.
45. Binyamin Majerczak, interview by author; Binyamin Meirtchak, *I Love You. Granpa Beniek*, 53-100.
46. Szulim Rozenberg, interview by author.
47. Rachel Patron, *Sunflowers in the Snow*.
48. Ivri Meridor (Heniek Napadow), interview by author.
49. Shlomo Pomerantz, interview by author.
50. Hanka Hornstein (Rydel), interview by author, Tel-Aviv, June, 2005.

51. Ada Horwitz (Gibraltar), interview by author, Tel-Aviv, May, 2005.
52. Richard Lubelsky, interview by author, Prague, September, 1999.
53. Ivri Meridor (Heniek Napadow), interview by author.
54. Binyamin Majerczak, interview by author; Binyamin Meirtchak, *I Love You. Grandpa Beniek,* 101-128.
55. Kazimierz Rutenberg, interview by author, Tel-Aviv, September 17, 2003; Yossi Elgazi, "My Grandpa's Fighter Plane," *Haaretz,* April 25, 2003.
56. Aharon Eynat (Zalkind), interview by author, Tel-Aviv, March 9, 2005; Testimony at the ZIH Archive, Warsaw, 301/3619.
57. Aleksander Klugman, *Strzepy zyciorysu,* 13-36.
58. Noah Flug, interview by author, Jerusalem, February 17, 2003; Noah Flug's testimony, Yad Vashem Archive, Jerusalem, 03/4069.
59. Fayvl Podeh (Podemski), interview by author, Herzliya, February 20, 2002; Fayvl Podeh (Podemski), "The Ken of Hashomer Hatzair in the Lodz Ghetto" (in Hebrew), *Yalkut Moreshet* Kaf Het (1979): 7-36.
60. Dziunia Dublin (Liberman), interview by author, Kiryat Motzkin, June 7, 2005.
61. Aleksander Klugman, *Strzepy zyciorysu,* 36-65; Binyamin Eckstein, "Ebensee," *Holocaust Encyclopedia* (in Hebrew), 2-3.
62. Noah Flug, interview by author.
63. Dziunia Dublin (Liberman), interview by author.
64. Natan Gross, *Who Are You Mr. Grymek?* (in Hebrew); Natan Gross' testimony for the Jewish Historical Commission in Krakow, 1945, the ZIH Archive, Warsaw, 301/237, 301/424, 301/428, 301/578, 301/597, 301/598, 301/616, 301/617, 301/621; Christopher R. Browning, "The Fate of the Jews of Krakow Under Nazi Occupation," in *Every Day Lasts a Year: A Jewish Family's Correspondence from Poland,* eds. Christopher R. Browning et al. (New York: Cambridge University Press, 2007), 45-59.
65. Dr. Alina Margolis-Edelman, interview by author, Paris, September 26, 2004; Alina Margolis-Edelman, "Ala From the Primer," *Polin* 11 (1998): 94-111.
66. Henryk Grynberg, interview by author, Omer, December 18, 2002; Henryk Grynberg, *The Jewish War and The Victory* (Evanston: Northwestern University Press, 2001).

6. THE ZIONISTS

1. Natalia Aleksiun, *Dokad dalej? Ruch syjonistyczny w Polsce (1944-1950)* (Warszawa: Wydawnictwo Trio, 2002), 107-127; Yitzhak Zuckerman ("Antek"), *A Surplus of Memory: Chronicle of the Warsaw Ghetto Uprising,* ed. and trans. Barbara Harshav (Berkeley-Los Angeles-Oxford: University of California Press, 1993), 593-594; David Engel, *Between Liberation and Flight: Holocaust Survivors in Poland and the Struggle for Leadership, 1944-1946* (in Hebrew) (Tel-Aviv: Am Oved, 1996), 77-78, 198 f 146, 190 f 55; Dorka Shternberg, interview by author, Lohamei Hagetaot, August 12, 2003.
2. David Engel, *Between Liberation and Flight,* 148-150.
3. David Engel, *Between Liberation and Flight,* 80,89; Sara Zyskind, *Stolen Years* (Minneapolis: Lerner Publ. Co., 1981), 277.
4. David Engel, *Between Liberation and Flight,* 124-125; Yitzhak Zuckerman

("Antek"), *A Surplus of Memory,* 610; Natalia Aleksiun, *Dokad dalej?,* 150-151.
5. Yitzhak Zuckerman ("Antek"), *A Surplus of Memory,* 626.
6. Shlomo Bar-Gil, Ada Schein, Dwell in Safety: Holocaust Survivors in the Rural Cooperative Settlements, 1945-1955 (in Hebrew) (Jerusalem: Yad Vashem, 2010), 29-33; Natalia Aleksiun, *Dokad dalej?,* 135; David Engel, *Between Liberation and Flight,* 79.
7. Stefan Grayek, *The Struggle* (in Hebrew) (Tel-Aviv: Am Oved, 1989, 97.
8. Levi Arie Sarid, *The Trial of Suffering and Redemption* (in Hebrew), Vol. 2, (Tel-Aviv: Moreshet, 1997), 287; Avner Holtzman, *An Image Before My Eyes* (in Hebrew) (Tel-Aviv: Am Oved, 2002), 181-233.
9. Yitzhak Zuckerman ("Antek"), *A Surplus of Memory,* 627; Shalom Cholawski, "The End of the War — Memoirs, 1944-1946" (in Hebrew), *Yalkut Moreshet* 70 (2000): 113-136.
10. IPN Archive, Lodz, pf 10\690, t.3, 249-254; *ZAP,* February 11, 1946, 11/148, 1 and 11\147, 4.
11. Yitzhak Palgi, "Military Cadres and Assistance from Poland", *The Hashomer Hatzair Book,* Vol. 3 (in Hebrew) (Merhavya: Sifriat Hapoalim, 1964), 143; Leszek Olejnik, "Lodz jako centrum spolecznosci zydowskiej w Polsce (1945-1949)," in Fenomen getta lodzkiego, 1940-1944, eds. Pawel Samus and Wieslaw Pu (Lodz: Wydawnictwo Uniwersytetu Lodzkiego, 2006), 414. Michal Mirski, Memoir, Yad Vashem Archive, 037/25 and in *Mosty,* March 9, 1948, 4, May 22, 1948, 8; and October 6, 1948, 3.
12. Yehuda Bauer, *Flight and Rescue: Brichah* (New York: Random House, 1970), 119-121, 146-147, 221-222; David Engel, *Between Liberation and Flight,* 88-89, 128, 134-135, 150-152; Yitzhak Zuckerman ("Antek"), *A Surplus of Memory,* 645-646, 675.
13. Yitzhak Palgi, "Military Cadres and Assistance from Poland," 142-145. Levi Aryeh Sarid, *The Trial of Suffering and Redemption,* Vol. 2, 425; IPN Archive, Lodz, pf 10/690, t3, 119-120, t1, 7-10; see also *Documents on Israeli-Polish Relations 1945-1967,* edited by Marcos Silber and Szymon Rudnicki. Jerusalem: State of Israel, Israel State Archives and The Head Office of the State Archives in Poland, 2009, 115-116: 133-135.
14. Joel Royzman, *The Borokhov Youth and the Dror Borokhov Youth in Post-Holocaust Poland* (in Hebrew) (Tel-Aviv: Yad Tabenkin, 1999), 35-47; Dorka Shternberg, interview by author, Lohamei Hagetaot, August 12, 2003.
15. Natalia Aleksiun, *Dokad dalej?,* 182; Shalom Cholawski, "The End of the War — Memoirs, 1944-1946," 123; N'ima Barzel, *Yearning and Reality: The Encounter Between the Leaders of the Ghetto Uprising and Israeli Society* (in Hebrew) (Jerusalem: The Zionist Library, 1998), 208, 214; Yad Yaari Archive, Givat Haviva, 150/14/9, 56/3/1-2, 69/4/1-2, 150/14/9, 50/5/1-2.
16. Natalia Aleksiun, *Dokad dalej?* 185, Yad Yaari Archive, 56/3/1-2, 65/5/1-2.
17. Yad Yaari Archive, 65/5/1-2, 14/4/150, 50/4/1-2.
18. *Mosty* 3(2), January 10, 1947; N'ima Barzel, *Yearning and Reality,* 215, 220; Yad Yaari Archive, 55/2/1-2.
19. The Gordonia Archive, *The Gordonia Movement in Lodz* (in Hebrew) (Maale Hachamisha: Hulda, 1998), 82-116; IPN Archive, Lodz, pf 10/690, t3, 116,159,161, 192; The Pinhas Lavon Archive, Hulda, Gordonia Collection 1/5.
20. David Engel, *Between Liberation and Flight,* 92-93; Yehuda Bauer, *Flight and*

Rescue, 120-121; Joel Royzman, *The Borokhov Youth and the Dror Borokhov Youth in Post-Holocaust Poland,* 35; Levi Aryeh Sarid, *The Trial of Suffering and Redemption,* Vol. 2, 287.
21. Yad Yaari Archive, 59/5/1-2, 63/5/1-2, 59/4/1-2, 14/9/150.
22. Natalia Aleksiun, *Dokad dalej?,* 159; David Engel, *Between Liberation and Flight,* 117; Emuna Nahmani Gafni, *Split Hearts: Redemption of Jewish Children from Christian Families in Poland After the Holocaust* (in Hebrew) (Jerusalem: Yad Vashem, 2006), 120-124; Stefan Grayek, *The Struggle,* 64; Kibbutz Lohamei Hagetaot, *The Redemption of Jewish Children from Christians in Poland After the Holocaust* (in Hebrew) (Lohamei Hagetaot: Lohamei Hagetaot House, 1989), 18; Nachum Bogner, *At the Mercy of Strangers: The Rescue of Jewish Children with Assumed Identities in Poland* (in Hebrew) (Jerusalem: Yad Vashem, 2000), 230-231.
23. David Engel *Between Liberation and Flight,* 83; Emuna Nahmani-Gafni, *Split Hearts,* 119; Leybl Kuriski, "The Jewish Coordination for the Redemption of Children in Poland in the Years 1946-1949," *Galed* 7-8 (1985): 259.
24. Natalia Aleksiun, *Dakad dalej?,* 159-160; David Engel, *Between Liberation and Flight,* 118-119; Nachum Bogner, *At the Mercy of Strangers,* 226-254; Leybl Kuriski, "The Jewish Coordination for the Redemption of Children in Poland in the Years 1946-1949," 260.
25. Lohamei Hagetaot House, *The Redemption of Jewish Children from Christians in Poland After the Holocaust,* 95; Nachum Bogner, *At the Mercy of Strangers,* 245; Emuna Nahmani Gafni, *Split Hearts,* 126, 129, 131; Joanna B. Michlic, "Who Am I? Jewish Children's Search for Identity in Post-War Poland, 1945-1949," *Polin* 20 (2008): 98-121.
26. Fayvl Podeh (Podemski), interview by author, Herzliya, August, 2002; Fayvl Podeh (Podemski), "The Liquidation of the Ghetto," *Yalkut Moreshet* Nun Het (1994): 173-174.
27. Fayvl Podeh (Podemski), interview by author, Hertzlia, August 2002; Recording of the Reunion of the Ghetto Fighters' Hebrew School in Lodz, Tel-Aviv, Fall 1997.
28. Wanda Rotenberg (Bela Elster), interview by author, Tel-Aviv, July 17, 2005 and telephone interview, October, 2003.
29. Sara Shner-Nishmit, interview by author, Lohamei Hagetaot, August 12, 2003; Sara Shner-Nishmit, *I Did Not Acquire Peace* (in Hebrew) (Tel-Aviv: Hakibbutz Hameuhad Publishing House, 1988), 189-204; *The Redemption of Jewish Children from Christians in Poland After the Holocaust,* 73-88.
30. Natan Gross, interview by author, Giv'atayim, February 21, 2002; Natan Gross, *Przygody Grymka w Ziemi Swietej* (Krakow: Wydawnictwo Rabid, 2006), 38.
31. Binyamin Majerczak, interview by author, Tel-Aviv, March 4, 2002; Binyamin Meirtchak, *I Love You Granpa Beniek* (published posthumously by the family, Tel-Aviv, 2007), 135-136.
32. Prof. Matityahu Mintz, interview by author, Herzliya, August 19, 2003; Yohanan Fein, *A Boy With a Fiddle* (in Hebrew) (unpublished memoir, Tel-Aviv, 2003), 154-156.
33. Aharon Eynat (Zalkind), interview by author, Tel-Aviv, March 9, 2005.
34. Rachel Patron, interview by author, Omer, September, 1999; Rachel Patron, "The Ticket: A Short Story," *Hadassah Magazine* 65/1 (1983): 24-25, 47-48.
35. Hanka Hornstein, interview by author, Tel-Aviv, June, 2005.
36. Ada Horwitz (Gibraltar), interview by author, Tel-Aviv, May 2005.

37. Shlomo Pomerantz, interview by author, Tel-Aviv, July 7, 2005.
38. Ivri Meridor (Heniek Napadow), interview by author, Beer-Sheva, May 2005.
39. Richard Lubelsky, interview by author, Prague, September, 1999.

7. THE OTHERS

1. Jaff Schatz, *The Generation: The Rise and Fall of the Jewish Communists of Poland* (Berkeley-Los Angeles-Oxford: University of California Press, 1991), 209-218; Israel Gutman, *The Jews in Poland After World War II* (in Hebrew) (Jerusalem: The Zalman Shazar Center, 1985), 63.
2. Jozef Adelson, "W Polsce zwanej Ludowa," in Najnowsze dzieje Zydow w Polsce (w zarysie do 1950 roku), ed. Jerzy Tomaszewski (Warsaw: Wydawnictwo Naukowe PWN, 1993), 434-435; Maciej Pisarski, "'Na zydowskiej ulicy': szkic do dziejow zydowskiej frakcji PPR I zespolu PZPR przy CKZP, 1945-1951," *BZIH* 2 (1997): 35; Krystyna Kersten, "Rok pierwszy," *Midrasz,* Lipiec-Sierpien (1998): 26.
3. August Grabski, *Dzialalnosc komunistow wsrod Zydow w Polsce (1944-1949)* (Warsaw: Wydawnictwo Trio-ZIH, 2004), 72-73, 79, 88-89, 116-118, 183-186; Jan T. Gross, *Fear: Antisemitism in Poland After Auschwitz. An Essay in Historical Interpretation* (Princeton and Oxford: Princeton University Press, 2006), 217-219; David Engel, *Between Liberation and Flight: Holocaust Survivors in Poland and the Struggle for Leadership, 1944-1946* (in Hebrew) (Tel-Aviv: Am Oved Publishers, 1996), 105, 144, 147.
4. Bozena Szaynok, "Problematyka zydowska w polityce komunistow w latach 1949-1953," in *Nusech Pojln: Studia z dziejow kultury jidysz w powojennej Polsce,* ed. Magdalena Ruta (Krakow-Budapest: Wydawnictwo Austeria, 2008), 9-17; Report by Anatol Wertheim, April 23, 1949, ZIH Archive, s/330/5; August Grabski, *Dzialalnosc komunistow wsrod Zydow w Polsce (1944-1949),* 307-308.
5. Daniel Blatman, *For Our Freedom and Yours: The Jewish Labor Bund in Poland, 1939-1949* (in Hebrew) (Jerusalem: Yad Vashem and The Hebrew University of Jerusalem, 1996), 277-299, 339-350; J.S. Hertz, *The History of the Jewish Labor Bund in Lodz* (in Yiddish) (New York: Unser Tsait, 1958), 464-471; Natalia Aleksiun, "Where Was There a Future for Polish Jewry: Bundist and Zionist Polemics in Post World War II Poland, in *Jewish Politics in Eastern Europe: The Bund at 100,* ed. Jack Jacobs ([city?]: Houndmills, 2001).
6. Grzegorz Berendt, "Michala Mirskiego rozrachunek z Polska Ludowa," *Niepodleglosc* 53-54 (2003-2004): 284-314; Klara Mirska, *W cieniu wiecznego strachu (wspomnienia)* (Paris, 1980), 152.
7. Grzegorz Berendt, *ibid.;* Michal Mirski, *Biegiem marsz* (Warsaw: Ksiega i Wiedz,a 1958); Klara Mirska, *ibid.,* 344-359, 450-451.
8. Grzegorz Berendt, *ibid.;* Klara Mirska, *ibid.,* 364-423; Michal Mirski, *Bez stopnia* (Warsaw: MON, 1960), 67.
9. Grzegorz Berendt, *ibid.;* Michal Mirski, *ibid.,* 150; Mirski's Report on the Jewish Committee in Lodz, YVA, 037/25, 1-2.
10. Grzegorz Berendt, *ibid.;* Mirski's Report on the Jewish Committee in Lodz, 3.
11. Klara Mirska, *W cieniu wiecznego strachu (wspomnienia),* 444-470; Mirski's Report on the Jewish Committee in Lodz, 22-23.
12. David Engel, *Between Liberation and Flight,* 82-83; Natalia Aleksiun *Dokad*

dalej? Ruch syjonistyczny w Polsce (1944-1950) (Warsaw: Wydawnictwo Trio, 2002), 258-259; Bozena Szaynok, *Ludnosc zydowska na Dolnym Slasku, 1945-1950* (Wroclaw: Wydawnictwo Uniwersytetu Wroclawskiego, 2000), 9; Marci Shore, "Children of the Revolution: Communism, Zionism, and the Berman Brothers," *Jewish Social Studies* 10(3) (2004): 23-86.
13. Klara Mirska, W *cieniu wiecznego strachu (wspomnienia)*, 467; Klara Mirska, *Pamietniki Klary Mirskiej: Kronika mojego zycia, 1907-66* (Warsaw: Biblioteka Narodowa, [Year?]), 1042-1048.
14. Alina Cala and Helena Datner-Spiewak, eds., *Dieje Zydow w Polsce, 1944-1968* (Warsaw: Teksty zrodlowe, Zydowski Instytut Historyczny), 139-141; Grzegorz Berendt, "Michala Mirskiego rozrachunek z Polska Ludowa:; Jan T.Gross, *Fear*, 217.
15. Maria Lorber, interview by author, Neve Ef'al, April 4, 2002.
16. Ewa Frenkel-Przemyslawski, interview by author, Jerusalem, November 23, 2005.
17. Noah Flug, interview by author, Jerusalem, February 17, 2003.
18. Aleksander Klugman, interview by author, Tel-Aviv, March 4, 2002: Aleksander Klugman, "Lodzkie impresje," *Midrasz* (July-August 2001): 6-7; Aleksander Klugman, *Strzepy zyciorysu* (Lodz: Biblioteka "Tygla Kultury," 2004), 66-74.
19. Dziunia Dublin (Liberman), interview by author, Kiryat Motzkin, June 7, 2005.
20. Szulim Rozenberg, interview by author, Paris, September 26, 2004; Szulim Rozenberg, "Lodz zydowska po wojnie," *Midrasz* (July-August 2001): 24-25; Jacob Metzer, "Arcadius Kahan, 1920-1982: Profile of a Scholar," in *Jews in Economic Life: Collected Essays in Memory of Arkadius Kahan (1920-1982)*, ed. Nachum Gross (Jerusalem: The Zalman Shazar Center), 1985, IX; Telephone interviews with Vivian Kahan, Peter Wiener, Abraham Zheleznikov, Izaak Luden and Rachel Rabin, December 2008.
21. Dr. Alina Margolis-Edelman, interview by author, Paris, September 26, 2004; Joanna Szczesna, "Marek Edelman i Antek Cukierman: losy powojenne," *Gazeta Wyborcza*, June 6, 2003; Hanna Kral, *Zdazyc przed Panem Bogiem* (Krakow: Wydawnictwo a5, 2003), 77-78; Marek Edelman, interview by author, Lodz, July 2, 2002.
22. Prof. Jacob Goldberg, interview by author, Jerusalem, February 9, 2004; Radoslaw Januszewski, Jan Strekowski, eds. *Polska w oczach cudzych* (Wroclaw: Towarzystwo Przyjaciol Ossolineum, 2003), 179-226.
23. Kazimierz Rutenberg, interview by author. Tel-Aviv, September 17, 2003.
24. Henryk Grynberg, interview by author, Omer, December 18, 2002; Henryk Grynberg, The Jewish War and The Victory (Evanston, IL: North Western University Press, 2001), 103-150; Henryk Grynberg, Zycie ideologiczne, (Warsaw: Zycie osobiste, Panstwowy Instytut Wydawniczy, 1992), 9-13; Joanna B. Michlic, "Bearing Witness: Henryk Grynberg's Path from Child Survivor to Artist. An Interview with Henryk Grynberg," Polin 20 (2008): 324-335; Henryk Grynberg, Kalifornijski kadisz, (Warsaw: Swiat ksiazki, 2005), 46; Henryk Grynberg, Ciag dalszy (Warsaw: Swiat ksiazki, 2008), 9-59.

EPILOGUE

1. IPN Archive, Lodz, pf/10/690 t.1, 213, 218; Leszek Olejnik, "Wojewodzki komitet zydowski w Lodzi — powstanie i glowne kierunki dzialalnosci (1945-1950)," *BZIH* 3/187 (1998): 21.

2. *Documents on Israeli-Polish Relations 1945-1967,* edited by Marcos Silber and Szymon Rudnicki. Jerusalem: State of Israel, Israel State Archives and The Head Office of the State Archives in Poland, 2009, 231-232; Natalia Aleksiun, *Dakad dalej? Ruch syjonistyczny w Polsce (1944-1950)* (Warsaw: Wydawnictwo Trio, 2002), 214; Levi Arie Sarid, *The Trial of Suffering and Redemption* (in Hebrew), Vol.2 (Tel-Aviv: Moreshet, 1997), 434; Letter by Eloni to Merhavya, December 1, 1949, Yad Yaari Archive, 150, 14(4); Helena Datner, "Szkoly Centralnego Komitetu Zydow w Polsce w latach 1944-1949," *BZIH* 1-3 (169-171) (1994): 114; Bozena Szaynok, *Ludnosc zydowska na Dolnym Slasku, 1945-1950* (Wroclaw: Wydawnictwo Uniwersytetu Wroclawskiego, 2000), 183; Joel Royzman, *The Borokhov Youth and the Dror Borokhov Youth in Post Holocaust Poland* (in Hebrew) (Tel-Aviv: Yad Tabenkin, 1999), 198; Israel Bialostocki, Rehabilitation of the Jewish Community in Poland After the Holocaust, 1944-1955 (Ph.D. diss., The Hebrew University of Jerusalem, 1990), A20; Letter from Michael to Fayvl, November 10, 1949, Yad Yaari Archive, (5)65, 1-2.

3. Joel Royzman, *The Borokhov Youth and the Dror-Borokhov Youth in Post Holocaust Poland,* 203, 205; Jozef Adelson, "W Polsce zwanej Ludowa," in *Najnowsze dzieje Zydow w Polsce (w zarysie do 1950 roku),* ed. Jerzy Tomaszewski (Warsaw: Wydawnictwo Naukowe PWN, 1993), 477; IPN Archive, Lodz, pf 10/690, t.1, 96; Yad Yaari Archive, (5)64, 1-2; IPN Archive, Lodz, pf 10/690, t.3, 30.

4. August Grabski, *Dzialalnosc komunistow wsrod Zydow w Polsce (1944-1949)* (Warsaw: Wydawnictwo Trio-ZIH, 2004), 326; IPN Archive, Lodz, pf 10/690, t.1, 95, 225, 18.

5. August Grabski, *ibid.,* 325; Jozef Adelson, "W Polsce zwanej Ludowa," 477; Helena Datner, "Szkoly Centralnego Komitetu Zydow w Polsce w latach 1944-1949," 103, 109; Bozena Szaynok, *Ludnosc zydowska na Dolnym Slasku,* 189-191; *Documents on Israeli-Polish Relations 1945-1967,* edited by Marcos Silber and Szymon Rudnicki. Jerusalem: State of Israel, Israel State Archives and The Head Office of the State Archives in Poland, 2009, 200-201.

6. Report by the Social Department of the Lodz Jewish Committee for January 1-March 11, 1950, ZIH Archive, Warsaw, 303/IX/1271, 1-5.

7. Albert Stankowski, "Nowe spojrzenie na statystyki dotyczace emigracji Zydow z Polski po 1944 roku," in *Studia z historii Zydow w Polsce po 1945 r,* eds. G. Berendt, A. Grabski, and A. Stankowski (Warsaw: Zydowski Instytut Historyczny, 2000), 115-117; Irena Hurwic-Nowakowska *A Social Analysis of Postwar Polish Jewry* (Jerusalem: The Zalman Shazar Center for Jewish History, 1986), 50; Leszek Olejnik, "Lodz wielonarodowa w pierwszych latach po II wojnie swiatowej," Rocznik Lodzki, 45, 1998, 197; Leszek Olejnik, "Wojewodzki komitet zydowski w Lodzi-powstanie i glowne kierunki dzialalnosci (1945-1959), 21.

8. Prof. Matityahu Mintz, interview by author, Herzliya, August 19, 2003.

9. Fayvl Podeh (Podemski), interview by author, Herzliya, February 20, 2002; Fayvl Podeh (Podemski), "The Ken of Hashomer Hatzair in the Lodz Ghetto" (in Hebrew), *Yalkut Moreshet* Kaf Het (1979): 7.

10. Natan Gross, *Przygody Grymka w Ziemi Swietej* (Krakow: [publisher?], 2006), 42-48; Natan Gross, *Who Are You Mr. Grymek?* (in Hebrew) (Tel-Aviv: Moreshet, 1986), 228-230.

11. Hanka Hornstein, interview by author, Tel-Aviv, June 2005.

12. Aharon Eynat (Zalkind), interview by author, Tel-Aviv, March 9, 2005.

13. Richard Lubelsky, interview by author, Prague, September 1999.
14. Ada Horowitz (Gibraltar), interview by author, Tel-Aviv, May 2005.
15. Ewa Frenkel-Przemyslawski, interview by author, Jerusalem, November 23, 2005.
16. Noah Flug, interview by author, Jerusalem, February 17, 2003.
17. Prof. Jacob Goldberg, interview by author, Jerusalem, February 9, 2004; Radoslaw Januszewski and Jan Strekowski, eds. *Polska w oczach cudzych* (Wroclaw; Towarzystwo Przyjaciol Ossolineum, 2003), 186, 196; "Na zajecia niose mape Polski Jagiellonow," Prof. Goldberg, interview by Radoslaw Januszewski and Jan Strekowski, *Nowe ksiazki* 6 (2002): 4-8.

Archives List

Archiwum Akt Nowych (Archives of New Documents), Warsaw.
Archiwum Panstwowe (The State Archive), Lodz.
Instytut Pamieci Narodowej (The Institute of National Memory), Lodz.
Yad Vashem Archives, Jerusalem.
Yad Ya'ari Archives, Giv'at Haviva.
Zydowski Instytut Historyczny (The Jewish Historical Institute), Warsaw.

BIBLIOGRAPHY

Adelson, Jozef. "W Polsce zwanej Ludowa." In *Najnowsze dzieje Zydow w Polsce (w zarysie do 1950 roku)*, edited by Jerzy Tomaszewski, 387-477. Warsaw: Wydawnictwo Naukowe PWN, 1993.

Aleksiun, Natalia. "Rescuing a Memory and Constructing a History of Polish Jewry: Jews in Poland, 1944-1950." *Jews in Russia and Eastern Europe* 1-2 (54-55) (2005): 5-27.

———. "The Situation of the Jews in Poland as Seen by Soviet Security Forces in 1945," *Jews in Eastern Europe* 3(37) (1998): 52-68.

———. "Where Was There a Future for Polish Jewry: Bundist and Zionist Polemics in Post World War II Poland." In *Jewish Politics in Eastern Europe: The Bund at 100*, edited by Jack Jacobs, 227-242. New York: New York Univ. Press, 2001.

———. *Dokad dalej? Ruch syjonistyczny w Polsce (1944-1950)*. Warsaw: Wydawnictwo Trio, 2002.

Altshuler, Mordechai et al., eds. *Soviet Jews Write to Ilya Ehrenburg, 1943-1966* (in Russian). Jerusalem: The Hebrew University & Yad Vashem, 1993.

Axer, Erwin. "Schiller w Lodzi," *Tygiel Kultury*, Lodz, nr. 7-9 (104-106) (2004): 110-130.

Bak, Samuel. *Painted in Words: A Memoir.* Bloomington and Indianapolis: Indiana University Press, 2002.

Bar-Gil, Shlomo and Ada Schein. *Dwell in Safety: Holocaust Survivors in the Rural Cooperative Settlement, 1945-1955* (in Hebrew) (Jerusalem: Yad Vashem, 2010).

Barzel, N'ima. *Yearning and Reality: The Encounter Between the Leaders of the Ghetto Uprising and Israeli Society* (in Hebrew). Jerusalem: The Zionist Library, 1998.

Bauer, Yehuda. *Flight and Rescue: Brichah.* New York: Random House, 1970.

Beevor, Antony and Luba Vinogradova, eds. *A Writer at War: Vasily Grossman with the Red Army, 1941-1945.* New York: Pantheon Books, 2005.

Berendt, Grzegorz. "Michala Mirskiego rozrachunek z Polska Ludowa." *Niepodleglosc* 53-54 (2003-2004): 284-314.

Berendt, G., A. Grabski, and A. Stankowski, eds. *Studia z historii Zydow w Polsce po 1945 r.* Warsaw: Zydowski Instytut Historyczny, 2000.

Bialostocki, Israel. Rehabilitation of the Jewish Community in Poland after the Holocaust, 1944-1950. Ph.D. diss. (in Hebrew). Jerusalem: The Hebrew University of Jerusalem, 1990.

Blatman, Daniel. *For Our Freedom and Yours: The Jewish Labor Bund in Poland, 1939-1949* (in Hebrew). Jerusalem: Yad Vashem and The Hebrew University of Jerusalem, 1996.

Bogner, Nachum. *At the Mercy of Strangers: The Rescue of Jewish Children with Assumed Identities in Poland* (in Hebrew) Jerusalem: Yad Vashem, 2000.

Brach-Czaina, Jolanta. "Kompleks." *Tygodnik Powszechny* 8 (1994): 23-27.

Browning, Christopher R. et al., eds. *Every Day Lasts a Year: A Jewish Family's Correspondence from Poland.* New York: Cambridge University Press, 2007.

Cala, Alina and Helena Datner-Spiewak, eds. *Dieje Zydow w Polsce, 1944-1968, Teksty zrodlowe.* Warsaw: Zydowski Instytut Historyczny, 1997.

Checinski, Michael. *Poland: Communism, Nationalism, Anti-Semitism.* New York: Karz-Kohl Publishing, 1982.

Chodakiewicz, Marek Jan. *After the Holocaust: Polish-Jewish Conflict in the Wake of World War II.* New York: East European Monographs, 2003.

Cholawski, Shalom. "The End of the War — Memoirs, 1944-1946." *Yalkut Moreshet* 70 (2000): 113-136 (in Hebrew).

Chroscielewski, Tadeusz, ed. *Tranzytem przez Lodz.* Lodz: Wyd. Lodzkie, 1964.

Datner, Helena, "Szkoly Centralnego Komitetu Zydow w Polsce w latach 1944-1949," *Biuletyn ZIH* 1-3 (169-171) (1994): 104-108.

Datner-Spiewak, Helena. "Instytucje opieki nad dzieckiem i szkoly powszechne Centralnego Komitetu Zydow Polskich w latach 1945-1946." *Biuletyn ZIH* 1, 3 (117, 119) (1981): 37-51.

Davies, Norman and Antony Polonsky, eds. *Jews in Eastern Poland and the USSR, 1939-46.* New York: St. Martin's Press, 1991.

Dawidowicz, Lucy S. *The War Against the Jews, 1939-1945.* New York: Holt, Rinehart and Winston, 1975.

Dobroszycki, Lucjan. "Reemergence and Decline of a Community." *YIVO Annual* 21 (1993).

———. "Restoring Jewish Life in Postwar Poland." *Soviet Jewish Affairs* 3(2) (1973): 58-72.

———. *Survivors of the Holocaust in Poland: A Portrait Based on Jewish Community Records, 1944-1947.* New York: M.E. Sharpe, 1994.

Dzigan, Shimon. *The Impact of Jewish Humour* (in Yiddish) (Tel-Aviv: The Public Committee for the Celebation of the 40th Anniversary of Shimon Dzigan's Acting in the Yiddish Theatre, 1974), 262-267, 280-295.

Elgazi, Yossi. "My Grandpa's Fighter Plane" (in Hebrew). *Haaretz*, April 25, 2003.

Engel, David. "Patterns of Anti-Jewish Violence in Poland, 1944-1946." *Yad Vashem Studies* XXVI (1998): 43-85.

———. "The Reconstruction of Jewish Communal Institutions in Postwar Poland: The Origins of the Central Committee of Polish Jews, 1944-1945." *East European Politics and Societies* 10 (1996): 85-107.

———. *Between Liberation and Flight: Holocaust Survivors in Poland and the Struggle for Leadership, 1944-1946* (in Hebrew). Tel Aviv: Am Oved Publishers, 1996.

———. " Warsaw as a Jewish Metropolis? Aborted Reconstruction in the Aftermath of the Holocaust." Paper presented at Warsaw-the History of a Jewish Metropolis, the UCL IJS Summer Conference, London, 22-25 June 2010.

Falkowska, Maria "Dzieci z Helenowka." In *Losy zydowskie, swiadectwo zywych* (Vol. 2), edited by Marian Turski, 31-53. Warsaw: Stowarzyszenie Zydow Kombatantow i Poszkodowanych w II Wojnie Swiatowej, 1999.
Fein, Yohanan. "A Boy with a Fiddle" (in Hebrew). Unpublished memoir, Tel-Aviv, 2003.
Finder, Gabriel N. "The Place of Child Survivors in Jewish Collective Memory after the Holocaust: The Case of *Undzere Kinder*." In *Nurturing the Nation: Displaced Children in Europe and the USSR, 1918-1953*, edited by Nick Baron. Leiden: Brill, 2010.
Friedlaender, Saul. *The Years of Extermination: Nazi Germany and the Jews, 1939-1945*. New York: Harper Collins, 2007.

Gasowski, Szczepan. *Panstwowy Teatr Zydowski im. Ester Rachel Kaminskiej: przeszlosc i terazniejszosc*. Warsaw: PWN, 1995.
Glowny Urzad Statystyczny Rzeczypospolitej Polskiej. *Rocznik Statystyczny 1946 r*. Warsaw: Glowny Urzad Statystyczny Rzeczypospolitej Polskiej, 1947.
———. *Rocznik Statystyczny 1949 r*. Warsaw: Glowny Urzad Statystyczny Rzeczypospolitej Polskiej, 1950.
Goldberg, Abraham. *A Long Way Home*. Kotarot Publishing, 2004.
The Gordonia Archive. *The Gordonia Movement in Lodz* (in Hebrew). Hulda-Maale Hachamisha: The Gordonia Archive, 1998.
Grabski, August. *Dzialalnosc komunistow wsrod Zydow w Polsce (1944-1949)*. Warsaw: Wydawnictwo Trio-ZIH, 2004.
———. *Zydowski ruch kombatancki w Polsce w latach 1944-1949*. Warsaw: Trio, 2002.
Grayek, Stefan. *The Struggle* (in Hebrew). Tel-Aviv: Am Oved, 1989.
Gross, Jan T. "In the Aftermath of the Kielce Pogrom: The Special Commission of the Central Committee of Jews of Poland." *Gal-Ed* XV-XVI,(1997): 119-136.
———. *Fear: Anti-Semitism in Poland After Auschwitz. An Essay in Historical Interpretation*. Princeton and Oxford: Princeton University Press, 2006.
———. *Upiorna dekada: trzy eseje o stereotypach na temat Zydow, Polakow, Niemcow i Komunistow, 1939-1948*. Krakow: Universitas, 1998.
Gross, Natan. "The Jewish Film in Poland After World War II, 1945-1950" (in Hebrew). *Kolnoa* 2 (1974).
———. *Przygody Grymka w ziemi swietej*. Krakow: Rabid, 2006.
———. *Who Are You Mr. Grymek?* (in Hebrew). Tel-Aviv: Moreshet, 1986.
Grudzinska-Gross, Irena and Jan Tomasz Gross, eds. *War Through Children's Eyes: The Soviet Occupation of Poland and the Deportations, 1939-1941*. Stanford, CA: Hoover Institution Press, 1981.
Grynberg, Henryk. *Ciag dalszy*. Warsaw: Swiat ksiazki, 2008.
———. *Kalifornijski kadisz*. Warsaw: Swiat ksiazki, 2005.

———. *The Jewish War and The Victory.* Evanston, IL: North Western University Press, 2001.
———. *Zycie ideologiczne. Zycie osobiste.* Warsaw: Panstwowy Instytut Wydawniczy, 1992.
Grynberg, Michal. "Lodz, 1945." *Folks-Sztyme* 5 (1974).
———. "Problemy zatrudnienia ludnosci zydowskiej w Polsce w pierwszych latach po II wojnie swiatowej." *BZIH* (1986): 97-114.
———. *Zydowska spoldzielczosc pracy w Polsce w latach 1945-1949.* Warsaw: PWN, 1986.
Gutman, Israel. "Jews in General Anders' Army in the Soviet Union." *Yad Vashem Studies* 12 (1977): 231-296.
———. "The Jews in Poland" In *Encyclopedia of the Holocaust,* edited by Israel Gutman, Vol. 3: 1155-1176. New York: Macmillan, 1989.
———. "Varsha." In *The Holocaust Encyclopedia* (in Hebrew), edited by Israel Gutman, Vol. 2: 470-475. Tel-Aviv: Yad Vashem and Sifriat Poalim Publishing House, 1990.
———. "Youth Movements in the Underground and the Resistance in the Ghettos." In *Jewish Resistance during the Holocaust. Proceedings of the Conference on Manifestations of Jewish Resistance*, Jerusalem, April 7-11, 1968 (in Hebrew). Jerusalem: Yad Vashem, (1970): 206-224.
———. *The Jews in Poland after World War II* (in Hebrew). Jerusalem: The Zalman Shazar Center, 1985.
———. *The Jews of Warsaw, 1939-1945: Ghetto, Underground, Revolt.* Bloomington and Indianapolis: Indiana University Press, 1982.

Hertz, J.S. *The History of the Jewish labor Bund in Lodz* (in Yiddish). New York: Unser Tsait, 1958.
Hitron, Hagai. "A Rare Glimpse of a Destroyed World." *Haaretz,* September 20, 2006.
Hoberman, J. *Bridge of Light: Yiddish Film between Two Worlds.* Philadelphia: Temple University Press, 1995.
Hoffman, Eva. *Exit Into History: A Journey Through the New Eastern Europe.* Penguin Books, 1993.
Holtzman, Avner. *An Image Before My Eyes* (in Hebrew). Tel Aviv: Am Oved, 2002.
Honoris Causa. Ksiega pamiatkowa dla uczczenia aktu nadania profesorowi Leszkowi Kolakowskiemu honorowego doktoratu Uniwersytetu Lodzkiego. Lodz: Wydawnictwo Lodzkie. Wydawnictwo Uniwersytetu Lodzkiego, 1994.
Horwitz, Gordon J. *Ghettostadt: Lodz and the Making of a Nazi City.* Cambridge, MA and London: The Belknap Press of Harvard University Press, 2008.
Hurwic-Nowakowska, Irena. *A Social Analysis of Postwar Polish Jewry.* Jerusalem: The Zalman Shazar Center for Jewish History, 1986.

Janowska, Anita. *Krzyzowka.* Wroclaw: Siedmiorog, 1997.
Januszewski, Radoslaw and Jan Strekowski, eds. *Polska w oczach cudzych.* Wroclaw: Towarzystwo Przyjaciol Ossolineum, 2003.

Kaminska, Ida. *My Life, My Theatre.* New York and London: Macmillan & Collier, 1973.
Kaminski, Lukasz. "Lodzkie protesty mlodziezy, 1945-1946." *Kronika Miasta Lodzi,* zeszyt 1-2 (1997): 176-185.
―――. *Polacy wobec nowej rzeczywistosci, 1944-1948: Formy pozainstytucjalnego zywiolowego oporu spolecznego.* Torun: Wydawnictwo Adam Marszalek, 2000.
Kenney, Padraic. *Rebuilding Poland: Workers and Communists, 1945-1950.* Ithaca: Cornell University Press, 1997.
Kersten, Krystyna. "Rok pierwszy." *Midrasz* July-August (1998): 26-29.
―――. *The Establishment of Communist Rule in Poland, 1943-1948.* Berkeley-Los Angeles-Oxford: University of California Press, 1991.
Kesari, Shulamit. "A Heroic Story" (in Hebrew). *Shiur Hofshi* (Israeli Teachers' Association) March (2003): 6-8.
Klugman, Aleksander. "Jak feniks z popiolow." *Kronika Miasta Lodzi* 2 (2006): 91-95; 3 (2006): 87-92; 4 (2006): 137-144; 2 (2007): 103-108; 3 (2007): 81-86.
―――. "Lodzkie impresje." *Midrasz* July-August (2001): 6-7.
―――. "Strzepy zyciorysu." *Tygiel Kultury* (2004): 66-74.
Kotkin, Stephen. *Magnetic Mountain: Stalinism as a Civilization.* Berkeley-Los Angeles-London: University of California Press, 1995.
Kowalska, Irena. "Kartoteka TOZ z lat 1946-1947." *Biuletyn ZIH* 3\95-2\96 (175-178) (July 1995-June 1996): 97-106.
Kozlowski, Janusz, ed. *Gorace dni, gorace lata.* Lodz: Wydawnictwo Lodzkie, 1976.
Krakowski, Shmuel "Lodz." In the *Holocaust Encyclopedia* (in Hebrew), 612-621. Tel-Aviv: Yad Vashem and Sifriat Hapoalim, 1990.
Krall, Hanna. *Zdazyc przed Panem Bogiem.* Krakow: Wydawnictwo a5, 2003.
Kugelmass, J. "The Rites of the Tribe: The Meaning of Poland for American Jewish Tourists." *YIVO Annual* 21 (1993).
Kuriski, Leybl. "The Jewish Coordination for the Redemption of Children in Poland in the Years 1946-1949." *Galed* 7-8 (1985): 253-261.

Langer, Lawrence L. "*Undzere Kinder*: A Yiddish Film From Poland." In *Preempting the Holocaust,* 157-165. New Haven and London: Yale University Press, 1998.
Lapicki, Andrzej. *Po pierwsze, zachowac dystans.* Warsaw: Proszynski i S-ka, 1999.
Lesiakowski, Krzysztof. "Nastroje mieszkancow Lodzi i wojewodztwa Lodzkiego w latach 1945-1948," *Acta Universitatis Lodziensis,* Folia Historica 71 (2001): 119-138.
―――. *Mieczyslaw Moczar "Mietek": Biografia polityczna.* Warsaw: Rytm, 1998.
Levin, Dov. *The Lesser of Two Evils: Eastern European Jewry Under Soviet Rule, 1939-1941.* Philadelphia and Jerusalem: The Jewish Publication Society, 1995.
Lewin, Nora. *The Holocaust: The Destruction of European Jewry, 1933-1945.* New York: Shocken Books, 1973.

Leyko, Malgorzata, ed. *Lodzkie sceny zydowskie: studia i materialy.* Lodz: Wydawnictwo Uniwersytetu Lodzkiego, 2000.

Litvak, Yosef. "Polish-Jewish Refugees Repatriated from the Soviet Union at the End of the Second World War and Afterwards." In *Jews in Eastern Poland and the USSR, 1939-46,* edited by Norman Davies and Antony Polonsky, 230-234. New York: St. Martin's Press, 1991.

———. *Polish-Jewish Refugees in the USSR, 1939-1946* (in Hebrew). Tel-Aviv: Ghetto Fighters' House, 1988.

———. "Jewish Refugees from Poland in the USSR, 1939-1946." In *Bitter Legacy: Confronting the Holocaust in the USSR,* edited by Zvi Gitelman, 123-150. Bloomington and Indianapolis: Indiana University Press, 1997.

Lodz urzedowa. Polska Agencja Prasowa. "Lodz urzedowa, spoleczna, przemyslowo-handlowa 1947." Lodz: PAP, 1947.

Loew, Andrea. *Juden im Ghetto Litzmannstadt: Lebensbedingungen, Selbsvahrnehmung, Verhalten.* Goettingen: Wallstein Verlag, 2006.

Lohamei Hagetaot House. *The Redemption of Jewish Children from Christians in Poland After the Holocaust* (in Hebrew). Lohamei Hagetaot: Lohamei Hagetaot House 1989.

Manley, Rebecca. *To the Tashkent Station: Evacuation and Survival in the Soviet Union at War.* Ithaca and London: Cornell University Press, 2009.

Margolis-Edelman, Alina. "Ala from the Primer." *Polin* 11 (1998): 94-111.

Meirtchak, Binyamin. *I Love You. Grandpa Beniek.* Tel Aviv: Published posthumously by the family, 2007.

Meyer, Peter et al., eds. *The Jews in the Soviet Satellites.* Syracuse: Syracuse University Press, 1953.

Michlic, Joanna B. "Who Am I? Jewish Children's Search for Identity in Post-War Poland, 1945-1949." *Polin* 20 (2008): 98-121.

———. "Bearing Witness: Henryk Grynberg's Path from Child Survivor to Artist. An Interview with Henryk Grynberg." *Polin* 20 (2008): 324-335

———. *Poland's Threatening Other: The Image of the Jew from 1880 to the Present.* Lincoln and London: University of Nebraska Press, 2006.

———. "Lodz in the Post-Communist Era: In Search of a Distinctive Identity." Center for European Studies, Program on Eastern and Central Europe. Working Paper Series #65. Cambridge, MA: Harvard University, 2006.

Milosz, Czeslaw. *Szukanie ojczyzny.* Krakow: Znak, 1992.

Mironowicz, Eugeniusz. *Polityka narodowosciowa PRL.* Bialystok: Wydanie Bialostockiego Towarzystwa Historycznego, 2000.

Mirska, Klara. "Pamietniki Klary Mirskiej: Kronika mojego zycia, 1907-66."

———. *W cieniu wiecznego strachu (wspomnienia).* Paris, 1980.

Mirski, Michal. *Bez stopnia.* Warsaw: MON, 1960.

———. *Biegiem marsz.* Warsaw: Ksiega i Wiedza 1958.

Mroczka, Ludwik. "Dynamika rozwoju i struktura spoleczno-zawodowa glownych grup etnicznych w Lodzi w latach 1918-1939." In *Polacy-Niemcy-Zydzi w Lodzi w XIX-XX w: Sasiedzi dalecy i bliscy,* edited by Pawel Samus, 99-117. Lodz: Ibidem, 1997.

Nahmani-Gafni, Emuna. *Split Hearts: Redemption of Jewish Children from Christian Families in Poland After the Holocaust* (in Hebrew), Jerusalem: Yad Vashem, 2006.
Nalewajko-Kulikow, Joanna. *Strategie przetrwania: Zydzi po aryjskiej stronie Warszawy.* Warsaw: Neriton, 2004.
Nussbaum, Klemens, "Jews in the Kosciuszko Division and First Polish Army." In *Jews in Eastern Poland and the USSR, 1939-46,* edited by Norman Davies and Antony Polonsky, 183-213. New York: St. Martin's Press, 1991.

Olejnik, Leszek. "Lodz jako centrum spolecznosci zydowskiej w Polsce (1945-1949)." In *Fenomen getta lodzkiego, 1940-1944,* edited by Pawel Samus, 407-419. Lodz: Wydawnictwo Uniwersytetu Lodzkiego, 2006.
———. "Lodz wielonarodowa w pierwszych latach po II wojnie swiatowej." *Rocznik Lodzki* 45 (1998): 185-210.
———. "Mniejszosci narodowe w Lodzi w latach 1945-1950." *Kronika Miasta Lodzi* 1-2, 1999): 193-203.
———. "Spolecznosc zydowska w Lodzi w latach 1945-1950: Zarys problemu." *AUL* (Folia Historica) 60 (1997): 125-147.
———. "Wojewodzki komitet zydowski w Lodzi—powstanie i glowne kierunki dzialalnosci (1945-1950)." *BZIH* 3/187 (1998): 3-22.
———. "Z dziejow teatru zydowskiego w Lodzi po IIej wojnie swiatowej." In *Lodzkie sceny zydowskie: studia i materially,* edited by Malgorzata Leyko, 143-152. Lodz: Wydawnictwo Uniwersytetu Lodzkiego, 2000.
———. *Polityka narodowosciowa Polski w latach 1944-1960.* Lodz: Wydawnictwo Uniwersytetu Lodzkiego, 2003.

Paczkowski, Andrzej. *Zdobycie wladzy, 1945-1947.* Warsaw: Wydawnictwo szkolne i pedagogiczne, 1993.
Palgi, Yitzhak. "Military Cadres and Assistance from Poland" (in Hebrew). *The Hashomer Hatsair Book,* Vol. 3, 142-145. Merhavya: Sifriat Hapoalim, 1964.
Patron, Rachel. "Flowers in the Snow." Unpublished memoir, 2005.
———. "The Ticket: A Short Story." *Hadassah Magazine,* 65/1, August-September 1983, 24-25, 47-48.
Paulsson, Gunnar S. *Secret City: The Hidden Jews of Warsaw, 1940-1945.* New Haven and London: Yale University Press, 2002.
Pietrzak, Jacek. "Hans Biebow-portret oprawcy." In *Fenomen getta lodzkiego, 1940-1944,* edited by Pawel Samus and Wieslaw Pus, 185-203. Lodz: Wydawnictwo Uniwersytetu Lodzkiego, 2006,.
Pisarski, Maciej. "Emigracja Zydow z Polski w latach 1945-1951." In *Studia z dziejow kultury Zydow w Polsce po 1945 roku,* edited by Jerzy Tomaszewski, 13-81. Warsaw: Trio, 1997.
———. "Na zydowskiej ulicy: szkic do dziejow zydowskiej frakcji PPR i zespolu PZPR przy CKZP, 1945-1951." *BZIH* 2 (1997): 35-48.
Podeh (Podemski), Fayvl. "The Ken of Hashomer Hatzair in the Lodz Ghetto" (in

Hebrew). *Yalkut Moreshet* Kaf Het (1979): 7-36.
———. "The Liquidation of the Ghetto" (in Hebrew). *Yalkut Moreshet* Nun Het (1974): 157-177.
———. *Memories from the Lodz Ghetto* (in Hebrew). Ra'anana: Docustory Publishers, 2004.
Prekerowa, Teresa. "Wojna i okupacja." In *Najnowsze dzieje Zydow w Polsce,* edited by Jerzy Tomaszewski, 273-384. Warsaw: PWN, 1993.

Redlich, Shimon. "Jews in General Anders' Army in the Soviet Union, 1941-42." *Soviet Jewish Affairs* 2 (1971): 90-98.
———. "The Jews in the Soviet Annexed Territories, 1939- 41." *Soviet Jewish Affairs* 1 (1971) 81-90.
Rivo, Sharon Pucker. "The Beginning of Holocaust Cinema: Contextualizing *Undzere Kinder* (Poland, 1948)." Presentation at the Annual Conference of the Association of Jewish Studies, Boston, 1994.
Roos, Hans. *A History of Modern Poland.* New York: Alfred A. Knopf, 1966.
Rosin, Ryszard, "Szkice z dziejow Lodzi — 1945 rok." *Kronika Miasta Lodzi,* zeszyt 1 2000: 115-129.
Rostworowski, Tomasz. *Zaraz po wojnie: wspomnienia duszpasterza (1945-1956).* Paris: Editions Spotkania, 1986.
Royzman, Joel. *The Borokhov Youth and the Dror Borokhov Youth in Post-Holocaust Poland* (in Hebrew). Tel Aviv: Yad Tabenkin, 1999.
Rozenbaum, Wlodzimierz. "The Road to New Poland: Jewish Communists in the Soviet Union, 1939-46." In *Jews in Eastern Poland and the USSR, 1939-46,* edited by Norman Davies and Antony Polonsky, 214-226. New York: St. Martin's Press, 1991.
Rozenberg, Szulim. "Lodz zydowska po wojnie." *Midrasz* July-August (2001): 24-25.
Rudnicki, Adolf. "Ojczyzna." In *Tranzytem przez Lodz,* edited by Tadeusz Chroscielewski, 93-106. Lodz: Wyd. Lodzkie, 1964.
———. *Niebieskie kartki.Slepe lustro tych lat.* Warsaw: Czytelnik, 1958.
Ruta, Magdalena, ed. *Nusech Pojln: Studia z dziejow kultury jidysz w powojennej Polsce.* Krakow-Budapest: Wydawnictwo Austeria, 2008.

Samus, Pawel, ed. *Polacy-Niemcy-Zydzi w Lodzi w XIX-XX w.* Lodz: Ibidem, Instytut Historii Uniwersytetu Lodzkiego, 1997.
Sarid, Levi Arie. *The Trial of Suffering and Redemption*, Vol. 2 (in Hebrew). Tel-Aviv: Moreshet, 1997.
Schatz, Jaff. *The Generation: The Rise and Fall of the Jewish Communists of Poland.* Berkeley-Los Angeles-Oxford: University of California Press, 1991.
Shapiro, Robert Moses. "Lodz." In *The YIVO Encyclopedia of Jews in Eastern Europe,* 1080-1086. New Haven: Yale University Press, 2008.
Shneiderman, S.L. *Between Fear and Hope.* New York: Arco Publishing Company, 1947.
Shner-Nishmit, Sarah. *I Did Not Acquire Peace* (in Hebrew). Tel-Aviv: Hakibbutz Hameuhad Publishing House, 1988.

Shore, Marci, *Caviar and Ashes: A Warsaw Generation's Life and Death in Marxism, 1918-1968*. New Haven: Yale University Press, 2006.

———. "Children of the Revolution: Communism, Zionism, and the Berman Brothers." *Jewish Social Studies* 10(3) (2004): 23-86.

Siedlecki, A. "How the Jewish Community in Lodz was Resurrected." *Bleter far geshikhte* 24 (1986): 200-204.

Siekierski, Maciej. "The Jews in Soviet-Occupied Eastern Poland at the End of 1939: Numbers and Distribution." In *Jews in Eastern Poland and the USSR, 1939-46*, edited by Norman Davies and Antony Polonsky, 110-115. New York: St. Martin's Press, 1991.

Siekierski, Maciej and Feliks Tych, eds. *Widzialem aniola smierci: losy deportowanych Zydow polskich w ZSRR w latach II wojny swiatowej*. Warsaw: Rosner i Wspolnicy, 2006.

Silber, Marcos and Szymon Rudnicki, eds. *Documents on Israeli-Polish Relations 1945-1967*. Jerusalem: State of Israel, Israel State Archives and The Head Office of the State Archives in Poland, 2009.

Smolar, Hersz. *At the Last Stand. With the Last Hope* (in Yiddish). Tel-Aviv: Y.L. Peretz Publishing House, 1982.

Sonnenberg, Sven. *A Two Stop Journey to Hell*. Montreal: The Canadian Foundation of Polish-Jewish Heritage, http://polish-jewish-heritage.org/eng/Ksiazka_Svena_Sonnenberg.htm (accessed 2009).

Spodenkiewicz, Pawel. *Zaginiona dzielnica: Lodz zydowska—ludzie i miejsca*. Lodz: Lodzka Ksiegarnia Niezalezna, 1999.

Sreniowska, Krystyna. "Warcholy w akcji: Sprawa Marii Tyrankiewiczowny." *Tygiel Kultury* 4-5 (1998): 96-100.

———. "Hotel Monopol." *Tygiel Kultury*, Lodz, 7-9 (1999): 49-53.

Stankowski, Albert. "Nowe spojrzenie na statystyki dotyczace emigracji Zydow z Polski po 1944 roku. " In *Studia z dziejow historii Zydow w Polsce po 1945 r.*, edited by G. Berendt, A. Grabski, A. Stankowski, 103-151. Warsaw: Zydowski Instytut Historyczny, 2000.

Strauss-Marko, Shlomo. *The History of the Jewish People in Poland after the War (Hebrew)*. Tel-Aviv: privately printed, 1988.

Swida-Ziemba, Hanna. *Urwany lot. Pokolenie inteligenckiej mlodzezy powojennej w swietle listow i pamietnikow z lat 1945-1948*. Krakow: Wydawnictwo Literackie, 2003.

Sword, Keith. *Deportation and Exile: Poles in the Soviet Union, 1939-1948*. New York: St. Martin's Press, 1994.

Szaynok, Bozena. "Bund i Komunisci zydowscy w Polsce po 1945 roku." *Midrasz* July-August (1998): 57-64.

———. "Problematyka zydowska w polityce komunistow w latach 1949-1953." In *Nusech Pojln: Studia z dziejow kultury jidysz w powojennej Polsce*, edited by Magdalena Ruta, 9-26. Krakow-Budapest: Wydawnictwo Austeria, 2008.

———. *Ludnosc Zydowska na Dolnym Slasku, 1945-1950*. Wroclaw: Wydawnictwo Uniwersytetu Wroclawskiego, 2000.

———. *Pogrom Zydow w Kielcach 4 Lipca, 1946*. Warsaw: Bellona, 1992.

Szczesna, Joanna. "Marek Edelman i Antek Cukierman: losy powojenne." *Gazeta Wyborcza,* June 6, 2003.

———. "Powszechna rzecz zabijanie. Rozmowa z Markiem Edelmanem." *Gazeta Swiateczna,* January 19, 2008.

Tec, Nechama. "Hiding and Passing on the Aryan Side: A Gendered Comparison." In *Contested Memories: Poles and Jews During the Holocaust and Its Aftermath,* edited by *Joshua* D. Zimmerman, 193-211. New Brunswick, New Jersey and London: Rutgers University Press, 2003.
Tenenbaum, Joseph. *In Search of a Lost People: The Old and the New Poland.* New York: The Beechhurst Press, 1948.
Terlecki, Ryszard. "The Jewish Issue in the Polish Army in the USSR and the Near East, 1941-1944." In *Jews in Eastern Poland and the USSR, 1939-46,* edited by Norman Davies and Antony Polonsky, 161-171. New York: St. Martin's Press, 1991.
Tomaszewski, Jerzy, ed. *Najnowsze dzieje Zydow w Polsce (w zarysie do 1950 roku).* Warsaw: Wydawnictwo Naukowe PWN, 1993.

Unger, Michal. *Lodz: The Last Ghetto in Poland* (in Hebrew). Jerusalem: Yad Vashem, 2005.
Urban, Jerzy. Jajakobyly. *Spowiedz zycia Jerzego Urbana.Spowiadali i zapisali Przemyslaw Cwiklinski, Piotr Gadzinowski.* Warsaw: "BGW," 1991.

Wechsler, Lawrence. "The Troll's Tale: Jerzy Urban." In *Vermeer in Bosnia: A Reader,* 151-181. New York: Pantheon Books, 2004.
Weinryb, Bernard D. "Poland." In *The Jews in the Soviet Satellites,* edited by Peter Meyer et al., 207-326. Syracuse: Syracuse University Press, 1953.
Wrobel, Janusz. "W cieniu Holocaustu: odrodzenie spolecznosci zydowskiej w Lodzkiem po II Wojnie Swiatowej." *Biuletyn IPN* 11(58) (2005): 26-36.

Yad Vashem. "Lodz and Lodz District" (in Hebrew). *Pinkas Hakehillot, Poland* 1 (1976): 1-40. Jerusalem: Yad Vashem, 1976.

Zajicek, Edward. Na rubiezach Grand Hotelu: Jak powstawala filmowa Lodz." *Odglosy* (Lodz), January 16, 1988.
———. *Nad Oka.* Film, 41 (1788), October 9, 1983: 3-5.
Zuckerman, Yitzhak. *A Surplus of Memory: Chronicle of the Warsaw Ghetto Uprising.* Berkeley, Los Angeles, Oxford: University of California Press, 1993.
Zyskind, Sara. *Stolen Years.* Minneapolis: Lerner Publications Company, 1981.

INDEX

1go Maja Street 1, 2, 6, 7, 9, 191

Abi men zet zikh (We Meet Again) 72
Abu Kabir 15
Afanasyevna — see Prokhorova.
Albatros cafe 42
Alek (Aleks) — see Klugman, Aleksander.
Alon, Yigal 156
Altai 87, 127, 131, 220
Alter, Viktor 183, 184
Amarant, Samuel 61
America 3, 33, 40, 100, 193
Anders, Wladyslaw, General 118
Andizhan 88, 133, 134
Andrzej, a door-keeper 164
Aniela 195
Anielewicz, Mordechai 94, 112, 121, 125, 219
Anna 130
Anski, S. 72
Antokolska Street 122
Ararat Yiddish Revue Theater 72
Argentina, 188
Aron (uncle Aron) 149
Atlas, Josef 63
Auerbach, Rachel 67, 68, 74, 168
Auschwitz 3, 33, 49, 71, 81, 95, 98, 99, 101, 104, 113, 114, 141, 143–145, 147, 190, 215, 218
Australia 100, 194
Austria 54, 87, 171
Austrian Alps 145
Avineri, Shlomo 2
Axer, Erwin 41
Azov Sea 132

Bagneux 219
Bak, Samuel 79
Baku 130
Baltic Sea 139, 141, 203, 207
Baltyk cinema 42, 63, 69

Baluty 33, 44, 72, 112, 170
Baranowicze 124
Barbanel, Fiszl 81
Barenholc, Pola 192, 199
Barzilai, Israel (Julek) 158, 161, 174
Basel 160
Bavaria 154
Bechtel, Delphine 101
Beer-Sheva 103
Belorussia 102, 124, 154, 183, 209
Belzec 1, 4, 114
Ben-Zion 21
Ben-Zvi, Isar 161
Bereza Kartuska 185
Berezovski, Shaul 68, 73, 75
Berg, Judith 78
Bergner, Yosl 102, 124
Berlin 103, 119, 194, 198
Berling, Zygmunt, General, 118, 138
Berlinski, Hersz 165
Berman, Adolf 69, 151, 158, 182, 188
Berman, Jakub 181, 182, 186
Biala Podlaska 123
Bialystok 36, 87, 89, 90, 100, 115, 122, 124–127, 132, 193, 209, 212, 216, 217, 219, 220
Biebow, Hans 63, 70, 71, 112
Biederman textile plant 38
Bielsko Biala 139, 187
Bierut, Boleslaw 63, 71, 160
Bilicka, Khasya 163
Binem, Simche 195
Birkenau 114
Biysk 87, 131, 220
Black Sea 102, 129, 132, 212
Blumenfeld, Diana 58, 68
Blumenthal, Nachman 67, 158
Boca Raton 87
Bolkow 157
Bomze, Nachum 68, 69
Borejsza, Jerzy 40

Boris Davidovich 129
Borokhov Zionist youth movement 69, 154
Borzykowski, Tuvia 70
Bossak, Jerzy 42, 51
Boston 18
Brandys, Kazimierz 39, 42
Brauner, Artur 51
Bremen 71
Breslau — see Wroclaw.
Brest 123–126, 218
Broner, Adam 78, 79
Broniewski, Wladyslaw 40, 69, 184
Brzezany 1, 4–6, 9
Brzezinska Street 164
Bukhara 136
Bursa 78–80, 83, 191, 193, 196, 211
Burzynski, father 7
Burzynski, Natek 7
Bytom 162

Calecka, Pola 79
Cambridge, Mass. 18
Canada 21, 87, 88, 177, 207, 208, 217, 218
Carpathian Mountains 93, 120
Caspian Sea 90, 118, 129, 130
CCPJ, the Central Committee of Polish Jews 51, 55–60, 62, 66, 67, 68, 72, 73, 78, 81, 82, 155, 163, 181–184, 187, 204
Cegielniana Street 41
Centralna Komisja Specjalna (the Central Special Commission for self-defence of the CCPJ) 82-83
Chazan, Yaakov 151
Chelmno 70, 71, 112–114
Chelyabinsk 127, 185
Chizhik, Moshe (Kalif) 162, 169, 206
Chojnow 5, 6
Cholawski, Shalom 154
Chorzow 163, 187
CKS — see Centralna Komisja Specjalna
Crimea 8, 90
Czaja, Jola 3, 105
Czaja, Ludwik 3, 105

Czechoslovakia 104, 195
Czestochowa 97, 114, 146, 151, 185, 189
Czytelnik Publishing House 40, 49
Czyzyny 146

Dabrowski Square 71
Danzig — see Gdansk.
Deblin 97
Dejmek, K. 52
Denmark 188
Diaspora Museum 4, 90
Dobre 105, 106, 150, 198, 199, 217
Dobroszycki, Lucjan (Lucek) 79, 142
Donbass 115, 124
Dos Naje Lebn 16, 59, 64, 67, 68, 71, 73, 78, 81, 186, 191, 218
Dresden 71
Dror Zionist youth movement 52, 67, 69, 151, 153, 154, 156–158, 160, 162, 166, 168, 179, 203, 220
Druker, Isaiah 60
Dublin, Dziunia 100, 143, 192, 215
Dumas, A. 18
Dusznicki — see Nishmit-Shner.
Dvar Hashavua 22
Dygat, Stanislaw 42
Dzialoszyce 99
Dziedzictwo (Inheritance), by Henryk Grynberg 105
Dziennik 44
Dzigan, Shimon 20, 28, 72, 73, 74, 117, 167, 168, 193
Dziwnow 203

Easter by Leon Schiller 41
Ebensee 98, 144, 145
Edelman, Marek 9, 10, 52, 70, 80, 82, 83, 101, 102, 148, 184, 193, 195, 196, 215, 219
Edelman-Margolis, Alina — see Margolis, Alina.
Efron, Ketty 71, 73
Ehrenburg, Ilya 7, 69
Eisenbach, Arthur 71
Eishyshok 92, 125
Ellenblum, Aron 80
Elster, Bela — see Rotenberg, Wanda.

INDEX

Emigration to Palestine/Israel 152, 160, 206, 208
England 55, 95, 120
Epstein, Dido 68
Eretz Israel 22, 151, 152, 162, 172
Erlich, Eliyahu 165
Erlich, Henryk 183, 184
Erol (the Turk) 8
Eugenia, the teacher 47
Europe 5, 88, 94, 109, 114, 156, 182, 188, 195, 211
Exit Into History, by Ewa Hoffman 3
Express Ilustrowan 39
Eynat (Zalkind), Aharon 26, 90, 91, 122, 170, 215

Fajnhaken, Henryk 79
Feiner, Leon 183
Feingold-Falkowska, Maria 76, 77, 187, 190, 192, 205, 209
Fergana 135
Fibich, Felek 78
Fichman (Mirski), Klara 185–188
Film Polski Studio 42, 50, 73, 168, 189, 207, 218
Fine, Yohanan 170
Finkelstein, Leo 183
Fishl (Grandpa Fishl) 1
Fiszgrund Salo 183
Florida 87
Flossenburg 99, 144, 218
Flug, Noah (Henryk) 52, 98, 141, 142, 144, 145, 190, 191, 209, 215, 216
Fogel, Gershon 184
Folks-Shtime 182, 186, 187
Forbert, Adolf 42, 51,
Forbert, Aleksander 51, 102, 124
Ford, Aleksander 42, 51, 192, 200
Ford, Wladyslaw 42
Frakcja, the Jewish Fraction of the PPR/PZPR 58, 181-183, 203
France 42, 120, 177, 208, 219
Franciszkanska Street 78, 112
Frania 167
Frankfurt 208
Fraszka, cafe 42, 49
Frenkel, Israel 100, 124, 127, 128, 216

Frenkel, Nadia 100, 128, 189, 190, 208, 216
Frenkel-Przemyslawski, Ewa 99, 100, 124, 125, 127, 128, 189, 190, 208, 209, 212, 216
Friedman, Philip 59, 63, 68, 188
Frydland 78

Galicia 1, 5, 47, 94, 114
Galili, Israel 156
Gasiorowska, prof. 49
Gazeta Wyborcza 9, 86
Gdansk 92, 207
Gdanska Street 1, 6–9, 16, 19, 21, 41, 67, 88, 173, 175
Gdynia 207
Germany 6, 13, 21, 29, 31, 33, 34, 54, 64, 70, 71, 76, 87, 96, 104, 111, 114, 115, 139, 143, 144, 154, 191, 218, 219
Gesia Street 148
Geverts, I. 19, 27
Gibraltar, Ada — see Horowitz, Ada.
Gibraltar, Mr. 90, 135, 136, 208
Gibraltars, family 136
Glantz, Israel (Igor) 19, 20, 75, 78, 174, 179
Glos Ludu 39
Glos Robotniczy 37, 39
Glueckel Hameln Demands Justice by Max Bauman 72
Gold, Lunia 192
Gold, Nusia 74
Goldberg, Jacob (Jakub, Kuba) 52, 79, 103, 195, 196, 209, 216
Goldberg, Leybele 166
Goldfaden, A. 20, 72
Goldmanowa, Mrs. 192
Goldstein, Bernard 183
Gordin, J. 59, 72
Gordonia Zionist youth movement 95, 154, 157, 160, 161, 168, 173, 203, 208, 217
Gorki 130, 131
Gorki region 102, 212, 220
Goskind, brothers 73
Goskind, Shaul 74, 167, 168
Grade, Chaim 68

Grand Hotel 8, 35, 42, 44, 50, 155, 170
Grandpa Fishl — see Fishl.
Greenbaum, Jack 72
Grenoble 136
Grodno 125, 185
Grodzisk 103, 148, 219
Grosman, Moshe 69, 158
Gross, Jerzyk 95, 123, 146, 147
Gross, Jozek 95, 123
Gross, Klara 95, 123, 146
Gross, Natan (Natek) 4, 20, 23, 28, 68, 73, 74, 94, 123, 146, 161, 167, 168, 192, 193, 200, 207, 216
Grosses, family 95, 146, 147, 207
Grossman, Vasily 35
Gruenbaum, Yitshak 69
Grynberg, Abram 105
Grynberg, Henryk (Herszek) 17, 77, 104–106, 146, 197, 199, 200, 217
Gunga Din, film 10
Guttenberg, J. 191

Habimah Theater 172
Haganah 83, 155–157, 169, 197
Haifa 100, 169, 207
Hakibbutz Hameuchad 154, 156
Halbstadt 101, 145, 215
Halinka 79
Halter, Marek 166, 191
Halter, Solomon 191
Hamburg 44
Hanoar Hatzioni Zionist youth movement 154, 160
Hans 144
Has, Wojciech 168
Hashomer Hatzair Zionist youth movement 7, 10–13, 15, 21, 22, 24, 26, 57, 59, 67, 69, 92–94, 101, 112, 120, 121, 125, 142, 143, 151, 153, 154, 157, 159–163, 165, 168–170, 174, 197, 203, 204, 206, 207, 213, 215, 219, 220
Hebrew University 1, 11, 14, 94, 103
Hehalutz Pioneer Center 57, 61, 155
Heidelberg 102
Hela (Aunt Hela) 173
Helenowek 12, 16, 17

Helenowek Children's Home 18, 20, 27, 74, 76–78, 82, 83, 85, 86, 100, 104, 112, 176, 187, 190, 192, 193, 198, 199, 205, 215, 217, 218
Helenowek Jewish orphanage 74, 75, 112
Heller, Binem 68
Helman, Michal 76, 200, 205
Hendel, Yehudit 2
Hershele from Ostropole, by Jacob Zonshein 59
Herzl 69, 143
Herzlia Pituach 93
Hesse, Herman 159
Hitler, Adolf 31, 49, 109, 110, 113–115, 117, 120, 126, 141, 143, 172, 191, 198
Hitlerstrasse 35
Hoffman, Eva 3
Hofrychter, Karol 45
Hornstein, Hanka, formerly Rydel 3, 88, 89, 134, 135, 172, 173, 207, 217
Hornstein, Romek 207, 217
Horowitz, Ada, formerly Gibraltar 27, 88, 171, 208, 217
Horowitz, Tamar 99
Horowitz, Zipora 12
Hotel Monopol 49
Hungary 208

Ianasovich, Isaac 68
Ichud Zionist party 57, 59, 67, 157, 205
Indersdorf 154
Iraq 15
Irtysh River 88, 136
Israel 1, 3, 9, 11, 13–15, 19–22, 27, 33, 43, 55–58, 65, 73, 76, 87, 88, 90, 93, 96, 98, 99, 101, 152, 154, 156, 157, 159–163, 165, 166, 169, 172, 173, 177, 183, 184, 188, 194, 196, 200, 201, 203, 204, 206–209, 212, 215–221
Italy 163, 206
Itatka 88
Itka (Aunt Itka) 121, 133, 134
Ivan 128

Ivanovo 129
Izabela 176
Izak 198

Jagiellonian University 95
Jakuba Street 65, 79, 82, 93, 164, 187, 192
Jakubowska, Wanda 42
Janion, Maria 40
Jaracza Street 49, 59, 66, 67, 72, 75, 193
Jaslo 4
Jastrun, Mieczyslaw 39
JDC, The American Joint distribution Committee 55, 56, 73, 116, 117, 163
Jelenia Gora 144, 191
Jerdens, Wilhelm 44
Jerusalem 11, 13, 14, 40, 69, 98, 99, 103
Jewish Committee in Lodz 155, 156, 161, 163–165, 167, 181–187, 190–193, 197, 203, 205, 220
Jewish Historical Commission 59, 68, 71, 74, 91, 95, 148, 187, 188, 213, 216
Jewish Historical Institute, Warsaw 91, 101, 204
Jewish Teachers Seminary 92, 96, 217, 221
Jewish Telegraphic Agency 70
Jewish Theater in Lodz 58, 59, 67, 71, 72, 73
Jewish Theater of Lower Silesia, in Wroclaw 58, 59
Jozek, Aleksander Klugman's friend 98, 141

Kaczerginski, Shmerke 68, 69, 188
Kagan 190, 205
Kahan, Arkadjusz (Avreml) 83, 180, 193, 194
Kahan, Pearl 194,195
Kahan, Vivian 180
Kahane, David 151
Kajtek — see Shor, Adam.
Kalif — see Chizhik, Moshe.
Kaminska, Esther-Rokhl 72

Kaminska, Ida 11, 59, 70, 72, 131, 205
Kaplinski, Baruch 3, 5, 23, 76, 91, 92, 161, 165, 217, 218
Kareni, Nadia 71, 74
Karol 1–3
Karola, the teacher 19
Kasyno cafe 42
Katowice 163, 187
Katta-Kurgan 134, 135
Katyn 38
Kaufman, Rachelka 78
Kawalerowicz, Jerzy 168
Kazakhstan 88, 115, 116, 136, 218
Kempinski, Hillel 195
Kenney, Padraic 47
Kermisz, Joseph 59, 67, 68
Khrushchev N. S. 188
Kibbutzim 151-154,157,160
Kielce, Kielce pogrom 39, 48, 50, 54, 58, 62, 64, 81–83, 99, 158, 163, 173, 181, 182, 184, 193, 196, 211
Kiev 127, 138
Kilinskiego Street 7, 11, 12, 18, 23, 45, 48, 67, 75, 158, 165, 173, 190, 197, 199
Kirgizstan (Kirghiz SSR) vi, 131
Klachko, Zeev ("Vovke") 13–15
Klugman, Aleksander 68, 84, 98, 99, 120, 141–144, 191, 218
Klugman, Dziunia 98, 141
Klugman, Hela 98, 141
Klugman, Masha 98
Klugman, Tosia 68, 84, 191
Kol Haam 14
Kolakowski, Leszek 40, 51, 52, 69, 191, 195, 196
Kolumna 16, 17, 93
Koluszki 169
Komi Autonomous Republic 102, 130, 212, 220
Koordynacja (Coordination) 90, 163, 165, 167, 170, 175, 176, 178, 213, 219, 221
Korczak, Janusz 192
Korn, Rachel 68
Koscielny Plac 33
Kosciuszko Boulevard 40 49, 50

Kosciuszko Division 118
Kotarbinski, Tadeusz 37, 40, 50, 191
Kott, Jan 39, 42
Koussevitski, M. 73
Kovel 184, 185
Kovner, Abba 151, 153
Kovno 96, 166
KPP, Polish Communist Party 181, 185
Krakow (Cracow) 14, 40, 42, 49, 50, 53–55, 61, 81, 82, 88, 95, 99, 104, 105, 110, 114, 123, 146–148, 153, 167, 168, 176, 181, 216
Krakowiacy i Gorale (Cracovians and Highlanders) 41
Krampf, Rudolf 70, 71
Krasinski Square 146, 147
Krasnodar 102, 131, 212, 220
Krasnovodsk 118, 130, 212
Krawiec (Rabbi) 70
Kreshchatik Boulevard 138
KRN, the Polish National Council 30, 182
Krosno 4
Kruczkowski, Leon. 200
Krupka — see Melamed.
Krupskaya, Nadezhda 128
Krzyzanowski, Henryk 198
KS in Lodz, the Special Commission for Jewish self-defense in Lodz 83, 169, 194
Kuban region 90, 132, 133, 219
Kuban River 132
Kula, Witold (Witek) 50
Kuron, Jacek 44
Kuznica 39, 50

Landau-Gutenteger, Gustaw 67
Lantzman, Claude. 70
Las Vegas 3
Lelushenko, D., General 34
Leneman, Helena (Hela) 164, 178, 213
Leneman, Leon68
Leningrad 107, 138
Lenino 92, 100, 118, 128, 138, 190, 216, 219

Lewin Moshe (Mishka) 12, 13, 158, 169
Liberman, Dziunia — see Dublin, Dziunia.
Liberman, Shaul 19, 76, 174, 179
Liberty Square — see Wolnosci Plac.
Lida 125
Limanowskiego Street 81
Lipman, Moshe 71, 74
Lipman, Natalia 73
Lipska-Librachowa, prof. 189
Lithuania 96, 116, 122, 166, 221
Liton, Eni 71
Litzmann, Karl, General 34
Litzmannstadt 34
Loberbaum, Maria — see Lorber, Maria.
Lodz, anti-Semitism in: 2, 4, 38-39, 79-82, 171-172, 174-175, 209; cafes in: 41-42; cinemas and films in: 10, 42, 44, 45; Jewish Committee of: 63-64, 165, 183, 186; "Jewish geography" of: 66-67
Holocaust commemoration in: 59, 60, 70
Lodz City Theater 41
Lodz Conservatory 41
Lodz Fabryczna railway station.
Lodz Film School 42
Lodz Ghetto 46, 63, 112-113, 141-143, 164, 207
Lodz Kaliska railway station 191
Lodz Komisja Specjalna 194
Lodz Municipal Archive 10
Lodz Pedagogical Institute 193
Lodz Polytechnic 190, 197, 216
Lodz School of Higher Education 50
Lodz Teatralna 39
Lodz University 9, 36, 39, 40, 49, 50, 51, 52, 69, 81, 103, 190, 191, 194, 196, 209, 215, 216
Loga-Sowinski, Ignacy 35, 191
Lohamei Hagetaot Archive 179
London 83, 184
Lorber, Henryk 97
Lorber, Maria 43, 44, 97, 189, 218
Los Angeles 194
Lower Silesia 53, 54, 58, 59, 61, 65, 87, 144, 157, 167, 170, 193

Lubelsky, Marika 208
Lubelsky, Richard (Rysiek) 27, 88, 136, 171, 176, 177, 208, 218
Lubetkin, Zivia 3, 153, 166
Lubianikier-Lavon, Pinhas 161
Lublin 40, 48, 58, 59, 60, 62, 63, 80, 94, 139, 151, 183, 186, 219
Lukow 123
Lutnia Hall 41
Lutomierska Street 170
Lutsk 125
Lwow 9, 29, 47–49, 87, 88, 92, 115, 121, 123, 125, 126, 133, 146, 167, 185, 192, 212, 218, 220
Lwow University 49

Magnitogorsk 90, 100, 124, 127, 132, 212, 216, 219
Majdanek 3, 12, 126, 173, 197
Majerczak, Binyamin 3, 10, 19, 91, 92, 107, 120, 123–126, 128–130, 138, 139, 168, 169, 179, 201, 212, 218, 219
Majerczak, Mareczek 126, 129
Malcia (Aunt Malcia) 4–6, 8, 16, 17
Malewicz 102, 124
Mann, Mendel 68, 69, 75
Marchacz, Mietek 177
Margolis, Alina (Ala) 52, 101–103, 146, 148, 195, 196, 215, 219
Margolis, dr. 102, 103
Margolis, Olek 103
Maria, educator 199
Mark, Bernard (Ber) 58, 68, 69, 158, 181
Marseille 220
Marszalkowska Street 43
Marusia, a nurse 129
Marysia 167
Mauthausen 98, 144, 190, 199
Mayn Shtetl Belz (My Town of Belz) 68–69, 198
Medem Center for Yiddish Culture, Paris 101
Meed, Vladka 63
Melamed, the teacher 19, 171, 174, 179
Melman, Marian 59, 72

Melnitzer, Zvi 156, 166
Mengele, dr. 101, 145
Meridor, Ivri — see Napadow, Heniek.
Miedzyrzec 124
Mijal, Kazimerz 35, 63, 78, 80
Mikhoels, Solomon 71
Mikolajczyk, Stanislaw 37, 38
Mila Street 96
Milstein, Maria 77
Minc, Hilary 181
Minsk 126, 194
Mintz, Matityahu 93, 94, 97, 121, 125, 162, 169, 170, 206, 213, 219
Mir Lebengeblibene (We, The Survivors), film 73, 216
Mirele Efros by J. Gordin 11, 59
Mirski, Maja (Majka) 185, 187
Mirski, Michal 16, 63–65, 68, 70, 71, 78, 83, 155, 156, 164, 181–189, 201, 204, 205, 213
Mittelman, Mordechai 204
Miznmacher, Beniek 12
Mocca, café 41
Moczar, Mieczyslaw 36
Montreal 3, 88, 89, 207, 217, 218,
Moscow 30, 71, 94, 131, 138, 183, 188, 194
Mostowa Street 195
Mostowicz, Arnold 74
Mosty 59, 67, 160
Muszkat, prof. 193
Mysl Wspolczesna 39

Nahir, Tsipora 213
Nalewki Street 101
Napadow, Heniek 7, 8, 10, 21, 25, 26, 89, 90, 121, 122, 127, 132, 133, 136, 137, 171, 172, 175, 176, 219
Narutowicza Street 2, 11, 18, 42, 46, 52, 67, 82, 157, 158, 163, 173, 175, 192
Neiman, Feliks "Fishke" 81, 86, 193, 194, 201
Neli, actress 128
New York 17, 72, 195, 208
Nie (No) 47
Nina Yakovlevna 130, 138, 139
Nishmit (Shner), Sarah 96, 166, 221

Nisko 139
Nizhni-Tagil 128
NKVD 36, 122, 126, 129, 131, 144
Novosibirsk 87, 131
Nowe Drogi 187, 188
Nowiny-Kurier 4
Nowotki Street 174
Nyse River 139

Obraztsov, Sergei 42
Odessa 94
Ogrodowa Street 90, 121
Oka River 138
Olek, pilot 139
Olicki, Mates 158
Opinia 59
Ordzhonikidze (Vladikavkaz) 129, 130, 212, 218, 219
Orsk 100, 128, 189, 212, 216
Oshres, Moshe — see Shmutter, Moshe.
Osobka-Morawski, Edward 182
Ossolineum Institute 215
Otwock 95, 147, 148, 216

Pabianice 80, 98
Pabianicka Street 45
Pahlevi 118
Palestine 2, 7, 11, 21, 33, 55–58, 61, 69, 76, 79, 83, 92, 94, 100, 113, 116, 117, 121, 125, 129, 151–163, 166–170, 176, 182–184, 187, 188, 197, 204, 212, 219
Palgi, Yitshak 157
Paris 97, 101, 166, 188, 208, 218–220
Patron, Rachel, formerly Rubinow 87, 122, 131, 132, 171, 220
Peltel, Feigele — see Meed, Vladka.
Pen, Alexander 14
Peretz Yiddish School 48, 75, 76, 77, 199, 205, 220
Persia 118
Petach-Tikva 15
Philadelphia 12
Pickwick Club cafe 42, 51
Picon, Molly 193
Pietrolesie 162
Pilsudskiego Street 80, 165

Piotr, the guard 207
Piotrkowska Street 7, 8, 19, 33, 35, 37, 40–45, 48, 49, 52, 67, 121, 155, 160, 163, 164, 170, 173, 178, 191, 195, 207
Piwkowska, Bozena 44–46
Poalei Zion 57, 63, 67, 76, 83, 96, 151, 157, 158, 165, 166, 168, 171, 182, 188, 190, 204, 220
Podeh Fayvl — see Podemski, Fayvl.
Podemski, Fayvl 11, 93, 101, 120, 121, 142, 143, 159, 164, 165, 206, 207, 220
Podlasie 106, 150
Polakiewicz, Ignac — see Palgi, Yitshak.
Poland-Israel Friendship Association, Warsaw 156
Polanski, Roman 42
Polish Army Theater 41, 70, 156
Polnocna Street 189
Polonia cinema 42, 44
Polska Zbrojna 39
Poltava 100, 127, 128, 212, 216
Poludniowa Street 4, 7, 8, 13, 19, 21, 75, 76, 81, 93, 100, 121, 157, 164, 165
Pomerantz, Hania
Pomerantz, Moshe (Moniek) 10, 26, 27, 28, 87, 171
Pomerantz, Shlomo (Salek) 26, 27, 87, 95, 107, 121, 174, 220
Pomerantzs 10, 88, 96, 107, 121, 134, 220
Ponary 140, 215
Poniatowski Park 35, 81
Potega, Jozef 43, 44
Poznan 29, 139
Poznanski Street 151
PPR, Polska Partia Robotnicza, Polish Workers Party 30, 35–38, 51, 57, 58, 68, 81, 156, 157, 181, 186, 187, 189, 190, 196
PPS, Polska Partia Socjalistyczna, Polish Socialist Party 30, 56, 57, 81, 156, 196
Praga, Warsaw 50, 149
Prague 88, 92, 169, 188, 208
Preter, Chaim 17, 18, 27, 77, 199

INDEX 261

Preter, Maurice 17, 18
Preter, Moshe 18
Prokhorova (Afanasyevna) 131, 132
Proport, Karola 27
Pruszkow 147, 149
Przemyslawski, Abraham 209, 216
PSL, Polskie Stronnictwo Ludowe, the Polish Peasant Party 3
Puszcza Bialowieska 209
PZPR, Polska Zjednoczona Partia Robotnicza, the Polish United Workers' Party 30, 58, 183, 203, 205

Radogoszcz 35, 103, 124, 141, 143, 144
Radomsko 38, 218
Radoszyna 105, 217
Raj 1, 6
Rala — see Patron, Rachel.
Rapoport, Natan 15
Rashal, Aharon 19, 76, 174
Ravensbrueck 49
Rav-Nof, Rachel — see Patron, Rachel.
Redlich, Franciszek (Fredzio) 9, 10, 197
Rela — see Patron, Rachel.
Rewolucji 1905 r. Street — see Poludniowa Street.
Reymont, Wladyslaw 32, 102
Robotnik 39
Roma Hall 156
Rostworowski, Tomasz, Academic Priest of Lodz University 37
Rotenberg, Wanda 95, 96, 157, 158, 165, 166, 220
Roth, Joseph 32
Rotman, Aizik 71
Rovno 104, 221
Roza 143
Rozenberg, Ksil 131
Rozenberg, Menashe 131
Rozenberg, Szulim 101, 124, 130, 201, 212, 220
Rozenstein, Fela 12, 169
Rozental, Chayele 69
Rozowski, Ryfka (Stasia) 148
Rozowski, Velvl 148

RTPD, Robotnicze Towarzystwo Przyjaciol Dzieci (Workers' Association of Childrens' Friends) 47, 49, 192
Rubinow, Rachel (Rala, Rela) — see Patron, Rachel.
Rubinow, Vovka 122
Rubinows 87, 122, 126, 131
Rubinstein, Arthur 33
Rubinstein, Joseph 68
Rudnicki, Adolf 39, 41–42
Rumkowski, Chaim 7, 76, 112, 113
Russia 7, 12–15, 21, 29–31, 46, 47, 53, 58, 59, 61, 66, 71, 74, 75, 80, 87, 88, 97, 99, 101, 102, 104, 109, 111, 113, 115–119, 121, 124–127, 131, 135, 140, 141, 146, 153, 156, 158, 163, 166, 167–169, 172, 174, 183–185, 188–190, 192, 196, 197, 199, 207, 211–213
Rutenberg, Kazimierz (Kazik) 104, 108, 138, 139, 196, 220
Rutka 192
Rybinsk 107, 129, 138
Rydel, Hanka — see Hornstein, Hanka.
Rydel, Hela 172
Rydels 89
Ryki 97, 98, 189, 218
Rykov, A. I. 139
Ryszard, Lodz guide 8
Rzeszow 186

Sadoul, Georges 42
Sala Spiewakow *(The Singers' Hall)* 68
Samarkand 76, 130, 135, 138, 190, 212, 219
Sander, mrs. 46
Sander-Janowska, Halina 46, 47
Sanders, family 46
Sarny 102, 124
Savoy, Hotel 32, 33, 42, 51
Schaff, Adam 40, 193, 196
Schiller, Leon 41, 52, 72
Schuld, Heinrich 46
Schumacher, Israel 20, 72, 73, 74, 117, 167, 168, 176, 193
Schumacher, Lidia 176
Segal, Louis 81

Sejny 96
Selbach, dr. 46
Selbach, frau 46
Semipalatinsk 88, 136, 218
Sepolowska, Stefania 148
Sfard, David 67
Shalev-Spokojny Josef (Yossi) 3, 27, 171
Shalom Aleichem 59, 68, 72, 102, 159
Sheptytski, Andrei (Metropolitan) 94, 95
Shmutter, Binyamin 13, 24
Shmutter, Moshe 11-15, 24, 158, 159
Shmutter, Rachel 13
Shmutters 12, 13
Shner, Sarah — see Nishmit-Shner, Sarah.
Shner, Zvi 221
Shoah, film by Claude Lantzman 70
Shor, Adam 137
Siberia 46, 88, 89, 90, 104, 116, 122, 127, 133, 134, 136, 172, 197, 217, 218, 220, 221
Siedlce 89, 173, 217
Sienkiewicza Park 40, 43
Sienkiewicza Street 187
Sierakowiak, Dawid 142
Singer, Isaac Bashevis 32
Singer, Israel Joshua 32
Skarzysko-Kamienna 114
Skidel 185
Skwarczynski, prof. 190
Slonim 124
Slowo Mlodych 161
Szpilki 39
Smolar, Hersz (Grzegorz) 58, 67, 181
Smolensk 18, 118, 138
Snow White, film by Walt Disney 44
Sobibor 97, 114
Sokolowski, Simcha 82
Solarz 16
Sommerstein, Emil 151
SOMS, Socjalistyczna Organizacja Mlodziezy Szkolnej (The Socialist Organization of School Youth) 103
Sonnenberg, Sven 77

Sosnowiec 104, 139, 220
Southern Urals 100, 128, 212, 216
Spain 97
Spokojny — see Shalev-Spokojny.
Srebnik, Shimon 70, 71
Sreniowska, Krystyna 48, 50
Sreniowski, Stanislaw (Staszek) 50
Sreniowskis 49
Srodmiejska Street 65, 67, 70, 154
Stalin, Joseph 14, 31, 38, 63, 109, 115, 143, 183, 188, 193
Stalingrad 132, 185
Starski, Ludwik 51
State Jewish Theater, Warsaw 104
Stawinski, Eugeniusz 156
Stefan, instructor 171
Sterling Street 71
Sternberg, Dorka 158
Stettin 53, 54, 56, 159
Strauss-Marko, Shlomo 206
Strzelecki, Jan 196
Stutthoff xv, 141
Stylowy cinema 63
Sudetenland 101, 145
Sutskever, Abraham 2
Swen, Sylvia 73, 78
Swida, Hanna 52
Swidnica 204
Syrena Theater 41, 43
Szaniecka, Emilia 52
Szczekacz (Rabbi) 63
Szczesna, Joanna 9
Szejnman, Wlodek 79
Szpigel, Jacob 83
Sztandar Mlodych 209
Sztrowajs, Hilary 63, 165
Szuldenfrei, Michael 183
Szwajger, Adina 148

Tabacznik, Hersz — see Mirski, Michal.
Tabenkin, Yitshak 154, 168
Tanka 6
Targowa Street 42
Tashkent 13
Tatra Mountains (Tatras) 3, 120
Teatr Polski, Warsaw 41
Teatr Powszechny 160, 200, 205
Tecza cinema 42

Teheran, 134, 135
Tel-Aviv 3, 13, 19, 20, 23, 28, 89, 90, 93, 94, 96, 97, 99, 172
Tel-Aviv Cinemateque 94
Tel-Aviv Hilton 89
Tel-Aviv University 94, 97, 206
Tene-Tenenbaum, Binyamin 69
Tevye the Milkman by Shalom Aleichem 59
The Brothers Ashkenazi, by I. J. Singer 32
The Chronicle of the Lodz Ghetto, ed. by Lucjan Dobroszycki 79
The Dibbuk by Anski 72
Tivoli Hall 63
TKZ, The Jewish Cultural Society 205
Toeplitz, Jerzy 42
Tomasz, Marko 206
Tomsk 104
Toronto 21
Torun 92
TOZ, Towarzystwo Ochrony Zdrowia Ludnosci Zydowskiej, the Jewish Health Care Society 52, 67
Traugutta Street 41, 42
Treblinka 3, 97, 111, 114, 173, 199
Trunk, Isaiah 59
TSKZ, Towarzystwo Spoleczno-Kulturalne Zydow w Polsce, the Cultural and Social Jewish Society 205
Tsukunft, the Bundist youth organization 57, 81, 104, 183, 184, 194, 216
Tsum Kamf 185
Tugentraich, Dorotka 191
Turkow, Jonas 58
Tuwim, Julian 33, 40, 98, 99
Tygodnik Powszechny 50
Tynenson, Issac 52
Tynenson, Tamara 52
Tyrankiewicz, Maria 36

Ukraine 4, 92, 100, 115, 126, 186, 212, 216
Ulica Graniczna (Border Street) film by Aleksander Ford 10, 42
Undzere Kinder (Our Children), film by Natan Gross 4, 17, 18, 20, 28, 73–75, 77, 78, 94, 95, 168, 176, 216
University of Chicago 193
UNRRA 14
Upper Silesia 53
Ural Mountains (Urals) 89, 100, 101, 115, 124, 185, 217
Urbach — see Urban.
Urban, Jerzy (Jurek) 47, 48
Ursynow 148
Uszer 199
U Turka cafe
Uzbekistan (Uzbek SSR) xvi, 76, 88–90, 139, 133–136, 172–174, 194, 212, 217, 219, 229

Venice 206, 207
Vera 130
Vienna 9
Vilna 12, 13, 29, 68, 69, 74, 79, 91, 92, 94, 96, 102, 114–116, 122, 124, 125, 140, 158, 165, 169, 170, 188, 194, 212, 215, 217, 219, 221
Vilna University 92
Vistula 92, 119, 149
Vladikavkaz — see Ordzhonikidze.
Volga River 92, 126, 128, 212, 218
Volhynia 102, 124, 184
Volkovysk xv, 124
Vovke — see Klachko, Zeev.
Vovo 4–6, 8, 16, 17, 21, 25

Wagszal, Lipa, dr. or Dr. 5
Wagszal, Pepka 5
Wagszals 5, 6
Wajda, Andrzej 42
Walbrzych 159, 204
Warsaw 1–3, 9, 15, 16, 22, 29, 31, 33, 36, 39, 40, 41, 43, 45–51, 53–55, 59–63, 65, 69, 70, 72, 73, 80, 89–92, 94–97, 99, 101–106, 109–112, 114, 115, 120, 121, 123–126, 131, 139, 146–151, 154–156, 160, 165–167, 173, 181, 183, 185, 187–189, 193,

195, 197, 199, 200, 204, 206–209, 212, 215–220
Washington, D.C. 105
Wasilewska, Wanda 138
Wazyk, Adam 39
Web, Marek 82
Weiner, Shayke 158, 161
Weiskopf, Bernard 63
Weiskopf, Daniel 63
Werner 102, 103
Wertheim, Anatol 63, 183
Wieckowskiego Street 161
Wiener, Bono 194
Wiener, Pinche 195
Wisla cinema 42
Wittlin, Benny 21
Wloclawek 92, 120, 129, 218
Wlokniarz cinema 42
Wohl, Stanislaw 42, 51
Wolczanska Street 2, 158, 160, 171
Wolna Lodz 39
Wolna Wszechnica 40, 50, 97, 218
Wolnosci Plac 33, 35, 49, 67, 82, 197
Woroszylski, Wiktor 50
Wroclaw 22, 55, 56, 58, 59, 100, 170, 184, 189, 193, 203, 215
Wschodnia Street 12, 76, 165
Wyspianski, S. 41

Yaari, Meir 151, 160
Yad Vashem 1, 95
Yaroslavl 92, 129
Yiddish Theatre 10, 11
Yiddishe Schriftn 59

Zacharczyk, Alicja 148
Zachariasz, Szymon 58, 181, 204, 205
Zachodnia Street 67
Zajicek, Edward, Prof. 50
Zakazane Piosenki (Forbidden Songs) film by Leonard Zuczkowski 10, 42, 51
Zakopane 3, 93, 95, 120
Zalkind, Aharon — see Eynat, Aharon.
Zalkind, Eliezer 26
Zalkinds 91, 122
Zambrowski, Roman 181

Zamenhofa Street 101
Zawadska Street 155, 163, 174
Zayonts, Pinhas 12
Zelda (Aunt Zelda) 170
Zeromski, S. 44, 45
Zeromskiego Street 102
Zgierska Street 33
Zgierz 89, 135, 136, 173, 174, 217
Zheleznikov, Avreml 195
Zhitomir 186
Zhukov, G.K, Marshal 34
Ziemia obiecana (Promised Land), by Wladyslaw Reymont 32
Ziemianska cafe 42
ZIH, Zydowski Instytut Historyczny, the Jewish Historical Institute, Warsaw 91, 101
Zionist Confederation House, Jerusalem 98
Zionist Labor movement 3
Zisman, Leon 190
Zisman, Miriam 190, 208
ZMP, Zwiazek Mlodziezy Polskiej (the Union of Polish Youth) 30, 48
ZOB, Zydowska Organizacja Bojowa, the Jewish Fighters' Organization 96, 148, 220
Zoliborz 165
Zonshein Jacob 59
Zosia 148
ZPP, Zwiazek Patriotow Polskich (the Union of Polish Patriots) 100, 118, 119, 131, 135, 136, 185, 186
Zuchowice 123
Zuckerman, Yitzhak (Antek) 3, 69, 76, 81, 83, 96, 148, 151–156, 164, 165, 166
Zwiazek Bialej Tarczy (The White Shield Union) 44
ZWM, Zwiazek Walki Mlodych, the Youth Fighting Union 191, 193, 215, 216
Zydowska Agencja Prasowa (ZAP), the Jewish Press Agency 59, 70, 155
Zygelbojm, Artur 83, 184
Zygelbojm, Yosl 83
Zyskind, Sara 64, 152

www.ingramcontent.com/pod-product-compliance
Lightning Source LLC
Chambersburg PA
CBHW050104170426
43198CB00014B/2455